Prenatal Testing and Disability Rights

EDITED BY
Erik Parens and Adrienne Asch

GEORGETOWN UNIVERSITY PRESS / WASHINGTON, D.C.

Georgetown University Press, Washington, D.C. 20007
© 2000 by Georgetown University Press. All rights reserved.
Printed in the United States of America
10   9   8   7   6   5   4   3   2   1
THIS VOLUME IS PRINTED ON ACID-FREE, OFFSET BOOK PAPER.

Library of Congress Cataloging-in-Publication Data

Prenatal testing and disability rights / edited by Erik Parens, Adrienne Asch.
     p. cm. — (Hastings Center studies in ethics)
   Includes index.
   ISBN 0-87840-803-7 (cloth : acid-free paper)–ISBN 0-87840-804-5
(paper : acid-free paper)
     1. Prenatal diagnosis—Moral and ethical aspects. 2. Prenatal diagnosis—Legal
status, laws, etc. I. Parens, Erik, 1957–II. Asch, Adrienne. III. Series.
RG628 .P745 2000
   176—dc21   00-026361

CONTENTS

Introduction

Against a background of burgeoning genetic discovery, rising consciousness of discrimination against people with disabilities, and the societal
debate about abortion, The Hastings Center undertook a two-year
project to explore the disability rights critique of prenatal testing for
genetic disability. When we began our project, this disability rights
critique had not yet met with a sustained, respectful analysis by the
bioethics or medical communities.[1]

The disability critique, which is articulated by people who are
ardently pro-choice, urges prospective parents to examine the meaning
of prenatal testing and selective abortion; it asserts that parents should
question the meaning of their and society's cumulative actions. Many
of those who voice this critique themselves live with disabilities or have
close relationships with disabled people, but other thoughtful people
without such direct personal experience also subscribe to these arguments. The critique seeks to persuade prospective parents and medical
professionals that they should re-examine stereotypes about life with
disability and about what it means to be the parent of a child who is
disabled. Proponents of this critique would like professionals who develop and provide tests—and prospective parents who use tests—
to question the assumptions that underlie prenatal testing. After such
questioning, perhaps providers and parents will think that testing is a less
important element of prenatal care and reproductive decision making.

Our group sought to understand both the logical arguments made
from a disability perspective as well as the social and psychological
context in which those arguments are made. Not only did we try to
understand the logic and feelings of people in the disability community,
but we also tried to understand the feelings of the people in the majority
community. If any one of us ever did, no one in our group can any
longer imagine having a view from nowhere. Those of us with disabilities
know that our particular experience of discrimination colors our critique
of prenatal testing. Those of us who used prenatal testing before or
during the project appreciate that this experience colors our responses to

those critiques. Those of us who are parents sometimes found ourselves justifying our own parental attitudes, whereas those of us who are not parents sometimes asked ourselves whether becoming parents might change our views about what constitutes an admirable parental attitude.

Though we came to the table with different experiences of both disability and parenting, we also came with a desire to hear each other and to identify areas of agreement and disagreement about how best to manage an emerging technology. Several members of our working group had personal or familial experience with disability, including scholars from disability studies, medical genetics, genetic counseling, medicine, law, the humanities, and the social sciences.

Over the course of our two-year project, we held five, two-day research meetings at The Hastings Center. Between meetings we engaged in a lively group e-mail conversation. In addition, through a grant from the National Institute for Disability and Rehabilitation Research to the Society for Disability Studies, our project members gathered with members of the Society at its May 1997 meeting in Minneapolis. Four conference sessions were devoted to discussing the project's work with many people who live with and study disability issues. This dialogue broadened our group's conversation by providing access to ideas from other interested and knowledgeable people. It also provided some members of the research group with their first contact—in a nonmedical setting—with disabled people.

Given the controversial nature of the subject and the diversity within our working group, it is not surprising that we could not reach consensus about all of the questions we discussed. We did not achieve unanimity on the major claims of the disability perspective—most specifically, that prenatal diagnosis is based on either morally problematic views about desirable parental attitudes and morally questionable views about people with disabilities, or on misinformation about the nature and consequences of disability. We did not reach consensus about what weight to give or how best to use the disability arguments about prenatal genetic testing in making public policy. Nor did we concur more specifically about whether it is wise public policy to draw lines between reasonable and unreasonable tests. Nonetheless, our project achieved two important aims. First, we aired and seriously considered the concerns of the disability community. Second, to the extent we achieved consensus about the merits in some of its claims, we recommended changes to ameliorate some of the problems associated with the customary ways of providing prenatal testing.

The Volume

Part one of this book introduces the practice of prenatal diagnosis and the arguments that form the disability rights critique. The first essay, written by Erik Parens and Adrienne Asch in extensive consultation with the project working group, presents a detailed account of what happened in our project—what we agreed and disagreed about and why. It lays out the claims made by those with a disability rights critique of prenatal testing, presents evaluations of group members, and proposes practice and policy recommendations flowing from those claims. The second chapter, written by medical geneticist Cynthia M. Powell, offers a brief history of prenatal diagnosis, describes the current state of prenatal testing in the United States, and speculates about the future of such testing.

Assessing the moral and policy ramifications of prenatal testing entails examining views of parenthood, views of disability, and views about the role of medicine and science in family life. The contributions that follow illustrate a variety of perspectives in our project group about parenthood (part two), disability (part three), and professional practice (part four).

Part two presents several perspectives on the implications of prenatal testing and selective abortion for the experience of parenthood generally. We begin with parenthood for two reasons. First, our project focused on the impact of this technology upon family life. Second, prospective parents benefit from the technology and must decide whether to use it and how to deal with the information it yields. The six chapters in this part grapple with what prenatal testing suggests for how prospective parents do and should think about disability and parenthood. We open with a chapter not commissioned by our project group, but one that echoed throughout our deliberations. Deborah Kent explores how it feels to learn that her parents and husband fear that her own child might inherit her disability. If they have loved her with this characteristic, how should she understand their responses to the possibility that her child might have the same characteristic? Project member and economist Mary Ann Baily's article offers a frank account of why she, as a prospective parent, chose to have an amniocentesis and why she thinks she would have had an abortion if testing had revealed a disabling trait. We follow these two personal reflections with empirical and theoretical examinations of the implications of a child's disability for family life and for the parent–child relationship. Three project members with extensive personal and professional experience of disability provide a synthesis of the qualitative and quantitative research on the experience of families who have children with disabilities.

Social scientists and educators Philip M. Ferguson, Alan Gartner, and Dorothy K. Lipsky suggest that the literature reveals that a child's disability does not cause the stress and family disruption so often portrayed by many bioethicists and physicians. Their article represents the disability critique claim that the desire for prenatal testing and selective abortion rests on misinformation about what a child's disability means for families. Philosopher William Ruddick takes up that part of the disability critique focused on norms of parenthood. He investigates three different, and in his view equally persuasive, conceptions of parenthood, which might motivate and delimit parents' different decisions about prenatal testing. Philosopher Bonnie Steinbock explores the claim that so-called disabling traits are neutral forms of variation that should no more be the basis for selective abortion than should traits like sex or eye color; against that line of argument, Steinbock contends that just as responsible parents try to avoid having children with disabilities by refraining from alcohol and tobacco during pregnancy, so do they try to avoid having children with disabilities by using prenatal testing and selective abortion.

We close this section with an essay that places parental decision making in a social context. Bruce Jennings, a political scientist, invites us to step back from examining the "free" choices of individuals and urges us to consider how genetic science increasingly frames and thus determines how people understand their experience of pregnancy and parenthood.

The chapters in part three all probe the contention that the creation and use of prenatal testing for disabling traits expresses negative views about people who live with those traits. Disability rights scholar and activist Marsha Saxton opens the section, discussing why many members of the disability rights movement believe that prenatal testing and selective abortion sends a hurtful message to and about people with disabilities. In the form of a dialogue between herself and her son, philosopher Eva Feder Kittay, whose adult daughter has multiple severe disabilities, presents the case that prenatal testing need not send the message received by many in the disability community. She argues that a woman's selective abortion is not best understood as a message to anyone; rather, it can be a reasonable response to her particular familial and social situation. In his article, philosopher James Lindemann Nelson also argues that individual decisions to use prenatal testing do not necessarily send disrespectful or hurtful messages. Like the others in this section, anthropologist Nancy Press reflects on the "messages" sent by prenatal testing. Rather than focusing on the choices made by individuals, however, Press examines the messages implicit in the choices made available by the very offer and routinization of such testing. Responding to the project discussions, bioethicist and disability rights scholar Adrienne Asch considers the challenges to the disability rights account of the messages sent by prenatal testing, as well as the meaning of such testing for the experience of parenthood.

The fourth and final part of the book addresses practical questions about how policymakers, courts, and professionals do and should determine appropriate prenatal testing practice. After reading these articles, readers hopefully will appreciate the difficulty of making policy in this area and the course our project took in making the particular recommendations outlined in the Parens and Asch chapter on pp. 3–43. These discussions demonstrate why our project could not reach agreement about whether prenatal testing should ever be limited to particular traits, and if so, on what criteria limits should be set. Sociologist Dorothy C. Wertz argues that even if in principle some lines might be drawn, in practice they will not make a difference; in her view, market and political—not "bioethical" or professional—forces will and should determine which tests are and are not offered. Pediatrician and bioethicist Jeffrey R. Botkin, however, argues that because medical professionals already set standards of care in other areas of medicine, they should in this one. He seeks to articulate a middle way between allowing prospective parents access to whatever tests they want or unfairly constraining their reproductive liberty. Law professor, bioethicist, and biologist Pilar N. Ossorio explores how the courts have dealt with cases where plaintiffs argue that they have been wronged by not receiving prenatal information. Though in the past there have been legal incentives for physicians to overutilize testing, Ossorio shows that courts have been attentive to "messages sent," and she offers a strategy for how legal incentives might be created to avoid such overutilization. In his contribution, obstetrician-gynecologist Steven J. Ralston gives a front-line view of what it is like to offer prenatal information to pregnant women (and their partners) and comments on how his personal encounters with disability before and during the project influence his work. As providers of the information yielded by prenatal diagnosis for the past thirty years, genetic counseling offers a valuable perspective from which to consider the disability rights critique. The book's concluding chapter, by genetic counselor Barbara Bowles Biesecker and her student-colleague Lori Hamby, calls for expansion and reform of prenatal genetic counseling in light of the disability rights critique and in line with the recommendations of the project.

Acknowledgments
Singly and together, we editors have many people to thank for their contributions to this book. When Erik Parens first thought to put together a project to examine the disability rights critique of prenatal testing, Eric Juengst was chief of the Ethical, Social, and Legal Implications of the Human Genome Project (ELSI) section of what then was called the National Center for Human Genome Research. Parens is deeply grateful to Juengst for supporting that idea—and even more for urging him to contact Adrienne Asch. Asch is not only the coeditor of this volume, but was centrally involved in every phase of the project. Parens would like to thank Hastings Center librarian Chris McKee and research assistant Rita Strobel, and their predecessors Marna Howarth and Eve DeVaro, for invaluable research support. Without the administrative support work of Jodi Fernandes, Nicole Rozanski, Mary Grace Pagaduan, and Mary Ann Hasbrouck, our research meetings would not have been as productive and pleasant as they were.

Adrienne Asch would like to express deep gratitude to all who have aided her participation in the project and in the creation of this book. Without the Luce Professorship at Wellesley College she would not have had the time available for such intense collaboration nor the funding for the research assistance and other expenses connected with the long-distance colleagueship. On campus many colleagues, staff, and students have supported her work. Maud Chaplin and Alison McIntyre discussed ideas throughout the years of the project. Caroline Moon not only provided research support for five years, but also provided probing questions and insightful observations. Patricia Cochran managed the office with a remarkable combination of efficiency, good humor, tact, and elegance. The loyal group of students/student-workers who retrieved library materials, scanned thousands of pages into computer code, and commented on what they heard and read, has been for her one of the great joys of the last several years. Rachel Price, Jeannie Lukacek, Jen Chau, Alice Kim, Bergen Nelson, Linda Cedeno, Simone Davion, Lili Schwan-Rosenwald, and Maggie Starr have been crucial to her work. She offers many thanks to Taran Jefferies for catching on, jumping into the work, hunting and gathering reading material, editing, proofing, and for getting her to quit sometimes obsessive research. All of these people have provided dedication and friendship that has made project collaboration from Wellesley a superb experience.

As with many collaborations, this one hit some bumpy spots. People who agree about many important matters can disagree about others. At one especially bumpy stretch of our project, we received critical help from working group member Nancy Press. We would like to thank Nancy for helping us to sort out what at the time felt like insurmountable disagreements about how to summarize the project's deliberations. Her judiciousness, insight, and equanimity got us over what at the time seemed more like the Rockies than a bumpy stretch of the road.

We would like to offer deepest gratitude to Jodi Fernandes. Without her huge and graceful administrative effort, this book would not have made it to John Samples at Georgetown University Press. Thanks, too, to associate editor of the *Hastings Center Report* Greg Kaebnick, who generously gave his work and insight to the creation of our overview of the project and the creation of this book. We are grateful to the National Institute for Disability and Rehabilitation Research for enabling several project group members to participate in and learn from the Society for Disability Studies conference, and we are deeply grateful to the members of that organization for sharing their ideas with our project in formal and informal sessions during the four-day 1997 annual meeting. We thank the National Institutes of Health for supporting our project through grant RO1 HG01168-02 and to Elizabeth Thomson, chief at the Ethical, Legal, and Social Implications section of the National Institute for Human Genome Research, for shepherding our project from grant application to completion.

We also offer deep thanks to all of the members of our project working group: Mary Ann Baily, Diana Bianchi, Barbara Bowles Biesecker, Jeffrey R. Botkin, Bette-Jane Crigger, Diane Dreher, Philip M. Ferguson, Alan Gartner, Eva Feder Kittay, Dorothy K. Lipsky, Bruce Jennings, Thomas H. Murray, James Lindemann Nelson, Pilar N. Ossorio, Cynthia M. Powell, Nancy Press, Diana Punales-Morejon, Steven J. Ralston, William Ruddick, Marsha Saxton, Bonnie Steinbock, Dorothy C. Wertz, and Benjamin Wilfond. We feel privileged to have worked with such a distinguished group of scholars and such a terrific group of people. Every member of our working group engaged our questions with seriousness, openness, and care. The intense engagement with ideas, the passionate but respectful arguments, the pain, laughter, and resulting friendships made the project a wonderful experience.

We believe that readers will find both resonance with and challenges to their own perceptions of what is important about parenthood and about what a child's disability signals for family life. We also believe that readers will be challenged to think about how society can support the desires of people with disabilities for social inclusion—while simultaneously supporting family privacy and reproductive liberty. Regardless of the particular decisions people make about using this technology or about acting on the information it can reveal, its very existence compels people to ponder parenthood anew. We hope that these essays will stimulate our readers to consider the norms and values they would promote in family and social life. As the visibility and respect enjoyed by the disability rights movement increases, and as prenatal testing technology leaps ahead, these issues will grow only more complex and significant.

ERIK PARENS,
The Hastings Center,
Garrison, New York

ADRIENNE ASCH,
Wellesley College,
Wellesley, Massachusetts

NOTE

1. Though not devoted exclusively to the disability critique, an important antecedent of our work is *Women and Prenatal Testing: Facing the Challenges of Genetic Technology,* ed. Karen H. Rothenberg and Elizabeth J. Thomson (Columbus: Ohio State University Press, 1994).

Part One

⚬

Overview and Context
of the Project

ERIK PARENS AND ADRIENNE ASCH

The Disability Rights Critique of Prenatal Genetic Testing: Reflections and Recommendations

The international project to sequence the human genome was undertaken in the expectation that knowing the sequence will offer new ways to understand and treat disease and disability. If researchers can identify the sequences of genes that code for the body's building blocks, then, it is hoped, they can identify and correct the sequences associated with disease and disability.

Thus far, researchers have enjoyed only minimal success in using gene therapy to correct such conditions, and no researcher has yet even attempted to use gene therapy to correct genetic impairments in a fetus. Rather, the discovery of abnormal or incorrect sequences has led primarily to the development of genetic tests that can reveal whether a person, embryo, or (in the usual case) a fetus carries an abnormality or "mutation" associated with disease or disability. It is now possible to test for gene mutations associated with some 400 conditions, from those universally viewed as severe, such as Tay-Sachs, to those that many might describe as relatively minor, such as polydactyly (a trait involving an extra little finger). The number and variety of conditions for which tests are available grow almost daily.[1]

Today we test for one trait at a time. In the future, however, with advances in biochip technology, it will be possible to test simultaneously for as many traits as one would like. In principle, we will be able to test for any trait we wish that has been associated with any given allele. Not only will the cost of such testing likely decrease as the diagnostic technology advances, but advances in the technology will make it possible to do the testing earlier in the pregnancy. One such technology will isolate the very small number of fetal cells that circulate in the maternal blood. Insofar as these earlier tests will be performed on fetal cells obtained from the mother's blood (rather than from the amniotic sac or chorionic villus) they will be noninvasive. Thus it will be possible to do many more tests, at once, and with less cost to the pregnant woman in time, inconvenience, risk, or dollars, than is now the case.[2]

As the ease of testing increases, so does the perception within both the medical and broader communities that prenatal testing is a logical extension of good prenatal care: the idea is that prenatal testing helps prospective parents have healthy babies. On the one hand, this perception is quite reasonable. Though no researcher has yet even attempted to correct a genetic impairment with in-utero gene therapy, increasingly there are nongenetic approaches to such impairments. At the time of this writing, more than fifty fetuses have undergone in-utero surgery to repair neural tube impairments (myleomeningoceles).[3] Moreover, negative (or reassuring) prenatal test results will reduce the anxiety felt by many prospective parents, and this in itself can be construed as part of good prenatal care. On the other hand, as long as in-utero interventions remain relatively rare, and as long as the number of people seeking prenatal genetic information to prepare for the birth of a child with a disability remains small, prospective parents will use positive prenatal test results primarily as the basis of a decision to abort fetuses that carry mutations associated with disease and/or disability. Thus, there is a sense in which prenatal testing is not simply a logical extension of the idea of good prenatal care.

Logical extension or no, using prenatal tests to prevent the birth of babies with disabilities seems to be self-evidently good to many people. Even if the testing will not help bring a healthy baby to term this time, it gives prospective parents a chance to try again to conceive. To others, however, prenatal testing looks rather different. If one thinks for even a moment about the history of our society's treatment of people with disabilities, it is not difficult to appreciate why people identified with the disability rights movement might regard such testing as dangerous. For the members of this movement, including people with and without disabilities and both issue-focused and disability-focused groups, living with disabling traits need not be detrimental either to an individual's prospects of leading a worthwhile life, or to the families in which they grow up, or to society at large. Although the movement has no one position on prenatal diagnosis, many adherents of the disability rights movement believe that public support for prenatal diagnosis and abortion based on disability contravenes the movement's basic philosophy and goals.

This document, the product of two years of discussions by a diverse group drawn from within and outside the disability rights movement, sets out the context within which the disability critique of prenatal diagnosis and abortion is located, and then frames, elaborates, and considers possible responses to that critique. It finds two broad claims: ← simply put, that prenatal genetic testing followed by selective abortion is morally problematic, and that it is driven by misinformation. The document then explores the prospects for distinguishing between acceptable and unacceptable testing and draws out of the ongoing debate recommendations to guide professional providers of genetic testing through this difficult terrain.

The Context: What Frames the Discussion

A History of Outright Discrimination Against and Unexamined Attitudes about People with Disabilities

We will not here review our nation's record of pervasive and invidious discrimination, which is only partly ameliorated by the passage of laws like the Individuals with Disabilities Education Act (IDEA) and the Americans with Disabilities Act (ADA). The history of discrimination against people with disabilities, including episodes of infanticide and compulsory sterilization, is long, ugly, and well documented.[4]

If Americans agree on the morality of little else, they agree that discrimination, including discrimination against people with disabilities, is evil. And most of us tend to be confident that we do not participate in such evil. But that confidence is illusory. Even with such important steps as the passage of the ADA and IDEA, discrimination is far from over. People with disabilities are still often treated as inferior to nondisabled people. As disability studies scholar Lennard Davis has pointed out, even the most educated of Americans, professors who make a living by writing about the nature of discriminatory practices and who decry discrimination against women, people of color, and other minorities, leave their attitudes toward people with disabilities largely unexamined. According to Davis, in the writings of these literary theorists, while "others" whose bodies are normal become vivid, others whose bodies are abnormal remain invisible.[5]

Of course, it is not just practitioners of fashionable literary theory who sometimes harbor unexamined and discriminatory attitudes toward people with disabilities. The bioethics and medical literatures of the last decade also reveal misinformation and stereotypic thinking about what disability means for individuals, families, and society. Many clinicians and bioethicists take it for granted that health status is mostly responsible for the reduced life chances of people with a disability, largely ignoring the role of societal factors such as educational and employment discrimination. Furthermore, these clinicians and bioethicists often discount data indicating that people with disabilities and their families do not view their lives in solely or even predominantly negative terms;[6] instead, they may insist that such data reflect a denial of reality or an exceptional ability to cope with problems.[7]

People who make policy concerning the dissemination of genetic information have reached a consensus that the purpose of prenatal testing is to enhance reproductive choice for women and families—not to decrease the number of children with disabilities who are born. Some have acknowledged, however, that there is a tension between the goals of enhancing reproductive choice and preventing the births of children who would have disabilities. Writing about screening programs for cystic fibrosis in the pages of the *American Journal of Human Genetics*, medical geneticist A. L. Beaudet observed: "Although some would argue that the success of the program should be judged solely by the effectiveness of the educational programs (that is, whether screenees understood the information), it is clear that prevention of CF is also, at some level, a measure of a screening program, since few would advocate expanding the substantial resources involved if very few families wish to avoid the disease."[8] Beaudet acknowledges that, in tension with the genetic professional's stated goal of educating individuals (without any investment in the particular decision those individuals might reach), those who pay for such education do so in part with a view to reducing the number of—and costs associated with—children born with cystic fibrosis.

Indeed, the profession of genetic counseling is based on a deep commitment to helping clients discover what course of action, upon reflection, is best for them. Some evidence suggests, however, that when disabilities are involved, both trained genetic counselors and others who deliver genetic information do not always live up to that commitment. A recent study designed to understand the experience of mothers who received a prenatal diagnosis of Down syndrome and chose to continue the pregnancy found problematic attitudes toward people with disabilities, evidenced in the way that medical professionals spoke to those prospective mothers. According to Helm, Miranda, and Chedd, one of the mothers who received a diagnosis of Down syndrome reported the following exchange:

> Obstetrician: *You have to move quickly. There is a doctor at [Hospital X] who does late-term abortions.*
> Mother: *No, I told you I'm not going to have an abortion.*
> Obstetrician: *Talk to your husband. You might want to think about it.*[9]

Because Helm, Miranda, and Chedd only provide this portion of a longer exchange, the rest of us cannot confidently interpret the exchange they report. Advising a patient to discuss a major life decision with her spouse is not prima facie problematic, much less discriminatory. According to their interpretation, however, these words reveal the physician's unwillingness or inability to respect this woman's already stated decision to continue the pregnancy with the fetus carrying a disabling trait. The reported exchange provides no evidence that this obstetrician understands the ways in which many families welcome and nourish—and are nourished by—children with Down syndrome.

As research has shown, obstetricians may be more likely than genetic counselors to urge particular actions upon their patients.[10] Helm, Miranda, and Chedd's study also reports, however, that some genetic counselors reacted negatively to women who intended to bear and raise children with Down syndrome. A woman who was told that the fetus she was carrying would have Down syndrome reported the following: "[The genetic counselor] treated me as though I couldn't accept this news, although I told her I could. She asked, 'What are you going to say to people when they ask you how you could bring a child like this into the world?' "[11] To say nothing of this counselor's failure to discuss the woman's decision without judging it, her words suggest that she has not thought deeply about what disabilities mean for individuals who live with them and for their families. At least from what we learn of her from Helm, Miranda, and Chedd, she does not seem to appreciate that welcoming a child with Down syndrome into a family is not a decision that needs to be defended; she does not seem to appreciate that parental attitudes differ, that traits that matter a great deal to one couple may seem inconsequential to another. Such exchanges are probably not rare exceptions; similar examples can be found in other discussions of genetic counseling practices in the prenatal testing situation.[12]

It is important to remember, however, that many genetic counselors and physicians work extremely hard to live up to the values of informed consent and nondirectiveness, and many of them are not only aware of but share the concerns voiced by the disability rights community. For example, at the New England Medical Center, women whose fetuses are diagnosed with Down syndrome are routinely scheduled to meet with a pediatric medical geneticist and a nurse clinician who specializes in the care of pediatric genetic patients. These women are scheduled to meet with pediatricians who specialize in genetics rather than obstetricians because pediatric geneticists understand better how Down syndrome influences the lives of children and their families. According to project member Diana Bianchi, who practices at the New England Medical Center, every attempt is made to introduce the pregnant woman and her partner to families who are raising infants, children, and/or young adults with Down syndrome. She reports that in her practice, only 62 percent of women who discover they are carrying a fetus with Down syndrome decide to have abortions. That rate of abortion upon a positive finding is believed to be relatively low. Disability critics point to such facts to suggest that when prospective parents obtain more accurate information about what life with disability is like, many realize that parenting a child who has a disability can be as gratifying as parenting a child who does not.

The disability critique proceeds from the view that discrimination results when people in one group fail to imagine that people in some "other" group lead lives as rich and complex as their own. The disability rights critics believe that everyone from literary theorists to bioethicists to obstetricians and genetic counselors are susceptible to such failures of imagination. Moreover, they think that the desire of prospective parents to avoid raising children with disabilities may depend on that same failure.

A Plurality of Disabling Traits and a Plurality of Attitudes toward Prenatal Diagnosis

As one begins to reflect on the meaning of using prenatal diagnosis to detect disabling traits, it is important to notice that the class of "disabling traits" is exceedingly heterogeneous. Prenatal diagnosis can now detect conditions as different as Lesch-Nyhan syndrome and ectrodactyly (a trait involving a partial fusion of the bones of the fingers and toes). Further, not only are the traits heterogeneous, but so are perceptions of their significance and/or seriousness. Nancy Press's research reveals that some generalizations can be made about what people take to be "serious": for example, mothers considering prenatal testing are most fearful of conditions like Lesch-Nyhan, which results in early and painful death.[13] But as the infamous Bree Walker Lampley case indicates, there is debate about the seriousness of ectrodactyly. In 1991, Bree Walker Lampley, a television newswoman in Los Angeles who had ectrodactyly, discovered that the fetus she was carrying had the trait ← and, when asked, made it known that she had no interest in terminating for such a minor trait; some suggested that it was "irresponsible" to bring a child into the world with such a serious trait.[14] Indeed, the research of Dorothy C. Wertz and colleagues suggests that even genetics professionals have very different ideas of what is and what is not "serious."[15] In one of Wertz's surveys, cleft lip/palate, neurofibromatosis, hereditary deafness, insulin-dependent diabetes, Huntington disease, cystic fibrosis, sickle cell anemia, Down syndrome, and manic depression were deemed serious by some professionals and not serious by others.[16]

A similar plurality of views exists within the disability community. Many groups representing people with disabilities, such as the National Down Syndrome Congress and Little People of America, have position statements affirming the value of life with disability for individuals and families.[17] However, there is considerable nuance and disagreement among groups, and in fact within some groups. This complexity is suggested by attitudes within the membership of Little People of America. Many of those who live with achondroplasia are concerned that prenatal testing, which can identify heterozygotes (that is, fetuses that will develop into long-lived people with achondroplasia), will be used to obliterate the Little People of America community. In fact, some members of that community might use the technology to select *for* the trait. Nevertheless, many couples who are heterozygous for achondroplasia would like to use prenatal testing to identify fetuses that are homozygous for the allele associated with achondroplasia. Homozygous achondroplasia is a uniformly fatal condition, and they would like to spare themselves the experience of bearing a child who will soon die. Adding to the complexity, discussions at the 1997 meeting of the ← Society for Disability Studies made it clear that some people with disabilities would use prenatal testing to selectively abort a fetus with the trait they themselves carry—and some people who would not abort a fetus carrying their own disability might abort a fetus if it carried a trait incompatible with their own understanding of a life they want for themselves and their child.

A similar diversity of views toward prenatal testing and abortion can be found among parents raising a child with a disability. Many such parents do not use prenatal diagnosis to determine whether their present fetus is affected.[18] The reasons for this are no doubt many; to some, the trait has come to be unimportant or irrelevant. Some may refuse it on the ground that using the technology would say something hurtful to or about their existing child. Other parents of children with disabilities decide to use these technologies.

We point to the plurality of traits and attitudes toward testing not to suggest that the terrain is too complex to be amenable to policy response. Nor do we think that public policy should be made by taking polls. The point is simply that people committed to ending discrimination and improving life for people who have disabilities are not monolithic on the prenatal testing issue, any more than all feminists are monolithic on a host of "women's issues" or than members of racial minorities are monolithic in their stance toward affirmative action or other practices that affect them. Such lack of unanimity does not negate the concerns that thoughtful people have brought to the attention of the bioethics and genetics communities. But a reasonable policy response must avoid simplifying the facts; it must take such complexities into account.

Health Care in a Changing Environment

Prenatal diagnosis has for the past few decades been offered by genetics specialists and some specially trained obstetricians or physicians in maternal-fetal medicine. Today prenatal diagnosis is often performed by obstetricians, who may or may not offer genetic counseling prior to performing a test. Obstetricians are expected to obtain consent for the diagnostic procedure, but there is debate among professionals about what constitutes sufficient consent for a procedure that will likely end with a pregnancy termination if a condition is identified. Again, some studies suggest that in getting consent for testing, many obstetricians seem to be more directive than the ethic of board-certified genetic counselors permits.[19]

Although genetic counseling can be performed by physicians, nurses, or social workers, typically it is performed by master's degree-level professionals educated in genetic principles and short-term psychosocial counseling. A professional corps of around 1,500 genetic counselors has existed for a quarter century in the United States, about 50 percent of whom provide prenatal counseling full time; another 300 or so provide prenatal counseling part time. In some regions, trained subspecialists perform prenatal diagnosis after genetic counseling, but increasingly obstetricians perform prenatal testing with minimal pretest counseling.

Board-certified genetic counselors emphasize the likelihood of carrying a fetus with a disabling trait based on the age and family history of the prospective parents. The counseling often includes discussion of how testing is performed, what it can detect (including descriptions of chromosomes and genes), and what the information may mean for an affected child. Currently, the ideal process entails an exploration of the prospective parents' views about family and children, a discussion of available economic and social resources, and an exploration of any experience prospective parents may have of people who live with the conditions being tested for. Anecdotal evidence and the few studies that have evaluated prenatal counseling suggest, however, this sort of in-depth discussion is rare.[20]

Most genetic counseling takes place (if it does) before an invasive test like amniocentesis. The presumption is that most people who attend prenatal counseling sessions will choose to undergo testing. Those who decline testing are typically not challenged by the counselor on that decision—although the setting lends itself to the assumption that individuals are there to get tests rather than to make decisions about whether to get tested. Often patients have been referred by physicians and do not understand that prenatal testing is an option that, in light of their values, beliefs, and needs, they may not want to use. Unfortunately, a health care system that emphasizes cutting costs more than truly informed decision making would likely encourage testing and discourage counseling. The latter is time consuming, not readily reimbursable by third-party payers, and can lead to fewer procedures and more births of children with costly medical needs.

In the future, computer-assisted education technologies and videos should be very helpful in communicating information—especially about predisposition or presymptomatic testing—that once was communicated by counselors. But again, in a health care delivery system ever more intent on keeping down costs, things are likely to get worse rather than better when it comes to fostering the dialogue and the counselor-patient relationship that ideally accompany prenatal testing. Improved access to prenatal counseling will compete with other demands on resources, and probably will lose out. It is likely, however, that the need for counselors who help people think through what to do with prenatal information will continue to grow. No one should rest easy with the hope that either alternative educational methods or alternative providers (physicians, nurses, or social workers) alone will be sufficient to meet the need on the horizon.

Reproductive Liberty

The proliferation of prenatal genetic testing has also occurred against the background of the controversy about abortion. Prenatal testing for genetic disability elicits unexpected responses from both sides of the abortion debate: many of those who are uneasy with abortion based on a prenatal finding of a disabling trait are pro-choice. And many who in general are against the right to abortion nonetheless approve of abortions performed on a fetus carrying a disabling trait.

Virtually all the major work in the disability critique of prenatal testing emerges from those who are also committed to a pro-choice, feminist agenda: Adrienne Asch, Marsha Saxton, Anne Finger, and Deborah Kaplan, for example.[21] Other pro-choice feminists, including Ruth Hubbard, Abby Lippman, Carole Browner, and Nancy Press, draw on the disability critique to question the impact of prenatal testing.[22] Like these scholars, our working group's reflections proceed from the premise that women (and men) have the right to determine when and how many children they will have; within the first two trimesters of pregnancy, abortion is a legally and morally defensible means of exercising that right.

What is new about prenatal testing is that it enables prospective parents to some extent to determine not only when and how many but also what kind of children they will have. With the exception of revealing the sex of the fetus, current prenatal testing is used to detect traits considered medically disabling—characteristics deemed undesirable departures from species-typical functioning. In the future it may be increasingly possible to select for traits we *do* value. That, however, is not the possibility that has motivated the disability critique; the motivation for the disability critique is the reality of using prenatal testing and selective abortion to avoid bringing to term fetuses that carry disabling traits. Thus, the issue we examined concerns a special way of using abortion: namely, to select against disabling traits.

Understanding and Evaluating the
Disability Rights Critique

The disability rights critique of prenatal diagnosis and selective abortion advances three claims. Critics contend that:

> (1) Continuing, persistent, and pervasive discrimination constitutes the major problem of having a disability for people themselves and for

their families and communities. Rather than improving the medical or social situation of today's or tomorrow's disabled citizens, prenatal diagnosis reinforces the medical model that disability itself, not societal discrimination against people with disabilities, is the problem to be solved.

(2) In rejecting an otherwise desired child because they believe that the child's disability will diminish their parental experience, parents suggest that they are unwilling to accept any significant departure from the parental dreams that a child's characteristics might occasion.

(3) When prospective parents select against a fetus because of predicted disability, they are making an unfortunate, often misinformed decision that a disabled child will not fulfill what most people seek in child rearing, namely, "to give ourselves to a new being who starts out with the best we can give, and who will enrich us, gladden others, contribute to the world, and make us proud."[23]

In these several contentions can be discerned two broad claims: that prenatal genetic testing followed by selective abortion is morally problematic, and that it is driven by misinformation.

Prenatal Testing Is Morally Problematic

Selective abortion is morally problematic, according to the disability critique, for two reasons. First, selective abortion expresses negative or discriminatory attitudes not merely about a disabling trait, but about those who carry it. Second, it signals an intolerance of diversity not merely in the society but in the family, and ultimately it could harm parental attitudes toward children.

The expressivist argument.   The argument that selective abortion expresses discriminatory attitudes has been called the expressivist argument.[24] Its central claim is that prenatal tests to select against disabling traits express a hurtful attitude about and send a hurtful message to people who live with those same traits. In the late 1980s, Adrienne Asch stated the concern this way: "Do not disparage the lives of existing and future disabled people by trying to screen for and prevent the birth of babies with their characteristics."[25] More recently, she has clarified what the hurtful or disparaging message is:

> As with discrimination more generally, with prenatal diagnosis, a single trait stands in for the whole, the trait obliterates the whole. With both discrimination and prenatal diagnosis, nobody finds out about the rest. The tests send the message that there's no need to find out about the rest.[26]

Indeed, many people with disabilities, who daily experience being seen past because of some single trait they bear, worry that prenatal testing repeats and reinforces that same tendency toward letting the part stand in for the whole. Prenatal testing seems to be more of the discriminatory same: a single trait stands in for the whole (potential) person. Knowledge of the single trait is enough to warrant the abortion of an otherwise wanted fetus. On Asch's more recent formulation, the test sends the hurtful message that people are reducible to a single, perceived-to-be-undesirable trait.

This observation about letting the part stand in for the whole is surely enormously important. In everyday life, traits do often stand in for the whole, and people do get looked past because of them. Indeed, one form of the expressivist argument has been regarded rather highly in another context. Many people who are concerned about supporting women's rights have argued that prenatal sex selection is morally problematic because it embodies and reinforces discriminatory attitudes toward women.[27] The sex trait is allowed to obliterate the whole, as if the parents were saying, "We don't want to find out about 'the rest' of this fetus; we don't want a girl."

Marsha Saxton has put the expressivist argument this way:

> The message at the heart of widespread selective abortion on the basis of prenatal diagnosis is the greatest insult: some of us are "too flawed" in our very DNA to exist; we are unworthy of being born. . . . [F]ighting for this issue, our right and worthiness to be born, is the fundamental challenge to disability oppression; it underpins our most basic claim to justice and equality—we are indeed worthy of being born, worth the help and expense, and we know it![28]

And as Nancy Press has argued, by developing and offering tests to detect some characteristics and not others, the professional community is expressing the view that some characteristics, but not all, warrant the attention of prospective parents.[29]

For several reasons, however, there is disagreement about the merit of the expressivist argument as a basis for any public policy regarding prenatal diagnosis of disability. Individual women and families have a host of motives and reasons for seeking out genetic information, and as James Lindemann Nelson and Eva Feder Kittay argue, it is impossible to conclude just what "message" is being sent by any one decision to obtain prenatal testing.[30] Acts (and the messages they convey) rarely have either a single motivation or meaning.

Some prospective parents no doubt have wholly negative attitudes toward what they imagine a life with a disability would be like for them and their child; others may believe that life could be rich for the child but suspect that their own lives would be compromised. Others who have disabilities perhaps see passing on their disabling trait as passing on a part of life that for them has been negative. Parents of one child with a disability may believe that they don't have the emotional or financial resources for another. The point is that the meaning of prenatal testing for would-be parents is not clear or singular. In any case, those sympathetic to at least some forms of prenatal testing point out that prospective parents do not decide about testing to hurt existing disabled people but to implement their own familial goals. In that sense, there is no "message" being sent at all.

To many in the disability rights movement, however, regardless of the parental motive to avoid the birth of a child who will have a disability, the parent may still be letting a part stand in for the whole. That prospective parents do not intend to send a hurtful message does not speak to the fact that many people with disabilities receive such a message and are pained by it.

A second criticism of the expressivist argument is that it calls into question the morality of virtually all abortions. The argument presumes that we can distinguish between aborting "any" fetus and a "particular" fetus that has a disability—what Adrienne Asch has called the "any-particular distinction." According to Asch, most abortions reflect a decision not to bring any fetus to term at this time; selective abortions involve a decision not to bring this particular fetus to term because of its traits. Pro-choice individuals within and outside the disability community agree that it is morally defensible for a woman to decide, for example, that she doesn't want any child at a given time because she thinks she's too young to mother well, or because it would thwart her life plan, or because she has all the children she wants to raise. The question is whether that decision is morally different from a decision to abort an otherwise-wanted fetus.

But it is not clear that the distinction is adequate. Sometimes the decision to abort "any" fetus can be recast as a decision to abort a "particular" fetus. James Lindemann Nelson, for example, argues that if parents of three children chose to end a pregnancy that would have produced a fourth child, such parents would not be making a statement about the worthwhileness of other families with four children, or about the worth of fourth-born children as human beings.[31] Rather, they would be deciding what would be right for their particular situation. If, as Asch and others have argued, prenatal testing is morally suspect because it lets a trait stand in for the whole potential person, precisely the same argument would apply to aborting a fetus because it was the fourth child. The trait of being fourth-born makes the prospective parents ignore every other aspect in which that fetus could become a child that would be a blessing to its family and community. Nelson's example of the potential fourth-born child suggests one reason to doubt the merit of the any-particular distinction; he thinks that the disability critics have failed to explain why traits like being fourth-born could be a legitimate basis for an abortion while disabling traits could not.

A third criticism of the expressivist argument is that it presumes selective abortion based on prenatal testing is morally problematic in a way that other means of preventing disability are not. Such other means include, for example, taking folic acid to reduce the likelihood of spina bifida or eschewing medication that is known to stunt the growth or harm the organs or limbs of a developing fetus. Such acts (or refraining from such acts) on the part of the pregnant woman are designed to protect the health of the developing fetus.

Disability critics hold, however, that abortion does not protect the developing fetus from anything. It prevents disability by simply killing the fetus. Proponents of this disability critique hold a strong pro-choice position. Their objection is only to a certain way of using abortion.

But those from the mainstream pro-choice community think of selective abortion in different terms. They do not see an important moral difference between selective abortion and other modes of preventing disability, in large part because they do see an important moral distinction between a born child with a disabling trait and an embryo or fetus with a disabling trait. They argue that parents of all born children have an obligation to love and care for those children—regardless of their traits. They also argue, however, that the pregnant woman and her partner are not "parents" before the child is born. Just as a woman or couple may decide during the first two trimesters of any pregnancy that becoming a parent to a first child, or to any child, is not in accord with their life plans, so may they make the same decision on the ground that the fetus has disabling traits. The woman may terminate the pregnancy and try again to become pregnant with a fetus that has not been identified as carrying a disabling trait. In this view, if it is reasonable to prevent disability in a developing child by adhering to a particular lifestyle, and taking specified medications or refraining from taking others, it is equally acceptable to opt for abortion to prevent the birth of a child with a significant disability.[32]

Even if expressivist arguments will not dissuade all people from using tests in making reproductive decisions for their own lives, policies that would in any way penalize those who continue pregnancies in spite of knowing that their child will live with a disabling trait must be avoided. Those prospective parents who either forego prenatal testing or decide that they want to continue a pregnancy despite the detection of a disabling trait should not have to contend with losing medical services or benefits for their child, nor feel obliged to justify their decisions. Further, the availability of prenatal testing in no way reduces our societal obligations to those people who are born with or acquire disabilities. Even if prenatal diagnosis says nothing to or about existing or future disabled people, we should as a society vigorously enforce antidiscrimination laws and improve services and supports for disabled people and their families.

The parental attitude argument.   The second argument that prenatal testing is morally problematic we call the "parental attitude argument." According to this argument, using prenatal tests to select against some traits indicates a problematic conception of and attitude toward parenthood. Part of the argument is that prenatal testing is rooted in a "fantasy and fallacy" that "parents can guarantee or create perfection" for their children.[33] If parents were to understand what they really should seek in parenting, then they would see how relatively unimportant are the particular traits of their children.

The parental attitude argument also involves the thought that in the context of prenatal testing, a part—a disability—stands in for the whole—a person. The prospective parent who wants to avoid raising a child with a diagnosable disability forgets that along with the disabling trait come other traits, many of which are likely to be as enjoyable, pride-giving, positive (and as problematic, annoying, and complicated) as any other child's traits. If prospective parents imagine that disability precludes everything else that could be wonderful about the child, they are likely acting on misinformation and stereotypes. The prospective parent has made biology destiny in the way that critics of the medical model of disability consistently resist.

According to the parental attitude argument, prospective parents should keep in mind that the disabling trait is only one of a fetus's characteristics. The activity of appreciating and nurturing the particular child one has is what the critics of selection view as the essence of good parenting. Loving and nurturing a child entails appreciating, enjoying, and developing as best one can the characteristics of the child one has, not turning the child into someone she is not or lamenting what she is not. If we were to notice that it is a fantasy and fallacy to think that parents can guarantee or create perfection for their child, and if we were to recognize what is really important about the experience of parenting, we would see that we should be concerned with certain attitudes toward parenting, not with "disabling" traits in our children. Good parents will care about raising whatever child they receive and about the relationship they will develop, not about the traits the child bears. In short, what bothers those wary of prenatal diagnosis is what might be called "the selective mentality." The attention to particular traits indicates a morally troubling conception of parenthood, a preoccupation with what is trivial and an ignorance of what is profound.

Those who connect acceptance of disability to what is desirable in any parent-child relationship will worry that our attitudes toward parenthood and ultimately toward each other are changing as a result of technologies like prenatal diagnosis.[34] Do these technologies lead us, one might ask, toward the commodification of children, toward thinking about them and treating them as products rather than as "gifts" or "ends in themselves"? Is it making us as a society less resilient in the face of the inevitable risks that our children face, and less willing to acknowledge the essential fragility of our species? When members of our project are confronted with, for example, sex selection or with the possibility of selecting for non-health-related traits like sexual orientation, concerns about the selective mentality come quickly to our lips. Indeed, those who want to reject the parental attitude argument in the context of disabling traits must recognize that they are criticizing an argument that they themselves may well want to use in the context of non-health-related traits. Certainly, many worry about the cumulative effect of individual choices, about the technologization of reproduction, and about a decreasing cultural ability or willingness to accept the reality of uncontrollable events. These concerns trouble even those who profess to be comfortable with genetic testing and selective abortion.

Nonetheless, many find significant problems with the parental attitude argument. One of the most important is that it makes what William Ruddick calls the "maternalist assumption," namely, that "a woman who wants a child should want any child she gets."[35] Ruddick acknowledges that many women do hold "maternalist" conceptions of pregnancy and motherhood, out of which that assumption grows. But he points out that there are other legitimate conceptions of pregnancy and motherhood that do not depend on or give rise to the same assumption. He suggests that some prospective parents may legitimately adopt a "projectivist" or "familial" conception of parenthood, and that either of these views is compatible with trying to ensure that any child they raise has characteristics that accord with these parental goals. In the projectivist parent's understanding of child rearing, the child is a part of her parental projects, and, within limits, parents may legitimately undertake to ensure that a child starts out with the requisites for fulfilling these parental hopes and aims. Ruddick is not claiming that projectivist parents could ignore a child's manifested commitments to things beyond the parents' life plans, but he is saying that, for example, the parent passionate about music may legitimately select against a future child whose deafness would make a love of some forms of music impossible. If a hearing child turns out to be tone deaf and enthusiastic about rock collecting and bird watching but not music, and if the parent views these activities as inimical to her parental values or projects, she need not support them, or (within limits) allow other people to do so.

According to Ruddick, the "familial" conception of parenthood highlights a parent's vision of her child as herself a parent or sibling— a participant in a nuclear and extended family that gives central meaning to life. For example, parents whose dreams of child rearing include envisioning their own child as a parent would be acting consistently with their conception of parenthood if they decided not to raise a boy with cystic fibrosis, whose sterility and shortened life span might preclude either biological or adoptive parenthood. A child of such a parent might, of course, reject family life in favor of solitude or communal adult companionship, but in using available technology to avoid raising a child who would never be able to fulfill a deeply cherished parental dream, the parent is acting in accordance with a legitimate conception of parenthood.

Although Ruddick is not alone in thinking that a selective mentality may be compatible with praiseworthy parenting, many share the disability community's worry that prenatal testing threatens our attitudes toward children, parenthood, and ultimately ourselves. Certainly, it would be to the good if we thought more deeply about our attitudes. If we want to be parents, why do we want to be parents? What do we hope being parents will bring for our children-to-be and for ourselves? And prospective parents would benefit from grappling with those questions in the context of prenatal diagnosis. However, such concerns could not undergird specific policies regarding prenatal testing for disabling traits.

Prenatal Testing Is Based on Misinformation

The second major claim of the disability critique is that prenatal testing depends on a misunderstanding of what life with disability is like for children with disabilities and their families. Connected with this claim is the question whether disability is one more form of "neutral" human variation, or whether it is different from variations usually thought of as nondisabling traits, such as eye color, skin color, or musicality.

There are many widely accepted beliefs about what life with disability is like for children and their families. Most of these beliefs are not based on data. They include assumptions that people with disabilities lead lives of relentless agony and frustration and that most marriages break up under the strain of having a child with a disability. Recent studies suggest, for example, that many members of the health professions view childhood disability as predominantly negative for children and their families, in contrast to what research on the life satisfaction of people with disabilities and their families has actually shown.[36] One strand of this project, then, involved wrestling with what to make of conflicting perceptions about how people with disabilities and their families experience life. Three disability researchers in the Hastings Center group—Philip M. Ferguson, Alan Gartner, and Dorothy K. Lipsky—analyzed empirical data on the impact of children with disabilities on families.[37] Their review, surprising to many, concludes that the adaptational profiles of families that have a child with a disability basically resemble those of families that do not.

According to Ferguson, Gartner, and Lipsky's reading of the data, families that include disabled children fare on average no better or worse than families in general. Some families founder, others flourish. Ferguson, Gartner, and Lipsky do not deny that families are often distressed upon first learning that their child has a disability. And they acknowledge that families with children who evince significantly challenging behavior experience more disruption than do other families. But recent research on raising a child with a disability offers happier news for families than many in our society have been led to expect. In the words of one leading family researcher, "The most recent literature suggests that families of children with handicaps [sic] exhibit variability

comparable to the general population with respect to important outcomes such as parent stress, . . . family functioning, . . . and marital
satisfaction."[38] Studies of family adaptation have begun to recognize the
prevalence of positive outcomes in many families.[39] Indeed, one recent
study found that parents of disabled adolescents reported more positive perceptions of their children than do parents of nondisabled
adolescents.[40]

In a 1995 study intended to learn how a child's disability affected
the work lives of dual-career families, the authors found that the needs
and concerns of families with and without children with disabilities
were "strikingly similar." They did, however, observe:

> What seems to distinguish families of children with disabilities from other
> working families is the intensity and complexity of the arrangements
> required to balance work and home responsibilities successfully. For exam-
> ple, parents of children with disabilities, particularly those with serious
> medical or behavioral problems, find it more difficult to locate appropriate,
> affordable child care. . . . Similarly, these families are more dependent
> upon health insurance policies with comprehensive coverage.[41]

This same study reminds us of a point that both Ruddick and Kittay
made: a child's disability may sometimes alter the customary parent-
child life cycle, in which parents gradually relinquish daily guidance
and caretaking and—if they are fortunate—see their children take on
adult productive and caretaking roles. Depending on the impairment
and on the social arrangements that parents help a growing child construct, some people with disabilities may require their parents' help
through adulthood in securing shelter, social support, and safety. Increasingly, adults with disabilities such as muscular dystrophy, spina bifida,
cystic fibrosis, Down syndrome, and other conditions do not stay "eternal
children," as they were once thought to do. Nonetheless, some, albeit
a small, portion of the population of disabled people will be more
vulnerable for longer than others and more in need of what Kittay
(borrowing from Sara Ruddick) described as "attentive, protective
love."[42]

Although it is important to demolish the myth that disability entails
relentless agony for the child and family, there is still considerable
disagreement about what conclusions to draw from the literature on
the family impact of a child with disability. In the view of the disability
community, this literature suggests that prenatal testing to select against
disabling traits is misguided in the sense that it is based on misinforma-

tion. That is, if prospective parents could see that families with children who have disabilities fare much better than the myth would have it, then parents would be less enthusiastic about the technology.

However, recognizing that there are erroneous beliefs that need to be dispelled may not show that the desire for prenatal testing stems from misinformation alone. The first problem with the misinformation argument has to do with the difference between retrospective and prospective judgments. It is one thing to look back on a stressful but ultimately rewarding experience and say, "I'm glad I did that." It is another to look forward to the possibility of a stressful and perhaps ultimately rewarding experience and say, "I'm glad to give it a try." To appreciate that many families respond well to stress does not commit one to thinking that it would be a mistake for families to try to avoid it. It may be true that, as one of the studies of working families points out, the concerns of working parents with disabled children very much resemble the concerns of any working parent—ensuring that children are safe, happy, stimulated, and well cared for at home, at school, and in after-school activities. But that study also acknowledges that working parents of children with special medical or behavioral needs find that meeting those needs takes more time, ingenuity, and energy than they think would have to be spent on the needs of nondisabled children. To appreciate that many families emerge stronger, wiser, and even better as a result of such an experience may not suggest that it is unreasonable or morally problematic to try to avert it. As Mary Ann Baily put it, child rearing is already like mountain climbing. That I want to climb Mount Rainier doesn't commit me to wanting to climb Everest. I appreciate that the rewards of climbing Everest might be extraordinary, beyond my wildest dreams, but I'd settle for Rainier.[43]

The disability researchers and theorists did not persuade everyone in the project group that raising a child with a disability is not more demanding than raising a child without this condition. As a specific type of life challenge, raising a child who has a disability may provide one individual of a particular aptitude or orientation with a life experience of great reward and fulfillment, perhaps with a positive transformation. For a different individual, who possesses a different character or aptitude, the overall experience may be negative. Parents may examine themselves and conclude that they are not choosing against a child's specific traits; they may be making an honest and informed acceptance of their own character and goals.[44]

Disability in Society

Perhaps the most fundamental and irreconcilable disagreement over the misinformation argument has to do with just what having a disability is "really" like for people themselves and for their families. Just how much of the problem of disability is socially constructed? Is it reasonable to say that in a differently constructed social environment, what are now disabling traits would become "neutral" characteristics?

Undoubtedly, more of the problem of disability is socially constructed than many people generally believe. But does that imply that having a characteristic like cystic fibrosis or spina bifida is of no more consequence than being left-handed or being a man who is five feet, three inches tall? According to the disability rights critique of prenatal testing, if people with disabilities were fully integrated into society, then there would be no need for the testing. In the world they seek to create, if a given health status turned out to be a handicap, that would be because of societal, not personal, deficits; the appropriate response would be to change society so that the person could live a full life with a range of talents, capacities, and difficulties that exist for everyone. In a society that welcomed the disabled as well as the nondisabled, there would be no reason to prevent the births of people with traits now called disabling.

In this project, those sympathetic to at least some forms of prenatal testing were struck by the fact that, for reasons that seem to be complex, members of the disability community speak at different times in different modes about the nature of disability. Sometimes, members of that community are clear about the fact that disabling traits have a "biological reality" or are not neutral. Adrienne Asch writes, "The inability to move without mechanical aid, to see, to hear, or to learn is not inherently neutral. Disability itself limits some options."[45] At other times, however—and this is the mode usually emphasized in critiques of prenatal testing—those in the disability rights movement speak as if those traits indeed are inherently neutral. Thus, Deborah Kent writes: "I premised my life on the conviction that blindness was a neutral characteristic."[46] In this other mode, the disability community argument often is that, different from what prospective parents imagine, these so-called disabling traits are not, to coin a term, "disvaluable" in themselves; they are disvaluable because of the way they are socially constructed.

Nora Groce's work illustrates the point about how social arrangements shape whether a characteristic is disabling.[47] In Martha's Vineyard in the nineteenth century, Groce argues, being unable to hear was not disabling because everyone spoke sign language. Groce's work establishes that much of what is difficult about having a disability stems from manifold facets of society, from architecture to education to aesthetic preferences. In choosing how to construct our societies, we do, as Allen Buchanan puts it, "choose who will be disabled."[48] We could choose differently than we have, and if we were to choose differently, what's disabling about what we now call disabilities would be largely eliminated. Plainly, then, the social constructionist argument is powerful. The objection concerns, rather, what appears to be a correlative claim of the disability position: that so-called disabling traits are neither disabling nor "disvaluable," but neutral.

Trying to delineate, understand, and come to consensus over this claim is perhaps the most contentious and difficult part of thinking about prenatal testing in the context of the disability critique. It is worth restating what Asch, Saxton, Lipsky, and others define as the "neutrality" of disability. Adherents of the disability critique acknowledge that some characteristics now labeled disabilities are easier to incorporate into today's society, or into a reconstructed society, than are others. Thus, no one would deny that disabling traits—departures from species-typical functioning—foreclose some options, or that some disabilities foreclose more options than others. A child with Down syndrome may never climb Mount Rainier because his strength, agility, and stamina may preclude it; he may also never read philosophy because he does not have the skills to decipher abstract material. Granting that people who can climb mountains and read abstract papers derive enjoyment and meaning from such activities, then being foreclosed from them, not by one's own choice, is regrettable. The lack of possibility is widely seen as disvaluable. In addition, these lacks of capacity stem from the characteristics of the individual who is not strong enough or agile enough to climb, or who is unable by any teaching now known to us to grasp complex abstract discourse. In that sense, disability community critics acknowledge that these facets of some disabilities are "real"—inherent in the characteristic itself—and not an artifact of any interaction with the environment. Even if all traits are to some extent "socially constructed," that is irrelevant to the fact that the existence of these traits forecloses for those who have them the opportunity to engage in some highly desirable and valuable activities; not being able to engage in those activities is disvaluable.

Disability community critics of the medical model of disability acknowledge that they would be going too far if they claimed that society should not value activities that some of its members cannot engage in; it is harmless to value the capacity of sight that permits people to behold Rembrandt's masterpieces, sunsets, or the faces of family members and friends. It is not offensive to prize intellectual accomplishment, athletic prowess, or the ability to appreciate visual beauty, and to regret that not everyone we know can enjoy them. To the extent that spina bifida, Down syndrome, blindness, or cystic fibrosis currently preclude people from undertaking some parts of life that people who do not have those traits might experience, the disability critique acknowledges that disability puts some limits on the "open future"[49] people seek for themselves and their children.

As Bonnie Steinbock argues, if we really thought disability "neutral," we would not work as we do to maintain, restore, and promote health in ourselves and others. We use medicine in the hope that it will cure or ameliorate illness and disability. We urge pregnant women to refrain from activities that risk harming the fetus. If we thought that disabilities were "neutral," then we could tell women who smoke or drink during pregnancy to rest easy, for developmental delay, low birth weight, and fetal alcohol syndrome would all be just "neutral variations," of no consequence to the future child.[50]

While disability community critics acknowledge that some disabilities foreclose some opportunities, they also hold that calling attention to the foreclosure obscures two important points. The first is that rather than dwell on the extent to which opportunities to engage in some activities are truncated, we should concentrate on finding ways for people with disabilities to enjoy alternative modes of those same activities. Philip M. Ferguson puts it this way:

> The point is not so much whether . . . a blind person cannot enjoy a Rembrandt . . . but whether social arrangements can be imagined that allow blind people to have intense aesthetic experiences. . . . People in wheelchairs may not be able to climb mountains, but how hard is it to create a society where the barriers are removed to their experiences of physical exhilaration? . . . Someone with Down syndrome may not be able to experience the exquisite joy of reading bioethics papers and debating ethical theory, but . . . that person can experience the joy of thinking hard about something and reflecting on what he or she really believes. . . . The challenge is to create the society that will allow as

many different paths as possible to the qualities of life that make us all part of the human community.[51]

The second fundamental point is that rather than concentrate on the truncation or loss of some opportunities, our society generally—and prospective parents in particular—should concentrate on the nearly infinite range of remaining opportunities. Indeed, every life course necessarily closes off some opportunities in the pursuit of others. Thus, while the disability critics of prenatal diagnosis acknowledge that disability is likely to entail some amount of physical, psychological, social, and economic hardship, they hold that when viewed alongside any other life, on balance, life is no worse for people who have disabilities than it is for people who do not. No parent should assume that disability ensures a worse life for a child, one with more suffering and less quality, than will be had by those children with whom she or he will grow up.

The claim then is that overall, there is no more stress in raising a child with a disability than in raising any other child, even if at some times there is more stress, or different stress. In that sense, the disability community claims that disability is on balance neutral. Even here, however, many find that the terms "neutral" and "normal" are either inaccurate characterizations of disability or are being used in confusing ways. Specifically, some worry that these terms are used sometimes only to describe or evaluate traits and at other times to describe or evaluate persons.

Evaluations of Traits versus Evaluations of Persons

As already mentioned, the disability community itself sometimes speaks about the descriptive and evaluative senses in which disabling traits are not neutral, not normal. Legislation like the ADA could not exist without recognition that in some sense disabling traits are neither neutral nor normal. Indeed, the societal provision of special resources and services to people with disabilities depends on noticing the descriptive and evaluative senses in which disabling traits are not neutral, and how the needs of the people who live with them are, descriptively speaking, not normal. Yet the recognition of the obligation to provide those special resources is rooted in a commitment to the fundamental idea that the people living with those traits are, morally speaking, "normal"; the people bearing the traits are evaluatively normal in the sense of deserving the normal respect due equally to all persons. Unequal or special funding expresses a commitment to moral equality. Recognizing the non-neutrality of the trait and the "ab-normality" of the person's needs is necessary for expressing the commitment to moral equality and equal opportunity. There is nothing paradoxical about appreciating the descriptive sense in which people with disabling traits are abnormal while also appreciating the evaluative or moral sense in which they are normal.

Some who are sympathetic to prenatal testing worry that people in the disability community (as well as others) often conflate descriptive claims about traits and evaluative or moral claims about persons, as for example when Deborah Kent, who is blind, writes:

> When I was growing up people called my parents "wonderful." They were praised for raising me "like a normal child." As far as I could tell, they were like most of the other parents in my neighborhood, sometimes wonderful and sometimes very annoying. And from my point of view I wasn't like a normal child—I was normal.[52]

What does Kent mean when she says that she "was normal"? As a descriptive claim, it is not reasonable to say that the trait of blindness is normal. Statistically speaking, it is not. Also, as an evaluative claim, insofar as the trait can make it impossible to enjoy some wonderful opportunities, it does not seem reasonable to say that the trait is neutral. The trait may indeed seem neutral and insignificant when viewed in the context of the whole person; but that is a claim about the person, not the trait. On the view of those sympathetic to testing, the descriptive and evaluative claims about the trait do not bear a necessary logical relation to evaluative claims about the person who bears it. As an evaluative or moral claim about the person, it makes perfect sense to say that a person who is blind is normal; she is normal in the sense that she deserves the normal, usual, equal respect that all human beings deserve.

But if it is easy to notice the difference between the descriptive and evaluative claims about traits and the evaluative claims about persons, why do people in the disability community (and others) keep slipping between the two? Erik Parens suggests that there may be an important reason for this seemingly imprecise slipping. Discrimination against people with disabilities often involves a tendency to allow the part to stand in for the whole; Parens's suggestion is that members of the disability community sometimes succumb to a similar, equally problematic error. The majority community sometimes uses the trait to deny the moral significance of the person; the disability community sometimes uses the moral significance of the person to deny the significance of the trait. The majority community slips from an observation about a trait to a claim about a person; the disability community slips from an observation about a person to a claim about a trait. At important moments, both groups fail to distinguish evaluations of traits from evaluations of persons. While such slippage may be easily committed in both communities, and particularly understandable on the part of the disability community, it may be equally counterproductive in both.

In the end, for all of the project group's disagreements about the appropriateness of employing selective abortion to avoid raising a child with a so-called disabling trait, and about the aptness of the distinction between aborting any fetus versus aborting a particular fetus with a disability, at least these disagreements forced the group to grapple with what many think is disvaluable or undesirable about these traits. Albeit uneasily, the majority of the working group seems to think that disabling traits are disvaluable insofar as they constrain or limit some opportunities. To say that a disability is disvaluable is only to say that, in the world we now inhabit and in the world we can imagine living in any time soon, to have a given trait would make it impossible or very difficult to engage in some activities that most people would want themselves or their children to have the option of engaging in. For this reason, then, the majority seems uneasily to think that traits are disvaluable insofar as they preclude what many find precious. This view was held "uneasily" because many are keenly aware of how limited our ability is to imagine alternative social constructions—as well as of the extent to which traits once thought unreconstructable are now thought to be nearly infinitely plastic. We are keenly aware of the extent to which the trait that is sex was constructed in the past in arbitrary and pernicious ways, as well as of past arguments that sex could not be constructed much differently. And we recognize how paltry our ability is to imagine what the experience of others is like. Few of us would have believed before the project meetings began that conjoined twins would report feeling about their lives pretty much like people with "normal" bodies report feeling about theirs.[53]

It is important to remember that the disability community arguments are not intended to justify wholesale restrictions on prenatal testing for genetic disability. Rather, they are intended to make prospective parents pause and think about what they are doing and to challenge professionals to help parents better examine their decisions. They are intended to help make our decisions thoughtful and informed, not thoughtless and automatic. In his book about his son who has Down syndrome, Michael Bérubé attempts to steer a path much like the one ultimately adopted here. He writes:

> I'm . . . not sure whether I can have any advice for prospective parents who are contemplating what course of action to take when they discover they will bear a "disabled" child. Obviously I can't and don't advocate abortion of fetuses with Down syndrome; indeed, the only argument I have is that such decisions should not be automatic.[54]

To some, the advice that such decisions shouldn't be automatic may seem wishy-washy and disheartening. But to those who, like Hannah Arendt, think that evil can arise from thoughtlessness, it seems neither.

Recommendations to Professional Providers

These reflections lead to a question that defied our efforts at consensus: Is there a helpful and rational way to distinguish, in light of the needs and interests of families, between tests that providers should routinely offer and those they should not?

From the beginning of this project, it was agreed that using tests for conditions like Tay-Sachs is reasonable. Families have a morally defensible interest in avoiding the stress and sorrow associated with having a child who has a uniformly fatal condition such as this. And at least in the beginning, many also agreed that it would be unreasonable for medical professionals to offer tests for non-health-related traits such as, say, eye color. Many agreed that medical resources should not be used to help individuals satisfy narcissism or gain advantage. Further, many agreed, at least initially, that whereas prenatal testing to avoid disability arguably is consistent with the goals of medicine, prenatal testing to produce advantage is not. As James Lindemann Nelson points out, just as most reject what might be called the unconditional demand to welcome the prospect of a child with Tay-Sachs, so most reject what might be called the unconditional demand for the so-called perfect child.[55] A desire for what has no conditions or constraints seems to be at work in both, and in both seems unreasonable.

If one thinks there are reasons to draw lines between reasonable and unreasonable tests, then the question becomes: How many and how clearly can and should such lines be drawn? Jeffrey R. Botkin has made one of the most sophisticated attempts to draw lines.[56] To undergird that attempt, Botkin offers the general principle that when inquiring about the traits of the fetus, parents should be able to get information "designed to prevent harms to parents that are approximately the same magnitude as the harms of an unwanted pregnancy" (p. 36). The reasoning goes something like this: we assume that the prospective parent's conception of the harm associated with an unwanted pregnancy is realistic and appropriate. And we recognize that beyond the abortion itself, no other scarce medical resources, such as prenatal testing and genetic counseling, are required. However, according to Botkin, we should worry that the prospective parent's conception of the harm associated with some disabling traits is neither realistic nor appropriate. "The disappointment parents may feel [in circumstances where the condition is minor] is real, but disappointment from unrealistic or inappropriate expectations need not be considered a harm worth preventing" (p. 37). That is, we should develop criteria to help determine when the harm associated with a disabling trait is realistic and appropriate enough to warrant using medicine's resources to prevent it.

Botkin offers four criteria to help distinguish conditions serious enough to warrant using those resources: the severity of condition, the age of onset, the probability that the genotype will manifest as disease, and the probability that the condition will occur in those without specific risk factors. For example, on Botkin's account, conditions such as hemophilia, Down syndrome, cystic fibrosis, and muscular dystrophy produce enough harm or burden for the family to warrant the use of the resources and the act of abortion. Among the conditions that are not serious enough to warrant the use and act are most cases of asthma (which can be effectively treated), Marfan syndrome (which has "limited impact on the life of the child and family in terms of effort, time, and financial resources" [p. 38]), Huntington disease (since "adult onset conditions do not constitute a burden to parents on the same magnitude as an unwanted child" [p. 38]), and schizophrenia (where a genotype may be a necessary but not sufficient cause for the disease).

Yet, however sophisticated Botkin's attempt may be to distinguish for policy purposes between serious and minor disabling traits, at least two sorts of objection can be raised to any such attempt. On the one hand, Dorothy Wertz's research shows that even among genetics professionals, there is deep disagreement about what constitutes a "serious" genetic trait.[57] In her view, therefore, Botkin's first and arguably most important criterion won't work for public policy purposes. On the other hand, proponents of disability rights object to attempting such precise distinctions, for several reasons. First, enlisting medical professionals to list the conditions approved for tests and exclude others as "not serious enough or burdensome enough" turns individual, private, parental decisions into socially supported ones. Also, it increases the likelihood that an explicitly devaluing message will be sent about people whose conditions are listed as "serious enough to avoid." Indeed, disability critics are horrified at the thought of officially identifying "bad" and "less bad" disabilities. Such lines would pit some members of the disability community against others. Some members of the community would end up on the right side of the tracks, others on the wrong.

To convey that disability is one characteristic (a normal, neutral form of human variation) the disability community may tolerate considerable parental autonomy to select against traits—in fact, more than it would like. In this project, at least, in rejecting the idea of drawing lines, members of the disability community came to occupy a position quite like the one occupied by proponents of parental autonomy. Ultimately, this preference that the decision be parental, not medical, prevented a consensus about one form of line drawing.

In the absence of a line between serious and minor disabling traits, perhaps there could be a line between disabling traits and other sorts of non-health-related traits. For example, would it work, as a public policy compromise, to say that it is reasonable for prospective parents to think carefully about testing for any traits that might be covered under the first part of the ADA, but unreasonable for them to test for traits that are not covered? The first or "functional" part of the definition would state that a disability is a physical or mental impairment that substantially limits one or more of the major life activities of an individual. The strength of this possibility is that such traits are associated with stresses that families might reasonably attempt to avoid. Thus, the distinction might be serviceable, in spite of the contestability of the phrases "substantially limits" and "major life activity."

Several features of this approach to determining the difference between reasonable and unreasonable tests are worth noting. First, it allows the people who will bear the consequences of the decision (that is, the prospective parents) to determine what disabling traits are sufficiently serious to warrant abortion. Second, it retains a clear connection between medical resources and health status. Third, it is not consistent with testing for non-health-related traits such as sex, sexual orientation, eye color, height, or similar traits.

However, our working group did not reach a consensus that it would be reasonable to offer tests only for traits covered under the

ADA, for roughly the same reasons that it resisted distinguishing among disabling traits of different severity. At least three reasons were given. First, those representing a disability rights perspective argue that while in the best of all possible worlds it perhaps would not be harmful to draw such a line, it would be in this world of rampant discrimination against people with disabilities. Unpersuaded by the critiques of the expressivist argument, and wanting to characterize disability as a form of human variation as acceptable as any other, they believe that drawing lines, whether among disabling traits or between disabling traits and nondisabling traits, will send a hurtful message to and about people with disabilities. Second, as explained by Dorothy Wertz, even if our group could reach consensus about how to draw such a line, what happens in practice will be determined by the desires of consumers and the decisions of health care delivery systems responding to those desires. Third, drawing a line between traits covered under the ADA and those not covered would be paternalistic; that is, doing so would be to make decisions for prospective parents that are rightly their own.

Each of these arguments has problems. Objections to the expressivist argument were explored above. The chief objection to the second argument is that it is really not so much a moral case against drawing lines as a prediction that such lines would fail. While ethical analysis has to take account of the facts and imagine how they will change, the point of such analysis is not to predict the future but to describe how the future ought to be—how it would be if our practices were more rational and just. An adequate response to the argument from paternalism would require analyzing what is at stake in selecting *for* desired traits, since the argument is rooted in the thought that parents should be free to choose whatever traits will be beneficial for their children. But our project did not systematically take up what is at stake in selecting for traits; thus, a response to that argument would be out of place here.[58]

For many in the project group, the refusal to accept any line drawing was a frustrating and disappointing result—as it will be for others. It will be disappointing to many in the mainstream medical community who would like to admit some but not all kinds of prenatal testing. And it will be disappointing to many proponents of disability rights, who while worried about increasing societal control over the characteristics of children, know that failing to distinguish acceptable from unacceptable testing will probably lead to more testing, to more attempts to screen out all sorts of attributes, and possibly to increasing intolerance of diversity in the human population and devaluing of adaptability to the unexpected in life.

Nonetheless, our project group could not reach a consensus about drawing lines between reasonable and unreasonable tests—nor did we have the opportunity to discuss alternatives to line drawing in the provision of prenatal diagnostic services. Clearly, additional discussion and research are needed to achieve a balance between competing visions of how best to use this technology in clinical care. When public policy-makers explore these issues in the future, we hope they will benefit from knowing in advance just how deep the disagreement can be about the wisdom of "drawing lines" in this context.

Genetic Counseling and Educating People about Disabilities

While this document is the record of disagreement over the substantive question about what traits may reasonably be tested for, on the procedural question about how prenatal tests are ideally offered and how the results of such tests are ideally discussed, there is considerable agreement.

Perhaps most important, in accordance with the ethic of genetic counseling, all genetics professionals must help prospective parents give truly informed consent to receive testing and equally must help patients reach truly informed decisions about how to use test results. Based on respect for persons, and as articulated in the National Society of Genetic Counselors Code of Ethics,[59] genetic counselors are committed to helping individuals understand genetic information and act on that information in accordance with their own values. Respect for the equality of persons and for the legitimate heterogeneity of their life projects is arguably one of the most substantive values available to us.

There are prenatal testing programs that help prospective parents gather information about what life is like for families with children who have disabilities. Such programs have begun to foster the sort of truly informed consent that the disability community is calling for and that the ethic of genetic counselors aspires to. Yet some evidence suggests that there are still physicians and genetic counselors who, for example, display surprise or distress upon hearing that a woman wants to bring to term a fetus identified as having a disability. If genetics professionals and obstetrical providers are to help individuals make truly informed decisions, then they, like everybody else in the "majority" community, must identify and overcome biases against people with disabilities.

The first, crucial step in helping patients achieve truly informed consent and make truly informed decisions is to give providers access to good information about what disability is really like for children with disabilities and for their families. Education about life with disability—as people who live with disabilities view it—is still too rarely offered to those who deliver genetic information. Indeed, according to one recent survey, many recent graduates of genetic counseling programs report that they think genetic counseling programs should highlight such education more than they do now.[60] Disability must become an important topic in the training of anyone who offers prenatal genetic tests, whether that person is a genetic counselor, medical geneticist, obstetrician, nurse, or some other health care professional. For those who desire to promote such education,[61] the resources are already available, and indeed some programs in genetic counseling and in medical genetics currently avail themselves of those resources. Increasingly, thanks to the work of people like Marsha Saxton,[62] genetic counselors receive education about disability and thus can help prospective parents receive the same, whether by visiting a family with a child who has the identified trait, by meeting adults with the trait, or by obtaining information produced by support groups for people with the trait.

In addition to this general point, we can offer some specific advice about the opportunities for presenting disability-relevant information to parents. There are three junctures at which health care providers could offer such information. The first is before a prenatal screening test. Increasingly, pregnant women first encounter prenatal diagnosis in the office of their obstetrician-gynecologist via the offer of a screening test (for example, triple marker screening for neural tube defects and Down syndrome or carrier testing for cystic fibrosis). Currently, prenatal screening is too often presented as a part of routine care, the purpose of which is purportedly to ensure the health of the baby, rather than as a test for potential disabilities that parents might choose to avoid. As more and more disabilities can be detected prenatally, perhaps all that is possible at this first, earliest juncture is for prospective parents to receive accurate information about the purposes of screening and brief but balanced information about the disabilities being tested for. Such a discussion, aided by well-prepared educational materials, need not take much time and could begin to help prospective parents ask the fundamental questions they should be asking: Why do I want a prenatal test? Do I understand what I think I am trying to prevent? What do I know about spina bifida, Down syndrome, or whatever? Will having a child with one of these conditions prevent me from gaining what I want in having a child? As new media are developed, particular attention should be paid to helping prospective parents grapple with those questions.

A second educational opportunity is in genetic counseling prior to amniocentesis. This opportunity arises for those women who requested a prenatal screening test (such as the triple screen) and received a positive result, and for those women (generally older than thirty-five) who may be referred directly for amniocentesis. During this session, the provider discusses with the patient whether she wants to undergo this invasive procedure.

The pretest sessions may not, however, be ideal times to explore what life with disability is like. Project member Barbara Bowles Biesecker put it this way:

> To make an informed decision about prenatal testing, clients need to understand what can and cannot be detected and what their options are if a condition is found. They also need to have their questions addressed and, as Mary White suggests, to engage in a dialogue about their values and beliefs.
>
> However, frequently in a prenatal setting there is limited time to explore the meaning of a life with disability. Further, most prospective parents defend themselves emotionally against the anxiety-provoking thought that a random, unlikely condition could affect their fetus. As this strategy for coping with the normal anxiety of pregnancy is healthy and largely unconscious, it may not be effective for counselors to challenge it. Parents may neither want nor be able to explore their fears about the future health of their fetus; indeed, they may resent being asked to engage in such a threatening exercise.[63]

However, if there is a positive result on the amniocentesis, then a further, posttest session should occur—a third opportunity for counseling. About the feasibility of providing disability-relevant information in the post-test genetic counseling, there is not yet a consensus. Diana Bianchi observed during one project meeting that "the post-test genetic counseling session is the ideal time to educate someone about the nature of disability. Most of the several hundred couples carrying a fetus with a chromosome abnormality that I have been involved with over the past twelve years of my genetics practice have welcomed information—the more, the better—prior to making any decisions."[64] Bianchi thinks that only the reality of a positive test result can make most people think hard about what it would mean to welcome a child with disabilities into their families. Others think, however, that the post-test session can be "an unteachable moment."[65] Many prospective parents will be sufficiently distressed by a positive test result that they will not be able to absorb new information about disability. As tests are performed earlier, it may be that more time will be available to think about the decision, and thus that there will be greater opportunity to get to a teachable moment. But for now, the time between receiving the test result and making the decision whether to abort is short—and fraught with anxiety for the woman or prospective parents, even those who find that they are able to learn.

If and at whatever point in the process clients indicate they want information about disability, they should receive it. The question then is what they need. According to the Down Syndrome Congress, prospective parents who learn that their fetus has a disabling trait need to receive: "(a) information that seeks to dispel common misconceptions about disability and present disability from the perspective of a person with a disability; (b) information on community-based services for children with disabilities and their families as well as on financial assistance programs; (c) materials on special needs adoption; and (d) a summary of major laws protecting the civil rights of persons with disabilities. [Also,] people with disabilities and parents of people with disabilities should be available to talk with future parents."[66]

It is crucial that prospective parents are offered both information about disability and the opportunity to explore the values, desires, fears, and dreams that enter into deciding what to do with prenatal genetic information. Equally crucial is that, in accordance with the ethic of genetic counseling, professionals who make such offers honor both acceptances and refusals of those offers.

As Nancy Press and Carole Browner have argued, the offer of prenatal genetic testing is not neutral;[67] in that context it means that the one who offers the test thinks that a reasonable person might go down the path of testing and selective abortion. Offering the post-test opportunity to explore information about disability, as well as the feelings and values that arise in the context of a positive test result, would convey that such exploration could be an important and worthwhile activity. In particular it would mean that the one who does the offering thinks that a reasonable person might not go down the path of selective abortion—even though when she accepted the test she tentatively thought she would. Yet just as providers in a pretest context must, in accordance with the ethic of genetic counseling, respect the decisions of those who do not want to receive testing at all, so must they respect the decisions of those who do not want to receive post-test counseling.

We strongly support providing such information about life with disability—although not because we think it will convince prospective parents to raise disabled children. It very well may convince them that that path is not the one they wish to travel. Much more research is needed into the most effective tools and counseling methods that will help prospective parents achieve truly informed decisions.

Even though it is crucial to make sure that the professional training of those who provide genetic information includes education about the nature of disability, it may be that neither pre- nor post-test genetic counseling sessions are the best places to help prospective parents learn about the nature of disabilities and think about the meaning of parenthood. If not, then when can individuals engage in the sort of reflection about the nature of disability and parenthood that we think needs to take place if decisions are to be truly informed? It may be, as James Lindemann Nelson has argued, that the best opportunities to educate people about disability are well upstream of the counseling session. Perhaps our best hope is that good information about disability will permeate our culture more thoroughly—that there will be more television and radio shows, more plays, more newspaper articles that accurately portray the lives of people with disabilities, and more books like Bérubé's *Life As We Know It*. Programs in genetic counseling, medical genetics, and obstetrics should integrate education about disability into their curricula.

Lives of Different Sorts

People with disabilities are a recent contingent in the civil rights march that is arguably the greatest moral achievement of the twentieth century. We fail our children if we do not educate them about the nature of disability and the history of the disability rights movement.

In the end, one of the most important points of agreement in this project is that ignorance about the nature of disability is widespread and that such ignorance is one of the primary sources of the discrimination suffered by people with disabilities. Our outrage at that discrimination is rooted in our fundamental commitment to the moral equality of all persons. Out of that same respect for persons grows our belief that prospective parents should have the liberty to make decisions about the uses to which they will put prenatal information about genetic disability. As those in the disability community have argued since they first launched their campaign to get medicine and bioethics to examine the assumptions behind prenatal diagnosis, those decisions will be truly informed—those exercises of liberty will be authentic—only when people in our society come to learn what disability really does and does not mean for individuals and their families.

Although the group as a whole does not accept every claim in the disability community's critique of prenatal testing, we do wholeheartedly endorse its central recommendation to reform how prenatal genetic information is communicated to prospective parents. Even with the best information about the meaning of disability to various individuals and families, and even if that information is made available to prospective parents many weeks before they must make any decisions about parenthood, many (perhaps most) will choose to forego raising a child with a disability. But if prospective parents comprehend what is possible given a disability, if they carefully ask themselves hard questions about what they want and will appreciate in a future child, then they and any future children they raise have a better chance for fulfillment and for mutual, rewarding family life. And if genetics professionals learn more about what raising disabled children can mean, rethink their approach to parents, and help those parents better imagine what a child's disability might mean for their family, then some progress will be made in honoring the disability rights movement's central message that our society must be able to value people and lives of many different sorts. Only as we take that message seriously can we be confident that our prenatal decisions will improve familial and communal life.

NOTES

1. Cynthia M. Powell, "The Current State of Prenatal Genetic Testing in the United States," in this volume.

2. Thomas H. Murray, *The Worth of a Child* (Berkeley and Los Angeles: University of California Press, 1996), pp. 116–17.

3. Diana W. Bianchi, Timothy M. Crombleholme, and Mary D'Alton, *Fetology: Diagnosis and Management of the Fetal Patient* (Blacklick, Ohio: McGraw Hill, forthcoming).

4. See Alan Gartner and Tom Joe, eds., *Images of the Disabled: Disabling Images* (New York: Praeger, 1987); Joseph Shapiro, *No Pity* (New York: Times

Books, 1992); and Jane West, ed., *The Americans with Disabilities Act: From Policy to Practice* (New York: Milbank Memorial Fund, 1991).

5. Lennard J. Davis, *Enforcing Normalcy: Disability, Deafness, and the Body* (London, New York: Verso, 1995).

6. National Organization on Disability, *National Organization on Disability / Louis Harris Survey of Americans with Disabilities* (New York: Louis Harris and Associates, 1998).

7. J. E. Tyson and R. S. Broyles, "Progress in Assessing the Long-Term Outcome of Extremely Low Birthweight Infants," *JAMA* 276 (1996): 492–93; and National Organization on Disability, *Survey of Americans with Disabilities.*

8. A. L. Beaudet, "Invited Editorial: Carrier Screening for Cystic Fibrosis," *American Journal of Human Genetics* 47, no. 4 (1990): 603–05, at 603.

9. David T. Helm, Sara Miranda, and Naomi Angoff Chedd, "Prenatal Diagnosis of Down Syndrome: Mothers' Reflections on Supports Needed from Diagnosis to Birth," *Mental Retardation* 36, no. 1 (1998): 55–61, at 57.

10. B. A. Bernhardt et al., "Prenatal Genetic Testing: Content of Discussions between Obstetric Providers and Pregnant Women," *Obstetrics and Gynecology* 91 (1998): 648–55; and T. M. Marteau, J. Kidd, and M. Plenicar, "Obstetricians Presenting Amniocentesis to Pregnant Women: Practice Observed," *Journal of Reproductive Infant Psychology* 11 (1993): 3–10.

11. Helm, Miranda, and Chedd, "Prenatal Diagnosis of Down Syndrome," p. 57.

12. Cara Dunne and Catherine Warren, "Lethal Autonomy: The Malfunction of the Informed Consent Mechanism within the Context of Prenatal Testing," *Issues in Law and Medicine* 14, no. 2 (1998): 165–202; and T. Marteau, H. Drake, and M. Bobrow, "Counseling Following Diagnosis of a Fetal Abnormality: The Differing Approaches of Obstetricians, Clinical Geneticists, and Genetic Nurses," *Journal of Medical Genetics* 31 (1994): 864–67.

13. Nancy Press et al. "Provisional Normalcy and 'Perfect Babies': Pregnant Women's Attitudes toward Disability in the Context of Prenatal Testing," in *Reproducing Reproduction: Kinship, Power, and Technological Innovation*, ed. Sarah Franklin and Helena Ragone (Philadelphia: University of Pennsylvania Press, 1998), pp. 46–65.

14. Aliza Kolker and B. Meredith Burke, *Prenatal Testing: A Sociological Perspective* (Westport, Conn.: Bergin and Garvey, 1994), p. 9.

15. Bartha M. Knoppers et al., "Defining 'Serious' Disorders in Relation to Genetics Services: Who Should Decide?" *American Journal of Human Genetics* 57, no. 4, supplement (1995): A296, abstract 1723.

16. Dorothy Wertz, "What's Missing from Genetic Counseling: A Survey of 476 Counseling Sessions," abstract, National Society of Genetic Counselors meetings, October 1998.

17. National Down Syndrome Congress, "Position Statement on Prenatal Testing and Eugenics: Families' Rights and Needs," available at http://

members.carol.net/ndsc/eugenics.html, and accessed in 1999; and Little People of America, "Position Statement on Genetic Discoveries in Dwarfism," available at http://www2.shore.net/~dkennedy/dwarfism_genetics.html, and accessed in 1999.

18. Dorothy C. Wertz, "How Parents of Affected Children View Selective Abortion," in *Issues in Reproductive Technologies* I, ed. H. Holmes (New York: Garland Publishers, 1992), pp. 161–92.

19. Bernhardt et al., "Prenatal Genetic Testing"; and Marteau, Kidd, and Plenicar, "Obstetricians Presenting Amniocentesis to Pregnant Women."

20. Barbara Bowles Biesecker, "The Future of Genetic Counseling: An International Perspective," *Nature Genetics* 22 (1999): 133–37, at 134.

21. Michelle Fine and Adrienne Asch, "The Question of Disability: No Easy Answers for the Women's Movement," *Reproductive Rights Newsletter* 4, no. 3 (1982): 19–20; Marsha Saxton, "Prenatal Screening and Discriminatory Attitudes about Disability," in *Embryos, Ethics and Women's Rights*, ed. Elaine Hoffman Barucch, Amadeo E. D'Adamo, and Joni Seager (New York: Haworth Press, 1988); Anne Finger, *Past Due: Disability, Pregnancy, and Birth* (Seattle, Wash.: Seal Press, 1987); and Deborah Kaplan, "Prenatal Screening and Diagnosis: The Impact on Persons with Disabilities," in *Women and Prenatal Testing: Facing the Challenges of Genetic Testing*, ed. Karen H. Rothenberg and Elizabeth J. Thomson (Columbus: Ohio State University Press, 1994), pp. 49–61.

22. Ruth Hubbard, *The Politics of Women's Biology* (New Brunswick, N.J.: Rutgers University Press, 1990); Abby Lippman, "Prenatal Genetic Testing and Screening: Constructing Needs and Reinforcing Inequities," *American Journal of Law and Medicine* 17, nos. 1–2 (1991): 15–50; Carole Browner and Nancy Press, "The Production of Authoritative Knowledge in Prenatal Care," *Medical Anthropology Quarterly* 10, no. 2 (1996): 141–56; and Martha A. Field, "Killing 'The Handicapped': Before and After Birth," *Harvard Women's Law Journal* 16 (1993): 79–138.

23. Adrienne Asch, "Reproductive Technology and Disability," in *Reproductive Laws for the 1990's*, ed. Sherrill Cohen and Nadine Taub (Clifton, N.J.: Humana Press, 1989), pp. 69–124, at 86.

24. Allen E. Buchanan, "Choosing Who Will Be Disabled: Genetic Intervention and the Morality of Inclusion," *Social Philosophy and Policy* 13 (1996): 18–46.

25. Asch, "Reproductive Technology and Disability," p. 81.

26. Adrienne Asch, "Why I Haven't Changed My Mind about Prenatal Diagnosis: Reflections and Refinements," in this volume.

27. Dorothy C. Wertz and John C. Fletcher, "Sex Selection through Prenatal Diagnosis: A Feminist Critique," in *Feminist Perspectives in Medical Ethics*, ed. Helen Bequaert Holms and Laura M. Purdy (Bloomington: Indiana University Press, 1992), pp. 240–53.

28. Marsha Saxton, "Disability Rights and Selective Abortion," in *Abortion Wars: A Half Century of Struggle, 1950–2000*, ed. Rickie Solinger (Berkeley and Los Angeles: University of California Press, 1997), pp. 374–95, at 391.

29. Nancy Press, "Assessing the Expressive Character of Prenatal Testing: The Choices Made or the Choices Made Available?," in this volume.

30. Eva Feder Kittay with Leo Kittay, "On the Expressivity and Ethics of Selective Abortion for Disability: Conversations with My Son"; and James Lindemann Nelson, "The Meaning of the Act: Reflections on the Expressive Force of Reproductive Decision Making and Policies," in this volume.

31. Nelson, "Meaning of the Act."

32. Bonnie Steinbock, "Disability, Prenatal Testing, and Selective Abortion," in this volume.

33. Asch, "Reproductive Technology and Disability," p. 88.

34. Murray, *Worth of a Child*, pp. 115–41; and Adrienne Asch and Gail Geller, "Feminism, Bioethics, and Genetics," in *Feminism and Bioethics: Beyond Reproduction*, ed. Susan M. Wolf (New York: Oxford University Press, 1996).

35. William Ruddick, "Ways to Limit Prenatal Testing," in this volume.

36. J. A. Blier Blaymore et al., "Parents' and Pediatricians' Views of Individuals with Meningomyelocile," *Clinical Pediatrics* 35, no. 3 (1996): 113–17; M. L. Wollraich, G. N. Siperstein, and P. O'Keefe, "Pediatricians' Perceptions of Mentally Retarded Individuals," *Pediatrics* 80, no. 5 (1987): 643–49.

37. Philip M. Ferguson, Alan Gartner, and Dorothy K. Lipsky, "The Experience of Disability in Families: A Synthesis of Research and Parent Narratives," in this volume.

38. M. W. Krauss, "Child-Related and Parenting Stress: Similarities and Differences Between Mothers and Fathers of Children with Disabilities," *American Journal of Mental Retardation* 97 (1993): 393–404.

39. D. A. Abbott and W. H. Meredith, "Strengths of Parents with Retarded Children," *Family Relations* 35 (1986): 371–75; and A. P. Turnbull et al., eds., *Cognitive Coping: Families and Disability* (Baltimore, Md.: Paul H. Brookes, 1993).

40. J. P. Lehman and K. Roberto, "Comparison of Factors Influencing Mothers' Perceptions about the Future of Their Adolescent Children With and Without Disabilities," *Mental Retardation* 34 (1996): 27–38.

41. Ruth I. Freedman, Leon Litchfield, and Marjl Erickson Warfield, "Balancing Work and Family: Perspectives of Parents of Children with Developmental Disabilities," *Families in Society: The Journal of Contemporary Human Services* (October 1995): 507–14, at 511.

42. Sara Ruddick, *Maternal Thinking: Toward a Politics of Peace* (Boston: Beacon Press, 1989).

43. Mary Ann Baily, personal communication to authors, October 1997.

44. Caroline Moon, unpublished paper on file with Luce Program at Wellesley College, 1999.

45. Asch, "Reproductive Technology and Disability," p. 73.

46. Deborah Kent, "Somewhere a Mockingbird," in this volume.

47. Nora Ellen Groce, *Everyone Here Spoke Sign Language: Hereditary Deafness on Martha's Vineyard* (Cambridge, Mass.: Harvard University Press, 1985).

48. Buchanan, "Choosing Who Will Be Disabled."

49. Dena S. Davis, "Genetic Dilemmas and the Child's Right to an Open Future," *Hastings Center Report* 27, no. 2 (1997): 7–15; Bonnie Steinbock and Ronald McClamrock, "When Is Birth Unfair to the Child?" *Hastings Center Report* 24, no. 6 (1994): 15–21; and Ronald Green, "Parental Autonomy and the Obligation Not to Harm One's Child Genetically," *Journal of Law, Medicine & Ethics* 25, no. 1 (1997): 5–16.

50. Steinbock, "Disability, Prenatal Testing, and Selective Abortion."

51. Philip M. Ferguson, personal communication to authors, May 1998.

52. Kent, "Somewhere a Mockingbird."

53. Alice Domurat Dreger, "The Limits of Individuality: Ritual and Sacrifice in the Lives and Medical Treatment of Conjoined Twins," *Studies in the History and Philosophy of Science* 29, no. 1 (1998): 1–29.

54. Michael Bérubé, *Life As We Know It: A Father, A Family, and An Exceptional Child* (New York: Pantheon, 1996).

55. James Lindemann Nelson, personal communication to authors, October 1997.

56. Jeffrey Botkin, "Fetal Privacy and Confidentiality," *Hastings Center Report* 25, no. 5 (1995): 32–39. See also Mary Terrell White, "Making Responsible Decisions: An Interpretive Ethics for Genetic Decisionmaking," *Hastings Center Report* 29, no. 1 (1999): 14–21.

57. Knoppers et al., "Defining 'Serious' Disorders in Relation to Genetics Services"; and Wertz, "What's Missing from Genetic Counseling."

58. See, however, Murray, *Worth of a Child;* and Erik Parens, ed., *Enhancing Human Traits: Ethical and Social Implications* (Washington, D.C.: Georgetown University Press, 1998).

59. National Society for Genetic Counselors, "National Society for Genetic Counselors Code of Ethics," in *Prescribing Our Future: Ethical Challenges in Genetic Counseling,* ed. Dianne M. Bartels, Bonnie S. LeRoy, and Arthur L. Caplan (New York: Aldine de Gruyter, 1993), pp. 169–71.

60. J. Teicher et al., "Disability Awareness Training in the Graduate Genetic Counseling Training Program: A Survey of Recent Graduates," *Journal of Genetic Counseling* 7 (1998): 498.

61. Asch, "Reproductive Technology and Disability," Appendix A, pp. 108–17.

62. Marsha Saxton, "Disability Feminism Meets DNA: A Study of an Educational Model for Genetic Counseling Students on the Social and Ethical Issues of Selective Abortion" (Ph.D. diss., Brandeis University, 1996).

63. Barbara Bowles Biesecker, personal communication to authors, May

1999. On parents' views of the future health of their fetus, see Barbara Bowles Biesecker and Theresa M. Marteau, "The Future of Genetic Counseling: An International Perspective," *Nature Genetics* 22 (June 1999): 133–37.

64. Diana Bianchi, personal communication to authors, May 1999.

65. Lori B. Andrews et al., *Assessing Genetic Risks: Implications for Health Policy* (Washington, D.C.: National Academy Press, 1994), p. 150.

66. National Down Syndrome Congress, "Position Statement on Prenatal Testing and Eugenics: Families' Rights and Needs," available at http://members .carol.net/ndsc/eugenics.html, and accessed in 1997.

67. Nancy Press and Carole Browner, "Collective Silences, Collective Fictions: How Prenatal Diagnostic Testing Became Part of Routine Prenatal Care," in *Women and Prenatal Testing: Facing the Challenges of Genetic Testing*, ed. Karen H. Rothenberg and Elizabeth J. Thomson (Columbus: Ohio State University Press, 1994), pp. 201–18.

Cynthia M. Powell

The Current State of Prenatal Genetic Testing in the United States

The last century has brought rapid advances in the ability to detect abnormalities in the fetus. With discoveries of human genes and their mutations, the number of disorders that can be tested for prenatally is increasing on an almost daily basis. This essay will review the history of prenatal testing in order to provide a deeper understanding of current testing practices. It will describe the types of tests that are being offered, the medical professionals who are offering and counseling patients about these tests, the costs of tests, and what is likely to be available in the future.

History of Prenatal Testing

The oldest reference to prenatal diagnosis is for anencephaly (absent skull and brain) diagnosed by x-rays in 1917 by James T. Case.[1] The first amniocentesis is attributed to Schatz in 1883 for the purpose of treating hydramnios (excessive amniotic fluid).[2] Amniocentesis to detect erythroblastosis fetalis (complication of Rh incompatibility) began in the 1950s. Prenatal testing with amniocentesis for genetic disorders began in 1955 when it was discovered that the sex of a human fetus could be predicted by analysis of fetal cells in amniotic fluid.[3] Initially the testing was used to determine fetal sex when a woman was at risk for having a child with an X-linked condition such as hemophilia.[4] In this situation she would have a fifty percent risk of having an affected male infant. If the baby were a female, she would have a fifty percent risk of carrying the gene, but be clinically unaffected. The sex chromatin body (Barr body) could be identified in nondividing amniotic fluid cells. A male fetus (absent Barr body) could be identified and the pregnancy terminated despite a fifty percent probability that it would be unaffected. The first report of the procedure being done for this purpose was in Denmark in 1960.[5]

It was reported in 1959 that Down syndrome is due to an extra chromosome (21), and amniocentesis to detect fetal chromosome abnormalities began in the 1960s.[6] Widespread use of amniocentesis for increased maternal age in the United States is partly attributed to lawsuit settlements in the late 1970s in cases where patients had not been referred for testing and gave birth to children with disabilities.[7] In 1983 the American Academy of Pediatrics and the American College of Obstetrics and Gynecology recommended that all pregnant women thirty-five or older at the time of delivery be offered amniocentesis; thus, amniocentesis became a routine part of obstetric care.[8] Other contributing factors to the rapid increase in demand for prenatal diagnostic services include the liberalization of abortion statutes, changes in cultural attitudes toward family size, quality of life issues, and extensive media coverage and publicity given to prenatal diagnosis.[9]

Chorionic villus sampling (CVS)—aspiration of tissue that will become the placenta—was first done in Copenhagen in the late 1960s.[10] Because of various technical problems it did not come into common use until the 1980s.[11] This test has the advantage of being performed in the first trimester of pregnancy (nine to thirteen weeks) as compared to amniocentesis, which is done in the second trimester (fifteen to eighteen weeks). CVS and amniocentesis are equally useful in obtaining fetal cells for metabolic and DNA studies. However, the spontaneous abortion rate following CVS is approximately 1 percent, which is higher than for amniocentesis (one in 300 to 400). There is also a higher rate of mosaicism (two or more cell lines with different chromosomal constitution) with CVS as compared to amniocentesis (0.5 to 1 percent for cultured CVS cells versus 0.2 to 0.3 percent for amniocytes).[12] In most cases the abnormal cell line is confined to the placenta, but a follow-up amniocentesis is often needed to look for the possibility of true mosaicism in the fetus. CVS performed earlier than nine weeks may be associated with an increased risk of limb and facial malformations. With CVS, alpha-fetoprotein levels cannot be measured to screen for neural tube impairments. Moreover, because CVS is a technically more difficult procedure than is amniocentesis, fewer obstetricians offer the test in their office. Not all tertiary care facilities or major medical centers offer it.

Screening for neural tube impairments was first demonstrated in 1972 by determining amniotic fluid concentrations of alpha-fetoprotein (AFP). Elevated levels were associated with spina bifida and anencephaly in the fetus.[13] Elevated levels of AFP were also found in maternal blood serum when the fetus had an open neural tube.[14] By the 1980s, most women were being offered serum AFP screening during pregnancy. Maternal serum AFP screening, ultrasound, and amniocentesis together are capable of detecting 100 percent of cases of anencephaly and 80 to 90 percent of cases of spina bifida.[15]

In 1984 it was reported that AFP values in maternal serum were lower than expected when the fetus had Down syndrome or trisomy 18.[16] AFP measurement along with age of the mother were used to detect pregnancies at risk for a chromosome abnormality in women under the age of thirty-five. This technique could detect 20 percent of cases of Down syndrome in this population who otherwise would not be identified as having an increased risk. Other biochemical markers were identified that varied from normal when a woman was carrying a fetus with Down syndrome or trisomy 18. These include unconjugated estriol and human chorionic gonadotropin. Use of these three markers to screen pregnancies is commonly referred to as the "triple screen" and is generally done at the sixteenth through eighteenth week of pregnancy. Abnormal values are followed by ultrasound to confirm dating. If dating is correct, amniocentesis is offered for definitive testing for chromosome abnormalities. Detection rates with use of the triple screen have been reported as 67 to 75 percent, with a false positive rate of 4 to 5 percent.[17]

Ultrasound was first developed in World War I as sonar, to seek underwater submarines. Using it to view fetuses began in the 1960s.[18] Ultrasound is used for determining gestational age, locating structures prior to invasive testing procedures, and identifying structural abnormalities in the fetus. Conditions such as anencephaly, spina bifida, congenital heart defects, hydrocephalus, and kidney abnormalities are detectable with ultrasound. Most women in this country have at least one ultrasound during their pregnancy. Studies have not shown a risk to the fetus as a result of ultrasound, but pregnancy outcomes have not been shown to improve through routine ultrasound use.

Fetoscopy, the direct visualization of the fetus by using an optical instrument, was first used in 1954 but is now rarely done except for fetal skin biopsy. Fetoscopy was used in the past to obtain fetal blood samples, but percutaneous umbilical blood sampling (PUBS)—also known as cordocentesis—is currently the method of choice. In this procedure ultrasound guides placement of a needle inserted through the maternal abdomen into the umbilical vein. PUBS is used for diagnosis of chromosome abnormalities, fetal infections, coagulation defects, hemoglobin and red cell disorders, and metabolic and immunologic diseases.

The first reported prenatal diagnosis established by molecular genetic techniques was for alpha-thalassemia by means of linkage analysis in 1976[19], and for sickle cell anemia by analysis of gene mutation in 1978.[20]

Today's Prenatal Tests

Prenatal diagnosis is available for hundreds of genetic conditions, including chromosome abnormalities, inborn errors of metabolism, neural tube impairments, and single gene disorders. Ultrasound detects many different structural defects, including hydrocephalus, congenital heart abnormalities, limb anomalies, skeletal dysplasias, and diaphragmatic hernias. The most recent edition of the *Catalog of Prenatally Diagnosed Conditions* lists 940 conditions that have been diagnosed prenatally, including chromosome abnormalities, congenital malformations, dermatologic disorders, fetal infections, hematologic disorders, inborn errors of metabolism, tumors and cysts, and multiple congenital anomalies of unknown etiology.

Methods of prenatal diagnosis include maternal serum screening with biochemical markers to look for neural tube impairments as well as chromosomal aneuploidies (i.e., abnormal numbers of chromosomes). The triple screen detects up to 75 percent of fetuses with Down syndrome. However, these are screening tests, and for definitive diagnosis they must be followed by additional procedures such as ultrasound in the case of neural tube impairments and amniocentesis or chorionic villus sampling for chromosome abnormalities.

According to estimates based on data from the Council of Regional Networks for Genetic Services (CORN) for 1989, 50 percent of pregnancies in the United States were being screened for MSAFP.[21] Based on results of a 1995 survey of laboratories performing maternal serum screening, an estimated 63 percent of annual births were screened for Down syndrome using one or more markers, ranging from 51 percent in the southeastern United States to 76 percent in the mid-Atlantic region.[22]

CORN data for 1989 showed that increased maternal age was the most common primary indication for genetics services for prenatal patients (62 percent), with abnormal MSAFP accounting for 14 percent; positive family history for 7 percent; previous spontaneous abortion or stillbirth, 1 percent; abnormal ultrasound, 1 percent; parental concern/anxiety, 1 percent; and "other" and "unknown/unrecorded," 11 percent.

These services include genetic counseling, ultrasound examination, and amniocentesis. In a survey of a university-based cytogenetics laboratory over a five-month period in 1997, of 476 amniotic fluid samples, 52 percent were obtained for increased maternal age; 34 percent, abnormal triple screen; 7 percent, abnormal ultrasound; family history of a genetic disorder, 3 percent; DNA testing, 1 percent; and elevated MSAFP, multiple miscarriages, and maternal anxiety, 3 percent. The DNA diagnostic testing included testing for achondroplasia, Rh, Kell antibody, sickle cell, and X-linked hydrocephalus (C. M. Powell, unpublished data).

Who Is Offering Tests

Most prenatal genetic testing is obtained through obstetricians in private practices or public health clinics. The remainder is obtained through tertiary referral centers such as university medical centers or private genetic centers. In a U.S. study that examined discussions between obstetricians or nurse-midwives and their patients during their first prenatal visit, it was found that time devoted to discussion of genetic testing averaged 3.7 minutes (range 0–25.3 minutes). A comprehensive family history was not taken in any of the visits. Discussion of topics such as abortion or continuation of pregnancy if an anomaly were detected, or a description of the disorders for which testing was offered, occurred in a minority of visits.[23] *Guidelines for Perinatal Care* (1997) of the American Academy of Pediatrics and American College of Obstetrics and Gynecology does not recommend referral for formal genetic counseling for women of advanced maternal age because it states that primary care physicians can explain the risks.[24]

When an abnormality is detected through prenatal testing, an obstetrician, genetic counselor, or nurse usually provides information and counseling. The information given varies depending upon the knowledge and experience the professional has regarding the specific condition. Many health professionals who offer prenatal genetic counseling have not had direct contact with children and adults with developmental disabilities and genetic disorders. Obstetricians often have had little contact with such patients since their medical school training, and even then, this contact may have been minimal. Few genetic counselors work in both prenatal and pediatric genetics. Few genetic counseling training programs give students an opportunity to work with children or adults with developmental disabilities. Therefore, most women who receive information about a specific chromosome abnormality, birth defect, or genetic impairment in their fetus receive this information from health care providers unfamiliar with the natural history and outcomes of the condition.

Cost of Tests

The cost of prenatal diagnosis using CVS or amniocentesis combined with a level II ultrasound is in the range of $1,500 to $2,000. Such diagnosis would include physician fees and laboratory costs. Laboratory costs alone for amniocentesis range from $500 to $800. CVS is an additional $100. A level II ultrasound alone costs $300 to $600. Maternal serum screening ranges from $20 to $30 for AFP alone, and from $50 to $75 for triple marker screening. The cost of DNA analysis for specific single gene mutations is usually in the range of $50 to $250, depending on the number of mutations tested for.

Who Pays for Testing?

In a survey of health insurance providers conducted in 1991 by the Office of Technology Assessment, it was found that 80 percent of HMOs were covering prenatal testing for Down syndrome when medically indicated, compared to 75 percent of Blue Cross/Blue Shield plans and only 34 percent of other commercial insurance companies defined as for-profit companies in the business of writing major medical expense policies. The percentages covering patient-requested testing ranged from 4 to 12.[25] Data were not obtained for coverage of abortion when an abnormality was found and the patient elected termination of pregnancy. Genetic counseling is not generally covered except through hidden charges in the physician's fee.

The federal Genetic Diseases Act, passed in 1976, funded state grants to provide genetic services. Funding for these programs derives from maternal and child health federal block grants that have been substantially reduced in recent years. These funds cannot be used to pay for abortion unless the pregnancy presents a threat to the life of the woman or was the result of rape or incest. None of these conditions is likely to be relevant in cases of abortions for genetic indications. Women who are poor and have no way to pay for an abortion can have prenatal testing paid for with federal funds, but only to obtain reassurance or prepare for the birth of an affected child.[26] There are also state regulations which, depending on the state, may limit use of state funds even for prenatal diagnosis. There is little consensus among states regarding these programs.

The federal government does provide some genetic services. The U.S. Public Health Service is directed to provide voluntary genetic disease testing, diagnosis, counseling, and treatment. Members of the Armed Services and their families can obtain prenatal diagnosis if the woman is thirty-five years old or older, or the couple already has a child with, or a family history of, a congenital abnormality.[27]

The Future

Any genetic condition for which the gene has been localized or mutation identified can be tested for prenatally by obtaining cells from the fetus either through CVS or amniocentesis. At the present time these include genes that cause deafness, dwarfism, adult-onset neurological disorders, treatable diseases such as phenylketonuria, and those that predispose to cancer. Although these tests are available through some laboratories, many prenatal diagnostic centers and laboratories do not offer them, citing ethical considerations. For example, if a fetus with a positive test result for a late-onset condition were allowed to go to term, then the child the fetus becomes would have had presymptomatic testing without having given informed consent. Data on the actual utilization of these tests are difficult to obtain. There are no official guidelines for the use of such tests. In the future, once all genes have been identified, thousands of additional conditions will be diagnosable. These conditions may include not only disease-causing genes but also those affecting complex traits, such as obesity, intelligence, and sexual orientation.

A technique to obtain fetal cells from maternal blood has been developed. It is still in experimental stages but may eventually offer a less invasive way of obtaining fetal cells for prenatal studies.[28] One of the reasons for limiting access to invasive prenatal diagnostic procedures is the argument that they are not justified if the risk of complications or fetal loss from the procedure outweighs the risk a woman has of having a child with a particular condition (usually a chromosome abnormality). Less invasive methods will decrease potential risks and increase the justification for pursuing prenatal testing.

It has been stated that "the fundamental philosophy of prenatal genetic diagnosis is to provide reassurance to couples at risk that they may selectively have unaffected children even if their procreative risk for having defective offspring is unacceptably high."[29] Although the technology to accomplish this has increased dramatically over the last decade, it remains impossible to ensure a "normal" outcome in a pregnancy. As more tests become available, the false impression the public has that such guarantee is possible is likely to increase. Pre- and post-test counseling aimed at obtaining true informed consent will become essential. There are not enough trained geneticists and genetic counselors to accomplish this task. Primary care physicians, nurse practitioners, physician assistants, and nurses will need the education and training to provide these services.

NOTES

1. David D. Weaver, *Catalog of Prenatally Diagnosed Conditions*. 3rd ed. (Baltimore, Md.: Johns Hopkins University Press, 1999), p. xi.

2. Weaver, *Catalog of Prenatally Diagnosed Conditions*, p. xi.

3. D. M. Serr, L. Sachs, and M. Danon, "Diagnosis of Sex Before Birth Using Cells from the Amniotic Fluid," *Bulletin of the Research Council of Israel* 5B (1955): 137; F. Fuchs and P. Riis, "Antenatal Sex Determination," *Nature* 177 (1956): 330; E. L. Makowski, K. A. Prem, and I. H. Kaiser, "Detection of Sex of Fetuses by the Incidence of Sex Chromatin Body in Nuclei of Cells in Amniotic Fluid," *Science* 123 (1956): 542–43; and L. B. Shettles, "Nuclear Morphology of Cells in Human Amniotic Fluid in Relation to Sex of Infant," *American Journal of Obstetrics and Gynecology* 71 (1956): 834–38.

4. Ruth Schwartz Cowan, "Aspects of the History of Prenatal Diagnosis," *Fetal Diagnostic Therapy* 8, supplement 1 (1993): 10–17, at 11–12.

5. P. Riis and F. Fuchs, "Antenatal Determination of Foetal Sex in Prevention of Hereditary Diseases," *Lancet* 279 (1960): 180–82.

6. J. LeJeune, M. Gauthier, and R. Turpin, "Les Chromosomes Humains en Culture de Tissus," *Academie de Sciences* 248 (1959): 1721–22; M. W. Steele and W. R. Breg, "Chromosome Analysis of Human Amniotic Fluid Cells," *Lancet* 1 (1966): 383–85; Henry L. Nadler, "Antenatal Detection of Hereditary Disorders," *Pediatrics* 42 (1968): 912–18; and C. B. Jacobson and R. H. Barter, "Intrauterine Diagnosis and Management of Genetic Defects," *American Journal of Obstetrics and Gynecology* 99 (1967): 796–807.

7. Cowan, "Aspects of the History of Prenatal Diagnosis," pp. 12–13.

8. American Academy of Pediatrics, American College of Obstetrics and Gynecology, *Guidelines for Perinatal Care* (Washington, D.C.: American Academy of Pediatrics, 1983), p. 210.

9. Weaver, *Catalog of Prenatally Diagnosed Conditions*, p. xiii.

10. J. Mohr, "Foetal Genetic Diagnosis: Development of Techniques for Early Sampling of Foetal Cells," *Acta Pathologica et Microbiolica Scandinavica* 73 (1968): 73–77; N. Hahnemann, "Early Prenatal Diagnosis: A Study of Biopsy Techniques and Cell Culturing from Extraembryonic Membranes," *Clinical Genetics* 6 (1974): 294–306.

11. Z. Kazy, I. S. Rosovsky, and V. A. Bakharev, "Chorion Biopsy in Early Pregnancy: A Method of Early Prenatal Diagnosis for Inherited Disorders," *Prenatal Diagnosis* 2 (1982): 39–45.

12. Canadian Collaborative CVS-Amniocentesis Trial Group, "Multicentre Randomized Trial of Chorion Villus Sampling and Amniocentesis," *Lancet* 1 (1989): 1–7.

13. D. J. Brock and R. G. Sutcliffe, "Alpha-Fetoprotein in the Antenatal Diagnosis of Anencephaly and Spina Bifida," *Lancet* 2 (1972): 197–99.

14. D. J. Brock, A. E. Bolton, and J. M. Monaghan, "Prenatal Diagnosis of Anencephaly through Maternal Serum–Alphafetoprotein Measurement," *Lancet* 2 (1973): 923–24.

15. Aubrey Milunsky, ed., *Genetic Disorders and the Fetus: Diagnosis, Prevention, and Treatment*. 4th ed. (Baltimore, Md.: Johns Hopkins University Press, 1998), p. 635.

16. R. Merkatz, H. M. Nitowsky, J. N. Macri, and W. E. Johnson. "An Association Between Low Maternal Serum Alpha-Protein and Fetal Chromosomal Abnormalities," *American Journal of Obstetrics and Gynecology* 184 (1984): 896–94.

17. Milunsky, *Genetic Disorders and the Fetus*, p. 709.

18. Aliza Kolker and B. Meredith Burke, *Prenatal Testing: A Sociological Perspective* (Westport, Conn.: Bergin and Garvey, 1994), p. 25.

19. Y. W. Kan, M. S. Golbus, and A. M. Dozy, "Prenatal Diagnosis of Alpha-Thalassemia: Clinical Application of Molecular Hybridization," *NEJM* 295 (1976): 1165–67.

20. Y. W. Kan and A. M. Dozy, "Antenatal Diagnosis of Sickle-Cell Anaemia by D.N.A. Analysis of Amniotic-Fluid Cells," *Lancet* 2 (1978): 910–12.

21. F. John Meaney, Susan M. Riggle, and George C. Cunningham, "Providers and Consumers of Prenatal Genetic Testing Services: What Do the National Data Tell Us?" *Fetal Diagnosis and Therapy* 8, supplement (1993): 18–27.

22. Glenn E. Palomaki et al., "Maternal Serum Screening for Down Syndrome in the United States: A 1995 Survey," *American Journal of Obstetrics and Gynecology* 176, no. 5 (1997): 1046–51.

23. Barbara A. Bernhardt et al., "Prenatal Genetic Testing: Content of Discussions Between Obstetric Providers and Pregnant Women," *Obstetrics and Gynecology* 91 (1998): 648–55.

24. American Academy of Pediatrics and American College of Obstetrics and Gynecology, *Guidelines for Perinatal Care* (Elk Grove Village, Ill.: American

Academy of Pediatrics and American College of Obstetrics and Gynecology, 1997), p. 81.

25. U.S. Congress, Office of Technology Assessment, *Genetic Tests and Health Insurance: Results of a Survey*, OTA-BP-H-98 (Washington, D.C.: U.S. Congress, Office of Technology Assessment, 1998), pp. 25–29.

26. Ellen Wright Clayton, "Reproductive Genetic Testing: Regulatory and Liability Issues," *Fetal Diagnosis and Therapy* 8, supplement 1 (1993): 39–59, at 40.

27. Clayton, "Reproductive Genetic Testing," pp. 40–41.

28. Diana W. Bianchi, "Progress in the Genetic Analysis of Fetal Cells Circulating in Maternal Blood," *Current Opinion in Obstetrics and Gynecology* 9 (1997): 121–25.

29. Milunsky, *Genetic Disorders and the Fetus*, p. 2.

Part Two

Parenthood, Disability, and Prenatal Testing

DEBORAH KENT

Somewhere a Mockingbird[1]

When I was only a few weeks old my mother realized that I couldn't see. For the next eight months she and my father went from doctor to doctor searching for answers. At last their quest led them to one of the leading eye specialists in New York City. He confirmed everything they had already heard by that time—my blindness was complete, irreversible, and of unknown origin. He also gave them some sound advice. They should stop taking me to doctors and give up looking for a cure. Instead they should help me lead the fullest life possible. Fortunately for me, his prescription matched their best instincts.

As I was growing up people called my parents "wonderful." They were praised for raising me "like a normal child." As far as I could tell, my parents were like most of the others in my neighborhood—sometimes wonderful and sometimes annoying. And from my point of view, I wasn't *like* a normal child—I *was* normal. From the beginning I learned to deal with the world as a blind person. I didn't long for sight any more than I yearned for a pair of wings. Blindness presented occasional complications, but it seldom kept me from anything I wanted to do.

For me blindness was part of the background music that accompanied my life. I had been hearing it since I was born and paid it little attention. But others had a way of cranking up the volume. Their discomfort, doubts, and concerns often put blindness at the top of the program. Teachers offered to lighten my assignments; Scout leaders discouraged me from going on field trips; boys shied away from asking me on dates. The message was clear. Because I was blind, these people saw me as a liability—inadequate, incompetent, and too strange to be socially acceptable. I knew that my parents ached for me when these situations arose. It hurt them to see me being prejudged and rejected. Yet they found it hard to do battle on my behalf. Though they shared my sense of injury, they also identified with the nondisabled people who sought to exclude me. "You have to understand how other people see things," my parents told me. "They're trying their best. You need to be patient with them." I struggled to show the doubters and detractors that they were wrong. Much of the time I felt that I was fighting alone.

Since one of my brothers, three years younger than I am, is also blind, it seemed more than likely that my unknown eye condition had a genetic basis. I never thought much about it until my husband Dick and I began to talk about having a child. Certainly, genetics was not our primary concern. We married late (I was thirty-one, Dick forty-two) and were used to living unencumbered. Since we both worked as freelance writers, our income was erratic. We had to think about how we could shape our lives to make room for a child, whatever child that might be.

But somehow blindness crept into our discussions. I don't remember which of us brought up the topic first. But once it emerged, it had to be addressed. How would I feel if I passed my blindness to our son or daughter? What would it mean to Dick and to our extended families? What would it be like for us to raise a blind child together?

I premised my life on the conviction that blindness was a neutral characteristic. It created some inconveniences, such as not being able to read print or drive a car. Occasionally it locked me into conflicts with others over what I could and could not do. But in the long run, I believed that my life could not have turned out any better if I had been fully sighted. If my child were blind, I would try to ensure it every chance to become a self-fulfilled, contributing member of society. Dick said he agreed with me completely. We were deciding whether to have a child. Its visual acuity was hardly the point.

Yet if we truly believed our own words, why were we discussing blindness at all? I sensed that Dick was trying hard to say the right thing, even to believe it in his heart. But he was more troubled than he wished me to know. Once when I asked him how he would feel if he learned that our child was blind, he replied, "I'd be devastated at first, but I'd get over it." It was not the answer I wanted to hear.

I was blind and I was the woman Dick chose to marry, to spend his life with for better or for worse. I was his partner in all our endeavors. He accepted my blindness naturally and comfortably, as a piece of who I was. If he could accept blindness in me, why would it be devastating to him, even for a moment, if our child were blind as well? "You know why," was all he could tell me. "You've got to understand."

What I understood was that Dick, like my parents, was the product of a society that views blindness, and all disability, as fundamentally undesirable. All his life he had been assailed by images of blind people who were helpless, useless, and unattractive, misfits in a sight-oriented world. I had managed to live down that image. Dick had discovered that I had something of value to offer. But I had failed to convince him that it is really okay to be blind.

Our discussions showed me a painful truth. No matter how close we grew, how much of our lives we shared, blindness would never be a neutral trait for him.

I wanted our child to be welcomed without reservation. I wanted Dick to greet its birth with joy. I did not know if I could bear his devastation if our baby turned out to be blind like me.

It was too painful to explore the implications any further. Instead I plunged into a search for information. After all, we didn't even know the real cause of my blindness. We couldn't make a decision until we gathered the facts. Surely the field of ophthalmology had learned something new over the past three decades. A series of phone calls led me to a specialist at New York University Medical Center. I was assured that if anyone could answer my questions, he was the man.

So, on a sunny morning in October, Dick and I set out for New York to learn why I am blind. We lived in a small town in central Pennsylvania at the time, and Dick wasn't used to driving in the city. He dreaded the horn-blaring, bumper-to-bumper traffic and the desperate search for a parking space. All of his energy focused on delivering us to our destination. As we packed the car he commented, "It's going to be a long, nervous day." I couldn't have agreed with him more.

Parking on the streets of Manhattan was as difficult as Dick had feared. Finally we squeezed into a spot a dozen blocks from the hospital and set out on foot. The city engulfed us with its fumes and bustle and grinding noise. We didn't try to talk above the traffic. Really, there was nothing new to say.

We had walked several blocks when I was dimly aware of a strange sound. It was remarkably like the song of a bird, the clear, warbling notes ringing out against the concrete walls around us. At first I assumed it was a recording turned full blast, or some mechanical toy worked by a child. But as we drew nearer Dick remarked, "There's a crowd of people standing by a tree. They're all looking at something. Oh hey, there's a bird up there!"

I've been an avid birder most of my life, and the song was unmistakable. It was a mockingbird. The mockingbird thrives in fields and gardens. It gathers scraps and snippets from the songs of other birds and braids them into a pattern all its own. The mockingbird sings exuberantly from April to June, but by late summer it usually falls silent. Yet this one poured forth its song on East 32nd Street in mid-October, out of place and out of season. It seemed utterly fearless and confident, staking a claim for itself in that inhospitable city landscape. It had something to say, and it was determined to be heard.

New Yorkers are used to almost anything, but the extraordinary song of this tiny creature brought them to a standstill. For a little while Dick and I paused too. We stood on the pavement, listening and marveling. Then we pushed through the revolving door and into the antiseptic halls of the medical center.

I expected a battery of tests, maybe a referral to yet another expert. But the doctor dilated my pupils, gazed into my eyes, and announced, "I'll tell you what you have, and I'm 100 percent certain. You've got Leber's congenital amaurosis." Leber's is a genetic condition, he explained, autosomal recessive in nature. Both of my parents carried the recessive gene, and each of their children had a one-in-four chance of inheriting the eye condition.

What were my chances of passing Leber's on to my own children, I asked. The doctor explained that I would inevitably give one recessive gene for Leber's to my child. But unless my partner happened to carry the same recessive gene, there was no possibility that our child would be affected. The chances were slight that Dick would prove to be another carrier.

The discussion could have ended with that simple exchange of information. But the doctor had more to say. "You have a good life, don't you?" he asked. "If you have a child with Leber's, it can have a good life, too. Go home and have a dozen kids if you want to!"

Even from a total stranger, those were wonderful words. They affirmed that I was not a liability to the world. I was a worthwhile human being with a variety of traits to pass on to future generations. To this New York physician my Leber's genes were not a curse. They need not be extinguished, any more than my genes for dark brown hair. I was valued for who I was. My child, sighted or blind, could be valued in the same way. I floated out of the doctor's office and found Dick in the packed waiting room. "Hey, guess what!" I cried in triumph. "I've got Leber's congenital amaurosis!"

The trip to New York cemented our decision to have a child. We left the city with a new certainty, a sense that we were ready for whatever came our way. Yet I knew Dick was comforted by the fact that Leber's is relatively rare, and that probably he did not carry the recessive gene. I wished that he didn't need that comfort.

Within the year we were parents-to-be. We awaited the birth of our child with the eagerness, wonder, and anxiety common to expectant parents everywhere. We seldom mentioned the possibility that our baby might be blind. Leber's congenital amaurosis seemed safely remote, a flash of lightning that wouldn't strike again. But it could reappear, I knew. I lived with the small unspoken fear that, if our child were blind, Dick would feel betrayed—by medical science, by fate, by me.

Dick had his doubts about coaching me through labor and viewing the birth. To support us both his sister came along to our Lamaze classes. She even stayed with us in the birthing room to help out in case Dick should faint dead away. But nobody fainted. When our daughter Janna arrived, we greeted her with greater joy than I could have imagined. Her welcome was boundless and wholly unreserved.

My parents flew out to visit us when we brought Janna home from the hospital. Mom helped with the cooking and housecleaning and insisted that I get as much rest as I could. I spent every conscious moment nursing, rocking, diapering, and marveling at the extraordinary new being who had entered our lives. I was too happy and excited to feel exhaustion.

I wasn't worried about Janna's vision or anything else. But one day my mother confided that my father had told her, "We've still got to find out if the baby's blind." I was stunned by his concern and by her sense that it was justified. My parents raised all three of their children, including my blind brother and me, with sensitivity and unwavering love. In all of us they tried to nurture confidence, ambition, and self-respect. Yet they felt apprehensive about the prospect that their granddaughter might also be blind. Blindness had never become neutral for them, any more than it had for Dick.

It was almost time for Mom and Dad to go home when Dick said to my mother, "You've raised two blind children. What do you think—can this kid see or not?" My mother said she really couldn't be sure. Janna was barely a week old; it was too soon to tell. The day after my parents left, Dick found the answer on his own. As Janna lay in his arms, awake and alert, he moved his hand back and forth above her face. Distinctly he saw her turn her head to track the motion. She saw his hand. She followed it with her eyes.

"She can see!" Dick exulted. He rushed to the phone and called my parents with the news. I listened quietly to their celebrations. I don't know if anyone noticed that I had very little to say.

How do I myself feel about the fact that Janna can see? I am glad that her world is enriched by color as well as texture and sound. When she snaps a picture with her new camera or poses before the mirror in her favorite dress, I draw pleasure from her delight. As her mother I want her to have every advantage, and I know that some aspects of her life are easier because she has sight. She can play video games with her friends; she can thumb through magazines and note the latest fashions. All too soon now she will be learning to drive a car.

Beyond that, I am glad Janna will never be dismissed as incompetent and unworthy simply because she is blind. I am grateful that she will not face the discrimination that threads its way through my life and the lives of most people with disabilities. But I know her vision will not spare her from heartbreak. She will still meet disappointment, rejection, and self-doubt, as all of us must.

I will always believe that blindness is a neutral trait, neither to be prized nor shunned. Very few people, including those dearest to me, share that conviction. My husband, my parents, and so many others who are central to my life cannot fully relinquish their negative assumptions. I feel that I have failed when I run into jarring reminders that I have not changed their perspective. In those crushing moments I fear that I am not truly accepted after all.

But in recent years a new insight has gradually come to me. Yes, my own loved ones hold the unshakable belief that blindness is and always will be a problem. Nevertheless, these same people have made me welcome. Though they dread blindness as a fate to be avoided at almost any cost, they give me their trust and respect. I don't understand how they live without discomfort amid such contradictions. But I recognize that people can and do reach out, past centuries of prejudice and fear, to forge bonds of love. It is a truth to marvel at, and a cause for hope and perhaps some small rejoicing.

Sometimes Dick reminisces about the day Janna turned her head to watch his moving fingers. In his voice I hear an echo of the excitement and relief that were so vivid for him on that long-ago morning. Each time I hear the story I feel a twinge of the old pain, and for a few moments I am very much alone again.

But I have my own favorite stories to recall. I remember our long, nervous day in New York, and the doctor who told me to go home and have a dozen kids. And somehow I have never forgotten the mocking-bird that sang so boldly in a place where no one thought it belonged, making a crowd of busy people stand still to listen.

NOTE

1. Previously published in Michele Wates and Rowen Jade, eds., *Bigger Than the Sky: Disabled Women on Parenting* (London: Women's Press, 1999).

MARY ANN BAILY

Why I Had Amniocentesis

I chose to have amniocentesis and I think I would have chosen to have an abortion if I had received a diagnosis of a significant genetic disability. This chapter is an explanation of why I made that choice.

Why do I feel a desire to explain? I am responding to the fact that many people in the disability community see my choice of prenatal testing for genetic disabilities as a personal rejection. They interpret it to mean that I do not value persons with disabilities (at least the disabilities I would have considered as sufficient reason for an abortion), that I believe that their quality of life is too low to make it worth living, that I believe raising a child with a disability would be an overwhelming burden on the child's family, and so on.

I can understand why they think this. First, they perceive (correctly, I think) that most Americans simply do not understand what life with a disability is really like. Most do not realize that the lives of people with disabilities can be filled with productive work, enjoyable play, and relationships with others in which they give as much as they take. It is true that to have a fulfilling life, a person with a disability may have to overcome obstacles. One thing I have learned from the disability community, however, is that often the greatest obstacle isn't the direct effect of a disability on the ability to manage the activities of daily life. Instead, it is the average person's belief that disability makes a fulfilling life impossible, and the impact this belief has on the way people with disabilities are treated.

Second, people with disabilities perceive (again, correctly) that many Americans who accept prenatal diagnosis and abortion do justify their position on the grounds that the life of the child with the disability would not be worth living and the child would be an overwhelming burden on his/her family and society. A woman says, with a shudder, "I would have an abortion because I could *never* do that," implying that parenting a child with a disability is only for self-sacrificing saints. A talk show host bears a child with the same genetic condition she has herself and receives hate mail accusing her of personal and social irresponsibility. Legislators outlaw abortion on the grounds that a fetus is a person so abortion is murder . . . but then make an exception for a fetus with a disability.

Acceptance of prenatal diagnosis and abortion certainly *can* express rejection of people with disabilities. But *must* it? Or can one look at it another way? I do, and I suspect that I am joined by many other women who have used prenatal diagnosis. I would like to think that understanding this point of view could ease some of the pain I hear in the voices of people with disabilities when they talk about prenatal diagnosis.

I think I should begin my explanation with a description of my general attitude toward reproductive choice. I had an extremely Catholic upbringing, in which God's will determined childbearing, and the woman was allowed virtually no say in it. Sex outside of marriage was prohibited, of course. Within marriage there was somewhat grudging acceptance of periodic abstinence (the "rhythm method" of birth control) but strong condemnation of artificial contraception, sterilization, and, of course, abortion, for any reason at all, including to preserve the health or even the life of the mother.

I have rejected these views. I am pro-choice, in two senses. First, I believe that a woman should have the legal right to make these reproductive choices, and that her decisions should not be interfered with, whatever they are. In this, I am joined by my mother, a devout Catholic and mother of five who accepts the Church's teachings herself but believes that these reproductive choices should be guided by a woman's own conscience, not the law. Second, and in this I am *not* joined by my mother, I believe that it is morally acceptable for a woman to exercise choice over whether to begin a pregnancy, and through the second trimester, whether to continue it. In other words, to me, abortion is not morally problematic in itself. There are good and bad reasons for having abortions, but it is not so much the abortion as the reason that I would condemn.

I have given serious thought to these views, and I hold them sincerely. There *is* a sense in which abortion remains morally problematic for me, however. Although I have tried to reason carefully about my position on abortion, I might be wrong. A Catholic upbringing is not easily discarded. (I call this the "I don't believe in God, and God is going to get me for that" syndrome.) Because of this, and also because of the emotional and physical aspects of having an abortion, especially in the second trimester, I think abortion is something to be avoided if possible, and I am glad I have never been in a situation in which I would want to choose abortion. Nevertheless, I do believe that in the first and second trimester it is a morally acceptable choice. (I don't, by the way, have the same uneasiness about contraception and sterilization, both of which the Church condemns as strongly as abortion and both of which I have used without any hesitation.)

In sum, I believe that I can (in fact, I should) make my own choices about reproduction rather than leaving them to fate. To me, this has meant having far fewer than the biological maximum of children I could have, and doing what I could to ensure that the children I did have were born into favorable circumstances—favorable for them and for me.

Now, suppose prenatal diagnosis, in a wanted pregnancy, reveals a genetic disability—Down syndrome, to be concrete—and I decide to have an abortion. One can say, "She doesn't want to have a child with Down syndrome" and interpret this as a rejection of children with Down syndrome as persons. What I would say is "I do not want my child to be born with Down syndrome," meaning, "If I have a choice, I want the person who will be my child to be born into a body without such potentially significant limitations."

At one meeting of The Hastings Center's "Prenatal Testing for Genetic Disability" project, there was a moment when, listening to Adrienne Asch speak about the expressive character of prenatal diagnosis and abortion, I found myself thinking, "It's too bad we don't believe in reincarnation." I had a vivid mental image of my impression of the difference between how I see prenatal diagnosis and abortion and how some members of the disability community see it. Their picture is of a line of babies waiting to be born, and a quality control officer coming along and throwing "people like them" out of the line so they never make it to earth. My picture is of a "disembodied soul," the essence of my yet-to-be-born child, waiting to be inserted into a baby-shaped container, with me standing there to make sure my child's soul gets into a well-functioning container.

This is, of course, utter nonsense from the scientific point of view. I know intellectually that every conception that continued to birth would result in a different child. Also, I am not at all sure what I mean by a "disembodied soul," since science and my own experience suggest that the physical, mental, emotional, and spiritual characteristics of a person are linked to one another and to the person's genetic makeup.

Nevertheless, at the point of prenatal diagnosis, all I know about my potential child is the result of the test. If the test indicates a disability that will cause significant limitations and I have an abortion, it does not feel to me like a rejection of the specific child that particular fetus might have grown into, with his or her unique personality traits. I will conceive another child—the same, generic, unknown child—and, with luck, this time the child will not have to contend with the physical or mental limitation that the genetic disability represents. The background to my decision is always my awareness that every month of my reproductive life I could conceive a child, and every one of those children would be unique, and before this child was conceived, I had already decided that I would actually give birth to at most only a few of those children.

The background to my decision is also my belief that, all other things equal, disability (specifically, a disability for which I would consider an abortion) would make life more difficult for my child, my family, and me. This is not the same thing as saying it would be an overwhelming burden or would make a fulfilling life impossible. It does not mean that my child, my family, and I could not handle the difficulties. It means only that *if I have a choice*, I would prefer to avoid them, for all of our sakes. And I believe I do have a choice.

I must confess at this point that I simply cannot see the any/particular distinction that Adrienne Asch draws. If I believed that abortion was wrong, then the moment of total commitment to the potential child would come at conception. But I don't believe that. If the moment of commitment comes later—if I can let information about the impact of pregnancy in general on my life and the life of the potential child influence my decision about continuing the pregnancy—I don't see why I can't let information about the impact of this *particular* pregnancy influence me. The distinction seems completely arbitrary to me.

Does my personal decision have an expressive character? It does not express my opinion on whether people with disabilities can have worthwhile, fulfilling lives (they can), whether parenting a child with a disability can be rewarding (it can), whether other people should be pressured into aborting fetuses with disabilities (they shouldn't), or whether societal resources should be devoted to improving the lives of people with disabilities (they should).

It also does not express my belief that I'm "entitled to a perfect child." Prenatal testing cannot eliminate the risk of giving birth to a child with a disability, it can only reduce it, and most disability isn't congenital anyway. Moreover, disability is far from the only circumstance that can make child-rearing more difficult than expected.

It expresses only the fact that given a choice, I would rather my child did not have a disability. That's all. For a person with a disability to take this as a personal rejection seems unreasonable to me. When people with disabilities say, "Prenatal diagnosis and abortion means people 'like us' will never be born," I want to say, well, of course they will, they just won't have the disability. To me, this objection only really makes sense if people with disabilities *are* their disabilities. This, in turn, seems inconsistent with the disability community's contention that a major part of the unnecessary, socially created burden of disability is the tendency of people who are not disabled to take a person's disability and make it the essence of the person, rather than simply one aspect, or attribute—to speak of "the blind," "the deaf," "the mentally retarded," "paraplegics," "amputees."

After all, by this standard, any intervention that prevents or cures disability eliminates people with disabilities. Suppose a serious genetic disability could be cured in utero by an operation about as burdensome to the woman as an abortion. Wouldn't we take it for granted that most women would have the operation (maybe even criticize the choice not to have it), but wouldn't the result be the same: a smaller number of children born with that disability?

Prenatal testing/abortion is sometimes made synonymous with eugenics and condemned as intolerant of diversity. My dictionary defines eugenics as "a science that deals with the improvement (as by *control* [emphasis added] of human mating) of hereditary qualities of a race or breed."[1] It is the control part, in my opinion, that gives eugenics such a bad name. Although I value diversity, it seems to me that pressuring women to continue pregnancies they would rather end, for the sake of diversity, sounds more like eugenics than leaving them to make their own reproductive decisions.

What of the concept that people with disabilities are, by virtue of their disability, members of a separate culture? From the little I have read about this, I think it is a useful way to approach some disability-related issues, and I would like to learn more about it. I'd like to describe an interesting reaction I had as a parent to one application of it, though. At one of the Hastings Center project meetings, in reference to fetuses with disabilities, Marsha Saxton said something like, "These are our children!" On one level, I think she was simply applying to children with disabilities the principle that children belong to all of us, not just to their parents (something I believe strongly myself), and saying that adults with disabilities recognize and embrace a special responsibility to mentor the children these fetuses would become. Nevertheless, my immediate, intense emotional response was "are *not!*" When I analyzed it, I realized that as a prospective parent, I would not be enthusiastic about having my child grow up to be a member of another culture, especially one that is on somewhat hostile terms with the one to which I belong. I pictured my disabled fifteen-year-old looking at me with angry eyes and saying scornfully, "I want nothing to do with you, you ableist pig!"

Parents want their children to become adult members of their own culture. Even when parents believe that joining another culture will give their children expanded opportunities and have made heroic sacrifices to make that possible, as in the case of voluntary immigrants to the United States, they often feel a sense of loss when it happens. Don't misunderstand: If I had a child with a disability, I would promote his/her involvement in disability culture (and the involvement of the rest of the family, to the extent the disability culture would allow), because I think it would be an important source of self-affirmation and support. What I am saying is, it is not a plus. The more disability rights advocates emphasize that people with disabilities form a separate culture, the less appealing raising a child with a disability looks to someone who is not already part of that culture.

What about the contention of the disability community that enthusiasm for prenatal diagnosis is fueled by misinformation about the impact of disability on life, and by a lack of social support that makes the impact greater than it needs to be? Misinformation and lack of social support are certainly problems that should be corrected, whether or not prenatal diagnosis is an option, for the sake of people with disabilities and their families. All pregnant women should have a realistic picture of the impact of disability, not only so that they can make informed decisions about prenatal diagnosis and abortion, but so that they are adequately prepared for the full range of possibilities in childbearing. I think this is especially important for people who do not consider abortion a morally acceptable choice. It must be very terrible to be a woman who believes that abortion is murder but nevertheless fears disability so much that she has one in violation of her deepest moral principles.

But would better information and social support eliminate the interest in prenatal diagnosis by people who do consider abortion morally acceptable—people like me? I don't think so. Even with substantial social support, life will still be more difficult for people with some genetic disabilities and for their families than it would be in the absence of the disability. People who believe they have a choice may still reasonably prefer to avoid the difficulties. Remember also that for most genetically diagnosed disabilities, there is a range of severity, and most people are risk-averse. A woman's decision may reasonably be influenced more by the "worst-case" Down syndrome scenario than by the average.

Let me close by saying that I think there may be an unappreciated danger in basing opposition to prenatal diagnosis and abortion on its expressive character. This may have an adverse effect on the broader goal of getting people without disabilities to appreciate and support the issues that are important to the disability community. Since people don't like to have their personal reproductive choices criticized as immoral and unfeeling, their natural impulse will be to defend themselves against such criticism. One way to justify the choice of abortion is to magnify the consequences of not having one—in this case, to insist on portraying life with a disability in the most negative of terms. As an analogy, consider the controversy about whether mothers should work outside the home. For a long time, women who chose to stay home demonized career women as unnatural mothers and their children as psychologically damaged. Women who went to work retaliated by denigrating housewives, extolling the socialization value of day care, and exaggerating the extent to which their work was an economic necessity. In this emotionally charged atmosphere, it became very difficult to develop balanced information on the consequences of different approaches to child-rearing.

Most people are not analytic thinkers; they tend to know what they want to do and then look for justifications. When the disability community says: "Prenatal testing/abortion expresses the belief that the lives of people with disabilities are not worth living," the average woman is not likely to say, "Oh, I certainly would not want to send that message, so I will not have prenatal diagnosis and abortion," as the disability community presumably hopes. Nor will she say, as I do, "I do want prenatal testing/abortion, but you are wrong in saying my decision expresses that belief." Rather, she may very well say, "I do want prenatal testing/abortion, so I guess I must believe the lives of people with disabilities are not worth living." This can then turn into, "If I acknowledge that the lives of people with disabilities are worth living, then I won't be able to use prenatal testing/abortion to make my own reproductive decisions." The unintended result may be to reinforce the distorted public perception of the impact of disability rather than to correct it.

NOTE

1. *Webster's Ninth New Collegiate Dictionary* (Springfield, Mass.: Merriam-Webster, 1986), p. 428.

PHILIP M. FERGUSON, ALAN GARTNER,
AND DOROTHY K. LIPSKY

The Experience of Disability
in Families: A Synthesis of
Research and Parent Narratives

One of the foundations of many discussions about prenatal genetic
testing and selective abortion has often been the sense that the birth
of a child with severe disabilities represents an unquestioned tragedy
and lasting hardship for the family of the child. Who could question
that the experience of raising a child with significant cognitive and
physical disabilities was unavoidably one of acute emotional distress and
disrupted lives (if the child died quickly), or of chronic sorrow, prolonged
economic hardship, foreclosed opportunities and, often, marital dysfunc-
tion or dissolution (if the child survived to adulthood)? Whatever ethical
decisions were to be made about terminating a pregnancy seemed
implicitly to assume that the birth of such a child would be more of a
burden than a blessing, to both the parents and the society. Even when
conclusions were reached that ethical considerations ultimately argued
against termination of the pregnancy, such conclusions were usually
embedded in a motif of sympathy and regret for the prospective parents.
From this perspective, the words of Hester Thrale in 1775 (a diarist
and friend of Samuel Johnson and well known to literary critics and
historians interested in that period) were almost as apt for our era as
they were two centuries earlier. Upon having a doctor confirm the
"dreadful sentence" of permanent fatuity (or intellectual disability) for
her newborn son, Thrale bemoans her fate:

> Oh how this dreadful Sentence did fill me with Horror! & how dismal
> are now the thought of all future Connection with this unhappy Child!
> A Thing to hide & be ashamed of whilst we live: Johnson gives me what
> Comfort he can, and laments he can give no more. This is to be sure

[one] of the great Evils Life has in it, and one had no business to prepare for a sorrow so uncommon—I shall therefore bear it the worse perhaps. Oh Lord give me patience to bear this heaviest of all my Afflictions![1]

Although technology may have changed, the assumption until recently by most geneticists and bioethicists has been that parental reactions have remained remarkably—if understandably—the same over the last 225 years.

However, over the last twenty years or so, there has been a steadily growing body of literature that has increasingly challenged this assumption. In both research on families and parent narratives themselves, the portrayal of family reactions to having a child with significant disabilities has become much more complicated and nuanced. Indeed, if assumptions have to be made at all about how families react, then the bulk of the literature now suggests one that the quality of their lives resembles that of families generally.

In this chapter we will review this literature on family adaptation and document how it has changed over the last few years. Our interpretation assumes that both disability and the reactions to it are socially constructed interpretations that inevitably reflect the personal and cultural context in which those interpretations are made. Whether through endorsement or resistance, both professionals and parents are obviously influenced by the beliefs and circumstances that hold sway at any given time. As the social circumstances of people with disabilities have undeniably improved over the last few decades in our country, it would be surprising if the familial response did not reflect that improvement. However, it is equally true that even more than simply documenting changed family reactions over the years, researchers themselves have shifted to a point where they "discovered" a host of more positively framed family outcomes that had previously gone unnoticed.

Of course, we cannot pretend that we, ourselves, are somehow unaffected by this process. All three of us have been actively involved in trying to speed this change in perspective and circumstance as researchers, advocates, and parents ourselves. We readily admit that this chapter is our construction of an immense body of research and personal accounts. There are always multiple interpretations possible of what even a single study means, much less the plausible summaries available to characterize the knowledge base as a whole. We find our version to be persuasive and useful when thinking about the ethical issues surrounding prenatal diagnosis and selective abortion. We do not claim to be neutral in our account, then, but have tried to be fair in analyzing the messages from the fields of family research and disability studies.

Regardless of their social origins, these changed messages about the experience of parents of children with severe disabilities have not yet been sufficiently heard by many of those participating in discussions about the ethics of prenatal diagnosis and selective abortion. In part, this is because too few of those in the disability community have been asked to join those discussions. Second, this lag may simply be the byproduct of an increasingly specialized research literature across multiple disciplines and methodologies. Research on families of children with disabilities (as with disabilities in general) is bewilderingly multidisciplinary and difficult to follow down all of the tributaries of specialized inquiry in the humanities and social sciences. Most of the participants in this area of genetics and bioethics understandably focus on research close to their own fields. Finally, this slowness to recognize the shifting consensus in the research on families may reflect a reluctance to dismantle some comfortable assumptions that have made this ethical discussion seem somewhat easier.

We will present our analysis in three sections. First, we will quickly review some of the main strands in the research on families since the days of Hester Thrale. Next, we will explore the evolution of what we call the "adaptational" approach in family research over the last twenty years or so and its conceptual grounding in family systems theory, models of stress and coping, and the important contributions of family narratives. Finally, we will review what we think are the key themes that emerge from this review of the literature.

The History of Family Research

Several years ago, Philip M. Ferguson and Adrienne Asch began a review of the published narratives written by parents and persons with disabilities with what struck us as some simple truths. "The most important thing that happens when a child with disabilities is born is that a child is born. The most important thing that happens when a couple becomes parents of a child with disabilities is that a couple becomes parents."[2] However, when we look at the history of professional responses to the birth of such a child, we find patterns of research and practice that have, until recently, assumed that the disability itself inevitably overwhelmed all other considerations. Whether seen as the cause or the outcome of the disability itself, the unfortunate family circumstances supposedly associated with such births were consistently presented as inherent and immutable.

Blaming Parents for the Disabilities of Their Children

Eighteenth-century London as portrayed in Hester Thrale's family journal actually represented something of a transition period in the emergence of professional explanations of parental responses to disability. As the Enlightenment took hold, the presence of disability in God's universe acquired newly scientific explanations. Yet burgeoning confidence in scientific knowledge co-existed with a persistent moralistic gloss on the occurrence of such blatant evidence of original sin. Even for someone of Thrale's elevated and educated social status, the sense of shame at having a disabled child was vivid and reinforced. She reflected the common belief that she must be responsible for her child's condition:

> In the midst of this Distress [i.e., the deaths of her mother and one of her other children] I have brought a Baby, which seems to be in measure affected by my Vexations; he is heavy, stupid & drowsy, though very large. . . . I see no Wit sparkle in his Eyes.[3]

For the poor, the assignment of blame for such births was even more blatant. The presence of disabled children was not so much God's plan as parents' sinful, or at least ignorant, behavior, now carefully couched in the discourse of biological discovery.

Throughout the nineteenth century, with the emergence of increasingly specialized medical and educational professions, both the causal direction and moral blame for most childhood disability were thought to begin with the parents (especially those with the bad judgment to be both poor and female). Indeed, the common link between the emergence of the kindergarten and the first asylums for the so-called "insane" and "idiotic" was a professional argument by the most respected researchers of the era. These facilities were needed to remove vulnerable children from the evil influence of the families and their "vicious habits of low-bred idleness"—to use the words of Henry Barnard, one of the earliest advocates of early and universal education.[4] Samuel Gridley Howe, a contemporary of Barnard's and one of the early founders of specialized asylums for people with intellectual disabilities, offered an even more explicit indictment of parents of so-called idiots, as he made a plea for money to the Massachusetts legislature. It was a characteristic combination of morality and biology that led Howe to the door of the poor household.

> The moral to be drawn from the prevalent existence of idiocy in society is, that a very large class of persons ignore the conditions upon which alone health and reason are given to men, and consequently they sin in various ways; they disregard the conditions which should be observed in intermarriage; they overlook the hereditary transmission of certain morbid tendencies; they pervert the natural appetites of the body into lusts of divers kinds,—the natural emotions of the mind into fearful passions— and thus bring down the awful consequences of their own ignorance and sin upon the heads of their unoffending children.[5]

Social policy reflected what the professionals said their research revealed. Reform schools, asylums, and residential schools for increasingly specific disabilities all began to appear in the nineteenth century as ways to get disabled or "vulnerable" children away from their parents. With the spreading optimism of the Enlightenment, the emerging professionals and specialized experts of the 1800s argued that the only way to break the connection between poor parents and disabled children was to allow them and their staffs to assume the parental role within the walls of their facilities. This carried over into the rapid spread of special education classes in public school systems after the turn of the century.[6] Even today, versions of this professional attack on family culture can still be seen in special education referral and placement practices that remain troublingly skewed and segregated along lines of race and class.

Shifting the Blame to the Child

For most of the last fifty years, the underlying assumptions of professional research have largely reversed themselves. No longer was the emphasis on how poor and probably disabled parents breed poor and inevitably disabled children (at least for most genetic conditions). Professionals now shifted their attention to how disabled children inevitably damaged the families to which they were born. Whether they preferred to use primarily attitudinal categories (guilt, denial, displaced anger, grief) or behavioral ones (role disruption, marital cohesiveness, social withdrawal), most researchers assumed a connection that was both intrinsic and harmful to the parent-child dyad.[7] The challenge for research was to catalogue and sequence the evidence of parental damage and to argue for the efficacy of this or that therapeutic intervention.

The medical model that dominated approaches to disability was extended to families.

The conclusion was also inescapable. Some researchers used primarily attitudinal categories to characterize the neurotic paths families followed. If families expressed displeasure with doctors or other professionals over the supposed lack of supports, this was presented as merely the displaced anger that was originally directed at the disabled child.[8] On the other hand, if the parent seemed too passive in the face of inadequate services, then this was seen as an outgrowth of underlying guilt or denial. Of course, other researchers attributed active parent involvement and dedication to the welfare of their child as prima facie evidence of a deep-seated need to compensate for the same underlying guilt complex. Apathetic or involved, angry or accepting: there was a professional explanation of the pathology behind any conceivable parental response.[9] In many ways the process is at the heart of the so-called "medical model" that many in the disability community have attacked as dehumanizing and reductive. The pathology becomes the focus of professional interest, whether the person involved is the child with the disability or the family of that child. The dominance of the process can be seen in educational as well as medical settings. Bruce Engel found the process repeatedly described by parents he interviewed about their interactions with professionals.

> Whereas parents tend to perceive the whole child and to emphasize capabilities, the professionals tend to perceive the child in terms of those "defects," those aspects of the child that deviate from the norm and justify the child's classification as "handicapped" or "disabled."[10]

The pathologizing is extended to the parents by dismissing their emphasis on a child's capabilities as merely the symptoms of denial rather than adaptation.[11] It is a therapeutic "Catch-22" in which whatever response parents provide, the assumption of damage can be seen as verified. As Dorothy K. Lipsky wrote some twelve years ago:

> Not only do the perspectives [of researchers and professionals such as those just discussed] have serious limitations, not only are they severely overgeneralized and overapplied, but they increase the likelihood that no matter which role a family plays, it will be deemed unsatisfactory by one or more professionals. In other words, both sides of the coin show pathological behavior.[12]

In the 1960s and 1970s, research on families reflected the larger shift in the social sciences to a preference for behavioral approaches and categories over the previously fashionable psychoanalytic tradition. However, despite the conceptual reorientation, the normative assumptions about family responses to a disabled child remained largely unchallenged. In one of the largest and best-known studies from this era, Barnard Farber and his colleagues found that the families who institutionalized their mentally retarded children were relaxed, harmonious, and integrated. They participated more in activities outside the house. However, subsequent studies showed the danger of professional assumptions about what was normative and what was not. The question unasked by Farber was whether the erratic or nonexistent support services for families in the 1950s and 1960s had more to do with the findings of marital disharmony and social isolation than did any inherently disruptive influence of the disabled child living at home. Indeed, a less well-known but revealing study from the same era discovered that when disabled children living at home were in day programs or schools, marital integration was much higher than in families without such services. What Farber interpreted as normative and unavoidable was, in fact, found to be situational and contingent.[13]

Nonetheless, in both attitudinal and behavioral research, the causal connections between disabled child and damaged family continued to dominate. The extremes to which this passion for pathology was taken can be seen in the title of one research piece that appeared in 1981, just before the tide of family research began to shift once again. In an article titled "Parentalplegia," the authors provide perhaps the most transparent version of the dominant logic:

> Children having conditions of mental retardation or other handicaps involving physical deficiencies are likely to be causes of a secondary handicapping condition involving the parents. . . . The authors have chosen the term parentalplegia to describe a secondary psycho-physiological (stress induced) condition that evolves among parents of handicapped children. Parentalplegia seems to be caused by an inability on the part of parents to adjust to the handicap of their children.[14]

Family and Disability in an Adaptational Context

These implicit and explicit assumptions that have guided family research in the past primarily reflect the social and historical context within which that research occurred. This is no real surprise, unless one assumes that the influence of cultural values and social policy somehow stops at the door to the lab. We assume, instead, that such influence is where the inevitability resides, not in some unbreakable connection of disabled child and parental pathology.

Of course, these social and historical forces continue to influence the questions that family researchers are asking today. What has changed over the two decades, however, in both policy and practice, is a dramatic evolution of our attitudes and supports for people with disabilities and their families. At levels of both culture and policy, disability analysts are making the case that impairment is part of the human condition.[15] As with all other features of the human condition, however, impairment can never remain unembodied in the cultural context. It is how we interpret impairment as a social construct that it comes to be "disability." In this critical analysis, disability advocates are challenging those unquestioned assumptions at the very heart of so many debates over disability and social policy. They are asking why it is that disability—rather than bad social policy—is always identified as the problem to be solved. They question the priorities of a society that spends more time and money on eliminating disability than on including people with disabilities alongside all other segments of our diverse communities. Martha Minow has captured the challenge that disability advocates (as well as other minority groups) are presenting us:

> From their own perspective, women, members of minority groups, and disabled people may not be abnormal; they may instead introduce more varied and more inclusive definitions of what is normal. The dilemma of difference will recur for them, however, in programs that presume the status quo to be natural, good, or immutable, where the status quo assigns the label of difference and its burdens to some and refuses to make room for a range of human conditions. Reframing social experience to transcend the difference dilemma means challenging the presumption that either one is the same or one is different, either one is normal or one is not.[16]

At the policy level, the emergence of the disability rights movement finds its legal reflection in legislation from Section 504 of the Vocational Rehabilitation Act to the Americans with Disabilities Act. The growth of inclusive education for children with disabilities in our nation's schools is traceable through the elaboration of legal concepts such as the "least restrictive environment" and "zero rejection" found in the Education of All Handicapped Children Act and its extension to early childhood in PL 99-457 (both now encompassed in the Individuals with Disabilities Education Act). Finally, the demonstration that people with even the most significant and multiple disabilities can be supported as active members of society, productively participating in the daily life of their communities has been increasingly acknowledged by Medicaid waivers for innovative state programs in community and family settings; conversion efforts to move from sheltered workshops to supported employment; and a reliance on smaller and smaller community-residential arrangements by almost all states. Charles Lakin and his colleagues have recently reported that these residential patterns have now passed the symbolically important halfway point in terms of people with developmental disabilities living in small (i.e., six or fewer individuals) community facilities across the country.[17]

It remains true that all too many people continue to live at home with their aging parents because of the wait lists for access to such community settings. It is equally true that public policy still maintains financial incentives to incarcerate thousands of people in large public institutions or private nursing homes. Still, the change in circumstance is measurable, steady, and seemingly durable despite the whims of politicians and bureaucrats.

All of these developments are part of the context that both generates and reflects the questions that today's researchers are trying to answer about families and disability. One of the most prominent of these researchers, Marty Krauss at Brandeis University, has summarized the implications well:

> For decades, researchers examining families of children with disabilities explicitly assumed a high degree of pathology in family functioning. . . . These studies may have served a useful purpose in focusing attention on the enormous difficulties experienced by families who received little or no public services to support their caregiving efforts. . . . However, substantial strides have been made in publicly supported early intervention systems, educational inclusion policies, and family support programs over the past decade. . . . [T]hus, studies conducted prior to the early 1980s are based on a different cohort of families than those who have participated in research conducted within the context of current service initiatives.[18]

Over the last two decades, perhaps the most influential developments in research on the effect of a child with a disability upon parents and other family members have come from two specific conceptual traditions: models of stress and coping (or adaptation), and models of family life course development. No more than a summary sketch of either of these research traditions is possible here. However, even a cursory outline reveals the important contribution that a sociohistorical approach has made to interpreting the meaning of disability in people's lives.

Within the broad field of social psychology, research has centered on developing a theoretical representation of how families more or less successfully adapt to the potentially refined and elaborated classic "ABCX model" originally developed by Reuben Hill. Essentially, this model describes "family crisis" ('X') as an interactive outcome of three factors: 'A', an initial "stressor event"; combined with 'B', a family's resources for dealing with crises; and 'C', how the family defines the stressor.[19] Recent work with families of children with disabilities has proposed refinements to this original model in three important ways.

First, over the last few years, the use of this or other models of family adaptation and resilience has allowed researchers to increasingly recognize and interpret the many successful coping strategies and positive adaptations that many families report.[20] The shift in emphasis is important. Most researchers have abandoned the sort of tally sheet mentality that seeks to add up responses to see how bad (or how good) it is for families to have a child with a disability. The question is no longer one of listing the "unfortunate consequences" of an "unquestioned tragedy." It has really moved, as well, beyond a simple counterbalancing quest for purely positive outcomes. Instead, most of the more sophisticated research on family stress today is trying to understand the factors that contribute to some families adapting more successfully than others. While there is certainly a range of results and opinions in this body of research as in any other, there is a level of agreement approaching consensus that the overall adaptational profile of families who have children with disabilities basically resembles the overall profile for families in general (including children with and without disabilities).[21] Again, Marty Krauss provides a summative judgment on the effect of this growing research base upon the field:

> There is increasing recognition that many families cope effectively and positively with the additional demands experienced in parenting a child with a disability. . . . The most recent literature suggests that families of children with handicaps exhibit variability comparable to the general population with respect to important outcomes such as parent stress . . . , family functioning . . . , and marital satisfaction. . . . Thus, although no one disputes the highly stressful effects on both mothers and fathers of learning that their child has a disability, research is now focused on understanding the factors associated with the amelioration of the "crisis" and on the similarities and differences between mothers and fathers in their perceptions of and responses to the experience of parenting a child with special needs.[22]

Second, researchers have made the model dynamic by recognizing that the ABCX cycle of responding to a perceived crisis is often cyclical and cumulative within a specific family. How a family responds to one stressor will influence how a family responds to subsequent stressors. Moreover, researchers have tried to capture not only the importance of a family's initial or "elementary" appraisal of the various elements of the "crisis," but also a "secondary" appraisal of their own capacity and resources. That is, the model now usually incorporates not only the resources for dealing with the crisis, but also how the family appraises its resources for dealing with a crisis.[23] What this more elaborated model allows is a dual focus. Not only do researchers look at how families respond differently in terms of their behavior, but they also look at the different cognitive interpretations and strategies that families use to shape their response.

For example, several interesting studies have compared families of children with Down syndrome to families of children with other disabilities, or with no disabilities. In one such study, Cahill and Glidden found that when they matched samples of families of children with Down syndrome with families of children with other disabilities, there were no significant differences in family and parental functioning. The authors suggest that this counters a persistent stereotype that children with Down syndrome are easier to raise than children with other disabilities. However, an ancillary finding indicated that not only was there no "adjustment advantage" to rearing children with Down syndrome,

> the average level of functioning for all families was quite good. On most variables, scores were at or near norms based on families in general, not those engaged in rearing children with developmental disabilities. . . . Most families who are rearing children with disabilities are demonstrating effective coping with this task.[24]

This shift has also allowed recognition of the importance of where a family is within its own life course. Phases of family development inevitably shape how family members perceive a specific source of potential stress. This development has supported the "discovery" of older parents by researchers. Until very recently, almost all research on family response to a disabled child focused on families with young children. Studies that followed families across the life span, or that specifically sought older parents of adults with disabilities, have opened up fascinating avenues for learning more about why some families are more resilient than others, and how extended coping with chronic illness or disability affects families over time. One unpublished study of parents over and under fifty-five actually found higher levels of adjustment in the older group, supporting the "adaptational" over the "wear-and-tear" hypothesis.[25]

A third important elaboration has been a distinction between internal and external resources that may be available to families. For example, this would recognize the obvious differences that the availability of effective family support programs might make in how well a family copes with the financial stress sometimes associated with having a child with a disability. Perhaps a more powerful argument that recent research has supported is that some external resources actually end up contributing to family stress. The process seems to work as follows for some families. We know that families of children with at least some disabilities, and most types of chronic illness, have greater contact with professionals in health, education, and human services. However, many families report that these interactions add to their stress rather than reduce it. In earlier research, this common expression of parental dissatisfaction with the formal support system has been called "the penalties of participation." Parents report a tradeoff of having to use a health-related or social service in paying a price in frustration, confusion, waiting lists, or lack of information. In a study of the families of over one hundred children with severe physical disabilities, Patricia Sloper and Stephen Turner supported the finding of other studies:

> It is possible that the conceptualization of use of services as an active coping behavior is not relevant to many professionally initiated service contacts which apply to families of children with disability. Equally, there is evidence that, even when contact is initiated by parents, they do not necessarily receive help . . . and that there is a considerable amount of parental dissatisfaction with the help received in managing children with physical disabilities. . . . Under these circumstances, services may exacerbate rather than moderate stress, particularly through the worry and difficulties regarding where to obtain help and information.[26]

Of course, the division of external and internal resources is embedded within a sociohistorical context of social policy and cultural assumptions.[27]

One obvious way to look at this cultural variability is to explore the area of cross-cultural comparisons of family reactions. Surely the differences in cultural attitudes, social supports, and personal beliefs across countries should be associated with different patterns of family response to disability. What is most surprising is how little of this type of comparative research has actually been conducted. Indeed, at least one study has argued that our research on families of children with chronic health problems has shown signs of cultural insensitivity that especially results in the underrepresentation of African American families in published studies. However, we do have a growing body of self-contained studies within individual countries that can be examined.

What existing research of this type suggests is that the anticipated differences do appear when one looks at separate studies done in different countries. For example, one study of Scandinavian mothers of children with Down syndrome found "little evidence of depression, [and] anxiety, revealed normal social and emotional contacts, and observed the negative feelings experienced at birth of the child almost invariably changing in a positive direction."[28] On the other hand, a study of mothers in India found evidence of much greater perceived burden and social isolation. The differences may not be solely related to levels of formal social support. There is some evidence that extended kinship networks are also effective in reducing perceived stress, and such networks are often stronger in non-European cultures.[29]

The problem for the more objectivist family researchers has been to move from acknowledgment of this larger context to operationalizing its components for comparative measurement. Some of the most exciting work here has been the study of so-called "ecocultural niches" by Thomas Weisner and Ronald Gallimore and their colleagues. This research uses "activity settings" as the unit of analysis for understanding the social construction process that families use to shape the meaning of disability in their lives.[30]

Those of us who rely on more interpretivist methods have been content to collect and analyze the stories that pack all of that history and culture into a shared family narrative. The elaboration of the stress and adaptation models has allowed researchers to rediscover the rich body of information available in the stories that families have always been willing to tell about their experiences. These stories are useful as more than simple accounts of the recent (or increasingly the not so recent) past. As anthropologists have always known, the stories and myths that we adopt to explain our origins—whether as part of a family or part of a culture—always tell as much about our current situation as our past. What we choose to remember and the stories within which we frame those memories always help to "clarify the circumstances at the time the story is retold."[31] In telling us about their lives "then," families are equally telling us about their lives "now."

Implications for Ethical Considerations

So, let us summarize the key points that we believe emerge from any fair and thorough reading of *recent* research on family adaptation to raising a child with a developmental disability.

- Perhaps the most universally agreed upon point is that family responses to disability are immensely variable. As one recent synthesis of the research concluded:

  What we are beginning to realize is that maternal and family reaction to disability, and to mental retardation in particular, is highly variable, so that it is difficult and inaccurate to talk about "families of children with retardation" in a general sense. Within the universe of families of children with retardation, there is a great range in the nature and extent to which individual mothers report maladaptation.[32]

- There is an increasingly dominant body of research that finds aggregate patterns of overall adjustment and well-being to be similar across groups of families with and without children with disabilities. This aggregate pattern, however, does show some developmental differences over the family life course (from birth of first child to death of last parent).

- There is increasing recognition and growing research that a significant number of parents actually report numerous benefits and positive outcomes for their families associated with raising a child with disabilities. These include coping skills (adaptability), family harmony (cohesiveness), spiritual growth or shared values, shared parenting roles, and communication.

- This is not to say that having a child with a disability is not a stressful event. The research continues to refine its understanding of why some families are more resilient than others in adapting to this stress. There is a growing amount of research indicating that factors such as the severity of the disability or chronic illness or family structure (single parents, family size) are not as predictive of stress on families as behavioral disruption (sleep problems, self-injurious behavior) or family income. There are also some differential patterns along ethnic and cultural lines that we do not understand well enough.[33]

Given this knowledge base, we wonder if this is the picture that is usually drawn for prospective parents as they are first learning to cope with a prenatal diagnosis of genetic disability for their prospective child. Through anecdotal information and some research, it is our impression that many (though certainly not all) medical professionals and genetic counselors—not to mention bioethicists—are either unaware of what the research shows about family adaptation patterns and the experience of disability or have difficulty translating that awareness into a balanced presentation for parents.[34]

Much about this situation has stayed depressingly unchanged since the 1970s when the debate over the selective treatment of newborns saw doctors and ethicists doubting the very humanity of infants with disabilities such as Down syndrome and spina bifida.[35] It was an era when respected journals such as the *Hastings Center Report* published arguments that openly questioned the "personhood" of individuals based on nothing more than an IQ score: "Any individual of the species homo sapiens who falls below the I.Q. 40-mark in a standard Stanford-Binet test . . . is questionably a person; below the 20-mark, not a person.[36] The philosopher Peter Singer (recently honored by Princeton University with an endowed chair in bioethics) took such arguments to their logical conclusion: "[K]illing a defective infant is not morally equivalent to killing a person . . . [and] very often it is not wrong at all."[37] Given this history of doctors and ethicists, can it be surprising that those of us advocating for disability equality hear disturbing echoes in the eugenic visions of some of today's geneticists?

There has been movement in the arguments as the discussion has moved from withholding treatment from newborns to aborting fetuses with genetic impairments. The argument has subtly changed. Twenty years ago, when the research on families predominantly seemed to support the medical predictions that such disabilities were unmitigated and chronic tragedies for the parents involved, the bioethical discussions cited this evidence at length. Now that the weight of family research has challenged this assumption, the evidence is seldom discussed. Instead, the claim is made that the issue all along has been parental choice. While there is apparently great variety from setting to setting, some data suggest that the majority of prospective parents, when presented with the diagnosis, choose to terminate the pregnancy. Even if it may not be deleterious to the family's well-being, raising a child with a disability is not the parenting experience that most couples anticipate. They should have the right to choose not to have that experience.

There are several possible replies to this shift in the argument. The first is simply to notice the shift. Why are the ethicists and geneticists not trumpeting the research results that parenting a child with a disability is apparently not nearly as bad as we said it was? Why are they not more fully incorporating into their counseling guidelines the ample evidence that some families report positive benefits to raising a child with a disability? If the issue is truly one of allowing parents to make an informed choice about what mountain they choose to climb as they start the trek of family life, then should not we be sharing the maps that show the topography to be pretty similar? Second, and to torture the metaphor a bit more, why are some mountains deemed avoidable (disability) and others just part of a path that parents should just accept (e.g., gender)? Instead, what we are left with is all too often the opposite of choice, where the prospective parents feel challenged if they select any other action but abortion.[38] At a minimum, then, regardless of how one ends up on the ethical options of responding to prenatal diagnosis of disability, surely we can agree that both parents and professionals should consider those options with full and balanced information about what the most recent research on families tells us. However, that agreement presents no small task. The health professions have historically been the last, not the first, to adjust to the evolving interpretation of the meanings of disability in our society.

Disability, like race and gender, is a complicated blend of physiology and culture inevitably viewed through the lens of our own personal history. Unlike race and gender, it is still permissible in our society to portray disability as clearly undesirable. The responses of pity and paternalism that allow us to distance ourselves while seeming sympathetic would be rejected out of hand if brought into ethical discussions of race or gender inequities. However, they remain central elements of the dominant discourse in ethical considerations of medical policy and practice toward people with disabilities and their families. Finally, it is now customary to recognize the social dimension to even the most private and individual decisions concerning ethnicity and sexual identity. The clarion call of earlier feminist battles is now a cliché that seems self-evident—of course "the personal is political." However, it is often portrayed as surprising and disruptive when members of the disability community suggest that the social valence of decisions affecting individuals with disabilities and their families is crucial contextual information.

It is ironic that the progress our society has made over the last twenty years to include disabled people in the midst of our communities is now increasingly threatened from the margins of life. From selective abortion to selective suicide, the disability community sees a mounting social threat to their existence just at the time when they are beginning to benefit from a generation of legislation and advocacy. Of course, none of this is meant to minimize the hard choices that specific couples must make in specific situations, with whatever resources and prospects they happen to have available. It is not so much the parental choices that we challenge, as it is the assumptions and contexts within which health professionals inevitably frame those choices.

NOTES

1. Mary Hyde, *The Thrales of Streatham Park* (Cambridge, Mass.: Harvard University Press, 1977), p. 115.

2. Philip M. Ferguson and Adrienne Asch, "Lessons from Life: Personal and Parental Perspectives on School, Childhood, and Disability," in *Schooling and Disability: Eighty-Eighth Yearbook of the National Society for the Study of Education, Part II*, ed. Douglas P. Biklen, Dianne Ferguson, and Allison Ford (Chicago: National Society for the Study of Education and the University of Chicago Press), pp. 108–40, at 108.

3. Hyde, *The Thrales*, p. 85.

4. Henry Barnard, "Extracts from the Sixth Annual Report of the Superintendent of Common Schools to the General Assembly for 1851," *Journal of American Education* 15 (1865): 293–313, at 294. Other valuable summaries of family/professional relationships during the nineteenth century can be found in Bernard Farber, "Historical Context of Research on Families with Mentally Retarded Members," in *Families of Handicapped Persons: Research, Programs and Policy Issues*, ed. James J. Gallagher and Peter M. Vietze (Baltimore, Md.: Paul H. Brookes, 1986), pp. 3–23; Philip M. Ferguson, "Mapping the Family: Disability Studies and the Exploration of Parental Response to Disability," in *Handbook of Disability Studies*, ed. Gary Albrecht, Katherine Seelman, and Michael Bury (Thousand Oaks, Calif.: Sage, forthcoming); Michael Katz, *Poverty and Policy in American History* (New York: Academic Press, 1983); and Nancy Tomes, *A Generous Confidence: Thomas Story Kirkbride and the Art of Asylum-Keeping* (New York: Cambridge University Press, 1984).

5. Samuel Gridley Howe, "Remarks on the Causes of Idiocy," in *The History of Mental Retardation: Collected Papers, Vol. 1*, ed. Marvin Rosen, Gerald Clark, and Marvin Kivitz (Baltimore, Md.: University Park Press, 1976), pp. 31–60, at 34.

6. Philip M. Ferguson, *Abandoned to Their Fate: Social Policy and Practice Toward Severely Retarded People in America, 1820–1920* (Philadelphia, Penn.: Temple University Press, 1994); Katz, *Poverty and Policy in American History*; David J. Rothman, *The Discovery of the Asylum: Social Order and Disorder in the New Republic* (Boston: Little, Brown, 1971); Joseph L. Tropea, "Structuring Risks: The Making of Urban School Order," in *Children at Risk in America: History, Concepts, and Public Policy*, ed. Roberta Wollons (Albany: State University of New York, 1993), pp. 58–90.

7. Roslyn B. Darling and John Darling, *Children Who Are Different: Meeting the Challenges of Birth Defects in Society* (St. Louis, Missouri: C. V. Mosby, 1982); Philip M. Ferguson and Dianne L. Ferguson, "Parents and Professionals," in *Introduction to Special Education*, ed. Peter Knoblock (Boston: Little, Brown, 1987), pp. 346–91; and Dorothy Lipsky, "A Parental Perspective on Stress and Coping," *American Journal of Orthopsychiatry* 55 (1985): 614–17.

8. P. Pinkerton, "Parental Acceptance of a Handicapped Child," *Developmental Medicine and Child Neurology* 12 (1970): 207–12; and Gerald H. Zuk, "The Cultural Dilemma and Spiritual Crisis of the Family with a Handicapped Child," *Exceptional Children* 28 (1962): 405–08.

9. R. McKeith, "Parental Reactions and Responses to a Handicapped Child," in *Brain and Intelligence*, ed. F. Richardson (Hyattsville, Md.: National Education Consultants, 1973), pp. 131–41; A. J. Solnit and M. H. Stark, "Mourning and the Birth of a Defective Child," *Psychoanalytic Study of the Child* 16 (1961): 523–37; and Lipsky, "Parental Perspective."

10. D. M. Engel, "Origin Myths: Narratives of Authority, Resistance, Disability, and Law," *Law and Society Review* 27 (1993): 785–826, at 811–12.

11. D. Drotar et al., "The Adaptation of Parents to the Birth of an Infant with Congenital Malformation: A Hypothetical Model," *Pediatrics* 56 (1975): 710–17. A more recent variation on this theme is the tendency of some professionals to dismiss parental reports of the positive impacts of having a child with a disability in the family as simply a defense or coping mechanism. As we discuss later, the persistence of this professional negativity toward disability can actually exacerbate rather than ameliorate family stress. One recent study summarized this point: "The findings suggest that these [negative professional] attitudes are deeply rooted in professional practice which often leads to professional intervention contributing to, rather than alleviating, the stress and difficulties faced by families." See Tim Stainton and Hilde Besser, "The Positive Impact of Children with an Intellectual Disability on the Family," *Journal of Intellectual and Developmental Disability* 23, no. 1 (1998): 57–70, at 68.

12. Lipsky, "Parental Perspective," p. 615.

13. Barnard Farber, "Effects of a Severely Mentally Retarded Child on the Family," in *Readings on the Exceptional Child: Research and Theory*, ed. E. P. Trapp and P. Himelstein (New York: Appleton-Century-Crofts, 1962), pp. 227–46; and M. Fowle, "The Effect of the Severely Retarded Child on His Family," *American Journal of Mental Deficiency* 73 (1965): 468–73.

14. J. N. Murray and C. J. Cornell, "Parentalplegia," *Psychology in the Schools* 18 (1981): 201–07, at 201.

15. Thomas Shakespeare, "Choices and Rights: Eugenics, Genetics and Disability Equality," *Disability and Society* 13 (1998): 665–81, at 678; and Jessica Scheer, "Culture and Disability: An Anthropological Point of View," in *Human Diversity: Perspectives on People in Context*, ed. Edison J. Trickett, Roderick J. Watts, and Dina Birman (San Francisco, Calif.: Jossey-Bass, 1994), pp. 244–60.

16. Martha Minow, *Making All the Difference: Inclusion, Exclusion, and American Law* (Ithaca, N.Y.: Cornell University Press, 1990), p. 95.

17. K. Charles Lakin, David Braddock, and Gary Smith, "Trends and Milestones: Majority of MR/DD Residential Service Recipients Now in Homes of 6 or Fewer Residents," *Mental Retardation* 34 (1996): 198.

18. Marty W. Krauss, "Child-Related and Parenting Stress: Similarities and Differences between Mothers and Fathers of Children with Disabilities," *American Journal of Mental Retardation* 97 (1993): 393–404, at 393.

19. Reuben Hill, *Families Under Stress* (New York: Harper and Row, 1949); and Hill, "Generic Features of Families Under Stress," *Social Casework* 49 (1958): 139–50. The literature on patterns of stress and coping by families under various types of circumstances is now immense. Other references that relate the concepts specifically to the disability of a child as the potentially stressful event include Shirley K. Behr, Douglas L. Murphy, and Jean Ann Summers, *User's Manual: Kansas Inventory of Parental Perceptions* (Lawrence: University of Kansas Press, 1992); Joan M. Patterson, "The Role of Family Meanings in Adaptation to Chronic Illness and Disability," in *Cognitive Coping, Families, and Disability*, ed. Ann P. Turnbull et al. (Baltimore, Md.: Paul J. Brookes, 1993), pp. 221–38; George H. S. Singer and Larry Irvin, "Family Caregiving, Stress, and Support," in *Support for Caregiving Families: Enabling Positive Adaptation to Disability*, ed. Singer and Irvin (Baltimore, Md.: Paul H. Brookes, 1989), pp. 3–25; and Lynn M. Wikler, "Family Stress Theory and Research on Families of Children with Mental Retardation," in James J. Gallagher and Peter M. Vietze, *Families of Handicapped Persons: Research, Programs and Policy Issues* (Baltimore, Md.: Paul H. Brookes, 1986), pp. 167–95.

20. Aaron Antonovsky, "The Implications of Salutogenesis: An Outsider's View," in *Cognitive Coping, Families, and Disability*, ed. Ann P. Turnbull et al. (Baltimore, Md.: Paul J. Brookes, 1993), pp. 111–22; Shirley K. Behr and D. L. Murphy, "Research Progress and Promise: The Role of Perceptions in

Cognitive Adaptation to Disability," in *Cognitive Coping*, pp. 151–63; Anne E. Kazak and Robert S. Marvin, "Differences, Difficulties and Adaptations: Stress and Social Networks in Families with a Handicapped Child," *Family Relations* 33 (1984): 67–77; Jean Ann Summers, Shirley K. Behr, and Ann P. Turnbull, "Positive Adaptation and Coping Strength of Families Who Have Children with Disabilities," in *Support for Caregiving Families: Enabling Positive Adaptation to Disability*, ed. George H.S. Singer and Larry Irvin, pp. 27–40; and Ann P. Turnbull and H. Rutherford Turnbull, III, *Families, Professionals, and Exceptionalities: A Special Partnership* (Columbus, Ohio: Charles E. Merrill, 1990). Finally, a rare look on fathers' takes on such positive parenting by Tim Stainton and Hilde Besser can be found in Garry Hornby, "A Review of Fathers' Accounts of their Experiences of Parenting Children with Disabilities," *Disability, Handicap, and Society* 7, no. 4 (1992): 363–74.

21. C. Baxter, R. A. Cummins, and S. Polak, "A Longitudinal Study of Parental Stress and Support: From Diagnosis of Disability to Leaving School," *International Journal of Disability, Development and Education* 42 (1995): 125–36; James Knoll, "Being a Family: The Experience of Raising a Child with A Disability or Chronic Illness," in *Emerging Issues in Family Support*, ed. Valerie J. Bradley, James Knoll, and John M. Agosta (Washington, D.C.: American Association on Mental Retardation, 1992), pp. 9–56; Krauss, "Child-Related and Parenting Stress"; Marty W. Krauss and Marsha M. Seltzer, "Current Well-Being and Future Plans of Older Caregiving Mothers," *Irish Journal of Psychology* 14, no.1 (1993): 48–63; H. R. Lie et al., "Children with Myelomeningocele: The Impact of Disability on Family Dynamics and Social Conditions: A Nordic Study," *Developmental Medicine and Child Neurology* 36 (1994): 1000–09; A. Taanila, J. Kokkonen, and M-R. Järvelin, "The Long-Term Effects of Children's Early-Onset Disability on Marital Relationships," *Developmental Medicine and Child Neurology* 38 (1996): 567–77; and in a study that included the families of children with diabetes, Taanila, Järvelin, and Kokkonen, "Cohesion and Parents' Social Relations in Families with a Child with Disability or Chronic Illness," *International Journal of Rehabilitation Research* 22 (1999): 101–09.

22. Krauss, "Child-Related and Parenting Stress," pp. 393–94. For a similar assessment, see Matthew K. Yau and Cecilia W. P. Li-Tsang, "Adjustment and Adaptation in Parents of Children with Developmental Disability in Two-Parent Families: A Review of the Characteristics and Attributes," *British Journal of Developmental Disabilities*, Part 1, 45, no. 88 (January 1999): 38–51. "In their well-intentioned efforts to document areas of difficulty in families with children with disability, researchers have sometimes neglected to describe ways in which differences may indicate successful family functioning within a different but not 'deviant' family structure. . . . Current studies indicate that families of children with disability, including those whose disabilities are severe, often believe their lives have been enriched by their children's presence" (p. 39).

23. H. I. McCubbin and Joan M. Patterson, "The Family Stress Process: The Double ABCX Model of Adjustment and Adaptation," *Marriage and Family Review* 6 (1983): 7–37; and Patterson, "The Role of Family Meanings."

24. B. M. Cahill and L. M. Glidden, "Influence of Child Diagnosis on Family and Parental Functioning: Down Syndrome versus Other Disabilities," *American Journal of Mental Retardation* 101 (1996): 149–60, at 158. See also Marcia Van Riper, Carol Ryff, and Karen Pridham, "Parental and Family Well-Being in Families of Children with Down Syndrome: A Comparative Study," *Research in Nursing and Health* 15 (1992): 227–35.

25. R. R. Fewell and P. F. Vadasy, eds., *Families of Handicapped Children: Needs and Supports Across the Life Span* (Austin, Tex.: Pro-Ed, 1986); Ann P. Turnbull, Jean Ann Summers, and Mary Jane Brothers, "Family Life Cycle: Theoretical and Empirical Implications and Future Directions for Families with Mentally Retarded Members," in *Families of Handicapped Persons: Research, Programs and Policy Issues*, ed. James J. Gallagher and Peter M. Vietze (Baltimore, Md.: Paul H. Brookes, 1986), pp. 43–65; Mary F. Hayden and Tamar Heller, "Support, Problem-Solving/Coping Ability, and Personal Burden of Younger and Older Caregivers of Adults with Mental Retardation," *Mental Retardation* 35 (1997): 364–72.

26. Patricia Sloper and Stephen Turner, "Service Needs of Families of Children with Severe Physical Disability," *Child Care, Health and Development* 18 (1992): 259–82, at 260. For similar comments involving cystic fibrosis and intellectual disability, see D. Staab et al., "Quality of Life in Patients with Cystic Fibrosis and Their Parents: What Is Important Besides Disease Severity," *Thorax* 53 (1998): 727–31, at 731; and Graeme Browne and Paul Bramston, "Parental Stress in Families of Young People with an Intellectual Disability: The Nurse's Role," *Australian Journal of Advanced Nursing* 15, no. 3 (1998): 31–37, at 34.

27. See Singer and Irvin, "Family Caregiving," p. 6, for a schematic version of this dynamic conception of family adaptation. An excellent discussion of research on disability and culture in a family context may be found in Alan Gartner, Dorothy K. Lipsky, and Ann P. Turnbull, eds., *Supporting Families with a Child with a Disability: An International Outlook* (Baltimore, Md.: Paul H. Brookes Publishing, 1991), especially chapter 3.

28. B. Ryde-Brandt, "Mothers of Primary School Children with Down Syndrome," *Acta Psychiatrica Scandinavia* 78 (1988): 102–08, cited in J. Shapiro, Jan Blacher, and S. R. Lopez, "Maternal Reactions to Children with Mental Retardation," in *Handbook of Mental Retardation and Development*, ed. Jacob A. Burack, Robert M. Hodapp, and Edward Zigler (New York: Cambridge University Press, 1998), 606–36, at 622–23.

29. For discussion of cultural incompetence in recruitment strategies for family research, see Barbara Holder et al., "Engagement of African American

Families in Research on Chronic Illness: A Multisystem Recruitment Approach," *Family Process* 37, no. 2 (1998): 127–51. Sickle cell disease presents an instance of a chronic illness that predominantly affects African Americans, and some of the family studies of the effects of this condition, therefore, do focus on this population. For example, see Ronald T. Brown and Richard Lambert, "Family Functioning and Children's Adjustment in the Presence of a Chronic Illness: Concordance between Children with Sickle Cell Diseases and Caretakers," *Families, Systems, and Health* 17, no. 2 (1999): 165–79; P. D. Singhi et al., "Psychological Problems in Families of Disabled Children," *British Journal of Medical Psychology* 63 (1990): 173–82; and Shapiro, Blacher, and Lopez, "Maternal Reactions."

30. Ronald Gallimore et al., "The Social Construction of Ecocultural Niches: Family Accommodation of Developmentally Delayed Children," *American Journal of Mental Retardation* 94 (1989): 216–30.

31. Engel, "Origin Myths," p. 797.

32. Shapiro, Blacher, and Lopez, "Maternal Reactions," p. 625.

33. M. Seren Cohen provides a thorough review of much of the literature on the experiences of families of children with chronic illness and affirms the lack of correlation with severity of the illness. See "Families Coping with Childhood Chronic Illness: A Research Review," *Families, Systems, and Health* 17, no. 2 (1999): 149–64. The notion that families with low incomes may have more stress related to a child with disabilities or chronic illness than families with moderate or high incomes may seem obvious. Most social problems affect the poor more than others. However, with disability, this impact seems especially contingent on American society's policy decisions about health care (or the lack of it) for low-income families. The extent of the problem is thoroughly documented in two recent studies on the economic impact of having a child with a disability: Barbara M. Altman, Philip F. Cooper, and Peter J. Cunningham, "The Case of Disability in the Family: Impact on Health Care Utilization and Expenditures for Nondisabled Members," *Milbank Quarterly* 77, no. 1 (1999): 39–75; and Marcia K. Meyers, Anna Lukemeyer, and Timothy Smeeding, "The Cost of Caring: Childhood Disability and Poor Families," *Social Service Review* 72, no. 2 (1998): 209–33.

34. An example of this can be found in M. Sandelowski and L. C. Jones, "Healing Fictions: Stories of Choosing in the Aftermath of the Detection of Fetal Anomalies," *Social Science and Medicine* 42 (1996): 353–61.

35. Raymond S. Duff and A. G. M. Campbell, "Moral and Ethical Dilemmas in the Special Care Nursery," *NEJM* 289 (1973): 890–94; John Lorber, "Results of Treatment of Myelomeningocele: An Analysis of 524 Unselected Cases, with Special Reference to Possible Selection for Treatment," *Developmental Medicine and Child Neurology* 13 (1971): 279–303; and Robert F. Weir, *Selective Nontreatment of Handicapped Newborns* (New York: Oxford University Press, 1984).

36. Joseph Fletcher, "Indicators of Humanhood: A Tentative Profile of Man," *Hastings Center Report* 2 (1972): 1–4, at 3.

37. Peter Singer, *Practical Ethics* (New York: Cambridge University Press, 1979), p. 138.

38. Brian Appleyard, *Brave New Worlds: Staying Human in the Genetic Future* (New York: Viking, 1998); Martha Nibley Beck, *Expecting Adam: A True Story of Birth, Rebirth, and Everyday Magic* (New York: Times Books/Random House, 1999); and Engel, "Origin Myths."

WILLIAM RUDDICK

Ways to Limit Prenatal Testing

How many prenatal tests should laboratories, genetics counselors, or physicians provide a prospective mother? The agreed answer seems to be, "Far less than the hundreds soon to be available." Otherwise, it is feared, women will soon swamp physicians and genetic counselors with limitless test demands in a quest for "perfect children" or "designer babies."

Some proposals would allow laboratories to conduct only tests with "analytical and clinical validity" and high predictive power.[1] Other proposals would allow physicians to offer patients only tests for pediatric conditions that gravely burden children and their family caretakers.[2] Other proposals would reduce test demand by reducing public ignorance and prejudice about disabilities[3] and by fostering a more unselective, all-welcoming conception of motherhood.[4]

I think that demand-reducing is more promising than test-curbing. Government and professional bodies rarely have power to restrict practices that physicians and patients endorse. The practices occur either sub rosa or under liberal reading of regulations. (Recall pre-Roe "therapeutic" abortions or current "compassionate" provision of experimental drugs.) I suspect that laboratories would so read "analytical and clinical validity" and "high predictive value," and physicians, "severe burdens on child and parents." Moreover, such regulations would surely be resisted as violations of physician and patient autonomy.

Some of the current proposals to reduce demand are, however, as dubious as these proposed curbs. Too few pregnant women, I suspect, will be moved to reject testing in favor of a maternal ideal of "welcoming into the world" any child they happen to conceive, whatever its actual or threatened disability. A campaign in schools and the media to show patients and families living with various disabilities might prove more effective in the long run, but would clearly face varied resistance, financial and psychological.

Women vary in their concepts of pregnancy and motherhood, each of which favors certain tests more than others. Moreover, none of these concepts especially favors unlimited testing. If, as I think, test demand varies with and is limited by those conceptions, then we have far less reason to take preemptive action against the predicted wave of women in "quest of perfect children" or "designer babies." Likewise, we would have less need to convert women to the ideal of the all-welcoming mother.

Several preliminary points about terms I do and don't use. For the sake of clarity, I will sketch these distinct concepts of motherhood (and pregnancy) as if women held them in single-minded, unvarying forms. Hence, I give the concepts an ideological suffix—"maternal*ism*," "project-iv*ism*," and "familial*ism*." Although some women may be conceptual purists, interviews, unprompted remarks, and maternal practices suggest that these concepts often co-exist, waxing and waning with children's development and other changing parental circumstances. This medley also reflects the fact that all three views have continuing appeal, as well as drawbacks, and hence their shifting mutual accommodation. Moreover, although deeply entrenched in thought and practice, these concepts are in no sense a priori concepts, immune from the influence of changing technology or cultural shifts. For this reason, we need to ask what bearing new multiplex prenatal tests, genetic interventions, and abortifacients might have on them, singly and jointly. Of course, any answers will be highly speculative, depending more on a sense of what is plausible or fitting than on systematic surveys or other evidence. (But then that is true of many important questions and answers.)

Concepts of disability are also deeply entrenched, as I have learned from participating in this Hastings Center project. Indeed, unless corrected, I still tend to use terms for disabilities as if they named pathologies well defined by undesirable symptoms. To counteract this tendency, I make very few references to disabilities by name and thereby hope to respect the point that disabilities are highly variable bodily and cognitive conditions to which people with those conditions and their families may respond in various ways.

This variability of condition and response also counts against proposals to rank disabilities and provide tests only for "the most severe," quite apart from the enforcement problems mentioned above. How burdensome a disability may be depends greatly on its particular features and the circumstances of children and parents, including the concept of parenthood they embrace. I understand the desire of professionals and administrators to have guidelines and limits to cope with all this variability and particularity, but I have gradually come to appreciate the risks of prejudicial and oppressive simplifications in disability matters.

But as someone with little first- or second-hand experience of disabilities, I have good reason to think that my own remarks are still subject to such criticism.

A last point. I refer throughout to *women's* concepts, hopes, and test selections. Men, of course, may share and influence these concepts and test selections, and rightly so to the extent that they can and will share parental responsibilities. Yet, since this sharing is rarely equal (and in pregnancy and nursing cannot be), it is better to speak of "women" and "mothers," not of falsely egalitarian "mothers and fathers," or "parents."

Now to the several notions of pregnancy and motherhood I shall sketch, I begin with the most immediately recognizable and often celebrated, "maternalism."[5]

Maternalism

Once a woman experiences fetal movements or the visible, burdensome weight of later pregnancy, she finds it hard to think of herself as other than a mother carrying a child.[6] What makes these maternal thoughts maternalist is the time at which they begin: Maternalists date motherhood from the moment of conception. Hence maternal responsibilities of care and protection begin as soon as they know or even suspect that they are pregnant.

This identification of pregnancy with motherhood has both religious and medical support. According to some religious doctrines, God participates in each conception, providing a woman with the "gift of a child" for whose well-being she is responsible. Some physicians themselves hold this view, but even atheist obstetricians may support maternalism as a way of getting patients to become concerned as early as possible about the vulnerability of the fetus, or even the embryo, to ingested or inhaled harmful substances.

There is also a more general inducement to maternalism. We tend to read into the earliest stages of a teleological process the very properties that will appear or be fully present only much later in the final stages of the process, or when it is completed. Thus, we speak of planting a tree, not planting a seed that we hope will produce a tree. By such "proleptic" means, we focus and motivate our protective efforts, regarding them as more certain of success than the facts may warrant in the earlier, formative stages of development.

Even for maternalists, however, there are some requisite prenatal tests, namely, those for maladies best treated prenatally (e.g., hydrocephalus and hydronephrosis). Likewise, maternalists might want tests for certain untreatable maladies whose burden of suffering is usually so great that abortion can, arguably, be a protective act (e.g., Tay-Sachs, Lesch-Nyhan). So regarded, the maternalist could think of abortion as justifiable infant euthanasia, sparing her fetus/child a future worse than death.[7] Maternalists could disagree about which conditions can be so regarded, due in part to varying degrees of optimism or pessimism. Optimists would focus more on the least severe cases of a particular condition, pessimists on the most severe. Nonetheless, they would agree that it is the child's burden only, not theirs, that determines whether to test and abort.

Such self-abnegation can, of course, be self-deceptive. Maternalists may be especially prone to casting their own well-being as that of the child. Within limits this may be harmless, or even necessary for sustained caretaking.[8] But the risks of such self-deceived, self-abnegation are obvious: sense of failure, resentment, anger, and burnout. There is also the contrary risk of maternalists' addiction to prolonged protective, nurturing care: maternalists may delay a child's maturing by excessive care, or burden a mature child with inappropriate care.[9] In a related fashion, a maternalist may neglect her other, older children whose needs may be less obvious and harder to address. This would, of course, be a failure in her own eyes, committed as she is to a principle of impartiality in responding to the needs of all her children, born and unborn.

Such impartial, equitable responsiveness is never simple, especially when needs arise that are more obvious and more easily addressed, even if not more serious than more subtle, complex needs. Hence, the risk that babies get more attention and older children get less than they need. So, too, perhaps is there such a risk with certain disabilities. Disability advocates insist that the needs of children with disabilities are no greater than—only different from—the needs of children without those disabilities. Yet, even if we had some way to judge this alleged equality, those differences may nonetheless elicit disproportionate responses from maternalists at the expense of other children.

Whatever the problems of maternalism, it does free women from many of the anxieties and emotional delays of the "tentative pregnancy"[10] that prenatal testing imposes. Accordingly, maternalism would seem an effective bulwark against the dreaded flood of multiplex prenatal testing, but the maternalists' restraint and resistance could quickly weaken. If gene therapy progresses at the rate of genetic diagnosis, maternalists may begin testing more—much more. This will not be prompted by desires "for a perfect child" but by a sense of obligation to "give my child every chance." Since maternalists regard even embryos as children, this testing and treatment might begin even early in pregnancies that now often end in spontaneous abortions.

Nonmaternalist physicians often regard such early abortions as "Mother Nature correcting her mistakes" and would, almost certainly, not take part in "rescue missions" that at best would preserve a fetus badly "compromised" at birth.[11] But with advances in fetal surgery and gene therapy, such interventions might prove more successful and physicians more willing to treat such cases.

In short, we should not suppose maternalists would remain test-averse. Indeed, they may prove at least as test-prone as some women they now criticize for excessive testing, or even more so. Let us turn to these nonmaternalists and their current and future testing rationales.

Projectivism

In contrast with maternalists, projectivists think of pregnant women as making a child, not as carrying or nurturing one. (The graphic term is "having one in the oven.") Like maternalists, pregnant projectivists will attend to diet and habits, but not as obligatory protection of a child, but rather as prudential protection of their maternal project. Likewise, an abortion would be regarded as termination of a failed project, rather than as early infant euthanasia.

It should not be supposed that projectivists would treat abortion lightly. Pregnancy may be a fully engrossing project whose failure or termination can cause prolonged mourning and delay before "starting over." It is true, however, that projectivists may have more grounds for abortion than a maternalist may, especially if their "project" is to raise a child to become a certain kind of adult. They would tend to test and abort for any condition that would end in premature death, even if not especially painful. On the other hand, a projectivist's project might be to bear and raise a child just so long as it did not have the specific illness or disability that, in her view, had ruined the life of her natal family. Accordingly, she might not abort for some other conditions that a maternalist might think warranted prenatal infant euthanasia and hence required testing.

Likewise, a projectivist might not test as widely as a maternalist intent on saving a pregnancy, by surgical or other interventions. Projectivists recognize no obligation to "rescue a child" who may spontaneously abort in early pregnancy, without intervention, nor an obligation "to give a child every chance." For them, the only therapies that matter would be those that fully correct whatever conditions threaten their maternal projects—fetal survival to term is not enough.

But how might multiplex testing, with or without fetal therapies, alter the kinds of project projectivists undertake? Perhaps projectivists might become more perfectionist, testing and aborting more, in "quest of the perfect child."

We need to distinguish several senses of perfectionism: high, low, and idiosyncratic. High perfectionists want a child with as many human excellences as technical and other resources allow, or so they might think. On reflection, they may fall back to a more realizable ideal, for high perfectionism has the problem familiar to Christian theologians of making various excellences compossible. (Can God be omnipotent, omniscient, and all loving? Can a child grow up to be both a good listener and a good talker, or both agile and strong?) Unlike theologians, however, parents have to work hard to foster a child's excellences, each of which takes devotion and resources to develop to the full.

A low perfectionism limited to a certain sphere of excellences, such as "perfect health," might seem a still more realistic goal. But even this relatively modest aim raises similar conceptual and practical problems. Would a "perfectly healthy" child need to be free of all genes that increase the likelihood of disease? Would it have to be free of all transmissible recessive genes, like sickle cell trait, but nonetheless have immunities (e.g., to malaria) some may confer? And if we could give a coherent account of "perfect health," would any parents have the resources and will to try to produce it?

By "the quest for a perfect child," critics may have a much more specific, idiosyncratic notion, namely, a child that has all the traits necessary for some particular achievement in later life. An example would be the man who responded to a positive Downs test, "If he can't grow up to be President, then we don't want him."[12] Will extensive testing increase the number of such idiosyncratic perfectionists who "select for success"? That may depend less on testing opportunities than on the extent to which parents become more competitive for whatever they regard as social prizes.

Not all such perfectionism need be competitive, or success oriented. Consider the musician who would test, treat, or abort in order to maximize her future child's musical capacities for pitch, rhythm, and musical memory. These efforts may not be motivated by thoughts of a child's future Carnegie Hall performances, but rather by a desire that the child be able to experience and share the activities and pleasures that give meaning to her own life. Critics will predict serious trouble ahead for both child and mother, given these shaping control efforts. Were illness or accident to deprive such a musical child of her capacities, they would expect the disappointed mother to lose or deny affection for the child—a risk of which the child might become anxiously aware.

This scenario and risk cannot be disregarded, but as far as I know they lack support from any systematic studies of children who have failed through illness or accident to realize parents' formative, realistic hopes. Of course, many children rebel against such hopes when the parents are obsessively overbearing martinets or when they have self-deceptively overestimated a child's capacities. Unless we accept the dubious theory that children must rebel to achieve maturity, I see no reason to think that a "well-designed" child couldn't grow up to share and fulfill realistic parental hopes, given parental tact, patience, and limited flexibility.

I have at times tried to define a "life-options provision principle" that allows such child-rearing efforts.[13] This principle steers between the Amish or Hasidic project of literally reproducing the parents' lives in their children, on the one hand, and the ultraliberal ideal that commits parents to suppress their own preferences in the interest of maximizing a child's "open future."[14] Roughly, my idea is that parents must help foster a range of life prospects or life options for a child, any one of which would be acceptable to both parents and child if realized. Conversely, they need not foster any life option that they themselves would find unacceptable if taken up by their child. Nor may they force a life prospect on a child that the child could be predicted in its maturity to reject.

We might try to extend this life-options provision principle to cover prenatal tests and abortions. Accordingly, a woman need not give birth to a child whose future she will not devote herself to helping the child realize or achieve. To apply this principle responsibly, however, presupposes self-knowledge of what one will and will not be able to accept in the future. Such self-knowledge requires a certain amount of experience and critical self-reflection, but, as disability advocates point out, most of us lack both, especially in our early reproductive years.

Such self-knowledge also requires some assumptions about future social developments, as well as one's reaction to them. (How many parents now adopting children with disabilities or racial ancestry different from their own could have predicted such changes in their own attitudes even a decade ago?) And, even without such general changes in social attitude, a woman would have to predict how accepting of a child she might become, once past the initial shock and disappointment of her projectivist goals.

For these reasons, I have come to doubt that this life-options provision principle can be of much use in responsible reproductive decisions involving disabilities.[15] Nor can the principle answer those critics who attack the very notion of parental selection as evidence of an ungenerous, unwelcoming spirit. In this "hospitality" view, women (maternalist or otherwise) who want a child should accept and welcome any child they happen to conceive, prepared to appreciate the child's developing individuality, however different from their own. This individuality, however, does not give children different values: all children are of equal value, whatever their differences. In monetary terms, all children are fungible. To attempt to produce a perfect child in the high sense would be akin to demanding that a bank teller give one only currency in "mint condition." To attempt to select a child's characteristics in the idiosyncratic sense would be like demanding currency of a certain design, or within a certain range of serial numbers—differences that anyone who understands currency knows to be irrelevant.

The idiosyncratic perfectionist or selectivist might reply that the proper analogy is with a woman who needs a particular foreign currency to make the (parental) trip she wants to take. The hospitality advocate will, of course, worry that banks will encourage such self-indulgent travel plans by merely making various foreign currencies available.[16]

Such speculations and analogies aside, let us turn now to a particular form of projectivism that deserves a name of its own and separate examination, namely, "familialism." It is, I think, even less prone to excessive prenatal testing than projectivism generally.

Familialism

This concept is reflected in the vernacular "being in the family way." For familialists, all mothers are in the family way; that is, embedded in family relationships that define the scope and limits of motherhood. What prompts a familialist to become pregnant is not some general desire to create new life, or to have a child to love and rear, but rather a particular desire to start a family, or to give her partner a child and her parents a grandchild, or to provide her first child with a sibling and playmate, and so forth. Accordingly, the specific constellation or demands of the family she wishes to begin, satisfy, augment, or alter will determine which prenatal tests to have and whether to abort or give birth to a child to be worked into her family life, new or preexisting.

Some familialist projects extend beyond the present family constellation. Like many other projectivists, a familialist may look to a child's maturity with the hope that the child will be suited and willing to carry on the family line, property, or enterprise, or, less grandly, to maintain family ties indefinitely. Accordingly, any condition that prevents or makes unlikely such an adult child would frustrate such familialist goals.

To which, if any, kind of perfectionism is a familialist prone, either now or with future multiplex testing? I think perfectionism is unlikely: high or low, perfectionism's demands on all family members are too great and, indeed, tend to subvert family cohesiveness. Even if parents can show the forbearance or make the sacrifice such perfectionist projects require of them, siblings rarely can. On the other hand, both parents and siblings may accept a maximizing project for a family member whose success would benefit everyone in the family. So, for example, a limited perfectionist project to produce a musical or athletic star might well unite a family.

Family solidarity with regard to an *im*perfectionist project, however, is less likely. Reportedly, some parents are prepared to test and abort in order to be sure that a child will have their own disabilities, such as achondroplasia or congenital deafness.[17] Their justification might be the familialist ground that they want a child to remain within the immediate family and/or within the larger "family" constituted by communities of Little People or the Deaf. Arguably, they would violate the life-options provision principle as well as a more general "open future principle."[18] They would probably also generate strong opposition from other members of the family. Grandparents or siblings—even if Deaf or Little—may well argue against such family confinement of a future child in favor of wider extra-familial possibilities than they themselves have had. In general, families are notably divided about the scope and limits of efforts at family cohesiveness.

In any event, we should not suppose that such extreme cases count against either familialism or projectivism generally. (Just so, maternalism would not be discredited by a few women who took steps to have a child with a disability that would ensure its lifelong need for the maternalist care that gives their lives meaning.) Nor do I think that such extreme familialist projects would multiply with multiplex testing: very few tests would identify new conditions that could become the basis for such family-confining projects.

Conceptual Mixing

Another brake on eccentric or excessive testing may arise from the interplay of the three concepts I have sketched. Although presented singly for clarity's sake, these concepts most commonly mix, waxing and waning with children's needs and ages. Primarily maternalists in pregnancy, women may tend toward familialism with infants and project-ivism with preteens, never becoming wholly single-minded. Thus, protective nurturance may reflect concerns about the child's future character traits ("Will nursing on demand encourage willfulness?"). Likewise, family makers may knowingly risk temporarily alienating one child in their attentive care of another in more apparent need. Even intense ballet mothers or soccer moms may recognize preteen children's continuing need for uncritical comforting.

In general, this conceptual mixing subverts single-minded excesses. A maternalist tempted to make a child perpetually dependent on her care would be checked by concern for a child's eventual self-reliance in her absence. Likewise, a projectivist would hesitate to maximize a child's chief talent at the risk of severing its feeling or connection with the family. Conversely, a fervent family maker would hesitate to sacrifice a talented child's prospects in order to keep her safely ensconced at home.

Even more moderating are the thoughts of disability advocates, summed up in the point that so-called "able-bodied" people are better regarded as *temporarily* abled, subject at any age to loss of abilities through injury and illness. In a related manner, it follows that so-called parental plans and goals are better regarded as parental *hopes*, with the recognition that even the most resourceful parents cannot fully control their children's safety or development. Whatever abilities parents foster pre- and post-natally, they need to recall that their children always are and remain "hostages to fortune."

Prenatal Counseling

How might this conceptual catalogue of pregnancies and mother-hoods bear on prenatal counseling in an era of multiplex testing? To the extent that a woman's concepts of pregnancy and motherhood determine the conditions she most fears and desires in a child, those concepts would help her decide which tests to select from the present and future test menu. Of course, she would need to be clear about which maternal concept(s) she does hold—a task in which genetic counselors could be most helpful. Such clarification would take extra counseling time but could save time overall: the concept-specific tests would be only a fraction of the whole menu of tests, and, hence, there would be far fewer tests needing explanation than there would be for women scanning the entire list. Third-party payers should not object.

Such concept-relative selection should also help select the materials or personal contacts a woman needs to become better informed about life with the particular disabilities that concern her. As with most educational efforts, the more tailored they are to a student's interests, the more immediate and effective they are likely to be.

Such concept-relative selection should also make nondirective counseling somewhat easier. Counselors should be less puzzled or disturbed by test requests that reflect an identifiable concept of pregnancy and motherhood, even if it is a concept they do not share.

I allow, however, that these suggestions are uninformed in ways that make them quite unfeasible. Even so, they may at least suggest that there is less to fear from multiplex testing and gene therapy than often supposed by those who propose strict curbs and radical moral reforms. The perfect child may well be a bugaboo, and the perfect mother an unnecessary, romantic ideal.

NOTES

1. Report of the Joint NIH/DOE Committee to Evaluate the Ethical, Legal, and Social Implications Program of the Human Genome Project, Washington, D.C., December 1999, available at http://www.nih.gov/Policy_and_public_affairs/Elsi/elsi_recs.html, and accessed December 21, 1999.

2. See Jeffrey Botkin, "Fetal Privacy and Confidentiality," *Hastings Center Report* 25, no. 5 (1995): 32–39; and Botkin, "Line Drawing: Developing Professional Standards for Prenatal Diagnostic Services," in this volume.

3. See Philip M. Ferguson, Alan Gartner, and Dorothy K. Lipsky, "The Experience of Disability in Families: A Synthesis of Research and Parent Narratives," in this volume, as well as the general recommendations of this working group.

4. See Adrienne Asch, "Why I Haven't Changed My Mind About Prenatal Diagnosis: Reflections and Refinements," in this volume.

5. I take some of Adrienne Asch's points to help define maternalism, but perhaps the better term for her view is "unconditional hospitality"—an ideal more appealing to maternalists, even if it does not presuppose maternalism as I once thought. In any event, it was her articulate, persuasive thoughts and inexhaustible patience that have inspired and corrected much of my original opposition, for which I am most grateful.

6. An example of maternal (and possibly maternalist) thought follows: "This thing [the needle] was stuck exactly where my baby is supposed to be the most protected. All that time, I kept thinking, '[T]his isn't right.' My womb is a sheltered place, a protected place, the only place my baby should be safe and undisturbed." In Rayna Rapp, *Testing Women, Testing the Fetus: The Social Impact of Amniocentesis in America* (New York: Routledge, 1999), p.117. Rapp's interviews with New York women from various ethnic, racial, class, and religious groups over a fifteen-year period are a valuable source of reflections on pregnancy, motherhood, and testing.

7. Another example derives from Rapp, *Testing Women, Testing the Fetus*, p. 144: "You ask me what to do if the baby is born sick? If the baby is born sick, very sick, then it is better for me to know now. If I know now, I can stop that baby from ever being born, born to suffer from being sick."

8. Caretakers often claim to detect responses in patients everyone else regards as completely amented, as in the case of the nurses who opposed her father's decision to withdraw Nancy Cruzan from feeding tubes after seven years in a persistent vegetative state.

9. Recall the old joke about the mother who, when her grown gangster-son suddenly appears at her door bleeding from police bullets, insists "Eat first, talk later!"

10. "Tentative pregnancy" is Barbara Katz Rothman's term in her attack on the medicalization of pregnancy in *The Tentative Pregnancy* (New York: Viking, 1986). Of course, in some traditional cultures, women do not fully commit themselves to a child's care until they are sure of its viability after birth. See Nancy Schepper-Hughes, *Death without Mourning* (Berkeley: University of California Press, 1992) for such practices in parts of Brazil where no physicians are found.

11. For the variety of parent-surgeon relations in fetal surgery, see "Are Fetuses Becoming Patients?" in *Biomedical Ethics and Fetal Therapy*, ed., Carl Nimrod and Glenn Griener (Waterloo, Ontario: Wilfrid Laurier University Press, 1988), pp. 107–19.

12. Rapp, *Testing Women, Testing the Fetus*, p. 92.

13. My most recent attempt appears in "Parenthood: Three Concepts and a Principle," in *Morals, Marriage, and Parenthood*, ed. Laurence D. Houlgate (Belmont, Calif.: Wadsworth, 1999), pp. 242–51.

14. The open future idea is described by Joel Feinberg in "The Child's Right to an Open Future," in *Freedom and Fulfillment: Philosophical Essays*, ed. Joel Feinberg (Princeton, N.J.: Princeton University Press, 1992), pp. 76–97.

15. I was more hopeful in an earlier draft of this chapter used in the *Hastings Center Report* special supplement, "The Disability Rights Critique of Prenatal Genetic Testing: Reflections and Recommendations," September–October (1999), pp. S6–7. Nonetheless, I still think the principle is helpful in certain child-rearing matters. It might, for example, justify a parent's opposition to intense ballet training (but not to the far less consuming hobbies of bird watching and rock collecting).

16. This monetary analogy is unrelated to the issue of "commodifying" children raised by Marsha Saxton in "Why Members of the Disability Community Oppose Prenatal Diagnosis and Selection Abortion," in this volume. Monetary analogies are not per se commercial analogies. As for "commodification," I would reserve the term for those few cases in which parents might actually trade or turn in a child for another they valued more, such as in adoption practices that allow adoptive parents a "trial period." Admittedly, prospective parents who test and destroy a fertilized egg or fetus are seeking a "better" replacement, but this is no commercial exchange, however costly the procedure.

17. See Bonnie Poitras Tucker, "Deaf Culture, Cochlear Implants, and Elective Disability," *Hastings Center Report* July–August (1998): 6–14, at 7.

18. See my essay, "Parenthood: Three Concepts and a Principle," in *Morals, Marriage, and Parenthood,* ed. Laurence D. Houlgate (Belmont, Calif.: Wadsworth Publishing Co., 1998).

BONNIE STEINBOCK

Disability, Prenatal Testing, and Selective Abortion

When Bob Dole addressed the international convention of B'nai B'rith a few years ago, he said that, as a member of a minority group himself— the disabled—he understands the wrong of discrimination. Some listeners were offended by this comparison. A professor of theology at Georgetown University was quoted in the *New York Times* as saying, "Most Jews today don't regard being Jewish as a handicap. They regard it as a privilege; it gives them roots and depth and a mission."

But some disabled people would argue that they do not regard their disabling condition as a handicap. It is not their medical condition that puts limits on what they can do, but rather the way in which society is organized. Some would go farther, arguing that disability makes one part of a community or culture, and that identification with that culture is as important to identity as being a member of a race or ethnic group. Erik Parens has characterized the position this way:

> Some people in the disability-rights community argue that so-called disabilities are forms of variation, which ought to be affirmed in the same way that most liberals want to affirm any other form of variation (such as being female or black).

Let us call this the "forms of variation" argument. Parens goes on to draw out an implication of this view for what physicians call "abortion for fetal indications":

> Some people in the disability-rights community argue that just as most liberals deplore sex selection (at least in part) on the grounds that it exacerbates discrimination against women, so should they deplore other sorts of selective abortion on similar grounds. While we can accept that being a woman in this culture can be disadvantageous (can in its way be "disabling"), we think that we ought to change the culture, not aggressively pursue the elimination of female fetuses. According to this line, having a "traditional disability" is like being a woman: the disadvantages it brings

are largely socially constructed; we should change how the culture treats people with disabilities, not try to eliminate fetuses with "disabling" traits.[1]

Let us call this view "the disability perspective on abortion."[2] The disability perspective on abortion is independent of the forms of variation argument: it is possible to reject the forms of variation argument while still holding the disability perspective on abortion. It is also important to note that the opposition to aborting fetuses likely to have a disability is not derived from a generally pro-life perspective. Some of the most passionate advocates of the disability perspective on abortion are generally pro-choice. However, they regard abortion for "fetal indications" as discriminatory and pernicious in a way that abortion for other reasons is not.

Needless to say, the disability perspective on abortion is not a mainstream view. For most people who regard abortion as justifiable, a serious disabling condition[3] in the fetus is regarded as one of the strongest reasons for terminating a pregnancy, far stronger than reasons like inability to afford a child, having to drop out of school, not wanting to marry the father, and so forth. Even among those who are almost always opposed to abortion, a severe disability in the fetus, like rape and incest, is often regarded as justifying abortion. The disability perspective challenges this popular view, and therefore must be addressed.

In this chapter, I will discuss five separate, though related, issues:

- Whether so-called disabilities are neutral forms of variation.
- Whether disabilities are best seen as medical problems or whether they are largely socially constructed.
- Whether attempts to reduce the incidence of disability are generally morally acceptable.
- Whether certain means of reducing the incidence of disability, and in particular, prenatal testing and selective abortion, are morally acceptable.
- Whether there is moral importance in the distinction between selective abortion and therapeutic interventions to prevent a person from developing a disabling condition.

Clearly, these issues are related. If disabilities are merely forms of variation, like sex or skin color, then it is hard to see the justification for reducing them by abortion or any other means. If disabilities are not intrinsically handicapping, but become handicaps only due to societal arrangements, then removing the obstacles would seem preferable to preventing the incidence of disabilities. Although related, these issues cannot be conflated into the same question. It is important to distinguish them, since individuals may agree on some of these issues but not on others.

In this article, I first consider the idea that disabilities are forms of variation. While the motivation for this idea is understandable—centuries of discrimination against people with disabilities—I argue that it is not a plausible position, nor is it intrinsic to a disability rights perspective. In the next section, I consider the claim that disabilities are socially constructed. I argue that while this claim has a great deal of truth to it, disability imposes real limitations, not all of which can be overcome through changing social institutions and attitudes.

If the argument in the second section is correct, then it follows that measures to prevent disability are in principle morally acceptable, and indeed, desirable. At the same time, measures intended to prevent disability may not be justified, on all sorts of grounds, including ineffectiveness, cost, and stigmatization. Next, I examine a few examples of preventive measures to illustrate some of the factors that are relevant to an assessment of prevention programs.

Finally, I consider specifically prenatal testing and selective abortion as a means of preventing disability. I discuss Adrienne Asch's view that, while abortion is morally acceptable to prevent the birth of any child, it is morally unacceptable to prevent the birth of a particular child because of some characteristic the child will have, such as sex or disability. I argue that the "any-particular" distinction does not have the moral force Asch claims, and that if abortion is a morally permissible means of avoiding other unwanted consequences (having a child too young, having to give up school or a job, etc.), it is also morally permissible to avoid the birth of a child with a serious disability.

Are Disabilities "Forms of Variation"?

The claim that disabilities are just forms of variation among others presumably means something like the following: most people get around by using their legs to walk, but some people use a wheelchair. The latter is not worse, just different. Most people communicate by hearing voices and speaking, but some people use sign language to communicate. The use of sign language is not worse, just different.

On the face of it, this is a surprising claim. With other deviations from normal functioning, there's no claim that these are just "forms of variation." If I get laryngitis and cannot talk, I don't regard my inability to speak as just different, nor will anyone call me "differently abled." Why should laryngitis be considered a medical problem, but mental retardation, paralysis, blindness, deafness, and so on be just forms of variation?

Perhaps the distinction between ill health and disability is that it is possible to have a disability (be mentally retarded, blind, deaf, paralyzed) and be perfectly healthy. In this view, laryngitis is not just a form of variation because it is a kind of ill health. Mental retardation, on the other hand, is not a form of ill health, because mentally retarded people can be healthy. So their mental retardation is not a health issue or medical problem but just a form of variation.

However, the fact that one can be mentally retarded or blind or deaf and healthy does not show that these conditions are not medical, much less that they are just forms of variation. Long-term medical conditions like high blood pressure, diabetes, and susceptibility to migraines are also compatible with good health. You can be healthy and have high blood pressure, which you control with medication. Why is there no group insisting that their blood pressure is just a form of variation, indeed, that the very term "high" blood pressure is offensive? Clearly, it is because people with high blood pressure are not usually subjected to discrimination and stigmatization. This suggests that the problem with the "medical model" is not that it sees a health problem where none exists, but rather the problem lies in the discrimination and stigmatization that people with disabilities have experienced over the centuries. Discrimination against people with disabilities is inarguably bad. It is a separate question whether the medical model in general, and prenatal testing and selective abortion in particular, either lead to or manifest discrimination against people with disabilities. I will return to this issue.

For now, however, let us return to the claim that disabilities are just "forms of variation." If we compare disability with a paradigm of the "form of variation" language, we see a significant difference: the absence of a norm. All human groups speak some language, but no language is "the norm." By contrast, a human being beyond infancy who cannot speak any language is a deviation from the norm; he or she lacks normal human abilities.

Sometimes the term "normal" itself is considered offensive, as if the claim that an individual lacks "normal" human capacities, like sight, hearing, and reasoning power was insulting. There is nothing in principle objectionable about references to what is normal. We speak of a "normal" body temperature, and this is useful in determining whether someone is sick and needs medical attention. It's only an average and you can be perfectly healthy with a body temperature of 96 or 99 degrees. But if you have a temperature of 104 degrees, you're sick and may need medical attention. Similarly, parents are told what is "normal" for a two-month-old, a six-month-old, or a nine-month-old baby. There can be wide variations of ability and temperament within normal variation. But if your six-month-old never smiles or your nine-month-old cannot sit up, this indicates not merely difference but a problem, a reason to check with the pediatrician.

In light of its initial implausibility, why would anyone put forward the idea that disabilities are just "forms of variation"? The answer is that this is supposed to counter all-too-prevalent stereotypical thinking about disability as inherently bad, inherently disadvantageous, inherently a problem. According to disability rights activists, this stereotypical thinking stems from an unthinking superiority on the part of the (temporarily) abled. As Anita Silvers writes:

> So habitual are our feelings of superiority to individuals with disabilities that we may automatically acquiesce in the . . . equating of disability with disadvantage. However, even though an impairment is no advantage, it does not follow that to be impaired or disabled is to be disadvantaged per se. For disadvantage is relative to both context and end. A specific impairment need have no natural or necessary deleterious impact on a life.[4]

However, Silvers appears to equivocate between something's being a *disadvantage* and its being *disadvantageous on balance*. Consider the example she gives of Itzhak Perlman. Due to polio as a child, Perlman walks with braces and canes. Is this a disadvantage? Surely it is. It limits his mobility and makes walking slow and cumbersome. It also means that he can leave the stage and return for a bow, as is customary, only with difficulty. Perlman handles this disability with great charm and good humor. In a concert I attended in London, he walked off the stage and returned, to tumultuous applause, for one encore; after that, he remained seated, saying to the audience, waving his hand in the direction of the wings, "Now I have gone off and come back on again."

Not being able to walk easily is certainly a disadvantage. But is Perlman disadvantaged on balance due to his disability? Surely not; we should all be so disadvantaged. To be sure, there are careers that are not open to him (boxer, mountaineer), but so what? His disability has not interfered with his being a great musician. So, on balance, Perlman is not disadvantaged; but at the same time, his disability is a disadvantage, and probably one he would prefer not to have.

There are times when a disability is not a disadvantage. Someone who is blind is unlikely to be drafted and therefore may survive a war. The fact that a disability can be under unusual circumstances advantageous is consistent with its being ordinarily a disadvantage. However, some disabilities may have their own positive advantages, even under ordinary circumstances. For example, many deaf people find they can concentrate better because they are not distracted by noise. One woman, when asked by her daughter if she would want cochlear implants, said, "Heavens, no! Why would I want all that noise?" A professor of animal behavior claims that her autism enables her to understand animals in a way that nonautistic people cannot. (She uses this skill to design slaughter houses that prevent panic among the cattle.) In 1997, the newspapers reported the story of an autistic boy who became lost while swimming in Turtle Creek in Florida. His parents believe it is possible that he survived the horrors of the swamp not in spite of his autism but because of it. His autism makes him impervious to fear and panic and helps him to focus totally on the situation at hand.

Clearly, there are some advantages linked to disability. Nevertheless, disabilities are not generally advantageous, not something to be hoped for; indeed, they are to be avoided, if possible. They are not merely neutral forms of variation.

Are Disabilities Socially Constructed?

It may be objected that while having a disability is usually disadvantageous (hence, the term "dis-ability"), nevertheless the disadvantage derives from the ways in which society responds to disability. That is, it is not the physical condition that is disabling, but rather the limitations imposed on the person.

The World Health Organization differentiates between impairment, disability, and handicap in ways useful to this discussion:

> An *impairment* is an abnormality or loss of any physiological or anatomical structure or function.
>
> *Disability* refers to the consequences of an impairment, that is, any restriction or lack of ability to perform an activity in the manner or within the range considered appropriate for nonimpaired persons.
>
> A *handicap* is the social disadvantage that results from an impairment or a disability.[5]

Thus, paralysis of the legs (perhaps resulting from polio or spina bifida) is the impairment; the inability to walk is the disability; but it is "the social consequences of that disability—the refusal of employers to hire the disabled person . . . that renders him or her handicapped."[6] A disability becomes a handicap due to the choices of individuals and organizations. Handicaps are the result of social choices; they are not part of the "fabric of the universe." Because they are chosen, they can be changed.

Harlan Hahn contrasts the medical approach that focuses on functional impairments or the economic approach that emphasizes vocational limitations with a new sociopolitical approach that regards the fundamental restrictions of a disability as located in the surroundings that people encounter rather than within the disabled individual.[7] Whether a disability becomes a handicap depends on many factors, including its prevalence and the attitudes of the nondisabled. Scheer and Groce use the example of hereditary deafness on Martha's Vineyard. The percentage of people born deaf was so great that the hearing residents found it advantageous to learn sign language, much as people who live near the U.S.-Mexico border find it advantageous to be bilingual in English and Spanish. They write:

> Unlike modern industrial societies, where the inability of the deaf to communicate effectively with the hearing population and the ignorance of the hearing population about the capabilities of deaf individuals limit the degree to which they can integrate into the larger population, in the Vineyard there were no barriers to overcome. Accordingly, Vineyarders who were born deaf were not considered handicapped. They were able and, in fact, expected to work, marry, hold public office, vote, and participate in all social events, in exactly the same manner as did their hearing family, friends, and neighbors. Deaf island residents were well integrated into community life, with a strong cultural tradition at least 300 years old to support their inclusion. In this island community, what to us today would be considered a substantial handicap was reframed as a normal human variation. As one woman stated, the difference between the hearing and the deaf was "like if you had brown eyes and I had blue ones."[8]

The example of deaf people on Martha's Vineyard is instructive in showing how something that might be a disability or even a handicapping condition in one context is not perceived as such in another. But the conclusion that all disability lies solely or even primarily in the environment is surely too strong. Not every disability can be overcome by social adaptation. As Wertz and Fletcher point out:

Much of the literature on effects of prenatal diagnosis on attitudes toward people with disabilities regards all disabilities as a generic class and treats them as if equal. This is not a realistic approach. Most physical and some mental disabilities can be overcome with social support and changes in the physical environment. Some mental and neurologic disabilities, however, require lifetime care and overwhelm the parents' lives. Such disabilities may never be overcome even with massive economic and social support.[9]

The motivation behind the claim that disability is just a form of variation is laudable: to end discrimination and make the larger community recognize that people with disabilities are people like the rest of us, with their own talents, abilities, and limitations. Disability rights activists have performed a much needed service in making the larger community aware that most people with disabilities find their lives rewarding and worthwhile. They do not wish they were dead, or that they had never been born. A disability rights perspective also forces us to recognize the extent to which socially constructed barriers, rather than natural conditions, prevent equal opportunity. At the same time, the claim that disability is completely, or mostly, a social construction is surely an exaggeration. Society can do a great deal to offer opportunities to people with disabilities, but not all disabilities can be overcome. Someone who is severely mentally retarded may have a life worth living but cannot go to college, hold a job, or raise children. This is not a matter of social prejudice but of reality. This is acknowledged even by disability rights advocates like Adrienne Asch, who writes:

> Not all problems of disability are socially created and, thus, theoretically remediable. . . . The inability to move without mechanical aid, to see, to hear, or to learn is not inherently neutral. Disability itself limits some options. Listening to the radio for someone who is deaf, looking at paintings for someone who is blind, walking upstairs for someone who is quadriplegic, or reading abstract articles for someone who is intellectually disabled are precluded by impairment alone. . . . It is not irrational to hope that children and adults will live as long as possible without health problems or diminished human capacities.[10]

Assessing the Morality of Various Means of Preventing Disability

If Asch is right that many, if not all, disabilities are not inherently neutral, that they limit people's lives in undesirable ways, then prevention of disability is, in itself, desirable. While some disability activists might contest even this claim, most would agree that prevention of disability is a good thing. Disagreement arises about the way in which disability is prevented. Many disability activists draw a sharp distinction between actions that prevent individuals from becoming disabled and actions that prevent individuals who would be disabled from coming into existence, such as prenatal testing and selective abortion. The former category includes, for example, putting iodine in salt to prevent mental retardation or enriching flour with folic acid to reduce the incidence of neural tube disorders. Such measures are not viewed as intrinsically morally problematic, although they might not be justified from a public health perspective if the cost or risks were high. For example, too much folic acid can be bad for elderly people. This might be a reason to provide pregnant women with folic acid supplements, rather than putting folic acid into a food everyone will eat.

Other noncontroversial forms of preventing disability include efforts to get women to avoid certain behaviors during pregnancy, such as smoking and drinking alcohol. Cigarette smoking in pregnant women has been shown to increase the risk of miscarriage, stillbirth, prematurity, and low birth-weight. Premature and low birth-weight babies are more likely to die during infancy than full-term and normal birth-weight babies and are at greater risk of developing neurological problems. Heavy and prolonged alcohol consumption (at least 5.0 ounces of absolute alcohol a day) during pregnancy, especially binge drinking, has been demonstrated to cause fetal alcohol syndrome (FAS), which usually results in neurological damage causing mental retardation, emotional problems, or learning disabilities. Even less heavy drinking (1.5 oz. of alcohol a day) during pregnancy has been found by some researchers to triple the risk of subnormal IQ.[11] Because the risks to the fetus and subsequently born child are serious, and the impact of refraining from smoking or drinking during pregnancy is not deleterious to the pregnant woman (in fact, it is better for her health, as well as her baby's), virtually everyone agrees that educational and noncoercive methods of getting women to avoid tobacco and alcohol during pregnancy are morally acceptable, and indeed, morally desirable, methods of preventing disability.

Are Prenatal Testing and Selective Abortion Morally Acceptable Ways of Preventing Disability?[12]

The disability perspective holds that prenatal testing for disability is as destructively discriminatory as sex selection. It maintains that the view that "fetal indications" justify abortion (or embryo discard) stems from the ignorant and prejudiced belief that having a disability makes life unbearable, and that those who are disabled are "better off unborn." Moreover, since prenatal screening cannot prevent all disability, such as disabilities caused during or after birth, an attitude of inclusion is better than an attitude of removal. Furthermore, prenatal screening leads parents to expect a "perfect baby." It increases intolerance of imperfection, and thus increases discriminatory attitudes toward disability.

Adrienne Asch is one writer who finds abortion for "fetal indications" profoundly troubling. This is not because she regards fetuses as persons and abortion as seriously morally wrong. Her view is that abortion is morally acceptable if the woman does not want to become a mother. However, she distinguishes between abortion to prevent having a child (any child) and abortion to prevent having this child. Why, Asch asks, would someone who wants to be a mother reject this pregnancy and this (future) child because of one thing about that child: that is, that he or she will have, or is likely to have, a disability? She believes that such rejection is likely to stem from inaccurate and prejudiced ideas about what it is like to have a disability or to parent a child with a disability.

Asch considers aborting to avoid having a child with a disability morally on a par with abortion to avoid having a child of the "wrong" sex. It embodies the view that there is something undesirable about being a person with a disability; so undesirable that it is better that such people do not get born. George Annas agrees that this is the rationale for prenatal testing but does not think that this makes such testing wrong. This is because he thinks that prenatal testing is used only to prevent the births of individuals whose lives would be so awful that they are better off not being born. He writes:

> Historically, prenatal screening has been used to find life-threatening or severely debilitating disease where a reasonable argument can be made that actually the fetus is better off dead than living a, usually, short life.[13]

But this is simply false. Prenatal testing has not been, and is not today, used only or even primarily to detect life-threatening, extremely severe fetal anomalies. One of the most common reasons for screening women over thirty-five in the United States is to detect trisomy 21 (Down syndrome). Down syndrome is not a fatal disease; many people with Down's live into their fifties and sixties. Moreover, it is compatible with a good quality of life, with appropriate medical treatment and educational opportunities. It is simply not true that someone who has Down syndrome would be better off dead or unborn.

What, then, should we say about most prenatal testing, which is used to screen for conditions that are serious but compatible with a life worth living? Should we say that such screening is wrong, comparable to screening for sex?[14] I do not think we need to concede this. There is another way to defend prenatal screening, one that does not require the fiction that it is used only to prevent the births of children whose lives will be so awful that they are better off unborn. Prenatal screening, along with abortion and embryo selection, can be seen as a form of prevention. It enables prospective parents to prevent an outcome they reasonably want to avoid: the birth of a child who will be sick or have a serious disability.

Admittedly, abortion prevents this outcome by terminating a pregnancy, by killing a fetus. In this respect, it differs from giving the pregnant woman folic acid, which does not kill, but rather promotes healthy development in, the fetus. Obviously, if fetuses have the same moral status as born children, then this difference is crucial. It is permissible to reduce the incidence of disability by keeping people healthy; it is not permissible to reduce the incidence of disability by killing people with disabilities. But if embryos and fetuses are not people (something a pro-choicer like Asch concedes), then the impermissibility of killing people to prevent or reduce the incidence of disability is irrelevant to the permissibility of abortion or embryo selection.

At the same time, most people find the termination of a wanted pregnancy troubling. Having an abortion at sixteen weeks, after an amniocentesis that reveals a serious, but not life-threatening, condition in the fetus, is not psychologically comparable to taking a folic acid supplement during pregnancy, and probably is not morally identical either. Even if fetuses are not people and do not have full moral status, they are potential people with some claim to our moral attention and concern—a claim that grows stronger as the fetus grows and develops. Most abortions for fetal indications take place in the second or even third trimester, when the fetus has many of the characteristics of a newborn, including human form, perhaps sentience, and some brain activity in the neocortex. All of these developments may incline us to extend the protection granted newborns to the late-gestation fetus.[15] For late abortions to be morally justifiable, the reason for having the abortion must be serious. In my view, abortion for fetal indications meets this requirement. It is reasonable for parents to wish to avoid having a child with a serious disability, like spina bifida or Down syndrome or cystic fibrosis, because these conditions may involve undesirable events, such as pain, repeated hospitalizations and operations, paralysis, a shortened life span, limited educational and job opportunities, limited independence, and so forth. This is not to say that everyone with a serious disability will experience these difficulties, only that they may, and that these are problems parents reasonably wish their children not to have. If abortion is permissible at all, it is permissible to avoid such outcomes, or the risk of such outcomes.

Asch rejects the idea that prenatal testing and abortion (or embryo selection) can be viewed as "prevention." She writes:

> What differentiates ending pregnancy after learning of impairment from striving to avoid impairment before life has begun is this: At the point one ends such a pregnancy, one is indicating that one cannot accept and welcome the opportunity to nurture a life that will have a potential set of characteristics—impairments perceived as deficits and problems.[16]

This suggests that there is something morally deficient in not being able to accept and welcome the opportunity to nurture a child with disabilities, a suggestion I want to rebut. First, the impairments may not merely be perceived as creating problems. This may be a realistic assessment of the situation. We do no one—not disabled individuals, not women, not families—a service by minimizing the physical, mental, and emotional burdens that may result from parenting children with disabilities.

Wertz and Fletcher outline some of these burdens in a discussion of the probable impact of having a mentally retarded child.[17] First, most of the care of the child tends to fall on the mother. Since most people with mental retardation live at home, she may have to stop working and adopt motherhood as her primary identification. She may have this role for the rest of her life. "It is not uncommon for parents in their eighties to be caring for children with Down syndrome who are in their fifties."[18] These are not trivial burdens, and the desire to avoid them does not indicate a character flaw, any more than wanting to avoid a hiatus in one's education or career. Whether a woman wants to terminate a pregnancy to avoid the burdens that come with being a mother, or whether she wants to terminate a pregnancy to avoid the burdens that come with being the mother of this child, the rationale for the abortion is the same: the avoidance of burdens that she finds unacceptable.

Asch points out that prospective parents cannot protect themselves from all burdens. A child may become disabled during or after birth. If a woman is unwilling to expend the extra effort to parent a child with a disability, how good a parent will she be? But even if we agree that a good parent will be willing to undergo burdens and sacrifices for a child, it doesn't follow that it is impermissible to try to avoid such sacrifices and burdens before becoming a parent. From a pro-choice perspective at least, a fetus is not a child and a pregnant woman is not yet a mother. Therefore, she does not have the same obligations to her fetus as she would to a born child.

In my view, a pregnant woman still has a choice whether or not to continue her pregnancy. She may change her mind because her circumstances change (e.g., the couple divorces). Although the pregnancy was wanted, she may not want to become a mother if this means being a single parent. Similarly, she may prefer to terminate a wanted pregnancy, because she wants a healthy, nondisabled child. Terminating the pregnancy gives her and her husband the chance to try again.

We can all agree that prospective parents should be fully informed about the problems and challenges they are likely to face, and that the decision to terminate should not be based on fear or ignorance. However, we can also recognize that parenthood itself is a very difficult job, even raising children without disabilities. If a woman or couple prefer not to accept the burdens and challenges that go with raising a child with special needs, that is a morally acceptable choice, and not one for which they need feel guilty or inadequate as prospective parents.

The Discrimination Argument

Another argument from the disability community focuses on the symbolic meaning of prenatal testing and its implications for people with disabilities. Sometimes this is expressed by saying that prenatal testing "sends a message" that "we don't want any more of your kind." Prenatal testing is seen, in this view, as a public statement that the lives of the disabled are worth less than those of the able-bodied. As John Robertson characterizes the view, "In short, it engenders or reinforces public perceptions that the disabled should not exist, making intolerance and discrimination toward them more likely."[19]

This is a powerful charge and one that needs to be taken seriously. If prenatal testing actually causes harm to disabled people by increasing discrimination or reducing opportunities, that is a strong policy reason against prenatal testing. Even if prenatal testing does not cause tangible harm to discreet individuals, but only makes a symbolic statement that the lives of disabled people are worth less, that is a reason to be troubled by prenatal testing.

However, I do not think that the argument is persuasive. From the fact that a couple wants to avoid the birth of a child with a disability, it just does not follow that they value less the lives of existing people with disabilities, any more than taking folic acid to avoid spina bifida indicates a devaluing of the lives of people with spina bifida. The wish to avoid having a child with disabilities does not imply that if that outcome should occur, the child will be unwanted, rejected, or loved less. There is no inconsistency in thinking, "If I have a child who has a disability, or becomes ill, or has special needs, I will love and care for that child; but this is an outcome I would much prefer to avoid." Allen Buchanan illustrates this point with a thought experiment:

> Suppose God tells a couple: "I'll make a child for you. You can have a child that has limited opportunities due to a physical or cognitive defect or one who does not. Which do you choose?" Surely, if the couple says they wish to have a child without defects, this need not mean that they devalue persons with disabilities, or that they would not love and cherish their child if it were disabled. Choosing to have God make a child who does not have defects does not in itself in any way betray negative judgments or attitudes about the value of individuals with defects.[20]

Disability activists have a laudable goal: to change society so that it is welcoming and accepting of people with disabilities. However, there is no reason why society cannot both attempt to prevent disability and to provide for the needs of those who are disabled. As a matter of fact, the rise of prenatal screening has coincided with more progressive attitudes toward the inclusion of people with disabilities, as evidenced in the United States by the passage of the Americans with Disabilities Act.

Conclusions

Prejudice and discrimination against people with disabilities are no more acceptable than racial or gender prejudice and discrimination. The sociopolitical model can help nondisabled (or temporarily-abled) individuals see how the world might be changed to make it more accessible to those with disabilities. The result might be a greater willingness on the part of prospective parents to accept the risk of having a child with a serious disability and might reduce the desire for prenatal testing.

On the other hand, it might not. Some couples will prefer not to have a child with a serious disability, no matter how wonderful the social services, no matter how inclusive the society. In my view, this is a perfectly acceptable attitude, one that does not impugn their ability to be good parents. Nor does this attitude imply a devaluing of the lives of existing people with disabilities, any more than do programs to vaccinate children against polio or ensure that pregnant women get enough folic acid. There is no conflict between respecting the rights of people with disabilities and respecting the rights of women to make their own informed decisions about whether to have prenatal testing, and if they have it, how to respond to the results of that testing.

NOTES

1. Erik Parens, personal correspondence to author, Briarcliff Manor, N.Y., August 21, 1996.

2. In calling this "the disability perspective on abortion," I do not mean to suggest that all people with disabilities embrace this view, or even that all people who are disability rights advocates take this view. At a meeting of the Society for Disability Studies (SDS), I heard one woman speak in favor of prenatal testing on the ground that it would not benefit a child with a disability to be born to parents who felt unwilling or unable to cope with raising such a child. Nevertheless, I think that the more prevalent view among disability activists is that abortion to prevent the birth of a person with disabilities is morally wrong, comparable to abortion for sex selection.

3. I limit myself in this chapter to "serious disabilities," leaving aside the question of abortion for trivial conditions. People will differ on what they consider a "serious" disability, and I do not attempt to define the term. In general, I consider a disability serious if most people would make strenuous efforts to prevent its occurrence.

4. Anita Silvers, " 'Defective' Agents: Equality, Difference and the Tyranny of the Normal," *Journal of Social Philosophy*, 25th Anniversary Special Issue (1994): 154–75, at 164.

5. Cited in J. Scheer and N. Groce, "Impairment as a Human Constant: Cross-Cultural and Historical Perspectives on Variation," *Journal of Social Issues* 44 (1998): 23–37.

6. Scheer and Groce, "Impairment," p.24.

7. Harlan Hahn, "The Politics of Physical Differences: Disability and Discrimination," *Journal of Social Issues* 44, no. 1 (1988): 39–48.

8. Scheer and Groce, "Impairment," p. 31.

9. Dorothy Wertz and J. C. Fletcher, "A Critique of Some Feminist Challenges to Prenatal Diagnosis," *Journal of Women's Health* 2, no. 2 (1993): 173–88, at 175.

10. Adrienne Asch, "Reproductive Technology and Disability," in *Reproductive Laws for the 1990's*, ed. Sherrill Cohen and Nadine Taub (Clifton, N.J.: Humana Press, 1989), pp. 69–124, at 73.

11. A. P. Streissguth, H. M. Barr, P. D. Sampson, B. L. Darby, and D. C. Martin, "IQ at Age 4 in Relation to Maternal Alcohol Use and Smoking During Pregnancy," *Developmental Psychology* 25, no. 1 (1989): 3–11.

12. Some of the material in this section comes from my paper, "Preimplantation Genetic Diagnosis and Embryo Selection," in *A Companion to Genetics: Philosophy and the Genetic Revolution*, ed. Justine Burley and John Harris (Oxford, U.K.: Blackwell Publishers, forthcoming).

13. George J. Annas, "Noninvasive Prenatal Diagnostic Technology: Medical, Market, or Regulatory Model?" *Annals of the New York Academy of Sciences* 731 (1994): 262–68, at 265.

14. While most people find sex selection generally morally problematic, there might be situations in which screening for sex would be morally permissible. Some genetic diseases affect only one sex, so it is reasonable to screen for sex to avoid having a child with the disease. In addition, there may be cultures in which being female is a disability. Ideally, those cultures should change, but until they do, I do not think it would be wrong for a woman to screen for sex, rather than undergo multiple pregnancies which might be damaging to her own health until she produces the required male child. Moreover, bringing female children into the world knowing they will be deprived of food and medical care is not necessarily a strike for feminism.

15. See Nancy Rhoden, "Trimesters and Technology: Revamping Roe v. Wade," *Yale Law Journal* 95, no. 4 (1986): 639–97, for a good explanation of the moral significance of late gestation.

16. Asch, "Reproductive Technology and Disability," p. 82.

17. Wertz and Fletcher, "A Critique of Some Feminist Challenges."

18. Ibid., p. 175.

19. John A. Robertson, "Genetic Selection of Offspring Characteristics," *Boston University Law Review* 76, no. 3 (1996): 421–82, at 453.

20. Allen Buchanan, "Choosing Who Will Be Disabled: Genetic Intervention and the Morality of Inclusion," *Social Philosophy & Policy* 13, no. 2 (1996): 18–46, at 33–34.

Bruce Jennings

Technology and the Genetic Imaginary: Prenatal Testing and the Construction of Disability

Curiosity and pregnancy go naturally together in human experience; indeed, the former is no less primal and fundamental than the latter. And for as long as humankind has enjoyed even a rudimentary understanding of the biology of childbearing, the wonder of that process has been inseparable from the wondering that has accompanied the period of invisible gestation—wondering if the pregnancy will persist until birth, worrying about how mother and child will fare, guessing what the child will look like, trying to discern if it will be healthy, imagining how it will change the life of the family, and wondering about its destiny. With wondering comes watchful waiting and an attitude of expectation tinged with uncertainty. Ordinary language still registers this set of linked attitudes when we say colloquially that a pregnant woman is "expecting."

These elements of the human experience of pregnancy and prenatal development cannot be merely fortuitous. Nor does it seem possible that they have no bearing on the reaction of adults—the mother, to be sure, but also the father and others who socially make up what will be the child's primary care-giving community—to the baby once it is born. The cultural meaning of pregnancy and the experience of it by closely attentive adults is not a mere prelude to the child-rearing practices of a society, but is inextricably bound up with them.[1] Expectation binds in advance. And while the traditional speculations of the prenatal period can lead to disappointment at birth, it is nonetheless remarkable how quickly adults will focus on newborn traits that fulfill hopeful expectations and tend to ignore those that do not. Bright eyes quickly replace big ears as the topic of conversation among relatives and visitors to the nursery. Of course, some traits are too serious or consequential to overlook, and some disappointments persist. But for the most part, the social/psychological time of pregnancy makes the family ready to accept the newcomer, who after all has been a presence in several adult lives (not only the mother's) for some time.

A moment ago, I referred to "invisible gestation." That notion requires qualification. The physically hidden aspect of pregnancy has certainly been a part of its human fascination and mystery. One can only speculate what course human culture and evolution would have taken if the female body were transparent and if fetal development had taken place in the public gaze. But from the earliest times people have found ways to make the invisible visible. Soothsaying and other arts of divination have been employed to make predictions about the future child. Looking for tell-tale signs by studying material thought to have some connection with the mother or the child, whether it be the entrails of spirit animals or the color or consistency of the woman's excrement, is an age-old practice. Among women in virtually all cultures a folk wisdom has developed concerning how a pregnant woman could glean information about her baby from its movements and from her own emotions and bodily responses during pregnancy.

The science of modern obstetrics and gynecology may have become the predominant means we have of making the invisible visible and the unknown known today, but it has not completely displaced other modes of knowledge and folk wisdom. Nor is there any reason why it should. Nonscientific—perhaps I should say nonmaterialistic—modes of knowledge may not be reliable guides to therapy and medical decision making, but pregnancy is too intimate and too significant an event within the family and within the culture to have its meaning exhausted by science. The curiosity it generates will not be satisfied by materialistic formulations and representations alone. The folk wisdom, personal interpretations, and tacit knowledge that are inevitably spurred by pregnancy continue to have psychological and cultural value and meaning even in an era when those forms of knowledge have been discredited by science and modern medicine.[2]

Thus, the inner workings of human pregnancy and gestation have never been entirely invisible or impenetrable to the prevailing forms of knowledge. This is far too important a topic for curious humans to leave alone. Nonetheless, there is a sense in which the veil covering gestation has been lifted more radically in recent years than ever before in human history. Physical technologies that generate images from reflected sound, so-called sonograms, and biochemical technologies that generate information about the fetus's genotype and chromosomal structures, prenatal genetic testing, are two scientific advances that have made gestation visible in unprecedented ways. As the Human Genome Project has prompted new research on gene sequencing and mapping, new genetic markers for disease and disabling conditions have been discovered. At present there are tests for genetic markers associated with some four hundred conditions. The number of such tests increases almost daily, and technological developments now in the offing suggest that future testing will be both less costly and less risky or invasive.[3] The pressure to use such testing even in the absence of other risk factors, such as family history or parental age, will surely mount. Making the invisible visible, and structuring our moral perception of pregnancy, childbearing, and disability in particular ways—these are the leitmotifs of prenatal genetic testing I explore in this chapter.

If we are attentive to these themes, we shall be reminded that sometimes the practice of ethical deliberation requires a strategy of indirection. One needs to defer a direct assault on specific moral and policy questions until we have taken stock of the tacit assumptions informing those questions and the way in which they are typically posed. How can society balance reproductive rights and procreative liberty against the equal recognition and respect due persons with disabilities? Should access to prenatal testing for certain conditions be curtailed or even prohibited altogether? Who should decide, and on what basis, which prenatal genetic tests will be made widely available and with what kind of counseling to accompany them?

Who among us has the wisdom to answer such far-reaching questions? They go to the heart of human choice, parental responsibility, and the exercise of conflicting freedoms in our society. Rather than attempting an answer to them, my purpose here is to circle around and behind them, while making the familiar seem strange. I do this because I am persuaded that there is something fundamentally amiss in the very way we have fashioned ethical and policy questions regarding the use of prenatal genetic testing technology. The problem is not so much that these questions are hard to answer (although they are), as it is that they are often framed in a peculiarly naïve way, a characteristically American individualistic way, if I may say so. The trouble with the ethics of prenatal genetic testing is that the more we talk about "ethics," the more our moral sensibilities and moral insights are attenuated, and the more our moral deliberations are blind to the background influence of the reality-constituting power of the technology itself. I believe that one task of a bioethical analysis should be to call that particular framing of the problem into question.[4] It is important to work toward the development of a different interpretative framework, a different angle of vision, that brings technological power more squarely and directly into ethical deliberations, both those conducted by expectant couples and their physicians and other counselors, and those conducted by the society as a whole at the policy-making level.

Before discussing prenatal genetic testing in more detail, I want to sharpen the distinction drawn above between two different types of ethical analysis. One approach, by far the most conventional and commonly found in the literature of the field of bioethics, takes the interpretative frame of individual freedom of choice for granted and proceeds from there. If the use of a particular technology is involved, the technology is assimilated into the universe of choices among which the individual agent can choose. The burden of discussion then falls into two parts. First, should any limitations or constraints be placed on the freedom of the individual agent in her choice making? Second, what should the agent choose, that is, what choice(s) should she make?

The Freedom of the Chooser

In consideration of the first question there are typically two outside agencies or forces pitted against the individual with his own internal values, desires, and conscience. The first of these forces is the coercive power of the state and the society with its laws, incentive systems, and rewards. The second of these forces is the influence of the surrounding culture and belief systems that affect the individual, including the norms of religion, custom, and tradition, and the pressures of conformity with the behavior of others.

These are classic questions of freedom in liberal political philosophy.[5] And insofar as our contemporary habits of mind in bioethics still bear the stamp of the liberal philosophical tradition, the burden of proof will be on these "outside" forces of law or custom. What consideration is important enough to justify overriding the freedom of choice and freedom of conscience of the individual? The only unambiguous answer to that question in our public morality today is some variant of the classic answer John Stuart Mill gave over a century ago, namely, harm to others.

Another sometimes persuasive form of justifying a social limit to freedom is the notion of harm to self. Here the issue is usually not so much whether freedom can be overridden as whether a free choice is really being proposed in the first place. In order to justify constraining the individual's preferred choice, it is necessary to show that the choice or action in question does not really express the values and identity of the agent himself, either because there is some deficiency in his information or understanding, because there is some background coercion at work, or because the agent's rational faculties are diminished and therefore the individual should be protected from doing harm to himself, even if there is no likely harm to others involved.

Thus, simply deferring to a person's assertion of freedom might not be the ethically justifiable thing to do in several types of situations. For instance, we might prevent someone from making a donation to a fraudulent charity. Or we might prevent a person from committing an action that we discover is being motivated by blackmail. Or we might prevent an intoxicated person from driving home after a party even though he insists on doing so.

What Should the Chooser Choose?

If no ethical justification can be found for outside forces to override the freedom of the individual to choose in light of his own values, interests, desires, and conscience, then the question that ethical deliberation must focus on is the justification of one choice rather than another. But by the time one gets to this point in the analysis, little remains to be done. By definition, the choice now in question is taken be a socially harmless, authentic, rational, and self-regarding one.

It is not clear what remains in the interior of a person's moral conscience since social and cultural norms have been treated as external constraints and have been determined to play no morally decisive role. Ethical deliberation, and the role of the ethicist as counselor or advisor to the individual, becomes little more than a rational balancing of competing desires, interests, or radically private, idiosyncratic values. An outward, public moral life that is conceived as essentially a struggle for power and control goes hand in glove with an understanding of an inner moral life that is hollowed out and a conception of moral deliberation that has more in common with techne in Aristotle's sense (the efficient manipulation of technical information) than phronesis (mature reflection and deliberation contemplating a practical action in the world).[6]

In sum, when bioethics adopts the frame of individual choice on any given issue involving the use of technology, the default assumption will normally be that the technology, having been shown to work and having been made available, is morally permissible; it is a prima facie moral option, so to speak. This individual choice frame assumes, in other words, that the technology will naturally and necessarily be in demand, that it is on balance better to have it than not to have it, and that individuals who have a reasonable interest in using the technology should be given access to it, subject to their sharing a fair burden of its cost and maintenance. The burden of proof will normally be on those who would justify limiting access to, or the use of, the technology for some reason. Bioethics will examine any and all arguments purporting to justify such limits on the technology, and bioethics will adduce the private moral reasons pro and con for an individual decision to use the technology in a given instance or life circumstance. From mechanical ventilators, kidney dialysis, and other life-extending technologies to experimental organ transplantation and genetic testing, across this spectrum of biomedical technologies bioethics has adopted this frame of individual freedom and rational choice and has deployed its armamentarium of concepts and categories drawn from various types of ethical theory and moral philosophy, mainly those growing out of the British analytic tradition.[7]

An alternative approach to ethical analysis would not focus on being altogether so "practical" or decision specific in the first instance, but would rather call attention to the very way in which the issue and the moral problem is being framed, both by those writing in the field of bioethics, and, more importantly, by the professional shapers of ideas in our society more broadly—voices from the medical and scientific professions, from government and private industry, and voices from special interest groups who adopt an adversarial interest in relation to the new technology or in relation to the underlying medical conditions the technology will affect.

This enterprise, as akin to social and cultural criticism as it is to ethics, will focus on the dynamics and implications of locating values questions about biomedical technology and its use in one conceptual frame rather than another.[8] How comprehensive a conception of "technology" does a given frame presuppose? What kind of relationship is postulated between the technology and those who make use of it? How are the conditions of choice and moral agency to be understood, and what is taken to be integral to those conditions and what is taken to be merely incidental? What alternatives to the frame of individual freedom of choice exist for social critique? Can such a frame and such a language of social critique be deployed without sacrificing important liberal and pluralistic values upon which a free and open society depends, and without unduly limiting the human right of all persons to improve the quality of their lives by availing themselves of the benefits of scientific and technological progress?

These are daunting questions. Hugging the shore with conventional liberal bioethics may seem an attractive option if it spares us the toil, indeed the danger, of exploring them. Yet the costs of forgoing this more ambitious exploration of the common sense behind the very questions we pose about biomedical technology, with the hypothesis that these questions are neither neutral nor innocent, are substantial. Chief among them, I think, is the illusion of freedom that is created when we underestimate the reality-shaping power of biomedical technology and its implications for the kind of parents, citizens, and human beings we are.

Assumptions Behind the Conventional Wisdom

I believe there would be widespread agreement in our society today with the following proposition:

> Prenatal genetic testing is a technology that can assist prospective parents in exercising their freedom of informed choice in reproductive decision making. The main problem with prenatal testing today is that the information the available tests provide is subject to inaccuracy and misinterpretation. False negatives are possible because genetic impairments can often originate from more than one site; positive findings often will not be sufficient to predict the probability, timing, or severity of symptomatic disease during the child's lifetime. Thus, no one course of action by prospective parents logically or ethically follows from most test results. Reproductive decision making in the face of predicted genetic impairment is highly personal and intimate.
>
> As the technology improves, the information it provides will become more accurate, specific, and reliable. And even though medical therapies to prevent or cure symptomatic disease may still be lacking, advance warning of the possibility or probability of genetically associated disease in the child's future is still valuable for prospective parents who may wish to factor it into their family planning, financial, and career decisions. Although painful, knowing about a prenatal genetic impairment is rationally preferable to not knowing.

This portrait of the moral situation posed by prenatal genetic testing amounts to the conventional wisdom in mainstream professional circles and even at the grassroots level among those who have some information about genetic testing. It contains several implicit assumptions that should be singled out for our purposes here.

One assumption is that genetic testing technology is a morally neutral tool or instrument of individual decision making and choice. The technology carries with it no intrinsic value commitments, either positive or negative, concerning whether to terminate the pregnancy or allow the child to be born and to undergo the predicted disease or experience of disability. Technology is a tool and hence not an appropriate object of ethical evaluation in its own right. Test results are true or false, but not moral or immoral. And human choices and actions can be judged from a moral point of view, but not the technology (or technologically mediated information) that informs them.

Another assumption is that the main technical problem pertinent to an ethical assessment of prenatal genetic testing is the quality of the information the technology provides. Indeed, the only role of technology (genetic testing and background theories of the genetic contribution to disease) in this story is to provide information. To be sure, the quality of this information leaves much to be desired and creates a number of moral quandaries due to its uncertain and probabilistic character. But it is never considered to have any morally significant role other than as a source of information about the child's future health. And the limitations in the knowledge provided are assumed to be a function of the undeveloped state of the technology itself, which in principle is subject to progressive correction and improvement. In other words, the ethically problematic nature of genetic knowledge is assumed to be a purely contingent feature of the current and corrigible state of science and technology rather than something inherent in this form of knowing per se.

Finally, the reality of genetic testing and reproductive decision making is seen as a radically private, intimate one. Like Mary before them, prospective parents in the genetic testing era ponder in their own hearts the information they receive about their forthcoming child.[9] On this account, it is easy to lose sight of the enormous public apparatus of scientific research and testing facilities, to say nothing of the enormous public (whether governmental or corporate) investment and expense that genetic testing technology represents. It is breathtakingly implausible, as a matter of fact, to characterize the use of genetic testing in obstetric practice in our society as a "private" act in any sense.

Even more telling is the assumption that each parent must somehow find her own meaning in the prospect of a predicted medical and social future for her child. Through years of social conflict and controversy over the woman's legal and moral right to have an abortion, our society, for good or ill, has come to rest on the belief that the decision to continue a pregnancy is a radically private one, and we assume an incommensurability of moral meaning among women in our pluralistic society on this existential question. This resting point on abortion has come to spill over and to color all of our thinking about reproductive decision making. If there are no broader cultural resources for a woman (or a couple) to draw on when it comes to terminating a pregnancy, if the woman must fall back upon her own moral interiority in the face of *that* decision, why should we expect it to be otherwise when a woman (or couple) has to contemplate the reality of rearing and caring for a child with a severe chronic illness or disability?

Given this framing of the issue, it must be the case that decisions about the continuation of pregnancy in light of prenatal genetic tests do not admit of questions of public morality at all. For there are no permissible paradigms of parental virtue or responsibility available in the public moral life of a secular, pluralistic society upon which parents can draw. Even most religious traditions are hesitant to insist on mandatory, prescriptive teachings in so emotionally fraught and theologically turbulent an area, allowing believers to fall back upon prayer and their own consciences as they struggle to decide how great a burden of caregiving they are able to shoulder and how much suffering they can permit their child to be subjected to.

In a culture where questions as fundamental as these are thought not to admit of public interpretation or social guidance, the pressure is enormous to turn to technologically mediated "facts" to push us in the direction of one decision or another. And the more this happens, the less plausible it becomes to maintain that the technology that generates these "facts" is merely a morally neutral tool that plays but an instrumental role in the decision-making process. The more secularized reproductive decision making becomes, the more technology ceases to be a side show and the more it becomes the main event.

Earlier I identified three assumptions implicit in the conventional wisdom concerning prenatal genetic testing. These were (1) the value neutrality of the technology; (2) the problem of unreliable knowledge; and (3) the radical privacy of contemplating genetic impairment in the unborn child. I propose to discuss the first two points now and then return to the third point at the end.

Technology as Tool, Technology as Power

Why has the understanding of technology as a value-neutral tool been so persistent in American thinking and the reality-shaping effects of technology so tenaciously overlooked? One important reason lies in the narrow, one-dimensional way the concept of "technology" is defined in most discussions and in the popular consciousness. Technology is equated with one aspect of its physical manifestation, namely, it is defined as machinery or gadgets. This leaves out a much more fundamental conception of technology as a system of knowledge, a system of institutional social organization, and a system of power.[10]

For example, the factory system of mass production manufacture is a "technology" in the proper sense of the term. It is an integration of various bodies of knowledge, from physics and chemistry to industrial psychology and time-motion studies, with various forms of hierarchical social organization (radically different from the organization work in preindustrial workshops or agriculture) and various types of machinery. This technology is held together by a form of authority and power that demonstrates its enormous capacity to structure human lives as well as to fashion natural raw materials into market commodities.[11] To equate the "technology" of the industrial era with devices such as the steam engine, the drill press, or the conveyor belt is far too narrow a perspective to be of much use for social or historical analysis. Even so, the "machine" can be a powerful symbol—technically a synecdoche (a rhetorical figure in which the part stands for the whole)—of the factory system as a technology or a system of power. In this regard, one thinks of the remarkable portrayal of the struggle between the worker and the giant cog wheels of the machine in Charlie Chaplin's "Modern Times."

To analyze technology and its effects in terms of a system of power and a specific pattern of socially institutionalized interaction among several persons is to depart from the perspective that puts discrete individuals (or dyads like the so-called "doctor-patient relationship") and separate decisions or choices at the center of attention. If Heidegger's work on technology arguably went too far in eliminating individual human agency altogether in favor of a superindividual force at work in history, contemporary American thought surely errs at the opposite extreme in its affection for market models and rational choice theories in which any notion of technology as system has no place.[12]

Prenatal genetic testing is not best understood as a value-neutral instrument of individual choice. It constrains choice in the subtle ways, and it helps to define the very situation as one that calls for choice making rather than some other mode of mental orientation and response (e.g., meditation or prayer and watchful waiting; or seeking out conditions of solace and mutual support with others). It calls forth the executive functions of our culture, in sometimes exaggerated degree: when the presence of technology presides over the scene, someone must take charge of the situation, no drift or indecision is to be allowed, logical order must be restored to behavior under stress and at risk of dissolution. Technology demands a response; it does not necessarily force any particular choice, but it does force choice in general. It is a commonplace to observe with virtually any technology that once it is available, then, like a genie out of its bottle, it cannot be undone or put out of the sphere of social reality. So the very existence of prenatal genetic testing for a given condition to some extent changes the moral status and cultural valance of that condition if it later appears.

Suppose a couple is offered a test for Tay-Sachs and decides to forgo it. If the child eventually becomes symptomatic with the disease, that cannot be considered a tragic surprise or shock to the parents, but rather stands as an example of willful and deliberate ignorance. No matter how understandable and justifiable the decision not to be tested may be, since the available cultural interpretation of what the onset of the disease means in the parents' life is not the same, the range of available cultural reactions to it cannot be the same either. There is a subtle cultural difference between, on the one hand, the kind of sympathy we give when someone receives sudden bad news that could not have been known in advance, and, on the other, the kind of sympathy we give when someone finds out something awful that could have been known before and could have been altered, albeit at a psychological and moral cost.

I am not suggesting that sympathy is unavailable to us as an appropriate response in the second case, only that its quality, to paraphrase Shakespeare, will be strained. So, to some extent the very existence of a prenatal test places a moral onus on those who choose not to use it because they cannot say later that they had "done all they could" to alleviate or avoid the trouble.[13] Of course, if they say at the time of refusing the test that they are prepared to accept either an impaired or an unimpaired outcome with their baby, then sympathy is probably the wrong cultural response to the outcome anyway. But even then their equanimity in embracing the baby regardless of its health status is not the same as the apparently identical response of surprised parents before the test was available. There is a reflective, calculated quality to the former case that is lacking from the more spontaneous temperament of the latter.

With testing, everything must be deliberate and everything is a decision. Nothing about the pregnancy seems just to happen by itself, to just be a given that we have no choice but to accept and deal with. Prenatal genetic testing technology shapes choice by in effect making everything into a choice. An ethical analysis that looks only at the dynamics of the interaction between the decision-making individual and others who seek to advise or shape those decisions is a fish that can't imagine water.

Knowledge and the Genetic Imaginary

A particular backward glance at a concern characteristic of the individual freedom of choice frame may be helpful at this point. Nothing I have said thus far relies on the violation of the principle of nondirective counseling that is a cardinal tenet in the genetic counseling field. I am talking about the influence of the background presence of testing technology on the space within which nondirective counseling is supposed to take place. I understand nondirective counseling to be a form of discourse and dialogue in which the professional counselor refrains from injecting his or her own personal biases or value judgments into the counseling dynamic. Nondirective counseling is also a norm of discourse according to which the professional does not exploit his or her professional authority in order to steer the client toward a decision that the counselor favors. So understood, I have no reason here to take issue with that professional ideal.

However, in a broader sense genetic counseling cannot be completely neutral or nondirective because the basic grounding of its professional discourse already derives from the genetic science and technology. The counselor (and the physician, who often takes on the role of counselor, *faute de mileux*) mediates between the client and the technology.[14] And this mediation is largely a one-way street. The genetic counselor's task is to adapt the attention and focus of the prospective parents to the information that the technology provides and to the way it structures that information. The counselor is in no position to make the genetic testing industry accommodate itself more fully to the educational and emotional needs of couples faced with the prospect of rearing a chronically ill or disabled child. Genetic test results do not come with psychosocial information or folk knowledge gained from experienced parents about how best to nurture and develop a child with a particular kind of disability.

All systems of knowledge focus and exclude, and genetics is no exception. It is the rare genetic counselor who supplements the order of this technology and this knowledge with technologies and bodies of knowledge from other realms of human experience. Of course, they are not trained to do this, there is not enough time in the clinical encounter as it is now structured in most programs, and like all specialists prenatal genetic counselors can make appropriate referrals. My purpose is not to fault genetic counselors, but these factors and limitations of their practice confirm my basic point. The counseling may be neutral as regards the personal beliefs of the counselor, but it cannot be neutral as regards the very context of genetic technology itself. Far from being neutral in that regard, genetic counseling is constituted by that technology. Indeed, prenatal genetic testing is itself an aspect of the broader medicalization of pregnancy that surrounds pregnancy with the discourse of disease, danger, risk, and defensive measures against misfortune.[15]

This being the case, when both the testing and the discourse of genetic testing and counseling enter the domain of the existential experience of pregnancy, important consequences follow. The technology and discourse of genetic testing create a new social and discursive reality, which then becomes the touchstone and the reference point for all the information the parents receive and all the decisions they make from that point forward. And it is a strong-willed parent who can resist having this powerful reality-shaping force become the *only* reality of the pregnancy. Those who can do so are those who have a previously affected child perhaps, or those who have a strong, principled commitment not to discriminate against or to undervalue the lives of those with disabilities, or those with a deep religious conviction against abortion. And those parents, a cultural and ideological minority in America today, may successfully resist the reality-shaping force of prenatal genetic testing technology because, having refused the testing a priori, they avoid exposure to this information and this discourse during their pregnancy.

For a majority of women and couples, however, prenatal testing, when indicated, will continue to be the rule. Many discussions of the ethics of genetic testing see nothing worrisome in this state of affairs that could not be cured by more complete genetic information and a better cognitive comprehension of that information. The underlying intuition is simple: good decision making depends upon accurate and reliable information. Improving the quality of information and enhancing the quantity of the information prenatal genetic testing can provide can do nothing other than lead to improved—that is, more rational and morally responsible—decision making by prospective parents. In the frame of individual freedom of choice, more information is always better than less.

Now, it is not easy to argue with this proposition without appearing to defend ignorance and irrationality. Making the case for these is not a promising task. Nonetheless, if we frame the meaning of genetic testing outside the perspective of individual freedom of choice and in a more communally oriented way, it is possible to argue that more information is not always better than less if the increase has the effect of narrowing our range of moral vision and attention to the point where some of the broader goals and interests of others or of the community as a whole are lost sight of.

Again, just as technology is not a mere instrument or tool for use by an agent, but is, in fact, an active force shaping that very agency itself, so, too, is information. Genetic tests do not provide simply "information" as some passive tool or raw material of decision making that individuals (either professionals or laypersons) are in complete control of during the decision-making process. Genetic tests provide a highly charged and theory-laden form of knowledge that structures our perception of our physical bodies, our social selves, and our temporal futures in selective and distinctive ways. And this form of knowledge also structures the perception of the bodies, selves, and futures of our unborn children.

Such knowledge is not only a benefit, although a benefit it may be. It is also a danger and a burden. As it shapes our intellectual and moral perception in one way, we need a counterpoise to shape that perception in another way, an internal gyroscope to keep our moral balance. For the practice of parenting begins during pregnancy, not at childbirth, and as a moral practice it requires a balance, a breadth, and a multifacet-edness of perception. Parenting requires white light, not light of a single color on the spectrum bent by the prism of a particular science and technology.

The kind of active, shaping knowledge that genetic testing provides creates a world within the human mind, a world validated by the leading intellects, scientists, and professionals of our time. Because it is an intellectually constructed world does not mean that it is not real. And because I stress the sense in which genetics constructs rather than reflects some underlying natural reality about human biology, this does not mean that genetics is somehow not true, real, or scientific. The notion that reality is theory laden does not mean that there is no reality, only illusion. On the contrary, the illusion is the positivistic one that believes science can offer something better, more pure, than this.[16]

The world that is constructed from the information provided by prenatal genetic tests is a "genetic imaginary" of the future child. Looking at it in this way will help us to better appreciate the morally two-edged character of this knowledge and give us a purchase on why more information of the same kind might not necessarily be better. Moreover, it suggests that the key ethical problem with prenatal genetic testing is not really incompleteness or unreliability of the information parents are offered, but the humanly one-sided and morally corrupting effects of this knowledge relative to the entire range of realities and possibilities that the moral imaginations of prospective parents should be exploring.

The genetic imaginary is not a picture of the child or even a fragmented image of what the child will be. It is not open to exactly the same epistemological critique that Susan Sontag leveled at realistic theories of photography and that can be applied in a rather straightforward way to show the fallacy of taking a sonogram to somehow be a picture or a direct representation of the unborn child.[17] (It also provides a way of critiquing the claims made by right-to-life groups several years ago on behalf of the sonogram-based video "Silent Scream.") Instead, the genetic imaginary is the basis for the possibility of conceiving the reality of the future child at all.[18] In this sense it has more in common with the art of caricature than it does with portraiture. It is a selective focus on certain traits to capture the essence of the self.

Another way to grasp what I have in mind by the genetic imaginary is to relate it to the homunculi produced by *Scientific American* in 1948 based on the work of Wilder Penfield, a Canadian neurosurgeon who pioneered the use of electrical stimulation to map functions on the human cerebral cortex. Using brain maps of both sensory and motor functions, images of the body were constructed with body mass roughly proportional to the area of the brain devoted to these functions. Both the sensory homunculus and the motor homunculus are wildly misshapen creatures. The sensory figure has enormous lips, enormous hands and feet, and an especially outsized thumb. The motor figure likewise has an enormous face and large hands with huge thumbs. In both cases the torso and lower body parts are withered and tiny.[19]

This is what the genetic imaginary based on the information given by prenatal genetic testing does. It offers to the mind's eye of the parent a homunculus shaped by the exclusive emphasis on some particular DNA sequence(s) and some particular biochemical processes associated with that sequence. If we look at our bodies only from the point of view of how much of our brain is devoted to motor coordination we will find that evolution has paid great attention to our facial muscles and to the musculature of our hands with dexterous fingers and an opposable thumb. These are surely excellent traits to have in a bipedal, social animal who fabricates and uses tools with its hands. But we would be very surprised when we met our first human being if this is all the information we had about her in advance.

The genetic imaginary does little mischief when the test results are normal, for in truth it evaporates from the parents' minds rather quickly as they turn to other sources of imagination in contemplating their future child. But in cases of abnormality and high likelihood of significant impairment and disability, the homunculus offered by the genetic imaginary can easily dominate the parents' vision. And this, as I indicated before, can have a morally corrupting effect.

Why? Not because the genetic information is invalid or is being misinterpreted. But because the imagined reality of the future child with a disability is being wrongly deformed and distorted. We are a society that gives women the right and the freedom to terminate a pregnancy, including those second trimester pregnancies that indicate the presence of severe genetic or congenital impairment. I support this right and believe this freedom on balance is a good thing. But one can support it more confidently in a context in which women are exercising a balanced and well-rounded moral imagination in their decision making concerning their pregnancies.

The reality and the experience of life lived with even severe disability is not simple or one-dimensional. It is certainly a far cry from the homunculus drawn by the genetic imaginary. Prospective parents contemplating abortion after an abnormal prenatal test must have the resources—through their own life experiences, the resources of their family and kinship network, their civic community, the assistance of health care professionals, or perhaps simply their own depth of character and empathy—to supplement the genetic imaginary with a fuller and more expansive moral imagination. Only out of that imagination can good judgment, sound practical reasoning (*phronesis*), and ultimately just prenatal decisions and choices flow. Only out of that imagination can we strengthen the fabric of solidarity, care, and respect that binds those with disabilities into full membership in our moral community.

The ethical use of prenatal genetic testing technology presupposes the existence of that community and that fulsome moral imagination. If these preconditions are lacking, we allow the wholesale introduction of prenatal genetic testing only at our own peril. In recent years we have made some progress at combating prejudice and discrimination against persons with disabilities, to be sure. Still, at present our society has few positive images of disability lives to bolster and nurture a well-rounded moral imagination. (It is something, by the way, that all temporarily able-bodied citizens, and not just prospective parents, need.) I am not certain that expanded prenatal genetic testing in our actually existing social and cultural environment in the United States will promote it, and there is a danger that increasing the power of this technology could hinder it.

Very few pregnancies go forward in a cultural silence, but medical and genetic discourse is not the only meaning-making language with which a pregnancy can be surrounded. Many parents and families still surround themselves with other types of discourse—religious, ethnic, genealogical, or kinship based—that carry very different interpretations of the pregnancy and that place it in the context of quite different narratives than those offered by medicine and genetics.

Here I confess to being torn. On the one hand, I recognize that inadequate access to excellent, state-of-the-art prenatal care is a major problem in our health care system today, and that universal access to such care is a moral imperative and a compelling public policy goal. At the same time, the plurality of narratives and discourses that surround pregnancy and make it meaningful to women, couples, and families is also a precious—and precarious—state of affairs. Greater homogenization of the prenatal care experience, greater univocality around the discourses of medicine and genetics, and greater exposure to an increasingly sophisticated and far-reaching array of prenatal tests as the technology advances—these are not prospects that we should embrace without significant moral reservation.

Clearly, work must be done to keep prenatal genetic testing limited to proper bounds within the standard of practice of universal prenatal care. Prenatal genetic testing as a technology (in the sense of a system of power) and corporate economic interest must be challenged and brought under reasonable regulatory control. The lack of systematic national regulation, the virtual frontier state, of this industry and this technology in the United States today is a scandal.[20] However, this is not the place to pursue a discussion of regulation and policy reform, and so let me return to the perspective of a broader critique.

Radical Privacy?

No matter how prenatal genetic testing is regulated and deployed in the years ahead, there are several dangers that we must be on guard against. One, already mentioned, is the growing exposure of the experience of pregnancy to a univocal discourse of genetics at the expense of other ways of conveying cultural meaning to human procreation and childbearing, motherhood, and parenthood.

A second related concern is the gradual attenuation of these other narratives of pregnancy and other languages to give it cultural significance and meaning. We must not underestimate the power of science and technology to colonize and dominate the contemporary imagination. As genetic therapy and prenatal, intrauterine surgery develop, and as the spectrum of genetic markers and genetic tests expands, what Abby Lippman has called the "geneticization" of pregnancy will spread and tighten its grip on our tacit knowledge and common sense assumptions.[21] The implications of this, particularly for those experiencing postnatal disability and chronic disease, will be profound. Indeed, what Lippman calls geneticization is the logical culmination of what I referred to above as the genetic imaginary. Her notion reminds us that many of the problems addressed in this chapter are not limited to imagining the body, the self, and the future of our children, but spread throughout the entire contours of our lives. A genetic understanding of a condition tends to "biologize" and localize what should be understood primarily in social and environmental terms. The Americans with Disabilities Act, for example, is based largely on a social-disability perspective that predates the current wave of geneticization in the popular media and culture. The rights and gains it secures for those with disabilities could be jeopardized if the opinion makers were to conclude that this public policy approach rests on false foundations. Indeed, the ADA is relatively vague when it comes to issues of genetic-related disability and genetic testing. It remains to be seen what future courts and legislatures will do in these areas.

A third concern is that the moral experience and sensibility that women (and their partners and families) bring to the experience of pregnancy will grow thin as a result of the breakdown of civic culture in the broader society and as a consequence of the generalized narcissism of our times.[22] In this case, the only life narrative a woman or a couple will have within which to place their pregnancy will be the narrative of self-interest and career. As this cultural narrative and form of moral imagination (if it can be called that) places a premium on the notion of molding or engineering one's adult life as a monument to the self, it will have a natural affinity with geneticization or the notion that we can exercise control, through genetic technology, over the very biochemical architecture of our bodies, or those of our children. This is not an interpretative frame that is likely to offer a place of intrinsic value and unconditional love for an imagined future child with a serious disability. But, at least to me, an essential question remains: Does the problem lie with the child's genetic make-up, or even with the later manifestation of disability, or does it lie with this interpretative frame itself?

It is natural for human beings to be cultural. It is everywhere and inevitably the case that people need to assimilate their experience into systems of ordered meaning and to surround the most biologically and socially important occasions with multiple layers of significance. Pregnancy is such an occasion par excellence. I am not prepared to say to what extent individuals' and couples' freedom to use prenatal genetic testing should be limited; but I do believe that such testing is neither socially nor morally neutral and must be socially regulated rather than treated as a medical market commodity.

Some may read these reflections as a call for constraining curiosity, information, and human knowledge. There are some things that people simply should not know, because the knowledge will lead them into moral pitfalls. In fact, I have little sympathy for that argument, and I do not intend that these reflections oppose the spirit of Prometheus. I simply remember the terrible burden inherent in his gift of foresight. Rather than curtailing the acts of curiosity, knowing, and projecting meaning during the prenatal period, I am concerned that they will become too univocal and one-dimensional. The new genetic discourse, linked as it is to science in a culture that is in love with science, is and will increasingly be a powerful voice in the making of prenatal meaning. It has the power to colonize and to permeate all our thoughts and feelings as we make decisions that will affect the futures of our families.

No fetus is merely a genetic homunculus; each contains many shapes of future possibility and many imaginable lives, with or without disability. Retaining among ordinary women and men in our culture the capacity to see that is the key. A fecund imagination and a rich moral life for all is the route to ethically sound prenatal decision making in a genetics age.

NOTES

1. For a penetrating discussion of the significance of what she calls human "natality," see Hannah Arendt, *The Human Condition* (Chicago: University of Chicago Press, 1959).

2. On the notion of tacit knowledge, see Michael Polanyi, *Personal Knowledge* (New York: Harper Torchbook, 1964).

3. Cynthia M. Powell, "The Current State of Prenatal Genetic Testing in the United States," in this volume.

4. On the concept of frame in social analysis, see Martin Rein, "Value-Critical Policy Analysis," in *Ethics, the Social Sciences, and Policy Analysis*, ed. Daniel Callahan and Bruce Jennings (New York: Plenum Press, 1983), pp. 83–112. See also Erving Goffman, *Frame Analysis* (New York: Harper and Row, 1974); and Robert N. Bellah, Richard Madsen, William M. Sullivan, Ann Swidler, and Steven M. Tipton, *The Good Society* (New York: Vintage, 1992).

5. See, for instance, Joel Feinberg, *The Moral Limits of the Criminal Law*, 4 vols. (Princeton, N.J.: Princeton University Press, 1984–88).

6. For a discussion of the Aristotelian distinction between *techne* and *phronesis*, see Richard J. Bernstein, *Beyond Relativism and Objectivism* (Philadelphia: University of Pennsylvania Press, 1983), pp. 109–70.

7. A more extended discussion of the account given in the preceding paragraphs can be found in Willard Gaylin and Bruce Jennings, *The Perversion of Autonomy* (New York: Free Press, 1996). In this work, however, insufficient attention is paid to the problem of technology and its impact on our understanding of freedom, autonomy, and coercion.

8. Michael Walzer, *Interpretation and Social Criticism* (Cambridge, Mass.: Harvard University Press, 1987) and *The Company of Critics* (New York: Basic Books, 1988).

9. Luke 2:1–20.

10. For an incisive discussion of various conceptions of technology and their use in social and political theory, see Langdon Winner, *Autonomous Technology* (Cambridge, Mass.: MIT Press, 1977). Classic works in this regard are Jacques Elluh, *The Technological Society* (New York: Knopf, 1964); and Lewis Mumford, *The Myth of the Machine*, 2 vols. (New York: Harcourt Brace Jovanovich, 1964–70).

11. E. P. Thompson, *The Making of the English Working Class* (New York: Vintage, 1963).

12. Martin Heidegger, "The Question Concerning Technology," in *Basic Writings*, ed. David F. Drell (New York: Harper and Row, 1977). See also Fred R. Dallmayr, *Polis and Praxis* (Cambridge, Mass.: MIT Press, 1984).

13. See Ruth Faden, "Reproductive Genetic Testing, Prevention, and the Ethics of Mothering," in *Women and Prenatal Testing*, ed. Karen H. Rothenberg and Elizabeth J. Thomson (Columbus: Ohio State University Press, 1994), pp. 88–97; and R. Alta Charo and Karen H. Rothenberg, " 'The Good Mother': The Limits of Reproductive Accountability and Genetic Choice," in *Women and Prenatal Testing*, ed. Karen H. Rothenberg and Elizabeth J. Thomson (Columbus: Ohio State University Press, 1994), pp. 105–30.

14. See Charles L. Bosk, *All God's Mistakes: Genetic Counseling in a Pediatric Hospital* (Chicago: University of Chicago Press, 1992).

15. Barbara Katz Rothman, *Recreating Motherhood: Ideology and Technology in a Patriarchal Society* (New York: W. W. Norton, 1989).

16. Richard Rorty, *Philosophy and the Mirror of Nature* (Princeton, N.J.: Princeton University Press, 1979).

17. Susan Sontag, *On Photography* (New York: Doubleday, 1990).

18. Cornelius Castoriadis, *The Imaginary Institution of Society* (Cambridge, Mass.: MIT Press, 1987).

19. These images are reproduced in Carl Sagan, *The Dragons of Eden* (New York: Ballantine, 1977), pp. 36–37.

20. Ellen Wright Clayton, "What the Law Says about Reproductive Genetic Testing and What It Doesn't," in *Women and Prenatal Testing*, ed. Karen H. Rothenberg and Elizabeth J. Thomson (Columbus: Ohio State University Press, 1994), pp. 131–78.

21. Abby Lippman, "The Genetic Construction of Prenatal Testing: Choice, Consent, or Conformity for Women?" in *Women and Prenatal Testing*, ed. Karen H. Rothenberg and Elizabeth J. Thomson (Columbus: Ohio State University Press, 1994), pp. 9–34.

22. Christopher Lasch, *The Culture of Narcissism* (New York: W. W. Norton, 1979).

Part Three

The Messages and Meanings of Prenatal Genetic Testing

MARSHA SAXTON

Why Members of the Disabil..y Community Oppose Prenatal Diagnosis and Selective Abortion

Prenatal tests have brought the revolution in molecular biology into the lives of ordinary people. Prenatal genetic tests promise to offer greater reproductive self-determination for families that carry genetic traits for serious disease. Originally intended to address "high-risk" pregnancies, prenatal diagnosis (PND) is becoming part of routine prenatal care. But these tests and the prospect of selective abortion raise many social and ethical concerns. Disability rights activists have begun to articulate a critical view of the practice of prenatal diagnosis with the intent to abort if the fetus appears to be destined to become a disabled person. Some people with disabilities, particularly those who are members of the disability rights community, perceive that selective abortion may be based on the assumption that any child with a disability would necessarily be a burden to the family and to society, and therefore would be better off not being born.

People with disabilities who have lived their lives creatively managing the logistics of a disability, as well as fighting disability discrimination, may regard these new genetic "options" as a way to promote selective abortion. As disability activist and lawyer Lisa Blumberg put it, "The social purpose of these tests is to reduce the incidence of live births of people with disabilities."[1] She describes a report which discussed, in the view of the authors, the troubling findings that some women would not have an abortion even if the fetus had "multiple, severe handicaps such as hemiplegia and incontinence." Blumberg writes: "Nowhere do the writers ask whether preventing the existence of people with spina bifida is an appropriate goal of a program funded by state taxpayers, including taxpayers with spina bifida." According to the disability rights paradigm, if suffering does indeed attend life with disability, then the place to begin ameliorating that suffering is with the eradication of social discrimination—not with the eradication of people with disabilities.

Lawyer and disability activist Deborah Kaplan contends, "If persons with disabilities are perceived as individuals who encounter insurmountable difficulties in life and who place a burden on society, prenatal screening may be regarded as a logical response. However, if persons with disabilities are regarded as a definable social group who have faced great oppression and stigmatization, then prenatal screening may be regarded as yet another form of social abuse."[2] This is the essence of the disability community's challenge to prenatal genetic testing. We believe that the current promotion and application of prenatal screening has a potent message that negatively affects people with disabilities, influences women in decision making about their own pregnancies, and reinforces the general public's stereotyped attitudes about people with disabilities.

The American public appears to have accepted the "common sense" assumption that prenatal screening and selective abortion can potentially reduce the incidence of disease and disability and thus is good. There are many misleading and mistaken views underlying this assumption: that the enjoyment of life for disabled people is necessarily less than for nondisabled people; that raising a child with a disability is a wholly undesirable thing; that selective abortion will save mothers from the burdens of raising disabled children; and that we, as a society, have the means to decide who is better off not being born. Using the literature written by people with disabilities, from the international disability community in the United States, Canada, Britain, Germany, and Japan, as well as feminist critics of PND, I will explore some of the current and historic origins of these pervasive assumptions and examine the views of people with disabilities about the message sent by prenatal diagnosis and selective abortion, as well as the impact of these technologies on the general population's attitudes about disability.

"The Medical Model" of Disability and the Need for Screening

Medical sociologist and disability activist Irving Zola explored the role that the medical system has in people's lives. Zola wrote:

> [Medicine] is becoming the new repository of truth, the place where absolute and final judgments are made by supposedly morally neutral and objective experts. And these judgments are made, not in the name of virtue or legitimacy, but in the name of health.[3]

The impact of the medical system's views and influence is especially prominent in the lives of people with disabilities, as a result of the additional time many disabled persons spend interacting with medical personnel. This may be due to the need for more extensive medical service, but also to the fact that many of the services and benefits available to disabled persons are controlled by medical "gatekeepers" who certify eligibility to various social institutions, such as the Social Security Administration (for income support, if disability affects employment), the division of motor vehicles (for special parking), or the housing authority (for eligibility to accessible housing programs).

Within the medical system's view, disability is defined as a biological problem or limitation.[4] Thus, the social consequences of disability, such as high unemployment and low educational levels of people with disabilities, resulting in low socioeconomic status, are thought to be caused by physiological limitation.[5] A fundamental assumption in the medical view is that greater degrees of disability (defined by medical standards as increased pathology) are associated with decreased quality of life.[6] This view is often referred to in the disability community's literature as the "medical model of disability." Inherent in this medicalized view is the assumption that the source of any problems related to the disability is located within the individual or within the individual's body. According to Adrienne Asch, the core of the medical model view is that "disability must be prevented, because disabled people cannot function within existing society."[7]

Tay-Sachs disease is often raised by medical professionals as justification for prenatal screening. But as a rare disease, it's a poor basis for a paradigm. As epidemiologist Abby Lippman says, "Rare cases make bad policies."[8] Conditions receiving priority attention for prenatal screening are Down syndrome, spina bifida, cystic fibrosis, and Fragile X, whose clinical outcomes are usually mildly to moderately disabling. Individuals with these conditions can live good lives. There are severe cases but the medical system tends to underestimate the functional abilities and overestimate the "burden" of these disabled citizens.

Medical language reinforces negativity, asserts Laura Hershey, a disability advocate from Tennessee: "Terms like 'fetal deformity' and 'defective fetus' are deeply stigmatizing, carrying connotations of inadequacy and shame. Many of us have been called 'abnormal' by medical personnel . . . who view us permanently as 'patients' subject to the definitions and control of the medical profession."[9] Says Diane Coleman, another activist from Nashville, "Maybe they see us as failures on their part."[10]

"The Disability Paradigm"

The view of disability developed by people with disabilities is very different from the medical view. The "disability paradigm" was made prominent in the late 1970s.[11] This view regards disability as a socially constructed phenomenon and is based on a view of disabled people as a minority group, much like women or persons of color targeted with social discrimination and denied full access to the mainstream life of the community. According to this perspective, once the oppression is revealed, the assumptions of the medical view (the more impaired, the less quality of life) are exposed as false.[12]

It is important to note that authors from within the disability community have conceded that disability itself is not inherently a neutral condition but constitutes a real loss apart from the socioeconomic loss that results from oppression:

> The inability to move without mechanical aid, to see, to hear, or to learn is not inherently neutral. Disability itself limits some options. . . . It is not irrational to hope that children and adults will live as long as possible without health problems or diminished human capacities.[13]

Among many socially stigmatized groups such as people of color and gay people, their "inherent characteristics" have been blamed by society for their lower socioeconomic status and/or used as justification for their social mistreatment or ostracism. The view expressed by Asch previously in this volume acknowledges that the experience of disability does not neatly reflect the experiences of these other social groups for whom negative judgments about their personal characteristic have been exposed as resulting solely from oppression. Acknowledging this does not confirm the medical model conceptualization of disability. One's options in life as a person with a disability may indeed, in some ways, be limited, but oppressive social conditions have so distorted the public's perceptions, as well as how disabled individuals themselves might internalize these perceptions, that it is difficult to assess the true impact of disability on the individual's life experience.

Explaining the Disability Experience to Social Researchers

Disability activists are concerned that the message of PND may have the effect of triggering additional oppression, reinforcing the general public's perception that disability is a tragic mistake (that could and should have been avoided) and that disabled people are therefore justifiably marginalized. Deborah Kaplan contends:

> Many leaders of the community of persons with disabilities have expressed concern that genetic testing and prenatal screening have a tendency to promote negative general attitudes about disability. They worry that these negative attitudes might result in . . . job discrimination, barriers to obtaining health insurance coverage, cutbacks on public support programs, and other similar negative actions."[14]

Perhaps in a very different world, a mythical world without sexism or disability oppression, prenatal predictive technologies could be useful, life-enhancing tools. That is not this world. The technologies can only be evaluated in the world the way it is, and on that basis, they have been and will be used in ways that devalue people with disabilities.

In our discussions during The Hastings Center project about the disability community's views of PND and selective abortion, I felt that some members of the group did not grasp the impact of stigmatization on disabled people's sense of self, and how that might affect our views of PND. Someone in the discussion once said that disabled people take PND far too personally. If someone aborts a fetus with a disability, she reasoned, what does that have to do with anyone else with a disability? In an attempt to lift the argument out of the emotionally charged context of disability discrimination, a hypothetical example was offered with a nonstigmatized "disability": lack of musical ability. The argument was made that this nonmusical person, call her Mary, would certainly not be devastated to learn of her musical parent's or musical husband's preference for children who are musical; she would be able to understand and not take it personally, if they prefer certain abilities or characteristics in a child. I argued that the social context, the day-to-day experience of discriminatory treatment, is essential and inseparable from any discussion of "choosing" or preferring characteristics in one's child. I offered the following illustration:

> Let's fill in some details in the typical life experience of someone in a marginalized constituency, such as nonmusical individuals, to further explore why Mary might be upset at her husband's and her own parent's preference for a musical child, why she might be disappointed that they don't regard her nonmusicality as neutral.
>
>   Mary reports that she had a generally happy childhood, but recalls some incidents where the other children in her neighborhood used to tease her, singing, "Mary isn't musical! Nya, nya, nya, nya, nya!" When

her mother took her to register for kindergarten, she was told, "We're sorry, we can't educate nonmusical children here. She must go to a special school." There are some public funds available for Mary's education, but the choice of schools is very limited, and mostly residential, so she must leave her family for months at a time, or else travel long hours on the bus every day to get a relatively decent education for the nonmusical.

When Mary walks down the street, going about her ordinary day, she sometimes hears people whisper, "There goes one of those nonmusical people. I wonder how they cope." Sometimes someone even comes right up to her and says something like, "You nonmusical people are such an inspiration! If I were ever to become nonmusical I would feel like killing myself. You must be so courageous!" Mary politely tolerates this intrusion from others, along with their awkwardness with the language to describe her condition, calling her "other-abled" and "musically challenged." She knows people mean well.

Sometimes she wishes she could tell one of these busybodies to go to hell, but she never does. She doesn't want to risk making others think badly of nonmusical people. She notices that the larger culture thinks all nonmusical people are just alike, even those from the full range of racial and ethnic groups. People are always assuming she prefers to be only with other nonmusical people, as if she were deeply ashamed of her nonmusicality, or felt she had little in common with those musical.

When Mary goes to the doctor for a sore throat or just to get a checkup, the doctor will often become very interested, but not in answering her questions. The doctor wants to know things like "How long have you been nonmusical? Were you born with this condition? Have you ever considered having experimental brain surgery to the auditory cortex?" Mary sighs, and reminds the doctor why she is there.

Mary has a job, which she'll admit wasn't so easy to find, not because she wasn't qualified, as she has many skills and an advanced degree. But every time she went to an interview the employer would bring up her nonmusicality, and ask probing questions that had nothing to do with the job or her skills. Eventually civil rights legislation prohibited employers from asking such questions. But Mary knows that since it is so hard to prove job discrimination, she and other nonmusical people will continue to have a high unemployment rate.

We might ask, is it any wonder that Mary's very sense of self might be affected by the world's negative views of her musical inability? Should someone from a stigmatized constituency, even a sophisticated, thoughtful person, be easily able to logically separate the effects of a lifetime of cruel mistreatment, both random and systematic, from one's self-concept, and then from one's feelings and beliefs?

If we hope to thoughtfully debate and form accurate and meaningful opinions about PND and selective abortion, and their impact on disabled people and everyone else, we must consider the full context of the issues, and we must strive to understand the real experience of disability in our society. We must explore both the stereotypes and the realities of disability, as best we can.

The Community of People with Disabilities

The objection to selective abortion from the disability rights community is ultimately related to how we define ourselves. As feminists have transformed women's sense of self, the disability community has reframed the experience of having a disability. In part through developing a sense of community, we've come to realize that the stereotyped notions of the "tragedy" and "suffering" of "the disabled" result largely from the isolation and exclusion of disabled people from mainstream society. While the limitations of a disability can be difficult, it is the oppression that is most disabling about disability.

Many disabled people have a growing but still precarious sense of pride in an identity as "people with disabilities." With decades of hard work, disability activists have fought against institutionalization and discrimination and have fought for access to employment, education, transportation, and housing. We have fought for rehabilitation and "independent living" programs and have proven that disabled people can participate in and contribute to society.

People with disabilities in the past twenty-five years have gained an identity as a social and political group, "[t]hrough an enhanced awareness of the significance of discrimination based on perceptible physical difference."[15] With the models of contemporary movements for civil rights, justice, and equality, disabled people also began to recognize that they had rights and could participate as full and equal members of society.

In an era that offers access to improved health, longevity, social mobility, and a political voice for disabled citizens, it is ironic that the growth of the new reproductive and genetic technologies of the 1970s and 1980s now provides the possibility of eliminating categories of people with certain kinds of disabilities, such as Down syndrome, spina bifida, muscular dystrophy, sickle cell anemia, and hundreds of other conditions. Laura Hershey suggests:

> The idea that disability might someday be permanently eradicated—
> whether through prenatal screening and abortion . . . has strong appeal

for a society wary of spending resources on human needs. Maybe there lurks, in the back of society's mind, the belief (the hope?) that one day there will be no people with disabilities. That attitude works against the goals of civil rights and independent living. We struggle for integration, access, and support services, yet our existence remains an unresolved question. Under the circumstances, we cannot expect society to guarantee and fund our full citizenship.[16]

Genetics Professionals

Genetics professionals, including genetic researchers, clinical MD geneticists, and genetic counselors, are motivated by a commitment to helping people with genetically related conditions. But the very nature of their work may reinforce certain stereotypes. Genetics professionals have been trained in a medical educational system that emphasizes worst-case scenarios of disease and disability, with virtually no attention to psychosocial factors in the experience of disability. The vast majority of articles and books from the genetics literature that addresses medical decision making about persons with chronic disease or disability completely omit reference to the social context of disability, ignoring the fact that persons with disabilities are subject to discrimination, which significantly affects the quality of their lives. Professionals who work with individuals with genetic conditions may have little familiarity with disabled people who are living independently and working in the community, and thus are unable to challenge pervasive cultural stereotypes about people with disabilities and illness.

In most genetic counseling training programs, students have internship placements in medical settings where they may observe disabled children. At Brandeis University a program was initiated that gave students a unique opportunity to interact with disabled adults more informally, outside of a medicalized encounter. Each student was assigned a disabled adult to interview for a minimum of three meetings over the course of a semester. My own study[17] focussed on these interactions; I interviewed the students and the disability consultants before and after they met. The students' reactions to these meetings were striking, revealing a significant shift after the meetings, where students reframed their view of disability as an experience informed by societal discrimination rather than personal tragedy. One student said:

> In talking with the other students, we all had these sort of mini-revelations about what disability is. I don't know if I would have ever done that if

we hadn't been required to. Everybody had a great experience—I mean, incredible. I've learned that you don't have to treat [disabled people] differently, get worked up, which is what I was doing. . . . It doesn't seem like it's such a different world. We build it up to be "us and them."

Students reported being struck at how little interaction with "real people with disabilities" they had before this program. As a result of these meetings, they experienced a newfound ability to perceive disabled people as potential friends and colleagues, and several stated their intention to utilize disabled persons as consultants in their professional work arenas to help educate colleagues. One student said: "I think it's ridiculous . . . all these professionals, talking and talking, but not with people with disabilities; this elite group makes decisions, but not involving anybody else. We don't want to admit this is a form of eugenics; don't want to be associated with that word. . . . I've brought it up before but people in my field don't really want to talk about it." Another said, "It scares me to think that I could have gone somewhere else [besides Brandeis] and never thought about any of this."

Doctors are facing a growing legal "duty" to test or to refer patients to genetic counseling. Milunsky writes: "An obstetrician who elects not to screen all patients in routine pregnancy or who fails to offer and discuss this screening test, invites a malpractice action should a patient deliver a child with a neural tube defect or Down's syndrome."[18] Thus, physicians' fear of wrongful life and wrongful birth suits became a "reason to test" and routine prenatal testing is built into the standard of care as a way to protect physician interests, unrelated to patient concerns.

Genetics professionals may feel the pressure to succumb to cost-benefit measures that implement screening as a way to save scarce health care dollars by eliminating fetuses carrying disabling traits. The cost-benefit argument starkly contrasts with "alleviating suffering" as a motive and justification for selective abortion. In the language of a recent Office of Technology Assessment report: "In the values and language of cost-benefit analysis, prenatal genetic testing programs in which fewer than 50 per cent of parents chose to terminate a fetus diagnosed with a genetic disorder are considered to be a 'failure.' "[19]

Critics argue that the value of a child's life cannot be measured in dollars, and some evidence suggests that families with disabled children who are familiar with the actual impact of the disabilities tend not to seek prenatal screening tests for subsequent children.[20] The cost-benefit argument is weakened in the face of the enormous resources expended to test for a few rare genetic disorders. Also within the cost-benefit argument for screening is the assumption of rational choice in decision making. Cost-benefit emphasizes outcomes, consequences, identification, and quantification of variables that operate in an individual's decision making. Gregg criticizes this view as poorly reflecting the actual decision-making process engaged in by the vast majority of women and couples facing screening, by neglecting the myriad influences on any decision maker. As Gregg suggests, the purported objectivity of screening "obfuscates its political uses and their consequences."[21]

The Reproductive Rights Movement

Fetal anomaly has sometimes been used by feminists as a "pro-choice" justification for legal abortion. This reinforces the idea that women are horribly oppressed by the existence of disabled children.[22] When disability is sanctioned as a justification for legal abortion, then abortion for sex selection may be more easily sanctioned as well. If "choice" is made to mean choosing the "perfect child," or the child of the "right gender," then children are turned into products perfectible through technology. Those who think that children are not commodities believe that real "choice" must include the choice to have a child with a disability.[23]

Some feminist writers defend the use of prenatal diagnostics as providing greater reproductive self-determination to women by reducing the incidence of birth defects, and therefore eliminating burdensome parenting experiences, and enabling greater self-determinism and resistance to patriarchal manipulation.[24] These assertions from feminists supporting prenatal diagnosis tend to be devoid of disability-positive language or conceptualization.

In the tradition of Shulamith Firestone,[25] who argued that reproductive technologies can free women from the constraints of biology, again, it has been argued that prenatal tests are feminist tools because they save women from the excessive burdens associated with raising disabled children. But critics argue that is like calling the washer-dryer a feminist tool; technological innovation may "save time," and even allow women to work outside the home, but it has not changed who does the housework.[26] Women do the vast majority of child care. Child care is not valued as real work. Raising children is regarded as "duty" and is not valued as "worth" paying mothers for. Selective abortion will not challenge the sexism of the family structure where women provide most of the care for children in general, for elderly parents, and for those disabled in accidents or from nongenetic diseases. Selective abortion is promoted in many doctors' offices as a "reproductive option" and "personal choice." But as anthropologist Rayna Rapp notes, "private choices always have public consequences."[27] A woman's individual decision, when resulting from social pressure, or colluding with "a trend," has repercussions for all others in the society.

Some feminists have been vocal in opposing prenatal testing and abortion for sex selection, pointing out that the rhetoric of "choice" can end up being used against women by encouraging women to "choose" to perpetuate their own devaluation.[28] For those with "disability-positive" attitudes, the analogy with sex selection is made, pointing out that oppressive assumptions, not inherent characteristics, have devalued who this fetus will grow into.

Pressure on Women to Test

Women are increasingly pressured to use prenatal diagnostic testing under a cultural imperative that undergoing these tests is the "responsible thing to do." Strangers in the supermarket, even characters in TV sit-coms, readily ask a woman with a pregnant belly, "Did you get your amnio?" While the ostensible justification is "reassurance that the baby is fine," the underlying communication to the mother is clear: screening for fetuses with disability traits is the right thing, "the healthy thing," to do.[29]

Another justification for testing is that it eases "maternal anxiety." Negative test results (that is, no detected anomaly) supposedly offer women reassurance of a good pregnancy; these results constitute a medical stamp of approval. This perspective supports the market for tests. But no test can guarantee a perfect pregnancy or child. A mother whose fetus was found to have a neural tube defect wrote about her experiences:

> As I was examined and interviewed by several different disciplines, I was left with the impression that continuing a pregnancy [of a fetus with spina bifida] such as mine was an unusual thing to do. It seemed as though every time I turned around another physician was asking me whether or not anyone had discussed my "options" with me. "Options" has clearly become a euphemism for abortion.[30]

Bringing to term fetuses with disability traits is widely seen to be the wrong thing to do. Micheline Mason, British disability advocate as well as the mother of a disabled child, put it this way:

The world, through its white-coated spokespeople, carries a value judgement into the new relationship [between mother and fetus] . . . even before the mother and child have met. The mother at this point may be armed only with what she has learnt about disabled people from charity posters, special school buses and the popular press. Everything, including these kind doctors who are looking after her, is telling her that the world does not want any more disabled babies and that she would never be able to cope.[31]

Sociologist Kitty Felker interviewed twenty mothers of children with Down syndrome. These mothers reported that before their babies were born, "clinicians had stressed the horrors of life with disabilities," while their families themselves described instead the satisfactions of parenting children with disabilities.[32] There is, as yet, little analysis of prenatal diagnosis written by parents of children with disabilities. A few recent films have explored the issues, including "The Burden of Knowledge," produced by Wendy Conquest and colleagues from Dartmouth College, which seeks to present a balanced view of the prenatal diagnosis decision-making process, by interviewing disabled adults and several sets of parents, some of whom did choose and others of whom did not choose selective abortion.

Selective abortion serves as a wedge into the broader issue of "quality control" of all humans. If a condition (like Down syndrome) is clearly unacceptable, how long before the line moves toward other (presumed genetic) characteristics fraught with a social charge: sexual orientation, race, attractiveness, height, and intelligence?[33] Preimplantation diagnosis, which can now be used with in vitro fertilization, offers the prospect of "admission standards" for all fetuses produced by such techniques.

Assessing the Value of the Fetus

It is important to distinguish between a woman who does not want to bring a fetus to term because she does not want any baby at this time, and a woman who does not want to bring a fetus to term because she does not want this particular fetus because of its disabling trait.[34] We see in the broader society that fetuses that are wanted are called "babies." Prenatal screening results can turn a "wanted baby" into an "unwanted fetus." The prenatal test result demands that the mother or couple face the moral task of identifying a potentially and justifiably rejectable "other," the "defective fetus."

The value ascribed to the disabled fetus depends upon the parents' and medical providers' views and attitudes about the disability, its survival potential, its potential to "become someone" (the expected child) and/or meet the parents' expectations of parenthood.[35] These attitudes and decisions about the potential disabled child are made largely by people (parents or medical professionals) with little or no exposure to actual people with the genetic condition in question.[36] Before genetic testing, parents got potluck; testing creates the illusion that parents are "choosing" the right fetus, and thus the right child, based on informed decision making.

Would my parents have "chosen" me? This is a question difficult to avoid for those of us with "screenable conditions." I was born before the era of testing, but the first generation of potentially "screenable" disabled people is just now coming of age. I have pondered the notion that "I might not have been born" and tried to assess how this informs the disability community's views on genetic technologies. That I or some other person with a screenable condition might not have been born certainly plays on people's emotions. The idea of selective abortion may trigger painful childhood and adult experiences of disabled people who were made to feel like burdens and "better off not being born."

Are those in the disability rights movement who question or resist selective abortion trying to save the "endangered species" of disabled fetuses? When this metaphor first surfaced years ago, I was shocked to think of disabled people as the target of intentional elimination, but I was also shocked to realize that I identified with the "disabled" fetus as one of my "species" that I must try to protect. I imagine this is often the initial response of people with disabilities or our close allies when first grappling with these complicated issues. When we refer to the fetus as "a disabled fetus" (rather than a "defective fetus"), we personify the fetus via a term of pride in the disability community. The fetus is named as a member of our community. The connection disabled people feel with the "disabled fetus" may seem to be in conflict with the pro-choice stance that the fetus is only a part of the woman's body, with no independent status as a person.

The notion of "it could have been me who got aborted" is ultimately a poor argument against selective abortion. Personalizing and individual-izing the issue has an unfortunate effect: it pits mother against fetus, in this case, the "able-bodied mother" against the "defective fetus," in a reverse twist of fetal rights, which tends to pit the "deviant" (defective) mother against the "perfect" (potentially able-bodied) fetus. It is not useful for disability rights activists to ally themselves with the "fetus as victim" kind of thinking of the pro-life right. Fighting for greater clarity about selective abortion is not the same as fighting to save the individual "disabled fetus." This is not to say that we as individuals wouldn't consider challenging an individual mother to reevaluate her disability-related attitudes with respect to a particular fetus.

Reduced to a Gene

A person with a disability could presumably ascribe any number of different meanings to the existence of PND. Yet there is remarkable congruence in the writing about this issue coming from people with disabilities around the world. All these writers identify this theme: "These technologies make us feel devalued as human beings." For people with disabilities, "the message" implicit in the practice of abortion based on genetic characteristics is, as Deborah Kaplan puts it: "It is better not to exist than to have a disability."[37] Your birth was a mistake. Your family and the world would be better off without you alive.

Again, it is important to state that this message is not coming from our families. Beeson and Dokum explored family reactions to genetic testing based on their relationships to disabled people and determined that families with a disabled child tend to go against the trend to test for subsequent children, resisting the pressure of "rationality and reason" from professionals.

> These families have come to appreciate the various dimensions of their [child's] existence, and the extent to which the quality of the "genetically imperfect" person's life is a result of social support. They become unwilling to reduce the meaning of the life of a person with a genetic disorder to their disease, or even to the suffering that may accompany it. In this context they reject reducing the issues to genetics and see many other dimensions of human experience. . . .[38]

In this era we people with disabilities have fought hard for acknowledgment of our being worth whatever extra effort may be needed from our families and providers, and for recognition that our contributions are meaningful and significant. For many of us, it has also taken effort to go ahead, despite the discriminatory attitudes, to get a job, to manage our lives despite the discrimination and the social barriers, to focus on what's true and what's possible. As a disabled person, you, yourself have the task of realizing that your disability is not the huge defining factor that the oppressive assumptions have pointed to. Your disability is a part of you, but really not that big of a deal in the totality of your being. And now we learn from genetic science that the particular characteristics, "the flawed part," that we fought against negative and learned stereotypes to accept, has now become the very factor identified by a technology as the excuse to eliminate potential people who might turn out "like you."

When we present the diagnosis of a genetic disease condition to the parents, do we also remind parents that this baby would also still come with a full set of other human characteristics? When medical students or genetic counseling students are shown slides of babies or adults with genetic conditions, do we also remind these students that these individuals will carry other human traits such as love and affection, humor and joy? Emphatically not: the diagnostic test reduces the entire set of human characteristics to one—the "flawed, imperfect" part.

With the example of racism we see that the whole complex, centuries-long history of fear of cultural difference, of white guilt at the horrors of slavery, of the economics of jobs and land, get projected onto one visible characteristic: dark skin. Analogously, we see with PND that the whole complex history and set of current social phenomena including the economics of dependence and interdependence, the politics of caregiving and gender roles, the fear of human difference and vulnerability, get reduced and projected onto one identifiable characteristic: a gene. We in the disability rights community resist the notion that our humanness can be evaluated and then reduced to a flawed gene.

It can be argued that the people with disabilities who are in a position to challenge mainstream cultural attitudes are exceptional: educated, privileged, with an unusual number of resources, and therefore not representative of the burdensome masses of disabled people. We would argue that we are exceptional as people with disabilities only in our confidence, our sense of ourselves as worthy human beings. We are privileged in having encountered and joined the community of other people with disabilities that offered us the unique opportunity to reflect on our position in society and to fight discrimination.

What changes do we disability rights activists want to accomplish in the process of prenatal screening and selective abortion? Simply put, we hope to educate genetics professionals, other medical personnel, and students to consider and learn from the views of the disability community, and to promote the inclusion of people with disabilities and their families as resource people and expert advisors in policy development and clinical services. (The Brandeis program mentioned earlier is one model that moves in this direction.) We want to educate the general public about the social issues of disability, so that families can make informed and meaningful decisions about prenatal screening, as these technologies reach more people. We are beginning to gain a voice in a few of these arenas.

In May 1998, National Public Radio aired a series of four hour-long radio shows on key disability issues, including one on genetic screening. That same week, the radio show "Talk of the Nation" requested that I and a clinical geneticist, Dr. Alan Gutmacher, be interviewed by Ray Suarez about the disability community's view of prenatal testing.[39] These radio programs were broadcast all over the country to an estimated four million listeners and were rebroadcast again in the spring of 1999.

Just a few years ago, I couldn't have imagined that the views of disabled people on this issue would reach this level of recognition. We are responding with our own message. "In order to imagine bringing a disabled child into the world when abortion is possible," Adrienne Asch offered, "one must be able to imagine saying to a child: I wanted you enough and believed enough in who you could be that I felt you could have a life you would appreciate even with the difficulties your disability causes."[40]

NOTES

1. Lisa Blumberg, "Eugenics v. Reproductive Choice," *The Disability Rag and Resource,* January–February (1994): 32.

2. Deborah Kaplan, "Prenatal Screening and its Impact on Persons with Disabilities," *Fetal Diagnosis and Therapy* 14 (1992): 122–35.

3. I. K. Zola, "Medicine as an Institution of Social Control," in *The Sociology of Health and Illness: Critical Perspectives*, ed. Peter Conrad and Rochelle Kern (New York: St. Martin's Press, 1978), pp. 511–27, at 514.

4. E. D. Berkowitz, *Disabled Policy: America's Programs for the Handicapped, A Twentieth Century Fund Report* (Cambridge, U.K.: Cambridge University Press, 1987).

5. Adrienne Asch, "Reproductive Technology and Disability," in *Reproductive Laws for the 1990s*, ed. Sherrill Cohen and Nadine Taub (Clifton, N.J.: Humana Press, 1989), p. 73.

6. Marsha Saxton, "Born and Unborn," in *Test-Tube Women: What Future for Motherhood?* ed. Rita Arditti, Renate Duelli Klein, and Shelley Minden (London: Pandora Press, 1984).

7. Asch, "Reproductive Technology and Disability," p. 98.

8. Abby Lippman, "Prenatal Genetic Testing and Screening: Constructing

Needs and Reinforcing Inequities," *American Journal of Law and Medicine* 17 (1991): 15–50.

9. Laura Hershey, "Choosing Disability," *Ms. Magazine*, July–August (1994): 26–32.

10. Diane Coleman, in Laura Hershey, "Choosing Disability," *Ms. Magazine*, July–August (1994): 43.

11. I. K. Zola, "Healthism and Disabling Medicalization," in *The Nation's Health*, ed. Philip Lee, Nancy Brown, and Ida Red (San Francisco, Calif.: Boyd and Fraser, 1979), pp. 101–10.

12. John Susman, "Disability, Stigma and Deviance," *Social Science in Medicine* 38, no. 1 (1994): 15–22.

13. Asch, "Reproductive Technology and Disability," p. 73.

14. Deborah Kaplan, "Prenatal Screening and Its Impact on Persons with Disabilities," *Clinical Obstetrics & Gynecology* 36, no. 3 (1993): 605–23.

15. Harlan Hahn, "Can Disability be Beautiful?" *Social Policy* 18, no. 3 (1988): 26–31.

16. Hershey, "Choosing Disability," p. 29.

17. Marsha Saxton, "Disability Feminism Meets DNA: A Study of an Educational Model for Genetic Counseling Students on the Social and Ethical Issues of Selective Abortion" (Ph.D. diss., Union Institute, Cincinnati, Ohio, 1996).

18. Aubrey Milunsky, ed., *Genetic Disorders and the Fetus* (New York: Plenum Press, 1986).

19. Institute of Medicine, Committee on Assessing Genetic Risks, *Division of Health Sciences Policy Assessing Genetic Risks: Implications for Health and Social Policy* (Washington D.C.: National Academy Press, 1994), p. 153.

20. Diane Beeson and Patricia Jennings, "Prenatal Diagnosis of Fetal Disorders: Ethical, Legal and Social Issues," in *Health Care Ethics: Critical Issues for the 21st Century*, ed. John F. Monagle and David C. Thomasma (Gaithersburg, Md: Aspen Publishers, 1998), pp. 29–44.

21. Robin Gregg, *Pregnancy in a High Tech Age: Paradoxes of Choice* (New York: New York University Press, 1995), p.15.

22. Kaplan, "Prenatal Screening and Its Impact on Persons with Disabilities."

23. Ruth Hubbard, *The Politics of Women's Biology* (Clifton, N.J.: Rutgers University Press, 1990).

24. Dorothy C. Wertz and John C. Fletcher, "A Critique of Some Feminist Challenges to Prenatal Diagnosis," *Journal of Women's Health* 2, no. 2 (1993): 173–88.

25. Shulamith Firestone, *The Dialectic of Sex: The Case for Feminist Revolution* (New York: Bantam, 1971).

26. Marsha Saxton, "Disability Rights and Selective Abortion" in *Abortion Wars: A Half Century of Struggle, 1950–2000*, ed. Rickie Solinger (Berkeley: University of California Press, 1998).

27. Rayna Rapp, "The Power of Positive Diagnosis: Medical and Maternal Discourses on Amniocentesis," in *Childbirth in America: Anthropological Perspectives*, ed. Karen L. Michaelson (South Hadley, Mass.: Bergin & Garvey, 1988), pp. 103–16, at 105.

28. Suneri Thobani, "From Reproduction to Mal[e] Production: Women and Sex Selection Technology," in *Misconceptions: The Social Construction of Choice and the New Reproductive Technologies 1* (Quebec: Voyager Publishing, 1994).

29. Saxton, "Born and Unborn," p. 298.

30. Alysoun J. Reichard, letter in *Insights Into Spina Bifida Newsletter*, March–April (1992): 4.

31. Micheline Mason, "The Breaking of Relationships," *Present Time 99*, no. 1 (1995).

32. Kitty S. Felker, "Controlling the Population: Views of Medicine and Mothers," *Research in Sociology of Health Care* 11 (1994): 25–38.

33. Hubbard, *The Politics of Women's Biology.*

34. Blumberg, "Eugenics vs. Reproductive Choice."

35. Asch, "Reproductive Technology and Disability."

36. Ibid.

37. Blumberg, "Eugenics vs. Reproductive Choice."

38. Diane Beeson and Teresa Doksum, "Family Values and Resistance to Genetic Testing," in *Bioethics in Social Context*, ed. Barry Hoffmaster (Philadelphia, Penn.: Temple University Press, forthcoming).

39. Laurie Block with Jay Alison, producers, "Beyond Affliction: The Disability History Project," in *Talk of the Nation*, National Public Radio, 1998. (Available at: http://www.npr.org/programs/disability/.)

40. Asch, "Reproductive Technology and Disability," p. 186.

EVA FEDER KITTAY WITH LEO KITTAY

On the Expressivity and Ethics of Selective Abortion for Disability: Conversations with My Son[1]

My daughter, Sesha, now twenty-seven years old, lives at home with us. It is sometimes easiest to describe her in the negative, what she is not and *does not do*, for these are the well-defined capacities: she doesn't talk, she walks only with assistance, she is not fully toilet trained, she can't feed herself, and so on. But what she *is* is so much more. She is a beautiful young woman with a winning smile, an affectionate nature, and a love for music, water, food, and the joys of physical affection. I had never before written of her or our relationship and had not used my knowledge of living with a disabled person directly in the service of my professional writing.

I was about to undertake the first of such writings when I was invited by The Hastings Center to participate in a project on prenatal testing for genetic disability. I had wanted my first forays into writing philosophically about my daughter to be about her and what her life means and has meant to me. I had to be persuaded to join the project, for it meant that instead I would have to reflect on the hypothetical of her nonexistence, and worse still, of the hypothetical of having had to choose whether or not she was to come into the world.

During the course of the project, I was asked to consider whether selective abortion for disability "sends a message" that devalues the life of the disabled. When some initial discussions on the question revealed differences between me and my twenty-one-year-old son, Leo, who has an undergraduate degree in philosophy, I chose to write a chapter by conducting a dialogue with my son. We carried on our conversation through e-mail over a period of a few months while my son was working at a ski resort. This article records our dialogue.

From My Diary[2]

I want to get some thoughts on paper before the intensity of this, the first of the four Hastings meetings, evaporates.

10/22. Reflecting now on one participant's memory of when her pediatrician told her that he didn't know if her underweight baby would be all right, and her recalling this as the most terrible moment in her life, I thought what I would answer had someone asked me, "was the moment you learned that Sesha was retarded the most terrible moment in your life." I would have answered, "No." The most terrible moment in my life was when I thought Sesha would die. The next most terrible moment was when my mother insisted (or tried to insist) that Sesha be institutionalized and that I give her up.

I was asked if my mother has changed her attitude toward Sesha, I said, "Yes," and said that had happened because she initially thought that keeping Sesha would ruin my life. She's seen that it hasn't ruined my life.

10/23. Wednesday morning I awoke feeling sore internally, somewhat nauseated, somewhat as if I were recovering from a physical torture. Tuesday evening, as I tried to cram the articles on psychological experiments on metaphors and idioms into my head for the upcoming class I teach, a dam burst and the floodgates came undone. I sobbed— deep, deep sobs from the interior of my soul. I cried, I cried for Sesha. I felt the hurt for her impairments, for the profound limits of the life she could experience, for the multiple aspects of life she could never know or even know that she couldn't know. I wept for Sesha—not for me, not for Jeffrey [my husband], not for Leo, but for her, her sweetness, her limitation, and the pain of knowing what a small aspect of human life she could inhabit. She, my daughter—the child I had brought into the world and the child I had raised and worked to nourish and protect. It is a hurt that doesn't dare to be felt, almost all the time, and it is a hurt that cannot be felt in her sunny presence. But it is there and at moments like post-Hastings it floods in.

Now what is this mysterious pain? Mysterious because who is hurt? I don't think Sesha is aware of her limitation. It is not like the sorrow for another's pain, because pain is felt by its bearer. So do I cry for myself and my expectations of the child I wanted to raise? That is not what those sobs were about—I know—I've had that cry as well. I need to think more about this mystery.

In debriefing Jeffrey and Leo on Tuesday, I spoke of the question posed at the conference: Whether aborting after learning that the fetus is impaired sends the message that a disabled life is not valuable. I asked Leo: If I had aborted a fetus based on disability, would it have sent the same message to him as would the message he'd receive if we had institutionalized Sesha. He said, "No." It wouldn't have sent the same message, but he did think that the message of an abortion would have been that the disabled shouldn't exist. I asked him, "Even in the face of Sesha and our life with her?" He answered that it still would, although it wouldn't be as strong as the message would be if I had aborted an impaired fetus in the circumstance that Sesha was not part of our life.

This surprised both me and Jeffrey. But it is information I must take seriously.

Dear Leo / Dear Mom

EFK's Letter #1

Dearest Leo, I've been asked to address the question of expressivity of a woman's decision to abort a fetus that has been diagnosed with a disability following amniocentesis or other prenatal testing. The question of expressivity is the question of whether such a decision signals the devaluation of the life of a person with disabilities. I thought I would send you excerpts of the letter I sent to Erik Parens when he first invited me to participate in The Hastings Center project. Tell me what you think.

Much love, Mom

Dear Dr. Parens:

I have a severely retarded daughter who also has cerebral palsy. As much as I value my daughter—she, together with my well son, constitute the single greatest joy in my life—I do not agree with the negative appraisal of prenatal testing that you say has been articulated by some members of the disability community.[3] I believe that our society does not provide the conditions that make raising and caring for a severely handicapped child, while otherwise living a full and fulfilling life, possible for most parents, and I am skeptical about the possibilities of any society reaching such an ideal state in the foreseeable future. To undertake to care for a child with severe disabilities has been a difficult and painful course, and yet to abandon such a child to the care of strangers was and continues to be, for both me and my husband, unthinkable. We have garnered tremendous joy and learned more than one can imagine from our daughter, and yet the decision to have a child with such severe and multiple handicaps is not one I could easily endorse. I think it is terribly cruel to burden a couple with the responsibility for a severely handicapped child when prenatal testing can determine in advance the condition of the fetus. Furthermore, as a feminist, I must underscore that the responsibilities normally fall to the mother, as fathers not uncommonly abandon the family with the advent of a severely disabled child, and in most instances the mother provides the daily care.

On the other hand, prenatal testing does not eliminate the tragedy of a child who is severely impaired, for I can also envision the agony of making a decision either to abort or not to abort. Rather, the testing shifts the tragic moment and the decisions to be made. But if the decision is made to go to term, even in the face of the impairment, at least there is a conscious choice, made with the possibility of a truly informed understanding of what such a decision requires of the future parents. Moreover, the availability of the technology to avert some of the consequences of genetic disabilities does not absolve the society at large of mitigating the difficulties of raising and caring for disabled persons. In any case, such is the line that I would take based on my own personal reflections.

Sincerely, Eva Kittay

Leo's Letter #1

Mom,

If we are to take the position that giving birth to a retarded child should be a choice in years to come, that is to say, that all parents will have their fetuses tested, and that the only fetuses to reach full gestation will be those whose parents have expressly chosen to raise them, then we must also be sure that some other changes are made. To begin with, it must be made public that raising a retarded child is equally, albeit differently, fulfilling than raising a normal child. If it ever feels more fulfilling, Mom, it is probably because we just expect it to be less so. Without such increased exposure to those different joys, sheer ignorance will cause the retarded population to become extinct. Anyone with the option would decide to abort a disabled fetus because they would not be able to imagine that the incredible burdens of raising a retarded child could be outweighed by the joys.

Why is this bad? Actually this is a hard argument to make. Social Darwinists might say that this is fine. This is a sort of "preemptive" survival of the fittest argument. However, a survival of the fittest argument is applied to fetuses or children only with difficulty. All babies are weak, and they tax parents and society. It might seem that we would all do better for ourselves in a world without the dependent young, but we all know such a world would be short-lived, if not absurd. Even Social Darwinists must take into account the dependents. They could argue that eventually "normal" children will grow big and strong. But, while many disabled children do not become strong and independent, some "normal" children do not either. This leads me to my next point. The argument you're making draws a major line between normal and retarded children, based on the difficulty of bringing them up. But beware the slippery slope, Mom. Are not all children a burden?

If, someday, we could determine that a fetus will develop into a hyperactive child, or into one with recurring ear infections, will these children's births also have to be expressly willed? Children are a burden. But it is incredibly important to keep making them and tolerating them. No, Mom? No human child is fit for survival without the help of elders. To start drawing the line about how much help they should need is extremely problematic. Some groups of children will start vanishing. And we do not even want a single species of animal to disappear. They are all intrinsically valuable. How do we show others how wonderful it can be to raise a retarded child, and how important and valuable her existence is? It is difficult! Especially if fewer retarded persons are being born.

What kind of message does aborting the retarded send to would-be siblings? I can only guess at this, Mom, because Sesha was born. But here are two different messages I could conceive of receiving:

1. The love my parents have for me is a condition of my being mentally and physically sound, not just of being a child of theirs. Rephrasing this: The only reason my parents want me is that I'm relatively smart and fit.

2. My parents chose me and therefore must really care about me. Again rephrasing: My parents wouldn't just love any child they might have, they love me because I possess the desirable properties or characteristics that make me who I am.

What I am trying to say is that the family starts to seem more like a club, and less like a family. In a club the members are selected based on one characteristic or another. This leads one to believe that if, for some reason, that characteristic is no longer attributable to the individual, or if anyone in the club comes to believe that this characteristic never applied, the membership in the group and the "love" that results can vanish. If a fraternity guy stops playing football well, he might be afraid he would not be wanted in the fraternity anymore. He was aware, after all, that his ability to play football allowed him entry into the club. If a child believes his membership in the family is contingent on not being retarded or otherwise disabled, he might at first value his place in it more highly because it was earned. (This goes hand in hand with the belief that those who are retarded or disabled are worth less. I think immediately of children who use the word "retard" on those they wish to insult and how this insult always seems to be underscored by the desire of the one doing the insulting to differentiate him- or herself from those who are retarded.) But the positive feeling that love has been earned can subside, and the child might instead feel a constant pressure to prove himself to be worthy of his place in the family. He will not view his family's love for him as unconditional love.

I hope these thoughts are helpful.

Love, Leo

EFK's Letter #2

Dearest Leo,

You raise many points, each of which is crucial and each of which I want to explore. My assignment was to consider the expressivity of prenatal testing with respect to disabilities generally, but you speak primarily of retardation. I will move from the one case to the next with some fluidity, although I will try to address the larger perspective of disability.

Parenthetically, let me say that in reading your letter, I realized why I have tended to speak of Sesha as "handicapped" rather than "disabled"— a designation for which I was called to task at the first meeting of The Hastings Center project on prenatal testing. Sesha's disabilities are so severe that in speaking of my child as disabled I think that I will be failing to communicate the particular condition that is Sesha's. That is, to speak of her as disabled puts her in the same category with persons with relatively mild disabilities, disabilities that do not prevent them from leading very independent and productive lives. By whatever our standards for independence and productivity, Sesha doesn't now and never will meet those. I feel more comfortable speaking of Sesha as "seriously disabled," although someone like Stephen Hawking is, by any standards, seriously disabled, and again by any standards is productive, though not independent. I recognize, of course, that "independence" too is a slippery notion because in some very important respects no one is independent.

The Americans with Disabilities Act speaks of a disability as "a physical or mental impairment that substantially limits one or more of the major life activities." Disability activists speak of handicaps as the *consequence* of a disability, where environment limits an individual with a given disability.[4] Many of these handicaps can be overcome with social interventions and modifications of the environment. It takes a social and political will to structure the environment so that it responds to the needs of those who are disabled. But Sesha's condition is such that most of her disabilities remain handicaps even with environmental modifications. In Sesha's case handicap and disability are nearly coincident. I think the distinction is nonetheless a very important one and speaks to the importance of how we express ourselves with respect to disability. I want to make it clear at the outset, that nothing I have to say is meant to deny the importance of how we speak with respect to the disabled. I think that Michael Bérubé is correct when he speaks of how representations of the disabled figure in their treatment and life prospects.[5]

Let me now summarize what I think are your main points. I will then address them.

First, you speak of the need to expose people to the joys and fulfillment of raising a child who is retarded (or severely disabled). Second, you address the possibility that with advances in prenatal testing all cases of retardation (and other serious disabilities) will be eliminated. You then ask us to consider what would be lost if we no longer had persons with mental retardation. Third, you point to the problem of arguing from the difficulties and burdens imposed in raising a seriously disabled child, and the slippery-slope problems connected to such a position. Finally, you address the message that the sibling gets if the family chooses to abort a fetus diagnosed with a disability.

I will start with the second point, the speculation that with advances in prenatal testing all cases of retardation (and other serious disabilities) will be eliminated. Most cases of retardation are not genetically based. Most cases of retardation result from something going wrong during the pregnancy itself or immediately after birth. This was probably the case with Sesha. Such cases could not be picked up in prenatal testing, which depends on examining genetic material. Even if all retardation or other disability were picked up prenatally, there would still be problems that occur during birth and immediately after birth. Then, of course, there is disease and trauma that leave children (and adults) disabled (and sometimes mentally retarded)—some of the children in

Sesha's early intervention program, for example, were casualties of car accidents or gunshot wounds. However, certain populations, such as those with Down syndrome and spina bifida, are likely to be diminished by selective abortion following prenatal testing.

Among fetuses diagnosed with Down syndrome upon results from amniocentesis, it has been said that 90 percent are aborted.[6] However, that figure has to be looked at more carefully. Prenatal testing, although increasingly available, is not available to large numbers of women—and even when it is available, not all women avail themselves of it. So when we get the 90 percent figure, we get the percentage of women who have taken the test, often having already concluded that they would abort if the results are that the child has a severe disability. The literature indicates that the reasons for aborting—whether or not they are well informed—are various and complicated. But we can discuss that later. My point now is only that I do not believe we will ever see a world without persons with disability, without serious disability, without mental retardation, or even without persons with Down syndrome or spina bifida—although there may well be fewer of the latter individuals, and we can certainly talk about the extent to which this would be undesirable.

Now you go on to ask what would be lost if it became the case that populations of significantly retarded persons and others with serious disabilities would be eliminated or significantly diminished through selective abortion. Let us confine this question to the case we know well, mental retardation. And qualify that case to include not all mental retardation, just all mental retardation that occurred before or even at the moment of birth. Well, I agree that the world would be a poorer place without persons with Down syndrome or other sources of retardation, without people like Jamie Bérubé, or Sesha.[7] Our household has been immeasurably enriched by Sesha. People like Jamie, Sesha, or Abbie [our neighbor's little girl], force us to think much more profoundly about what it is to be human, what our obligations are to others, why we have these obligations, what the source of human joy and human sorrow is. I haven't begun to plumb the depths of these questions with respect to Sesha, but they are my measure of the truth, and the value, of all philosophical theories. If they cannot include Sesha in their universe, they are at best incomplete, at worst faulty. And that is not because Sesha is so different from us, or even because she is so much like us, but that at the very core, we are so much like her.[8] We understand so much more about who we are and what moves us, when we see what moves Sesha. I understand so much more of what it is to be a parent and love a child like you, when I know what it is to love Sesha. (But, of course, there are also limits to that. If I kissed you as much as I kissed Sesha, you would have been gone from this house much sooner!)

And yes, Bérubé is right. Sesha's value, like Jamie's value, is not in what they teach us. They are of value in and of themselves, in the same way that you are of value in and of yourself. Perhaps the world is always diminished when that which has value in and of itself, intrinsic value, is lost to the world. Perhaps Wittgenstein was wrong when he wrote, "The world is the totality of facts."[9] Perhaps he ought to have said, "The world is the totality of intrinsic value." Because our world— our lived world—does not consist of facts, but of our understanding of facts and the value those facts have in our life.

Now, if I choose to abort a fetus that would grow into a child with disabilities, have I diminished the world? That is a painfully difficult question. Yet I cannot see that it is necessarily a very different question from the question: "If I abort have I diminished the world?" For to abort any fetus will be to abort a being that would have intrinsic value in this world. Perhaps I deviate from some feminists in thinking that a decision to abort is itself a difficult one; often, psychologically painful and ethically problematic (not necessarily wrong, but not easily right.) Yet I do not deviate from the feminist position in believing that the moral choice must be the woman's to make. I remain convinced that the same must be said, though perhaps with more poignancy (and you will be right to ask why), when the phrase "with disability" is inserted. Let me end this letter for now. Perhaps you want to reply before I move on to the other points. Hope the skiing continues to be wonderful.

All my love, Mom

Leo's Letter #2

In response, Mom:

I think that your summary doesn't highlight my point that it is only through exposure to actual retarded people that anyone can really appreciate how much they contribute to our lives, at least with the most severely "disabled." (Here I don't include Stephen Hawking because we can measure at least some of his value on the same scale that we measure the abled.) Not all disabled people are wonderful, though, and we would not want to put together an argument that is based on that premise. (Bérubé makes this point, his most memorable in my opinion. The story of *My Left Foot* also contains wonderful examples of this, when the disabled protagonist is often less than charming.) We could argue that severely disabled persons are pivotal to our world because they too add to it. Yet evil people, boring people, everyone adds to a culture in some way, and probably in some positive way to boot. No one tries to suggest that we attempt to abort these groups. You are right though, Mom, when you say we will never have the choice, or at least not in the conceivable future, of whether or not to *allow* disabled people to exist. So I don't know if this is an interesting line of argument at all.

Two possibilities might result if there were fewer retarded persons. The first is that fewer people will know what joys can come from being around someone like Sesha. More ignorance, and this is never a good thing. But here is another way of looking at it: a smaller population of this minority would be less threatening socially, politically, and economically (like the single African American child in an all-white school, or the sole Jewish family in a town of Christians). Sometimes it is easier for a minority to prosper under these conditions. But I tend to buy the first result more readily. The second feels too artificial and, in circumstances like these, the danger of stereotyping remains substantial.

You point out that I would want to consider why you say that aborting a disabled child is more poignant. I think it is because it feels, for a moment, to be an easier question than that of aborting a normal child. We fear that it will not get the same weight as the other question; that our system of values weighs the death, or (sorry) the lack of life, of one as less meaningful than the other. I think the way we will have to argue this point is to equate the value of the disabled with that of the normal. Maybe this is obvious to you, but it is not to me. Just as you are arguing that there is no difference between aborting a normal fetus and aborting a fetus with a disability, so we have to say that Sesha is not special—she is equal. Yes, she takes more money, more time, more patience maybe, but these needs should only be an adjustment in the mental figuring of the would-be parents. This is and must be separate from any appraisal of the child's worth.

Love, Leo

EFK Letter #3
Dearest Leo,

I want to respond to the point that people need exposure to disabled persons if they are to understand that the value of disabled people is, as you say, equal to the value of those not impaired. But I want to start by addressing the equally serious matter of the slippery slope argument.

You write that the argument I'm making draws a major line between normal and retarded (and other seriously disabled) children, "in the sense of them being difficult to raise." And while you acknowledge that this may be the case, you argue that we have to watch out for slippery slope arguments that would have us ask if, whenever detectable, other conditions which make a child more difficult to raise would make such conditions eligible for selective abortion as well. So if a child has a condition which would, for example, lead to recurring ear infections, that would be a condition for which parents may choose to abort. And you ask, "Are not all children a burden?"

A slippery slope problem is always hard. One doesn't even need to move into science fiction to face some of these dilemmas, since, although most genetic disorders detectable by prenatal testing today are potentially severely disabling, the tests cannot tell us how severe these disorders will be. In the language of genetics, test results cannot tell us the degree of expressivity of the genetic anomaly. Some conditions, such as Turner's syndrome, can result in a life that is little different from the life of persons without this disorder, except that the individual cannot bear a child.

Then again, women are already free to abort a fetus irrespective of any manifestations of disability. Some disability rights activists, who consider themselves to be feminists and pro-choice, argue against selective abortion on the grounds that there is an important distinction to be made between "aborting *any* fetus" and "aborting *this* fetus." That is, they maintain it is one thing to determine that you do not want to have a child, or to have a child at this time, or even with this man (that is, abortion *simpliciter*), and another to say that you do not want to have this particular child because it manifests such and such a trait (that is to say, selective abortion).[10] Perhaps this is the argument you would like to endorse?

Well then, here is my question. Why do women choose not to have a child? Or not to have a child at a particular time? Or not to have the child of a particular man? Well, for many reasons. But whatever the reasons (unless the decision is that they do it for ideological reasons— for example, "I do not believe it is right to increase the population of an already overcrowded world, but I will adopt and raise a child already born" or "I will not raise cannon fodder for a war state," or "I think this is too evil a world into which to bring new life"), the reason to abort involves some decision not to assume the burden, yes, *burden* of raising a child, now or under the current conditions of the woman's life. For yes, my dearest son, children are a burden.

Children, however, even in terrible times, under terrible conditions, are also a source of the deepest joy and satisfaction imaginable. Even under slavery, many women had their babies and raised them in spite of the near certainty that these children would be slaves, as abject as they themselves. Harriet Jacobs was a young slave woman who wrote of an old slave woman who chided her for shedding tears over her children: "Good old soul! She had gone through the world childless. . . . No sweet little voices had called her mother; she had never pressed her own infants to her heart, with the feeling that even in fetters there was something to live for."[11]

We can add that even where a child is as profoundly disabled as Sesha, there is so much to treasure. Does my assertion that "I think it is terribly cruel to burden a couple . . . with the responsibility for a severely disabled child when prenatal testing can determine in advance the condition of the fetus" belie the value of a child like Sesha, a child who requires very extensive resources, material and emotional, to survive and thrive, whose care is so burdensome, even as it has such special rewards? Children are a burden, but we each engage in numerous decisions about when and how to assume the burden, responsibility, and privilege of raising a child. We choose a mate or defer or decide against marriage (or cohabitation); we engage in or avoid sexual intercourse; we refuse or use contraception; we choose whether or not to take the pregnancy to term, when abortion is a choice; we commit to raising the child, or have family members raise the child temporarily or permanently, or give it up for adoption, and so forth.

Women have been thwarted in making such choices at various points along the way. As in all matters, we make choices but circumstances foil us and we are faced with unanticipated consequences of our actions or the actions of others. At each fork in the road, we have to decide. And when the matter is the care of a child, well or sick, able-bodied or disabled, we have to think if and how we can assume that burden and if the sacrifices required, at this time in our life, under these life circumstances, and given our current estimate of what our capacities are, what resources we can muster (remember how Bérubé quotes Janet declaring to him, "We can do this"), and what this child will require to survive and thrive. Rayna Rapp, an anthropologist studying women who have refused amniocentesis or who sought (or submitted to) it, and then based on a fetal diagnosis decided to abort, writes of the different decisions women make.[12] They are based on the women's perceptions and understandings, both of their circumstances and of the kind and extent of the disability.

The choices are enormously complex. An unmarried woman in her late thirties, whose pregnancy is "an accident" but who is delighted to be pregnant, chooses not to have amniocentesis because she knows that she will not have another opportunity to have a child. She knows she can welcome the child, whether or not there is a disability, as long as she has the support of the church she once left, the Seventh Day Adventists. Another woman, in her forties and with two sons and a daughter, chooses to abort a fetus diagnosed with Down syndrome because she is concerned about having a child with a disability at her advanced age. She fears that she will not live long enough to care for the child as the child ages. She is further concerned that such a major and unending responsibility will fall to her daughter alone. Another family, which includes a cousin with Down syndrome, in learning that the child will have a disability that may result in the child's being "slow," but outwardly normal in physique, decides to bring the pregnancy to term. They would have aborted if the child had Down syndrome because they were witness to the exertions on the part of their family in caring for the physical aspect of the disability of their cousin.

Many of these decisions are inflected by experience of race and the history of racial oppression. One African American family, whose fetus was diagnosed with Down syndrome, was told of farm communities where adults with Down are cared for and where they can participate in farmwork. The father's response was, "Sounds too much like slavery to me." They decided to abort. Many urban white families, in contrast, find the thought of a rural life for their Down syndrome children a comforting notion.

So yes, all children are a burden, and maybe you are quite right to say that to argue for the permissibility of abortion when the fetus is diagnosed with a severe disability on the grounds that a disabled child presents greater burdens is untenable, since the question of where we draw the line is an inevitable and unavoidable one. Perhaps the best rejoinder (if there is one) is to say that because having a child, any child, is a great burden and a great responsibility, our obligation as a society and as prospective parents is to go into that great adventure with our eyes open and with as much forethought as we can muster about whether we can assume that burden in a responsible way. Because a disabled child poses special burdens and responsibilities, a mother and a family must know that it is a challenge that they are prepared and willing to meet, when, that is, foreknowledge of an impairment is an option.

In fact, judging from the accounts that Rayna Rapp has accumulated, it is just such thinking that does, in fact, predominate. These thoughts and these facts have a great bearing on the question of the expressivity of selective abortion, which I would like to sort out in a future letter. But for now, I want to mention two things. First, the stigmatization of the disabled. Doesn't that play a big part in the decision making of families and in their thinking of what they can and cannot handle (and so, argue those opposed to selective abortion, permitting such abortions only reinforces the very stigmatization that is a causal factor in the decision). If so, the question you raise, whether stigmatization increases or decreases with a greater or lesser population of the disabled, is pertinent.

Second, a very important part of the decision making around testing and abortion has to do with the resources that the society itself makes available. For many women, the idea of raising a child with disabilities is weighed against her own ambitions, the ambitions she has for her other children, the prospects for her disabled child when she can no longer care for her. Perhaps it is more appropriate to question how the larger society values or devalues the disabled life—by looking at the resources it withholds or devotes to children with disabilities and their families—than to impute a disregard for the value of the life of disabled persons to the pregnant woman who tests for and aborts a fetus with impairments. I want to talk more about this social dimension later.

Must go now. Call us tonight, and let us know if you are going to remain in Taos.

Much love as always, Mom

EFK's Letter #4

Dearest Leo,

I am now going to try to respond to the first point, which you have been pressing throughout: The need to expose people to the joys and fulfillment of raising a child who is retarded (or severely disabled).

And you want to add, rightly, that not all who are disabled are wonderful nor that anyone who is disabled needs to be wonderful or sweet or whatever positive attribute we want to put in, in order to be valued. Again, I have no argument. I also have no argument with the need to expose all of us to more persons who are disabled, whatever the disability. That educating ourselves and others about differences in abilities, in the rewards of raising a severely disabled child, is crucial if women are to make a well-informed and genuine choice. Perhaps it is especially important to become aware of those who are severely cognitively impaired, and of their presence as being crucial to enriching all of our lives. Increasing such awareness is vitally important if we want those who have had no intimate contact with disability to open their hearts and devote resources to improving the lives of the disabled and their families.

I think few things are as difficult for humans to face as disabilities they themselves do not have; few "differences"—not race, not gender, not sexuality—are as threatening to a person's notion of self. Most characteristics that put us in a relatively privileged position are ones that it is difficult for us to imaginatively transmute. A man won't turn into the devalued woman; the white into the devalued black; the Christian into the devalued Jew. But the able-bodied can in fact turn into the devalued disabled at the next turn in the road. You would think therefore that prejudice against the disabled would be contained, confined, because, after all, at any time "I" could turn into "them." But, instead, such a possibility only increases the prejudice, the avoidance, and the stigma.

I don't know how to get past this, except to show people our love for Sesha, to recognize the difficulty others have with Sesha and simply, by our example, help them past this. But does this mean I have gotten past all my prejudices concerning the disabled? No. The first thing is to recognize them, know where they come from, and then relate to the person and not the disability, except as you can be of service or learn from the person who has had to engage in struggles you yourself have not faced. I think that all the kids in your high school who watched your friend's sister participate in high school performances and athletics will have more understanding about what it means to have the Down syndrome that marked her as "different." They will not automatically respond to a pregnancy with, "If there's Down, we'll abort." But I also am sure that among special education teachers, who have a deeper knowledge of what retardation and severe disability mean, there will be those who decide that, while they value every one of their students, they themselves cannot take on the challenge and responsibility of raising a child with a severe disability. In fact, among the women in one of Rapp's studies, there were two women who were special education teachers who chose to abort.

Rayna Rapp cites another woman, on the other hand, who upon receiving the diagnosis visited a group home for the mentally retarded and chose to bring the pregnancy to term. Knowledge is crucial. I agree. And the time to get informed is not just when you are facing the decision. We need to be active in integrating persons with disabilities into every aspect of life, to seeing that our society devotes the resources that can facilitate such integration and facilitate the lives of disabled persons and their families. Only when this is the case will people have the exposure to children such as Sesha and Jamie Bérubé that will permit prospective parents to truly understand what is involved in raising a child with severe impairments.

However, when that is the case, raising a child like Sesha will also be different. Raising a child with developmental delays and deficits today is so very different than it was when Sesha was born. What was available to Jamie was not available, or only becoming so, when Sesha was born. "Early intervention" was an entirely new concept then. New York City sidewalks didn't have a cut in their curbs that made using a wheelchair so much less cumbersome—an improvement that helps not only the disabled but also every parent who has an infant or toddler in a carriage and every shopper with a shopping cart.

Still, we live in a society without guaranteed health care for every child, much less every adult. How would Janet and Michael Bérubé have paid for Jamie's care if they didn't have generous insurance plans through their employment? During Sesha's recent back operation, her surgeon alone cost $25,000, paid for through the generous health care plan my job provides. One professor I know who has a severely disabled child has an ongoing battle with his university because they set a one-million-dollar limit on her medical insurance, and in the time he has been employed there (their daughter is now an adult), they have already exceeded the limit! So our society has done little to provide for even as basic a need as health care for the disabled. While this is also a difficulty for families with unimpaired children, for families with a disabled child, where medical emergencies are so much more frequent, having to consider cost can be devastating. The story that Bérubé tells of Jamie's early years is about par for the course—for some it's better, for some it's worse.

Then there is the question of the daily care of the severely disabled. There are now some respite programs that provide care for a disabled child so that a parent may have some time away from her disabled child, but these are woefully inadequate, as are the facilities for the severely retarded once they "age out" of the mandated school programs. If we want to speak of acts that are expressive of the devaluation of the life of the disabled, then to direct our attention to selective abortion is to direct us away from acts that are most egregiously expressive of this devaluation. The devaluation of the disabled life is expressed over and over again in the failure of our society to provide adequately for the disabled and their families. A woman who decides that she must make what is an excruciatingly difficult choice to abort (see Rapp's account of her own decision) may not be expressing that devaluation except in a secondary sense. She acts thus because she is faced with Hobson's choice—this or not at all: To raise a child with disabilities with only minimal social support (this) or to abort (not this child at all). It is an act motivated in part, at least, by the difficulties created in a society that fails to accord full humanity and citizenship to the severely disabled.

This isn't to say that in a utopian society not a single fetus will be aborted because of disability. Society can make available certain material resources, but individual emotional resources will vary from family to family. Perhaps some people shouldn't be parents at all, and some shouldn't be parents to disabled children, at least when that situation can be foreseen. Some parents cannot love unconditionally. I have heard parents say that their love for a child was diminished because the child wasn't as smart as they wanted their child to be. How sad for that child, I think. How much more devastating for a child not to get the love and the special love that she needs to sustain the illnesses, the pain, the loneliness that so often accompany a disability.

People who come into our house say Sesha is lucky to have parents who love her so much. And our standard response is that we are lucky to have Sesha whom we can love so much. But, in truth, they are right. As lovable as Sesha is, not every family may have allowed themselves to find out how wonderful she is. It's hard to imagine since she touches your soul so, but I just know it's true. To be able to love her so, to find it hard to imagine that anyone couldn't love her so, is to be touched by a bit of grace, and it has been our good fortune to be granted that grace. But what would her life be like if she didn't have people to love her as we do?

That, my dear, is the most painful thought—the thought of what happens to her when we are no longer around. No, these are things no one has any right to tell a family—no one has a right to say to a family: You must take this on and if you don't you are immoral, you don't value a life that is disabled.

Finally, I am ready to address some of your concerns as a sibling about the expressivity of the act of abortion in the case of disability. I'll write this tonight and tomorrow and e-mail you tomorrow night.

Love, Mom

EFK's Letter #5

Dearest Leo,

You ask, "What kind of message does aborting the retarded send to would-be siblings?" And you say that there are two possibilities to consider. The first is a negative message, that parental love is conditioned on "soundness" and accomplishment, or as you put it: "The love my parents have for me is a condition of my being mentally and physically sound, not just of being a child of theirs." And you provide an alternative formulation of this idea, that "the only reason my parents want me is that I'm relatively smart and fit." I see your alternative formulation as one that has to do not with the infant when born (a time when we cannot assess intelligence or athletic ability, but only good health and absence of anomalies) but has rather to do with the child's realization of the potential that good health and soundness make available.

The other possible message seems at first more positive, but contains a hidden explosive that can shatter a child's sense of well-being. This is a very disturbing message that we need to explore. You suggest that the message received might go something like this: "My parents chose me and therefore must really care about me." Or, "My parents wouldn't just love any child they might have, they love me because I possess the desirable properties or characteristics that make me who I am." But this seemingly positive message becomes just another statement of a conditioned love. For then, as you say, "the family starts to seem more like a club, and less like a family," in which the members are selected based on some desirable features. But if a person starts to fall short of the desirable characteristics, she knows that she is no longer welcome in the club. In a family, this would lead a child to feel "that if I don't toe the line and exhibit the desirable characteristics, I'll no longer be valued." You continue: "If a child believes his membership in the family is contingent on not being retarded or otherwise disabled, he might at first value his place in it more highly because it was *earned* . . . . But the positive feeling that love has been earned can subside, and the child might instead feel a constant pressure to prove himself to be worthy of his place in the family. He will not view his family's love for him as unconditional love." We need to address these two possibilities separately.

First, however, we need to think a bit about what it means to send a message. You are asking about the kind of message the act of selective abortion based on disability sends to the sibling. Opponents of this sort of selective abortion ask, "What kind of message does it send to society about the value of the life of persons with disabilities?" Many opponents of selective abortion (see, for example, Saxton[13]) claim that something is communicated in the decision to abort selectively for disability— that we say we want a child, but we do not want this child. They ask us to consider the claim that aborting that life sends the message that a disabled life is not one worth living; very much the way feminists have claimed that selective abortion for gender, which is generally a choice against having a girl, is a statement devaluing the life of females. They ask us furthermore to consider the impact of this sort of message on those who are female, in the one instance, and disabled, in the other instance. In focusing on the message that the sibling receives, your point is more specific, yet some of the considerations are the same. Some others, I'll try to show, are different.

The first thing we have to consider is whether the act of selective abortion is a "*saying.*" Is it an act of communication at all? What are we committing ourselves to when we claim that it is? Can we base an ethical evaluation of the act of selective abortion on the claim that the message sent is a devaluation of the life of those possessing the properties that determined the choice to abort?

When we say things, we are generally thought to mean what we say. I say, "It is raining," and mean by it that it's raining. Sometimes we speak of something meaning something when there is no one who is speaking, or when someone is not speaking but doing something. For example, we can say that lightning means thunder, or that a bear's paw prints mean that a bear has been here recently. Philosopher of language H. P. Grice makes the distinction between "natural meaning," as in "thunder means lightning," and "nonnatural meaning," as in *U* meant something by *uttering x*. Now if we have an agent that is capable of meaning something, then we can ask what that agent meant by her action, even if that action was not a piece of verbal behavior. Let's say this is a case in which *U* meant something, by *doing a*. So, if the footprints are those of a person and not of a bear, we might wonder if the person meant something by leaving those footprints. But the person may have meant nothing at all by leaving footprints. In that case, we can legitimately conclude nothing more from those footprints than what we can from a bear's prints. Nonetheless, when we have an agent who has intentions we are tempted to ask about a given act *a* if *U* meant something by act *a*.

Now if we take the term "utterance" to include acting as well as saying, then the utterance *x* could be an action. Grice goes on to analyze nonnatural meaning of utterances as follows:

"*U* meant something by uttering *x*" is true if and only if:

(1) *U* intended, by uttering *x*, to induce a certain response in *A*

(2) *U* intended *A* to recognize, at least in part from the utterance of *x*, that *U* intended to produce that response

(3) *U* intended the fulfillment of the intention mentioned in (2) to be at least in part *A*'s reason for fulfilling the intention mentioned in (1).[14]

So if in uttering the words "It is raining," *U* intended *A* to believe that it is raining (condition 1), and *U* intended *A* to recognize that *U* intended *A* to believe that it is raining, at least in part from *U*'s utterance "It is raining" (condition 2), and finally that *U* intended *A* to believe that it is raining because of *A*'s recognition that that is what *U* intended (condition 3), then we can say that *U* meant that it is raining when he said it is raining. Otherwise, for example, *U* could simply have been reading a script in which the words "It is raining" appeared. In other words, for *U* to mean something by the utterance *x*, *U* must have the intention of communicating that something, of so communicating by that very utterance, and to be communicating to someone who would understand both the utterance and the intention with which it was uttered. Otherwise it falls short of nonnatural meaning.

Now when we say that an action "sends a message," do we mean that this is a communication, and so a form of nonnatural meaning, or do we mean that it is something that has meaning in the sense that thunder means lightning. Well, if we are going to say that an action is unethical or immoral because it sends a certain message, I take it we mean that the action has meaning in the nonnatural sense, for if the action is to be either moral or immoral then it must be carried out by those who intentionally carry it out. Can we say of those who choose abortion following a diagnosis of fetal anomaly that they mean that the life of the disabled is not worth living? Not in the Gricean sense of nonnatural meaning. The utterer, in this case the woman, would have to intend to induce in another the belief that the life of the disabled is not worth living; she would have to intend to communicate this, in part at least, by aborting her impaired fetus; and she would have to intend her interlocutor to believe that she intended to produce that belief, in part at least, by aborting her impaired fetus. I don't think we need dwell on this point further than to note that none of those conditions are met in the case of most women who abort a fetus with disabilities.

Nonetheless, someone could deduce from this situation a conclusion: that a woman aborting a fetus (because it has an extra 21st chromosome, for instance) doesn't value the life of one with Down syndrome. But this would be a conclusion drawn not from a message sent but something inferred from an action taken. And then we could ask, are we correct in concluding this? Well, we'd have to ask the woman why she chose to abort and then, if Rapp's studies are indicative, we can see that there are many reasons women abort under these circumstances, few of which are that they believe that disabled persons shouldn't have the opportunity to live a life.

One could argue that the woman does not deny that she is aborting the fetus *because* it has this anomaly, so why then can we not conclude that her action itself bespeaks a devaluation of the life of the disabled— regardless of what else she says? Because this causal "because" need not express the *meaning* of the act. Let us say, for example, that I have ten dollars to spare today, and that I tell you that I am going to the movies because I have ten dollars to spare. However, this does not allow you to conclude that what it means to me to have a spare ten dollars is that I go to the movies.

Perhaps using the Gricean model puts too strong a set of constraints on what we can call a communication. Communication, nonnatural meaning, is perhaps too tightly connected to intentional acts. Is there another model? The great early modern linguist Roman Jakobson spoke about what it means to send a message or to communicate something in our use of semiotic systems.[15] Perhaps we can adapt his analysis to the case of communicating by an action. He identified six elements described in a communication. The first requirement is an addresser or speaker. The second is an addressee. A third is an open channel of communication between the addresser and addressee. When, for example, we establish eye contact with a potential interlocutor, we open a channel for communication. The fourth requirement is a "message" (we'll call it an "utterance") that the addresser sends to the addressee. Fifth, we need the "context" in which the message was sent, and sixth, we need a "code"—that is, a medium in which the message is encoded and which is understood by both the addresser and the addressee. The code, as Jakobson understood it, is normally a language or some system of signs (e.g., semaphores). If we want to include complex acts such as an abortion, we will need to consider the code as a set of conventions or social practices that are widely shared and by means of which such acts carry a commonly understood meaning.

While on a Gricean account we cannot say that an act of selective abortion sends a message, if we mean by that "means something in a nonnatural sense," we might find this looser notion of communication—one that does not rely so heavily on the intention of the addresser—a more apt model. But, in Jakobson's model, what we have is at best (as people in information theory would say) a "degraded" form of communication.[16] If selective abortion is an act of communication in which the message arrives in a degraded form, then I fail to see how it can provide grounds for any ethical judgments or moral (much less legal) prescriptions.

First, in the case of selective abortion, we identify the addresser as the woman who decides to abort the fetus and the addressee as society in general (alternatively, the disabled community). Now, it is not clear that a contact is ever established between addressee and addresser. A woman rarely says: "Listen up, world. I am having an abortion based on a diagnosis of fetal abnormality and I am about to tell you why I choose to abort a fetus with such an abnormality." (There are, of course, exceptions.[17]) When we learn that someone had such an abortion, we may not be in a position to query that decision, and the woman may not be in a position to query the addressee about the correctness of the "message" received.

Second, there is no established code by which to decipher the "meaning" of such an act. That is, there is no established code or convention or practice to which both addressee and addresser can appeal when determining the meaning of that act. When I tell you, "It is raining," you (if you speak English) know how to understand that statement, and I know that you know. There is a common code that allows us to communicate a statement such as that. But such codes are not always available. If, given the conventions of foot apparel, I wear one green sock and one blue sock, you don't know how to interpret that action. Perhaps I dressed before dawn in the dim light and failed to discern the colors of my socks. Perhaps I lacked a clean pair of matching socks. Perhaps I was engaging in a flight of fancy. Or costumed myself for a play. Or dressed according to a preestablished code, thereby signaling to a comrade the start of a revolution.

The failure to discern a univocal—or indeed any—meaning of the act of selective abortion partakes of the ambiguity of all those actions which fail to be situated in practices that have an agreed upon meaning. (The same may be said about abortion itself, an act whose meaning remains contested.) I may already spend my life caring for persons with disabilities. I may have decided to adopt a retarded child once I have health insurance. I may feel that I can take on the care of a healthy child now, but a disabled child only at a later time in my life. Or I may think that even a limp makes life not worth living. There is no established code by which you can interpret my action and so understand what my abortion means to me, nor by which I can discern what my action might mean to you.

Third, we have to consider the extent to which the context influences the act of communication. If I am in a drought-stricken area, the statement "It's started to rain" carries an emotional charge very different from one carried by the same utterance in a flood-torn area. Context will affect the cognitive meaning or emotive charge of an utterance. The newspaper headline announcing the crash of Hemingway's plane, when the writer was assumed dead, ran: "Hemingway Lost in Africa." When it was learned that he was still alive but missing, the headline remained, but with a different meaning.[18] The less developed the code, the more ambiguity the code itself permits, the more the context will determine meaning. Because codes concerning acts of abortion and selective abortion are so underdeveloped and so contested, context is virtually, though not entirely, determinative. In the case of selective abortion, the context includes both the particulars of the individual lives affected by the decision and the larger social setting in which the decision is made. Most contestations over this new technology and the decisions people make with it are struggles over how to understand and determine the context that, in turn, contributes to the meaning of the act. For many in the disability community, the context is one in which disability is stigmatized and persons with disabilities are devalued. That context, they argue, inevitably means that we interpret the act of selective abortion as another sign of the devaluation of a disabled life. That is to say, they believe society in general (the addressee) interprets the "utterance" of selective abortion in the context of the stigmatization of disability and that the message sent is that a child with disabilities will not be welcomed into a family. Therefore, they argue that the act of communication that results is that the disabled life is not worth living.

In response, we have to ask, "If we alter the context, is it the same message or not?" If we utter, "It's raining," to folks in a sodden Seattle and make them more miserable, is it the utterance (and what that utterance refers to, the fact that it is raining) or the context in which it is uttered that is the source of the misery? If we issue the same utterance to drought-stricken East Africa, are we uttering a message that makes people miserable? No.

If we are concerned with the devaluation of the life of the disabled (and that is something we should each be concerned about, regardless of whether we ourselves are disabled or have a disabled family member or if disability has never personally touched our lives), then we need to fix on, and fix, the context, not the utterance. Still, you might argue, to abort fetuses with disabilities is itself to further devalue the disabled. But that can't be the reply, because that is exactly what is at issue. What I will grant is that it is reasonable to infer that if many persons choose to abort fetuses with a particular characteristic, it is fair to make a hypothesis that those characteristics are devalued. But that is again, at best, a conclusion hypothesized about the causal factors that lead to the abortion and not a message that is sent out by the abortion. Only further questioning of actual motives can establish whether this woman aborted because she devalues disabled life. But even so, we should not confuse a message sent with a causal determinant of an action.

Now you may want to respond, "Look, Mom, it is only through exposure to actual retarded people that anyone can really appreciate how much they contribute." With selective abortion, "fewer people will know what joys can come from being around someone like Sesha. More ignorance, and this is never a good thing."

But if we could fix those conditions in utero, if we could have Sesha without the retardation, would we balk, even for one moment? And maybe, probably, Sesha wouldn't have the incredible sweetness she now has, a sweetness that is perhaps, in part, the result of her not encountering conditions that most of us encounter—an innocence of intentional evil, of senseless nastiness and stupidity that humans are capable of, of corrosive ambition, of frustrated dreams, of biting competition, and so on. What of it? Would we hesitate one moment to exchange her for a Sesha with all her mental faculties intact. Although every day I lay eyes on her, Sesha melts my heart with the purity of her joy, her laughter, I would not hesitate. Truly, I wouldn't hesitate.

Sesha's condition isn't just a difference, only it is that too. Sesha's condition is an impairment. If I can contemplate a Sesha without her impairments, or another child in her place, does this mean that I think that a disabled life is not worth living—that Sesha's life is not worth living? Absolutely not.

My life is worth living. Nonetheless there are conditions, ones that those I love would have rejoiced in, under which I would not have been born. Had my mother left Poland before the war and been spared the horrors of Auschwitz, I would not have been born. Does this mean that I cannot wish with all my heart that she had married the man from Toronto who had betrothed her and sent her the papers to leave Poland before the war? The fact that she didn't, of course, says nothing about the value she placed on my life. She could know nothing of what that life would have been like. But if she had had a crystal ball, and had foreseen it all—yet had no idea of what awaited her if she went off with the beau from Toronto—foreseen both surviving Auschwitz and me and would still have chosen Toronto, could I blame her? Could I say she devalued my life—could I blame her for not choosing this child? But these are fantasies, and she could never know.

We can know no more of the life we do not conceive or the life we choose to abort. Would I have aborted Sesha if I had known of her condition? I don't know. It might depend on the level of attachment I felt at the time I learned that the fetus had some problem. If it was already my child in my heart and mind, I may not have. I may have thought just as I did once Sesha was born—our own version of Janet Lyon's "We can handle this."[19] But maybe that is not what I would have said. Maybe I would have investigated further, learned something of the lives of the retarded. Our decision (because *both* Dad and I would make this decision) may well have depended on where our investigation led us: to a home like the Bérubés' or to a day treatment program like the one Sesha is currently in? These considerations reinforce some of the powerful points Bérubé makes with respect to the representation of the disabled. But it is also a confirmation of what I have wanted to underscore—namely the importance of the commitment of the society in general to the disabled.

So maybe we would have decided that there is joy enough for us here, and that we can make a good life for ourselves and our child. Maybe, and it is hard to think of it, I would have aborted. And we would never know Sesha. And that loss seems unimaginable. But I may have given birth to another child, whose nonexistence would seem equally unfathomable, and I would have wondered about the child I aborted. I would have stopped every time I saw a mentally retarded child or adult and wondered, with tears in my eyes. Just as now, with tears in my eyes, I think about the young woman of twenty-seven who might be a graduate student like my wonderful graduate students, or be thinking about marriage, or be out on the ski slopes with you. In each case there is a loss. It is a human tragedy.

No one can judge the choices of another in these cases based on what is at best a degraded form of communication. No one can make a moral evaluation based on this incomplete communicative situation. There is no singular utterance enunciated through a clear channel in an accepted code, in a nonambiguous context. It is a moral wrong to utter the word "nigger" in speaking of or to a person of African descent. It is a moral wrong to produce degrading and demeaning portrayals of women as sex toys for men. It is a moral wrong to reduce services for the disabled poor (doubly wrong). All these send vile messages that some people do not possess the value that others possess.

But to selectively abort because the fetus I carry is likely to develop into a child with profound disabilities does not send any clear and unambiguous message. And the morality of that choice must be weighed in the conscience of the woman who makes that choice. She alone can know just what her act meant and if it was carried out as a consequence of moral sloth and uncaring, or through a responsible choice.

Now, at last, we get to your point about the message that the sibling receives. First, let's consider this situation of communication with the six factors that Jakobson delineates. The situation here is quite different than that of an undefined audience, "society in general." Why? First, because in this case one can establish that channels of communication are open, and second, because one can adopt a code by which to interpret this utterance. Furthermore, we can delimit the context, or at least specify the relevant contextual features. Put more simply, one can discuss the matter through an exchange, not unlike the exchange you and I are now having. I wonder, however, if such exchanges do take place. Were I an empirical scientist, I would like to conduct a study in which to ask this question. But I think it is a parental duty to explain to one's child why one makes, or why one has made, such a decision. Otherwise, all sorts of misinterpreted, unintended, or garbled messages are an inevitable outcome.

Let's take the first scenario you envision. The sibling assumes that the parent's love for him is conditioned on his sound mind and body and is concerned that if anything should happen to him that would cause him to be disabled, the parent would want to discard him, as, once before, she had aborted his disabled unborn sibling. The first distinction I would want to put into place is the distinction between a born child, and the commitment a parent has to a child that has been born, and an unborn fetus. I believe that the concern you raise is a concern a child might raise in the case of any abortion. If the reason for the abortion is "I can't afford another one," a child may wonder, "What if we have less money than we have now? Will my parents want to be rid of me, too?" If the reason is, "I have my hands full with the children I have now," the child may wonder, "If I'm more trouble than I am now, will my parents want to be rid of me, too?" I think you see how it can go.

Remember, without discussion, with only the act of the abortion itself, we have not a true act of communication but a very degraded one. Once we have the distinction between the commitment to the born child and the tentative commitment to the unborn fetus, we are able to develop other features of the code and the context. We can make the case that the decision to abort was in significant measure a question of the parent's commitment to children already born, or to the other children the parents were likely to have. If there is a decision to bring the fetus to term, there is also considerable parental input that is demanded. A child may view any sibling as a rival, but a sibling that requires the additional attention a disabled child does may raise the level of resentment and jealousy. It is the job of the parent to open the channels of communication, to explain the decision (or the fate, as the case may be), and to integrate the normal and disabled siblings into one cohesive, caring family.

Too often we think that the message is obvious. We needn't check with our addressee if the intended message has been received. Your dad and I thought that it was obvious that our love for Sesha would give you the clear message that we love our children, unconditionally, irrespective of achievement. You might have gotten the unconditional part, but I'm not so sure about the "irrespective of achievement" part. Instead, you thought the message was that you had to compensate for the fact that Sesha would never have accomplishments, as those are normally tallied. Because we presumed the message was clear, we never made the effort to be certain that it was being received. (How dangerous to make moral judgments based on such bad communication channels.) I recall how as a four-year-old you mistook our affectionate responses to Sesha as a sign that we loved you less. We had to explain to you that Sesha understands only kisses and hugs—it is our sole means of communicating with her—whereas we could play and talk with you. Again, how careful we have to be in explaining our messages.

Now let's move to the second case: the sibling who first bathes in the love garnered for his particular characteristics and then comes to fear that such love is too unstable—that the family based on such love is more like a club than like a family. Here too one can invoke the distinction between commitment to the unborn and commitment to the born. But here I think the important point is that a family must not be like a club, whose membership is based on a set of desirable features. That is not how a family nurtures. We need a place where love is unconditional, where our mistakes are forgiven, where our imperfections are accepted and even cherished. We need such a place if we are to be emotionally whole. If the "message" that selective abortion for disability sends is that a disabled child is of less value, then it cuts into the sanctity of such a space and is corrosive. So here we have to be very clear. But once again, clarity comes from how we treat those with disabilities and not with a family's (and especially a woman's) decision to bring a fetus, any fetus, or this fetus to term. If we treat persons with disabilities with care and respect; if we attend to need when we see it and listen to the voices of those who wish to speak; if we treat all persons as moral equals, irrespective of ability or accomplishment; and if a household reflects this in all that it undertakes, then no child should think that it is valued merely for having certain desirable traits. If a child comes into a household where these values predominate, then the child comes into a home that welcomes her for the person she is, not for the traits that she bears. And if the message isn't getting through, then it's time to clear the channels of noise.

I love both you and Sesha with all my heart. Mom.

Leo's Letter #3

Mom,

Yes, the lines of communication must be open. And this is incredibly difficult. As open and honest as our family is, only in my twenty-first year have you and Dad and I discussed at any length many of the more painful, difficult aspects of having Sesha in the family. I have not even allowed a healthy dialogue to take place in my own head about Sesha until recently. Tremendous issues of anger and guilt have been lurking within me regarding Sesha, and coming to grips with them has been a big part of my postcollege soul searching. You said that the act of aborting a disabled fetus will convey a harmful message of conditional love to the sibling unless the following condition is met: "If we treat persons with disability with care and respect; if we attend to need when we see it and listen to the voices of those who wish to speak; if we treat all persons as moral equals, irrespective of ability or accomplishment; and if a household reflects this in all that it undertakes, then no child should think that it is valued only for having certain desirable traits."

There is only one problem, Mom. No child is consistently under the impression that the above condition is the case. In fact, no person for that matter thinks that his or her family is always treating him or her in such a way all the time. Even a family as wonderful as ours, *n'est-ce pas?* This passage does help me answer one thought that has been plaguing me throughout our discussions. Even though you did not abort Sesha, I remember experiencing every feeling that we have discussed a would-be sibling goes through as a result of a selective abortion. Just because you had Sesha and raised both of us honestly, better than I can imagine, I still managed to feel quite frequently and strongly throughout childhood, and even during many of my most formative moments, that Dad's and your love for me is a condition of my physical and mental abilities. Without these, I often felt, on some level, that I would not command your love and respect.

But when you break down the manner in which these messages get communicated in the case of an abortion, it helps me to see how this message could have been communicated so counterintuitively in the case of the elected birth, Sesha. It was in those moments in my upbringing when I felt treated as more than equal, when I got more attention than Sesha, or alternatively when I did not feel treated with the same care and respect as Sesha, that my young mind sometimes interpreted this nonequal treatment in terms of the inequalities and not the equalities. I thought I must be getting more attention than her because I can do more, or that I was getting less because she needed more. I think to some extent this phenomenon exists between all siblings, even between a child and a parent's career, between a child and the other spouse, whenever a parent's energies have to be distributed fairly. Anytime a child feels his status change, he is constantly searching for the cause of the change. Only a completely open line of communication continually sending a message of equally high value to all can truly do away with a mixed message. So, yes, Mom, I think you have hit on the secret of how not to send the wrong message to one's children when one decides to abort. I think it also happens to be a secret of parenting in general.

This leads me to my final thought. Let me say I do fear that allowing abortion based on prenatal screening will result in many abortions that are decided more quickly and based on less information than is ideal. Some women will even elect to have an abortion because they think less of disabled people, or because they want their children to be perfect. But, and this is my thought, parents make lousy decisions all the time. Some spend their money irresponsibly, some raise their kids to think they're worthless, others raise their kids to think they're worth more than everyone else, some beat their children. While sometimes I think it would be great to make laws that put a stop to such behavior, I know that in general that would not be a good idea. To insist that parents have children they are not thrilled about doesn't strike me as the best way to give children a great start in life. After all, the great burden of deciding whether or not to abort the child is small compared to the burden of raising the child. And if someone is not going to handle the decision responsibly, I would hate to see how they would handle the child.

Might they become thrilled before the nine months are up? Might having the child shatter their prejudice against the disabled? Yes, but it also could take longer. And what messages would be sent out meanwhile?

Love, Leo

NOTES

1. This chapter was prepared for The Hastings Center project, "Prenatal Genetic Testing for Genetic Disability," funded by the National Center for Human Genome Research of the National Institutes of Health, grant 1-R01-HG116801A2. It is a revised version of a chapter in *Norms and Values: Essays on the Work of Virginia Held*, ed. Joram G. Haber and Mark S. Halfton (Lanham, Md.: Rowman and Littlefield, 1998).

2. These diary entries were written prior to the correspondence that follows them.

3. Erik Parens, personal correspondence to Eva Feder Kittay, Briarcliff Manor, N.Y., May 21, 1996.

4. Adrienne Asch, "Reproductive Technology and Disability" in *Reproductive Laws for the 1990's*, ed. Sherill Cohen and Nadine Taub (Clifton, N.J.: Humana Press, 1988), pp. 69–124.

5. Michael Bérubé, *Life as We Know It* (New York: Pantheon Books, 1996).

6. Bérubé, *Life as We Know It*, p. 76.

7. Bérubé, *Life as We Know It*.

8. See Elizabeth Spelman, *Inessential Woman: Problems of Exclusion in Feminist Thought* (New York: Beacon Press, 1988), who speaks of the practice of saying about some people who are viewed as Other "but they are just like us" as "boomerang perception," one in which we only can see the other as "just like us," and never see ourselves as "just like them."

9. Ludwig Wittgenstein, *Tractatus Logico-Philosophicus* (London: Routledge & Kegan Paul, 1921).

10. Marsha Saxton, "Why Members of the Disability Community Oppose Prenatal Screening and Selective Abortion," in this volume; and Adrienne Asch and Gail Geller, "Feminism, Bioethics, and Genetics," in *Feminism and Bioethics: Beyond Reproduction*, ed. Susan Wolf (New York: Oxford University Press, 1996), pp. 318–50.

11. Harriet Jacobs, "Incidents in the Life of a Slave Girl: Written By Herself," in *The Classic Slave Narratives*, ed. Henry Louis Gates (1861; reprint, New York: Penguin, 1987), pp. 333–513, at p. 427.

12. Rayna Rapp, "The Ethics of Choice: After My Amniocentesis, Mike and I Faced the Toughest Decision of Our Lives," *Ms. Magazine* April (1984): 97–100; "The Power of 'Positive' Diagnosis: Medical and Maternal Discourses in Amniocentesis," in *Childbirth in America: Anthropological Perspectives*, ed. Karen Michaelson (South Hadley, Mass.: Bergin & Garvey, 1988), pp. 103–16; "Women's Responses to Prenatal Diagnosis: A Sociocultural Perspective on Diversity," in *Women and Prenatal Testing: Facing the Challenges of Genetic Technology*, ed. Karen H. Rothenberg and Elizabeth J. Thomson (Columbus: Ohio State University Press, 1994), pp. 219–33; "Refusing Prenatal Diagnosis: The Uneven Meanings of Bioscience in a Multicultural World," in *Science, Technology & Human Values* 23 (1998): 45–71; and "Risky Business: Genetic Counseling in a Shifting World," in *Articulating Hidden Histories*, ed. Rayna Rapp and Jane Schneider (Berkeley: University of California Press, 1995), pp. 173–89.

13. Marsha Saxton, "Disability Rights and Selective Abortion," in *Abortion Wars: A Half Century of Struggle, 1950–2000*, ed. Rickie Solinger (Berkeley: University of California Press, 1997), pp. 374–95.

14. Paul H. Grice, "Utterer's Meaning and Intentions," *Philosophical Review* 78 (1969): 147–77, at 153.

15. Roman Jakobson, "Linguistique et poétique," in *Essais de linguistique générale*, ed. Roman Jakobson (Paris: Edition de Minuit, 1963), pp. 209–48.

16. For an argument that comes to a similar conclusion on Wittgensteinian grounds, see James Lindemann Nelson, "The Meaning of the Act: Reflections on the Expressive Force of Reproductive Decision Making and Policies," in this volume.

17. Rapp, "The Ethics of Choice."

18. Donald Davidson, "What Metaphors Mean," in *Inquiries into Truth and Interpretation*, ed. Donald Davidson (Oxford: Oxford University Press, 1984); and Eva F. Kittay, *Metaphor: Its Cognitive Force and Linguistic Structure* (Oxford: Oxford University Press, 1987).

19. Bérubé, *Life as We Know It*.

JAMES LINDEMANN NELSON

The Meaning of the Act: Reflections on the Expressive Force of Reproductive Decision Making and Policies[1]

As these words are written in the early spring of 2000, on a clement morning in Columbia, South Carolina, three flags are fluttering colorfully over the dome of the State House—the Stars and Stripes; the palm and crescent moon of South Carolina; and the flag of the Confederate States of America, the Stars and Bars.

The presence or absence of a piece of colored cloth on a pole might seem irrelevant to the central concerns of state government— the education, health, safety and welfare of its citizens. But whether or not that third flag flies inspires heated demonstrations, numerous petitions, both action and pointed inaction in the State Senate and House of Representatives, and a good deal of bitterness. For some South Carolinians, the flag's display duly honors a rich heritage for which their ancestors fought and died. For others, it sends the despicable message that killing and dying in the defense of slavery is a heritage worth honoring.

The kind of dispute illustrated by flying the Stars and Bars over the State House is not rare. Human actions can express meanings, as well as have causal consequences, and people often care deeply about what those meanings are. Another site where the meaning of particular acts has become hotly contested is preconception and especially prenatal testing for genetic and chromosomal conditions that may give rise to disabilities. Several disability theorists and activists claim that the use of medical technologies to detect flaws in parental genes or fetuses, leading to the avoidance of conception or abortion, is just a way of saying "we don't want your kind here"—a sort of technologized medium for a kind of hate speech. The philosopher and disabilities theorist Susan

Wendell makes the point in virtually these terms when she says "the widespread use of selective abortion to reduce the number of people born with disabilities . . . sends a message to children and adults with disabilities, especially people who have genetic or prenatal disabilities, that 'we do not want any more like you.' "[2] Laura Hershey puts a similar point just as bluntly: "I believe the choice to abort a disabled fetus represents a rejection of children who have disabilities."[3]

In this chapter, I want to consider whether Hershey, Wendell, and others of like mind are correct in construing efforts to avoid the birth of such children as expressing a lack of respect for people with disabilities. This will involve paying fairly close attention to what has to be the case for nonlinguistic behavior to express a particular message—closer attention than typically has been paid by those who have raised this concern. Amniocentesis is a different sort of deed than is hoisting a banner; abortions are not flags. The semantic force of diagnostic tests and pregnancy termination is not well defined within our shared symbol systems, and whether one can be justified in attributing to such practices clear messages, disrespectful or not, needs careful consideration.

A characteristically authoritative paper by Allen Buchanan, "Choosing Who Will Be Disabled: Genetic Intervention and the Morality of Inclusion," is a good place to start, largely because it offers a fairly rigorous account of what has to be the case for an action to express a meaning.[4]

Buchanan calls the view that genetic testing and abortion send negative messages the "expressivist objection." He puts it like so:

> [T]he commitment to developing modes of intervention to correct, ameliorate or prevent genetic defects expresses (and presupposes) negative, extremely damaging judgments about the value of disabled persons.[5]

Buchanan draws this version of the objection from the work of the "radical disabilities rights position," particularly as developed in an issues paper by the International League of Societies for Persons with Mental Handicaps.[6] He is unimpressed with it, and in this formulation, that's hardly surprising. As it stands, it suggests that developing even the simplest intervention to cure or prevent even the most horrendous disease is morally dubious, and surely that comes close to a *reductio ad absurdum*. But the objection takes on much more force if it is restricted to interventions which, rather than preventing, curing, or ameliorating an individual's disease, prevent or eliminate a diseased individual. As Adrienne Asch and Gail Gellner put it, "What differentiates preventing disability by abortion from preventing it by immunization is that the abortion indicates that the disability makes the child unacceptable."[7] Buchanan, however, remains unswayed even by this version of the objection, raising what is clearly a key question: just how does an abortion "indicate" that the child is unacceptable?

As he sees it, the claim that an action conveys a meaning only has force if the actors involved meet two conditions. The first concerns the content of their beliefs. In order for an action to convey a certain meaning, the actor must have the beliefs purportedly expressed by the action. Thus, a person deciding to avoid the birth of a baby with disabilities must believe that life with the disabilities in question would not be worth living, or that only "perfect individuals" (i.e., those without disabilities) should be born. The second condition is that those beliefs must play a certain role in a person's decision making. In the case of a person who avoids having children she expects might have disabilities, her decision must either be motivated by such beliefs, or cannot be a rational decision absent her accepting such convictions.

But, as Buchanan points out, those who choose to abort or to avoid procreation as a result of prenatal or preconception testing simply do not meet this two-part test. To argue convincingly that these actions convey such a negative meaning, objectors would have to show that people making these decisions believe that disabled people lead lives not worth living, and are motivated by that belief. Claiming that people who make such decisions must necessarily have such beliefs and motivations, however, just will not hold up; many motivations can be imagined for trying to avoid the birth of a baby with disabilities, and many reasons can be provided for such action that do not involve either the belief that a life with disabilities is not worth living, or that only the "perfect" should be born. One may, for example, "simply wish to be spared avoidable and serious strains on one's marriage or on one's family" or "one may wish to avoid putting additional pressure on limited social resources to support disabled individuals."[8]

Buchanan thinks that people are perfectly at liberty to avoid having children on such motivations, since doing so wouldn't violate anyone's rights; there is, after all, "no existing individual who has rights that might be violated."[9] Avoiding conception clearly doesn't violate anyone's rights, and abortion violates rights only if fetuses have a right to be born, a view Buchanan thinks highly implausible. Yet even were it the case that fetuses had a right to be born, the expressivist objection to abortion would be beside the point. Abortion, on this assumption, would be wrong because fetuses are rights holders, not because abortion would express disrespectful messages about the disabled.[10]

I think that Buchanan's strategy of examining the conditions required for expressivity is key to assessing the expressivist objection. I also must agree that, at the end of the day, the expressivist objection does not succeed in showing that avoiding the conception or birth of children with disabilities devalues people with disabilities. However, I think the expressivist objection is more complex than Buchanan allows for. In what follows, I will try to show why the expressivist objection has more to it than Buchanan thinks, why it ultimately fails as a grounds for justifying restricting access to testing and abortion, and what it has to teach nonetheless.

The Semantics of Sterilization

Shortly after the birth of my third child—this would be in 1982—I was sterilized. In retrospect, I think I made a good decision, all things considered. At the time, though, there was one thing that did worry me a bit. It wasn't the thought that I might change my mind about wanting more children. Indeed, I thought it more likely that even if I had a change of heart, I would still believe that considerations of global and intergenerational justice (to say nothing of justice within the family) entailed that I was not entitled to bring more children into the world. My worry was a different one. It was what deliberately destroying my ability to procreate would say about my attitude to Eric, Laura, and Melissa, the three children I already had.

What I *wanted*, of course, was to live so as to convey plainly and consistently to my children that they were deeply loved and most welcome. But I wondered whether that message would be distorted or deflected by the steps I had taken to make as sure as I possibly could that I would never have another child. Even more disturbingly, I wondered whether my desire to be sterilized was really fully consistent with the welcoming attitude I professed.

As it happened, I don't think any of my children have ever had a moment's anxiety or discomfort about my sterilization. What's more, I ended up parenting six children, which only goes to show how fate can get a good chuckle out of one's attempts to control the dimensions of one's life. But although my concerns turned out to be, so far as I can tell, misplaced, I don't believe that they were hopelessly confused.

I tell this story because I think it illustrates how one can intelligibly have concerns related to the expressive character of one's reproductive decisions that do not fall within Buchanan's construal of this matter, and are not quieted by his arguments. In being concerned about the expressive character of my sterilization, I was not wondering whether I was *necessarily* or *solely* motivated by objectionable attitudes towards my children. Nor was I concerned that, in the absence of objectionable beliefs, my action was *necessarily* irrational; I was concerned about what my *contingent* motivations and reasons might be, particularly about the possible motivations and reasons that might not be altogether manifest to me. And I was not troubled about the moral claims of the children I might have had had I not been sterilized; that's not a confusion to which I was tempted. The discordant, disrespectful message I feared I might be sending was not directed to merely possible individuals; I was concerned that it might be addressed to, and perhaps received by, quite real individuals—my children.

Perhaps Buchanan is correct in suggesting that behavior expresses meaning only if it satisfies his two conditions of content and role; grant, for sake of argument, that the actor has to believe what the behavior expresses, and her belief must provide her with motivation or reason for what she does. Further, he is no doubt correct in pointing out that "selective abortions" can be chosen for many reasons. But, as my story indicates, the in-principle availability of other, benign reasons or motives doesn't preclude the possibility that the effective motives, the reasons actually informing the behavior, may not be benign. They may be just the ones that send the objectionable message. Nor is it clear how Buchanan's observation about the unconceived and the unborn as unpromising candidates for being rights holders is to the point; it isn't, after all, fetuses or merely possible people of whom Hershey or Wendell spoke. Their concern was with already existing people with disabilities and the insult to their dignity of the message "we don't want any more like you."

Abortion, Expressivity, and Asch's "Any / Particular" Distinction

So a successful challenge to the expressivist objection must do more that judge it against Buchanan's strict content/role conditions, and more, too, than dismiss the concern altogether on the ground that fetuses are merely possible people who possess no rights. But for the expressivist objection to be useful from disabilities rights perspectives, it will have to pass yet another difficult test: can objectors show in any convincing way that abortions (or other ways of avoiding birth) that have an objectionable expressive character are distinguishable from those that do not?

People plying the objection seem to want to claim that if an abortion is motivated by a belief that the fetus would be born with a disability, that abortion, unlike most others, is not a private event. As such abortions are not fully private affairs, it is permissible to consider restricting access to the diagnostic technologies that provide women with information about their fetuses. Perhaps there should be no such testing. Perhaps it should be restricted to only conditions incompatible with life, such as Tay-Sachs. Or perhaps women seeking to use such tests, or to act on the basis of what the tests reveal, must at least learn more about what's involved in caring for children with disabilities, before they are allowed to end their pregnancies.[11]

Yet this is a tricky business. Many disability rights proponents are not foes of abortion *tout court* and want to resist other efforts to impede women's control over their own reproductive lives. Can the expressivist objection cleanly sort out the dubious prenatal-diagnosis-inspired abortions from all the rest, which are to be regarded as "just" the woman's business?

Adrienne Asch has made an important suggestion about a way of making such a distinction. She notes that some women who find themselves pregnant wish to end the pregnancy for reasons that do not seem to involve properties of the fetus they are carrying; they would end *any* pregnancy, no matter what properties the fetus possessed, because of considerations that pertain to their own situations. Such a woman is merely rejecting pregnancy or parenthood as such. As fetuses are not rights holders, and as no woman should be forced to remain pregnant against her will, abortions in such instances are morally unproblematic. Other women wish to end a pregnancy on the basis of the properties they believe to be possessed by the *particular* fetus they are carrying. Such people have made something of a commitment to parenthood; they would be willing to parent some children in some contexts. But now they are picking and choosing among possible recipients of their parental care, on the basis of what those fetuses would be like were they to come into the world. Again, such picking and choosing may not violate any right held by the fetus, but it does express a negative attitude toward those who are already morally considerable, and are like the fetus in the relevant respects.[12]

While I think this is a very interesting effort to distinguish between "properly private" abortions and those that raise wider moral questions, I haven't been able to bring myself to think it does the work it seems to be trying to do. In part, my reservation is rooted in my story: if *any* reproductive decision is a matter of rejecting *any* possible child, as opposed to some particular child or child-precursor, sterilization would seem to be it. And yet, I was concerned about what my decision *represented*, about what I was *saying* about the worth of a child.

Perhaps an adequate account of what must be the case for nonlinguistic behavior to convey sense would show that my concern here was confused. But such an account has not been forthcoming from Asch or anyone else who has employed the expressivist objection. Nor has Buchanan's reconstruction, resting on what the agent *must* rationally believe or what *must* be motivating her and pointing out possible alternative beliefs, resolved the matter either, at least if it is possible for a person to be moved by many considerations, not all of which may be perfectly clear to her. Remaining at an intuitive level, then, it seems as though even very general kinds of reproductive decisions, such as sterilization, or the abortion of "any" fetus, might well have at least some of the same kind of implications for wider constituencies that more particular acts do. That is, they might express morally objectionable attitudes. Restricting the force of the expressivist objection to disabilities seems rather *ad hoc*.

There is a possible response here. Sterilization—at least, if we exclude the case of sterilization motivated by concerns about one's chances of procreating a child with disabilities—may have many meanings, some objectionable, some not. The same might be said about the abortion of "just any" fetus. One might so despise disabilities that the bare chance that a child might be born with handicaps would be enough to motivate an abortion, but this would be an odd circumstance, to say no more. It is morally responsible to give the benefit of the doubt to people seeking sterilization, or the abortion of any fetus they might be carrying, as there is so much their action might mean. But if a woman were to end a previously wanted pregnancy on finding out that she is carrying a fetus who she can anticipate will become a child with disabilities, there is, so this rejoinder might proceed, only one way to take that.

Buchanan has anticipated this response. He points out that a woman choosing an abortion after prenatal testing need not be saying to herself, "people with disabilities have no right to exist." Rather, she need only believe that fetuses with presumed genetic defects have no right to be born, and might well be motivated by concern about the effect that raising a child with special needs might have on other features of her life, or on other people with disabilities, for that matter. But again, a riposte is possible. Such concerns themselves bespeak an objectionable attitude. If the woman believed her pregnancy would issue in a "normal" child, the stresses involved in rearing would have been acceptable. Not so with the stresses involved in caring for a disabled child. What can be concluded except that the person whose decision pivots on this consideration is saying that people with disabilities aren't worth the time and trouble that they require?

The short answer is that many things could be concluded. The woman may believe that the character of the stresses involved in nurturing a child with disabilities would be markedly different, in degree or in kind, from those she was willing to undertake. Further, if choosing not to parent a child with disabilities entailed a belief that people with disabilities aren't worth the support they may require simply to live, then the vast majority of people who are capable of being parents, and yet have not sought to adopt disabled children, must be committed to such a repugnant belief as well, and this, too, looks uncomfortably like a *reductio*.

But this last point, at least, won't seem a satisfying reply to the objectors; the pregnant woman who refuses to bear and subsequently nurture a child she believes will have disabilities is pointedly and vividly refusing an opportunity with which she is directly presented, and that must make a difference. So, rather than continue to discuss whether women in such a position might not have adequate, nondisabilities demeaning reasons for ending pregnancies, I want, for sake of argument, to leave open the possibility that abortions subsequent to prenatal testing might express objectionable messages to disabled people and return to the question of whether or not other practices might also send equally objectionable messages. I focus on whether abortions done for reasons other than specific genetic indications are really so "nonparticular" as Asch requires.

If a woman decides not to carry a fetus to term, she will, at least in very many instances, have a reason or set of reasons for making this decision. For example, a woman may decide that her family is quite large enough. This seems precisely the sort of thing that Asch would likely regard as a matter of "the situation of the woman," rather than of the "characteristics of the fetus or would-be child."[13] The difficulty, however, is that if this woman should become pregnant, the fetus she is carrying does seem to have a property that is squarely involved in her decision to abort: the property of being the "n + 1" fetus, where "n" was this woman's highest acceptable number. Suppose her "n" is three; does that suggest that this woman is sending a message that she devalues fourth-borns, or that she is expressing contempt about large families? While it is not easy to imagine how we could keep women from knowing how many children they have—the technology for making such determinations is already in wide use—the options for proponents of large families are not exhausted. Would it be in order to mandate that this woman study accounts of the joys of mothering more than three children, or visit happy homes with big families before she is allowed to obtain her abortion?

Imagine now a woman who decides not to complete her pregnancy because she thinks herself too poor to have a child. The fetus she aborts, then, seems to stand to the property "indigence" much as a fetus with a genetic defect stands to the property "disability." That property, then, becomes her reason for the abortion. Does this action say something disturbing about this woman's attitude regarding poverty and poor children? Should poor women undergo special education about raising poor children before they abort? Are the stresses of raising such children enough in excess of those involved in raising middle-class children to justify the abortion without the need to assume that the woman does not sufficiently value poor people?

We can also readily imagine instances in which a woman is initially ambivalent about her pregnancy, or even welcomes the idea of becoming a mother, but changes her mind during pregnancy. She loses her job, or her partner, or her health. In such cases one could raise the same kinds of questions about what her reproductive decision says about poor kids, or kids raised by single mothers, or by ill mothers, with the added circumstance that such a person was clearly not saying she didn't want to be a parent at all; she just didn't want to be a parent when it turned out that the child she would be bearing would have certain traits and not others.

I have a suspicion that those who think that a sharp line can be drawn between "the situation of the woman" and the "characteristics of the fetus" think of genetically based disabilities as monadic properties, ones that inhere in the fetus itself, depending on no consideration of context, and which, moreover, are essential to the fetus's basic identity as the thing that it is. Being a fourth-born, or being poor, in distinction, are regarded as relational properties that hold only contingently of the individuals in question. But if proponents of the expressivist objection are tempted down this path, they should dig in their heels. Why couldn't I express contempt for someone because of her circumstances as much as for something essential about her? Further, on reflection one would not expect this distinction to be very attractive to many disabilities theorists and activists. For many of their most powerful insights have revolved around the idea that disability is socially constructed, that "being disabled" is precisely a relational property. As Asch has put it, "If some portion of the difficulty of disability stems from the biological limitations, the majority does not and is in fact socially structured . . . . [E]ven those characteristics we label as 'disabling' are at least partly socially determined . . . [and] . . . disability's all-too-frequent consequences of isolation, deprivation, powerlessness, dependence, and low social status are far from inevitable and within society's power to change."[14]

I conclude then that the "any/particular" distinction fails as a basis upon which to separate abortions that may remain private from those which have social implications because of what they seem to say. But this doesn't resolve the issue. For it is still open that, as a matter of fact, people who abort pregnancies on grounds of concerns about disabilities too often harbor offensive attitudes toward disabled people, or are negligently ignorant about them, and that such attitudes are part of the explanation of their reproductive decisions. And it is open as well that termination decisions for other reasons—poverty, or partner-lessness, say—also involve similarly objectionable attitudes. Or, of course, that they do not, or do not do so with the same frequency. More needs to be said about these possibilities. Finally, I want also to consider the possibility that the meaning of an act may not be tied so tightly to what is going on in the head of the actor as Buchanan's account suggests.

Intention and Meaning

I believe the discussion up to this point has undermined the view that preconceptual or prenatal testing, and abortion or other ways of avoiding the birth of children with disabilities, have an essential meaning. There is no good reason to think that such practices can only be taken as expressions of disrespect for people with disabilities. Buchanan has pointed out other possible motives, and I have tried to show that one could make an equally good case for saying that virtually any abortion expresses disrespect for people who share with the fetus the traits that motivated the woman to end the pregnancy. But neither Buchanan nor I have precluded the possibility that some or many acts of testing and abortion, if not *necessarily* expressing objectionable meanings, *may* do so. The question is whether or not in fact they do.

To address this question, I want to go back again to my own case and try to get clearer about what I was worrying about back in 1982. I was concerned that my children might take what I did to be an indication that I didn't want them in my life as wholeheartedly as I do. I was afraid that they might mistake my intentions. Now, as it turned out, this was not a realistic fear. It might have made sense for my children to interpret my behavior in this way if I had been otherwise abusive or neglectful. If I had tried to make their lives harder than they needed to be, or showed in a myriad of ways that I just didn't want to be bothered with them, then sterilization might well have been seen as yet another kind of repudiation. This is, of course, a halting analogy to the relationship between people with disabilities and the general society. It does hint why advocates for people with disabilities might be very concerned about what prenatal diagnosis and abortion mean to the women who seek out such services, as well as to the society that sponsors their availability. But it also suggests that the proper response to this concern may have little directly to do with reproductive decision making and a great deal to do with how people with disabilities are incorporated into social life.

But there are other possibilities, too. I was worried then about what my actions expressed to myself. Did they reveal that, unbeknownst to me, I had really harbored negative feelings about my children, about the ways they had complicated my life, added to my burdens, reduced my disposable income? Here, of course, the crucial problem wouldn't be what my children took from my actions, but rather what was there to be taken. This is more complicated, because it suggests that what my actions mean is not altogether a matter of what I want or consciously intend them to mean. My actions may express things about me— perhaps hateful things—even if nobody picks them up, things that even I cannot be sure about. Analogously, women facing decisions to continue or abort pregnancies may think of themselves as perfectly accepting of people with disabilities, when in fact they may have feelings and beliefs of which they are not fully aware, and would not reflectively endorse if they were fully aware of them, and which at the same time affect their behavior.

There is no reason to dismiss this possibility out of hand. But again, what seems to follow is that the problem isn't testing or screening programs, or abortions for genetic indications, but rather generally entertained beliefs, attitudes, and policies toward people with disabilities in general. In trying to right those beliefs, attitudes, and policies, interfering with reproductive liberties—an activity about whose expressive force we may also have reason to wonder—may be just the wrong thing to do. If the goal is to reduce the chance that people often harbor false and disrespectful beliefs about people with disabilities, it isn't clear why educational efforts ought to concentrate on a practice in which relatively few people will engage, trying to force them to reconsider a kind of behavior that has only an expressive impact. On this account, the complex of prenatal diagnosis and abortion is at worst the symptom, not the disease. It would seem more reasonable to educate more widely, focusing particularly on areas in which ignorance and disrespect will play themselves out directly in the lives of people with disabilities. What we need is not pregnant women being compelled to attend to certain information, but people generally being presented with more movies and television programs featuring people with disabilities realistically. And we need more books such as Michael Bérubé's powerful *Life As We Know It*, that make the reality of life as a parent of a child with a disability more vivid to more people.[15]

Social Meanings

Individual actions of obtaining various tests and making various reproductive decisions proceed from many motives and with many different understandings; any meanings such actions have will be fraught with ambiguity. Insofar as the motives or beliefs are disrespectful of people with disabilities, the most effective way to challenge them is probably not by making access to abortion harder, or by scheduling mandatory counseling sessions.

But rather than individual choices, consider the general social practice of developing and disseminating more and more tests for more and more conditions: Does that practice not express a clearer and plainly objectionable meaning, one that needs to be dealt with directly by trying to stop or at least restructure such practices?

A glance back to Columbia, South Carolina, might be useful here. Despite polls indicating that a majority of South Carolina voters support lowering the flag, the view of the dome is unchanged; the Stars and Bars continue to wave. Governor Jim Hodges has proposed—thus far unsuccessfully—to have the flag removed from its position atop the State House. In sending his proposal to the legislature, was Governor Hodges admitting that the individuals who advocated flying the flag were motivated by racist beliefs, or that their actions were only intelligible in the light of such beliefs? Possibly, but not likely; Hodges still wants the flag to fly on state property, after all. Perhaps his action was just an attempt to defuse a controversy by coming up with an acceptable compromise, one not committed to any particular view of what that flag expresses, much less any view of what has to be the case for a flag to express anything whatsoever. But there is, I think, another possibility. The issue between those who are offended by the display of the flag and those who wish to continue flying it as a symbol of a rich heritage is not exhausted by considerations of sincerity or even transparency about what those who wish it to fly mean in so doing. The flying of the Confederate flag, over the seat of state government, might convey an offensive meaning, even if no one involved in running it up the pole did so under the influence of offensive thoughts; the relationship between meaning and intention may be less direct than suggested by Buchanan's analysis.

Some recent currents in the philosophy of language suggest that meaning and intention are indeed more complexly related. For example, in a footnote in the *Philosophical Investigations*, Wittgenstein writes: "Can I say 'bububu' and mean 'If it doesn't rain I shall go for a walk'?"[16] While it is brash to be sure about Wittgenstein, I think he clearly expects his imagined interlocutor to say, "No, I can't," and to learn something about meaning from this thought experiment. I take Wittgenstein here to be drawing our attention to the extent to which meaning is a social phenomenon, not determined solely by what goes on, as we might say, in our heads. Of course, even if Wittgenstein is right, all he shows is that meaning isn't completely determined by our own intentions; for all he's shown here, it might be necessary to my meaningfully using the phrase, "If it doesn't rain I shall go for a walk," that I have certain accompanying beliefs and intentions. Still, this work, and others in like vein, does at least hint that practices might have expressive content in a way that is not solely a function of our beliefs.

What does determine meaning then? One possible response, again associated with Wittgenstein, is that the meaning of a symbol is a matter of how it is used, its role in a publicly shareable system of symbols. It is on the basis of considerations of this sort that flying the Stars and Bars over a state house could be reasonably taken to constitute an expression of contempt for African Americans, even if there were no conscious or unconscious racist beliefs or feelings motivating its (contemporary) appearance. The meaning of that symbol, it might be maintained, stems both from the conventional role of flags as symbols for collectivities and their aspirations, and from this particular flag's place in America's tragic history of slavery and the defense of slavery. It cannot, then, be used as a state symbol (as opposed, say, to a museum exhibit) without expressing contempt for African Americans, any more than we can say "bububu" and mean "If it doesn't rain I shall go for a walk."

So, the possibility that abortion as a response to disability expresses contempt for the disabled seems opened anew, since it now seems at least possible that "selective abortions," or policies that promote their occurrence, can have semantic properties in a way that does not essentially refer to mental states, open or hidden, of those choosing to terminate pregnancies or institute the relevant prenatal testing practices. Such practices take place against a very disturbing historical backdrop concerning the place to which people with disabilities have been assigned in American society. Given this, the widespread, partly publicly funded development and employment of prenatal and preconceptual tests, and pregnancy terminations because of their results, might seem to be the equivalent of flying the Confederate Battle Flag over the South Carolina State House.

My own view, however, is that even considered as a social practice, the meaning of testing and abortion remain both vague and ambiguous, and insofar as this practice does enfold objectionable meanings, the way to unseat them is not by restricting access to information and medical services. Reproductive policies and practices motivated by disability considerations occupy a different semantic position than do the Stars and Bars. Consider what Wittgenstein has to say immediately after the "bububu" passage. "It is only in a language that I can mean something by something."[17] Again, this is not a perfectly clear claim—particularly because it isn't evident just what would be countenanced as a language and what would not. But this sentence does call attention to how languages are settled social practices that, among other things, include devices for selecting sounds, images, or movements that more or less precisely have semantic significance, and that (interacting with context) thereby keep possible ambiguities and vagueness under some control. And it is the absence of these elements in individual acts or general practices of screening and abortion for disability that lead me to doubt whether such behavior expresses morally objectionable attitudes independent of the attitudes of individuals who engage in them.

Flags, and where and how they are flown, are unambiguously symbols; it doesn't stretch matters too far to say that they have a role in a language. While there is surely room for dispute about just what might be symbolized by a particular instance of display, any such dispute takes place against the backdrop of an entrenched practice of seeing flags as expressive of a nation and of what characterizes that nation most fundamentally. One simply couldn't say that flying the Battle Flag over the state house means whatever "we" want it to mean; if the South Carolina legislature had passed a proclamation saying, "the flying of Stars and Bars over the State House Dome has nothing whatsoever to do with slavery or racism," that would not have settled the question of what it means to fly that flag in that place.

Programs of screening and abortion, on the other hand, do not take place against a settled practice of seeing them as expressing what a community is and with what it identifies. It is not, unfortunately, inconceivable that certain kinds of social backdrops—say, states with Nazi-style policies—might make it unmistakable just what such programs aim at. But this sort of situation would be analogous to the person who seeks an abortion out of a general and professed policy of expressing contempt for children at every possible turn. But as things stand, there is no reason to claim that screening programs must, or even typically will, be motivated by Nazi-like assumptions. There are other possible motivations for both the social deployment and the individual use of screening, testing, and aborting for potentially disabling conditions than hatred or contempt for people with disabilities.

Conclusions: Context, Context, Context

What, as a matter of fact, does stand behind the social and professional interest in prenatal screening, testing, and abortion? The failure to take people with disabilities with full moral seriousness? Or an effort to increase the effective reproductive choices of women and try to give them a further measure of control over how they will live their lives? How do such practices fare in the competition for social support vis-à-vis efforts to construct a society more welcoming to people with disabilities or more empowering of women? Are they leading to the kind of situation feared by Bérubé, where, rather than allowing people more control over the circumstances in which they take up the challenges of parenting, prenatal testing and abortion are seen as part of what it means to be a good parent and a responsible citizen?[18]

Screening and aborting do not wear their meaning on their sleeves; if we want to work out what they express, then questions like these are the right ones to ask. Tracking them down will likely lead to mixed answers, leaving us confused as to whether such practices express anything clearly enough to be called a meaning. The meanings of decisions, practices, and policies that involve screening and abortion cannot be determined outside the context of a broader set of decisions, practices, and policies as they affect people with disabilities, as well as women and family life more generally. Examining that context will no doubt reveal some disturbing things. But in the end, whether the best way to improve social attitudes and practices regarding people with disabilities is to put pressure on prenatal screening and pregnancy termination may not be a matter of principle on the model of a right to be untroubled by hate speech, or by a racist symbol displayed over the seat of government. It may be, rather, a strategic question of where to invest energies to increase the probability of admirable changes in the way we live our lives. Looked at in this way, tactics other than intervening in women's reproductive decision making seem both less problematic and more meaningful.[19]

NOTES

1. This chapter is a slightly revised version of an article that first appeared in the *Kennedy Institute of Ethics Journal* 8, no. 2 (1998): 165–82.

2. Susan Wendell, *The Rejected Body* (New York: Routledge, 1996), p. 153.

3. Laura Hershey, "Choosing Disabilities," *Ms. Magazine,* July–August (1994): 30.

4. Allen Buchanan, "Choosing Who Will Be Disabled: Genetic Intervention and the Morality of Inclusion," *Social Philosophy and Policy* 13 (1996): 18–46.

5. Buchanan, "Choosing Who Will Be Disabled," p. 28.

6. L'Institute Roeher, *Just Technology?* (North York, Ontario: L' Institute Roeher, 1994).

7. Adrienne Asch and Gail Gellner, "Feminism, Bioethics and Genetics," in *Feminism and Bioethics: Beyond Reproduction*, ed. Susan M. Wolf (Oxford and New York: Oxford University Press, 1996), pp. 318–50.

8. Buchanan, "Choosing Who Will Be Disabled," p. 31.

9. Buchanan, "Choosing Who Will Be Disabled," p. 31.

10. Buchanan, "Choosing Who Will Be Disabled," p. 35.

11. Adrienne Asch makes a suggestion of this sort in her "Reproductive Technology and Disability," in *Reproductive Laws for the 1990's*, ed. Sherill Cohen and Nadine Taub (Clifton, N.J.: Humana Press, 1988), pp. 69–124.

12. Asch, "Reproductive Technology and Disability," p. 82. It should be underscored that Asch has been clear that, while richer information about the rewards as well as burdens of rearing children with disabilities should be provided women contemplating abortion after prenatal diagnosis, "a woman has the right to decide about her body and her life and to terminate a pregnancy for this or any other reason." (Michelle Fine and Adrienne Asch, eds., *Women With Disabilities: Essays in Psychology, Culture and Politics* (Philadelphia, Penn.: Temple University Press, 1988), p. 302. It also is worth pointing out that Asch's concerns here may not be limited to issues highlighted by the expressivist concern—she also seems to think that parental virtues include maintaining an attitude of wholehearted and uncritical acceptance of one's children; the selectivity involved in prenatal screening and abortion are taken to be incompatible with that virtue. While I will not deal with this objection explicitly, it should be tolerably clear why I find it implausible as a grounds for criticizing decisions to end pregnancies.

13. Asch, "Reproductive Technology and Disability," p. 82.

14. Asch, "Reproductive Technology and Disability," p. 73.

15. Michael Bérubé, *Life as We Know It: A Father, a Family and an Exceptional Child* (New York: Pantheon, 1996).

16. Ludwig Wittgenstein, *Philosophical Investigations* (New York: Macmillan, 1958), p. 18.

17. Wittgenstein, *Philosophical Investigations*, p. 18.

18. Bérubé's concern is worth spelling out: "The danger for children like Jamie does not lie in women's freedom to choose abortion; nor does it lie in prenatal testing. The danger lies in the creation of a society that combines eugenics with enforced fiscal austerity. In such a society, it is quite conceivable that parents who 'choose' to bear disabled children will be seen as selfish or deluded. Among the many things I fear coming to pass in my children's lifetime, I fear this above all: that children like James will eventually be seen as 'luxuries' employers and insurance companies cannot afford, or as 'luxuries' the nation or the planet cannot afford (Bérubé, *Life as We Know It*, p. 52).

19. My work on this article was supported by grant 5R01HG01168-02, "Prenatal Testing for Genetic Disabilities," made by the ELSI division of the National Human Genome Research Institute to The Hastings Center. I am grateful to Erik Parens, principal investigator, and to all members of The Hastings Center project, from whom I have learned a great deal (although by no means enough, as many will think). I am also grateful to participants at a meeting of the Society for Disabilities Studies held on May 22, 1997, in Minneapolis, for their very valuable comments on earlier versions of this chapter. For help in turning these remarks from a talk into an article, I am indebted as usual to Hilde Lindemann Nelson, and for their close attention to later drafts, to Cynthia B. Cohen and Elizabeth Leibold McCloskey.

Assessing the Expressive Character of Prenatal Testing: The Choices Made or the Choices Made Available?

One of the most powerful critiques of prenatal testing comes from disability theorists.[1] A particularly important aspect of this critique is the claim that using prenatal tests to detect fetal anomalies has an expressive character that is hurtful to and rejecting of individuals who live with disability. In this view, the choice to abort an otherwise desired fetus on the basis of one trait or characteristic sends the message that the lives of those with disability are not valuable and that "the disability makes the child unacceptable."[2]

Several well-argued objections have been proposed to this disability critique of prenatal testing, a critique that has been termed "the expressivist argument."[3] Objections to the expressivist argument share a skepticism about the ability of individual acts to constitute a message. One of the most forceful rejections of the expressivist argument comes from bioethicist Allen Buchanan.[4] Buchanan holds to stringent criteria for the manner in which an act can send a message. For Buchanan, an action can only convey the meaning that the actor holds in regard to that action, and, in addition, those meanings must have played a conscious role in the actor's decision.[5] James Lindemann Nelson rejects the necessity for an actor to have full consciousness of the message conveyed, allowing that, in reality, actions are polysemous and some meanings may be unknown to the actor. But precisely because the meanings of actions are often ambiguous even for an individual actor, and are certainly variable across the universe of multiple actors, Nelson also questions the expressivist argument.[6] He asserts that there are rare instances in which broad cultural agreement about the symbolic meaning of an act means that the act can send a specific message. His example is flying the Confederate Flag over a public building in the southern United States.

This flag is so linked to slavery, segregation, and southern separatism, that Nelson believes flying it in a public space legitimately constitutes a message. However, such clarity is rarely the case. Thus, Nelson notes that abortions can take place for many reasons, with many different intentions, yet these abortions are all similar as acts. Nelson contends that in order for selective abortions for disability to have the expressive character claimed by the expressivist argument, there would have to be some way to demonstrate clearly how abortions for disability, especially with the intention of rejecting those with disability, are distinguishable from other abortions.

But Nelson's challenge does not acknowledge the important nuance of Asch's argument, based on women's experiences of pregnancy, between the meaning of abortions for disability and abortions for other reasons. For Asch there is, virtually from its inception, a perceived difference between a wanted pregnancy and one that is not wanted at that time. In the first case there is an immediate, imaginative sense of carrying a baby; in the latter, the pregnancy remains a fetus. For Asch, the negative message of selective abortion for disability is that it is a decision to terminate a pregnancy, which was previously experienced as wanted, on the basis of knowing only one new fact about that baby— that it will have some sort of disability. To Asch this is fundamentally different from the termination of a pregnancy that was always unwanted based on characteristics of the woman's life at that time. Asch calls this the "any/particular" distinction.[7] This distinction has been critiqued by some contributors to this volume. Nelson, for example, claims that it is impossible to distinguish the characteristic of being the fourth-born child of a woman who feels she can only afford three children and that of being a fetus found to have a disabling condition.[8] I am not persuaded by Nelson's argument. Although one's place in the family birth order may come to leave a mark on a child, it is not an intrinsic attribute of that child, but rather of that pregnancy. Put up for adoption and raised in another family, the fourth-born, biological child may become the first-born, adopted child. But a disability is intrinsic to the child. A fetus definitively diagnosed with a disability will have that disability, whatever family raises it.

An interesting, literary example of Asch's "any/particular" distinction can be found in Simon Mawer's novel, *Mendel's Dwarf*. In this novel, the protagonist, Benedict Lambert—who is an achondroplastic dwarf as well as a Ph.D. geneticist—impregnates a married woman with whom he is having an affair. The woman, Jean Piercey, is of "normal" stature.

In the following passage, which depicts a conversation where Ben and Jean discuss what to do about the pregnancy, Ben states:

> "There's a fifty percent chance of it being"—[he pauses], loathing the word, finding no other—"normal. At present, prenatal diagnosis . . . isn't possible at all until after the twenty-fifth week, which is rather late. . . ."
> "Then we've got to stop it."
> "Of course. If that's what you want. I can hardly plead on the part of the child." Her eyes . . . blistered with tears. "You're not being fair." . . . Abruptly she changed tone, like changing gear in a car. "But we're responsible. And the situation that we're in. I mean, I'm still married. And we're not. So how could we possibly. . . . It'd be a terrible problem for the child, Ben," she said. "Our situation. . . ."
> "Me, that's what you mean. Me. The child might be like me."
> "That's being unfair. . . . All right, Ben," she said. "If you want to force me to say it I will: *the child might be like you. And I wouldn't want that*" [emphasis added].[9]

The "change of gear" marks Jean's attempt to turn a discussion of the particular fetus to a consideration of a topic the author clearly considers less interpersonally and morally problematic—the discussion of any pregnancy given the couple's relationship. Ben Lambert, however, will not allow this and states that it is not "our situation" that is at issue but "me . . . the child might be like me." Jean, defeated in her attempt to be kind, finds herself forced to agree that it is the particular child— which might be like her lover—that she does not want. This example from one novel does not, of course, "prove" that the "any/particular" distinction is logically valid. It does, however, seem to provide a very powerful, imaginative representation of the lived experience of Asch's point.

Linguistic anthropologists might in a different way help Asch respond to critiques of the expressivist argument. That is, linguistic anthropologists might fault all the above critiques of the expressivist argument for having too limited a view of the message—a view which ignores suprasegmental parts of utterances (e.g., body language, word choice), the order in which utterances in a "text" are put together, as well as the institutional setting and power relationships surrounding "sender" and "receiver."[10] By drawing attention to the broadest context of the message, these insights by linguistic anthropology raise an even more fundamental question: What is the message in the case of prenatal testing and who are the senders and receivers?

Most critiques of the expressivist argument implicitly assume that the "message" is having an abortion and the "sender" is the woman/couple who terminate the pregnancy. But this is only one possible way to construct the message to which those with disability may be reacting, and, I would contend, it is not the most useful way. Another way of thinking about it is that the offer of prenatal testing itself is the message and the institutional structures through which the offer is made constitute the senders of the message.

Following this lead, the focus of this chapter is on the social character of an *offer* of prenatal testing. As opposed to a focus on the message sent by the individuals, this analysis will move back in time and space to examine the message sent by specific social systems. As opposed to a focus on an individual's actions following a positive prenatal test, the focus will be on the social meanings of developing and offering prenatal tests. As opposed to simply assuming that the central meaning of prenatal testing is selective abortion, this analysis will look at how the relationship of prenatal testing and abortion is socially constructed and contested. Ultimately, I will contend that the strongest support for the expressivist argument comes not from an examination of the choices made by individuals, but rather by considering the meanings and cultural tensions of the choices made available by the increasing number and routinization of prenatal testing for a growing number of diseases and conditions.

How Silences about Abortion Shape the Expressive Character of Prenatal Testing

James Lindemann Nelson contends that the actions of individuals may have meanings that are contingent or hidden. This implies that asking an individual "what did you mean by that?" does not ensure a complete answer. In the same way, social actions may have unacknowledged, contingent, and even hidden meanings. When bioethicists discuss prenatal testing, the meaning, ethics, and politics of terminating or not terminating a pregnancy following a positive test result are generally central to their consideration. It would be a mistake, however, to assume that the public discourse mirrors that of these scholars. In fact, it may not go too far to say that certain silences in the public discourse have actually enabled the routinization and rapid growth of prenatal testing in the United States. They have done this by obscuring or limiting the need for public debate on two topics about which Americans are deeply conflicted but which lie at the heart of prenatal testing: abortion and disability.

Noninvasive Prenatal Screening: What's Abortion Got to Do with It?

My perspective on prenatal testing is shaped by the research I conducted with Carole Browner on a particular prenatal screen: the maternal serum alpha fetoprotein (MSAFP) test.[11] MSAFP screening was developed to detect neural tube defects (NTDs) in the fetus. NTDs are among the most commonly reported of serious birth defects, leading to varying degrees of physical and cognitive impairment and, in the case of anencephaly, are incompatible with life. Alpha fetoprotein is a substance produced by the developing fetus. In the early 1970s research suggested that levels of alpha fetoprotein in maternal serum could be used as a noninvasive, inexpensive modality of screening for NTDs.[12] Population-based screening seemed desirable, since over 90 percent of NTDs occur to women at no known risk. Ultrasound and amniocentesis would then be available for women who had abnormal MSAFP levels in order to arrive at a reasonably definitive diagnosis. The initial research was done in the United Kingdom where some of the highest worldwide incidences of NTDs are found (approximately 5 to 6 per 1,000 births);[13] researchers in the United Kingdom saw this as a public health problem and acted quickly to investigate the usefulness of MSAFP as a population screen in actual practice.

The subsequent story of the rapid adoption of MSAFP screening as a part of routine prenatal care has been chronicled elsewhere.[14] Today it is estimated that close to 60 percent of pregnancies in the United States are screened by MSAFP, making it the most widely used population-based screening intended to directly indicate possible fetal anomalies.[15] But the real importance of MSAFP screening is that it introduced the idea of noninvasive screening in young pregnant women with no known risk factors for possible genetic and congenital problems with their fetuses. In addition, the blood of pregnant women soon turned out to carry other information about the fetus—information that is now routinely, and without societal debate, acquired by the MSAFP test.

In 1986, California became the only state to mandate that all health care providers offer MSAFP testing to all their pregnant patients. It was in the context of this state program that Carole Browner and I undertook research into pregnant women's use of, attitudes toward, and understandings about prenatal screening. The findings from this research support a view that there is a crucial difference between a woman who enters the world of prenatal testing via an offer of amniocentesis and the much larger group of women who today start down that road with the offer of MSAFP or multiple-marker screening. In the case of the typical woman who is offered amniocentesis, the offer is based on advanced maternal age, usually due to delayed childbearing. This woman, even now, is statistically anomalous and is generally aware that she is considered "high risk." Many such women state that they would not have felt comfortable becoming pregnant at their age were it not for the option of prenatal testing *and* pregnancy termination. In contrast, the typical woman being offered MSAFP screening is the typical pregnant woman—young and at low risk for bearing a child with any birth anomaly. She did not begin pregnancy with an expectation of an offer of amniocentesis; in fact, to the extent that she is aware of amniocentesis, it is likely to be as something she doesn't have to worry about yet.

Carole Browner and I contend that the routinization of this screening—especially in concert with California's legal mandate—led to a paradoxical result: the test came to be viewed as routine and acceptable in the same measure as its actual meaning and purpose were obscured. In our research sites in California, MSAFP screening had been completely routinized as a part of standard prenatal care and, in the process, had become imbued with the same meanings and perceived purposes as the rest of routine prenatal medical care. We found that the women we interviewed described routine prenatal care and MSAFP screening—using remarkably similar phrases—as responsible maternal actions that provided useful information and were reassuring. For some women, the identity of meaning between standard prenatal care and prenatal testing was so complete that MSAFP was described in terms of helping to protect the fetus. The actual purpose of MSAFP screening—to find cases of untreatable birth defects in order to allow women and couples the opportunity to terminate a pregnancy—appeared to be obscured from view.

Browner and I have described elsewhere[16] the various steps in this process of subsuming the meanings of MSAFP screening under the rubric of routine prenatal care. The effect of this process may be most succinctly illustrated, however, by the participants we termed "reluctant acceptors." This small group of women was set apart by the fact that, unlike the vast majority of participants, who said they had accepted

MSAFP testing with little or no thought, reluctant acceptors had rumi-
nated a lot about this decision and then agreed only with some reluctance.
One of these women described her thought process in remarkable detail:

> I went back and forth [about taking the test]. . . . "I should do this; I
> don't know why I'm going to do this. . . ." [What if you get a positive
> result] and then you're panicked because you think that there is some
> kind of problem . . . and if there is no problem you feel better but there's
> been a lot of undue stress. [But] if there is a problem, well—you're
> already 24 weeks pregnant. So then you have to make a choice and I
> can't make that choice. For me the choice has already been made. We're
> going to have this child. . . . So now I've gone through all of this to find
> out something is wrong but I'm not going to do anything about it anyhow.
> So then I figure, why am I taking this test? I don't know, and then I say
> [to myself], "I'm not going to take it" and then I come [for my appointment],
> and I go, "Fine here's my arm, take my blood. . . ." [In the end] it was
> a matter of needing to know everything you can and do everything you can.

Much of this woman's action in holding out her arm could be
explained by the fact that the testing process at this HMO made it very
easy to accept, and rather difficult to refuse, MSAFP screening. But
perhaps the most striking thing about this statement is not the ultimate
action but the way one can watch the meaning of MSAFP being transformed. By the time she agreed to testing, MSAFP was no longer a
special kind of test that could diagnose untreatable birth defects and
thus present her with a decision she did not want to have to make.
Her final comment—"[In the end] it was a matter of needing to know
everything you can, and do everything you can"—is very telling. Who
is the object of the final phrase? For whom is everything possible being
done? Is it for the parent who needs the opportunity, denied earlier in
the statement, of terminating the pregnancy if there is a "problem" with
the fetus? Is it, somehow, the fetus itself? Is the protection even more
magical? Is this woman somehow protecting the imagined child from
the reality of the life that might ensue with a birth defect? Or is it
less individually based and simply that in contemporary U.S. culture,
"knowing" is part of an assumed package with "doing"? Knowing is a
kind of doing and knowing will inevitably lead to doing. For if there is
a culturally specific cognitive schema underlying our participants' approach to and understanding of MSAFP testing, it seems to have little
to do with abortion and a lot to do with the value of information.

It is impossible for us to know—and probably would be impossible
for this participant to parse—all the meanings packed into her statement.

However, by placing MSAFP screening so firmly under the rubric of routine prenatal care—care that our participants told us was valuable primarily because of the information it provided—it enabled the aspect of abortion to recede from view. Only a handful of participants mentioned the topic of abortion when discussing either the reasons they had accepted or what they thought was good about MSAFP testing. When asked directly what they would have done if all tests had shown that their fetus had a serious birth anomaly, less than 15 percent said they were certain they would have terminated the pregnancy. This is not to say that the women interviewed were unaware that pregnancy termination was one option that might follow a positive MSAFP test. And, in fact, aggregate figures from the state of California show that over 85 percent of women with a confirmed positive result following from an MSAFP test do terminate.[17] But this discrepancy still presents a conundrum that seems too important to dismiss by saying that these women are simply unwilling to admit what they know they would have done all along. Certainly the period between getting the first positive result and the point of termination is crucial and can shape a woman's perceptions and decisions in many ways. But even if we concede for the sake of argument that, on some level, the women accepting testing knew all along what they would do, the fact remains that they were allowed, and even encouraged, to begin down a path that can lead to a selective abortion without having to really face, think through, or even admit this endpoint. Health care providers in our study, and state officials who had created informed consent materials for the California MSAFP program, were often quite open about the fact that the link between abortion and prenatal screening was intentionally avoided. They cited as reasons behind this omission both political conflict over abortion and the observed discomfort of pregnant patients when abortion was mentioned in this context.

Avoiding honest discussion of the meaning and purpose of prenatal screening exists not only at the level of patient-clinician interaction but in the "hard" and "soft" scientific literature as well. In general, a truly open approach to the centrality of abortion to prenatal screening is found almost exclusively in the cost-benefit analyses done on MSAFP and other prenatal screening. This literature contains up-front calculations of the minimum number of pregnancy terminations that can be done before screening ceases to be cost effective.[18] In more general articles, however, the goals of MSAFP screening merit little attention and must, at best, be gleaned from a brief sentence or two in the introductory paragraph.[19]

However, a close examination of these brief statements reveals two, logically separate, types of goals. These might be called *societally approved goals* and *controversial goals*.

The societally approved goals of the MSAFP program are generally stated first. They include offering reassurance to pregnant women; providing information to the physician about the state of the pregnancy; allowing time for parents to prepare psychologically in the case where an abnormality is found; permitting special medical preparation for such a birth; and the possibility of in-utero treatment.

These goals share the following characteristics: (1) they focus on benefit to the individual or family, rather than to the society; (2) they focus on *joint* good to the mother and fetus, rather than raising the possibility of conflicting interests between the mother and the fetus; and (3) they are, in the broadest sense, "for life." However, all are also, ultimately, ancillary goals. They are ancillary in that they apply to statistically rare situations, involve information that could be found out in other ways, or describe either future situations or ones for which no guidelines for action currently exist. Fundamentally, they are ancillary because it is so unlikely that the MSAFP test would have become routinized if they were the only, or even the major, goals.

There are only two controversial goals: the ability to terminate pregnancies where the fetus is found to have an anomaly, and the concomitant cost savings to society. These goals, which are so central to the public health purposes that make population-based prenatal screening viable, are also so controversial that they are often stated indirectly. For example, two major public health proponents of widespread MSAFP screening wrote in the journal of the American Society of Human Genetics that, "MSAFP screening has proved to be a . . . cost-effective way of improving pregnancy outcome."[20] Verging on "newspeak," this is an excellent example of the encoded quality of much of this discussion, for it is certainly not the outcome of any particular pregnancy that is improved through MSAFP screening.

Such encoded language is explicable by the fact that, in opposition to the societally acceptable goals, these controversial goals imply things that are not comfortable for most Americans. They logically imply that not all life is worthwhile, and that the interests of society may be in conflict with those of the fetus. These goals also raise the specter of eugenics in regard to prenatal diagnosis. This encoded language also poses challenges to those who believe that the expressive character of prenatal diagnosis is hurtful, and even potentially dangerous, to those with disability: if the goals of prenatal testing are obscured and denied, it is difficult to demonstrate harm coming from those goals. The anecdotes below—although only the experiences of individuals—show what happened to two pregnant women who openly confronted the systematic silences surrounding prenatal testing. I believe each provides a powerful example of the expressive character of prenatal testing as it is offered in contemporary U.S. society.

That procedure would be done downtown . . .   A woman is pregnant for the first time at age thirty-eight. She is educated and affluent. She has waited a long time to have this child and is very happy to find herself pregnant. She is, in other words, a woman who would be expected to have amniocentesis. However, she has concerns about prenatal testing, wondering whether she shouldn't perhaps be willing to accept whatever child she is given. However, ultimately her fear of bearing a child with a disability is stronger than her reservations and she elects to have testing. She chooses chorionic villus sampling (CVS) as an earlier, technologically advanced alternative to amniocentesis.

She arrives at the building where the CVS will take place. It is a beautiful, modern building in an upscale part of a major western city. There is support staff in abundance and a great deal of gleaming, "high tech" equipment. She is treated with great courtesy by the staff who are concerned for her comfort and cognizant of the value of her time. Eventually she asks what seems to her the logical question given what is taking place: *What would happen if they detected a problem?* The first responses are to not worry about that—the chances of a problem are very small. But she persists: *Who, for example, would do the pregnancy termination? Should she meet that physician now? Where in the facility are terminations done?* Oh no, they answer, no pregnancy terminations are done at this facility; in fact, no physician directly affiliated with their program does abortions. The very occasional woman who needs this procedure is referred to another facility. This other facility turns out to be "downtown," not in the same "upmarket" area in which this prenatal testing is being done. It is, in fact, a "clinic" where the primary procedure done is abortion. *"Everything about this division of the CVS from the termination told me that I was doing something wrong in being here in the first place . . . ,"* she says.

Why else was I offered the test?   An affluent, white woman living in a major metropolitan area. She is forty-two, recently married for the second time and pregnant for the sixth time. She has two living children and has, over the years, had two spontaneous miscarriages and a previous abortion unrelated to prenatal testing. She and her new husband want to have a child together, and she attempts it because she knows she has the option of amniocentesis and abortion. She feels that it would be unfair to her other children and to the family's resources to try to raise a child with Down syndrome. If pressed, she will tell you that she thinks no one should have children with Down syndrome or any other disability that can be avoided through prenatal testing and selective abortion. She is, by training, a sociobiologist and feels that the biological progenitors lose selective advantage by bearing offspring who are ill or disabled. When her amniocentesis reveals trisomy 21, she cries, and then schedules a pregnancy termination through her long-term ob-gyn who performs abortions in a large teaching hospital. By the time she tells me this story she has had another baby, conceived within months of the amniocentesis and termination. This baby is now a healthy six-month-old and she is a very happy mother with absolutely no regrets about any of her decisions.

Nonetheless, she remembers the pregnancy termination following amniocentesis with anger and bitterness. She tells me that she entered the hospital in a state of grief over the necessity of ending a wanted pregnancy and was immediately put in a ward on the maternity floor. Nothing was done to protect her from the very different and happy experiences of these other pregnant women.[21] She reports treatment by nursing staff that was brusque and rude. In addition, she remembers being severely undermedicated for the physical pain she was going through during the protracted delivery of a nearly six-month fetus. Despite the fact that she was certain she was doing the right thing— *and really, why else was I offered amnio?*—she feels that there was a deeply punitive edge to the way she was treated. Such treatment makes no sense to her because she feels that what she did was not only morally all right but, in fact, also morally superior to bearing a disabled child. For her, this is the purpose of amniocentesis, but it did not fit with the more subtle message she received during her hospital stay.

What, then, does this analysis of the silences, ellipses, denial, and submerged negative attitudes toward abortion say about the expressivist argument that prenatal testing sends a negative and hurtful message to those living with disability? One might say that it indicates merely that abortion is simply, by the very fact of it, difficult for many people.

What then about the other central piece of prenatal testing—attitudes toward disability?

The Two Faces of Disability

It has been observed, for example, by Philip Kitcher[22] that increased prenatal testing has not, in fact, led to a reduction of resources available to people with disability, despite expressed fears that such would likely occur. A parallel objection could be made to the expressivist argument on the grounds that at the same time that the use of prenatal testing has increased, so have the resources and legal protections for people with disabilities. This, the argument would go, would seem to express an increasingly congenial and accepting message about people with disabilities concurrent with the increasing use of prenatal testing.

This argument seems very logical but is based on a rather thin view of the way people hold complex and contradictory beliefs. Claudia Strauss,[23] for example, has compellingly critiqued the theory that holding two, opposed views on a subject will lead to an uncomfortable "cognitive dissonance." In her work on the views of social mobility held by working class Americans, Strauss has shown that those she interviewed often held differing and internally contradictory opinions on the subject. These varying opinions, according to Strauss, are "filed" in different cognitive schema and are accessed via different questions that she asked. Since any one question elicits only one domain, cognitive dissonance does not occur.

Data that Carole Browner and I collected exhibit precisely these types of contradictory beliefs.[24] We interviewed a group of pregnant women at no particular risk for bearing a child with a disability, but who had all been offered MSAFP screening, about their images of disability and their attitudes toward bearing a child with a disability. As we believed this might be a multifaceted arena, we tried to access women's images and beliefs via several pathways. These included a short series of questions about their experiences and relationships with people with disabilities. We prompted them to discuss the problems they think a disability might have caused for the person and for the person's parents, as well as what they may have admired about the person with disability and/or the person's parents. Finally, we asked them how they think they might react themselves to the experience of raising a child with a disability. What we found reveals some very positive attitudes toward disability, which seems to show the effect of the disability rights movement, alongside some very negative views of disability as stigmatizing and deeply feared.

Perhaps the most striking discontinuities were seen between the upbeat, strongly positive, and almost romanticized attitudes women frequently expressed about people with disabilities versus their extremely fearful and negative attitudes regarding the possibility that their own child might be disabled. Thus, one woman, pregnant with her first child, said, "[H]andicapped kids are probably the most beautiful beings in the world; they have a bigger heart than anybody and they know what love is all about more than anybody." Another woman also spoke of "the handicapped" as special. She stated, "[A]ctually you can learn a lot from a handicapped person. . . . They become better than the average person." Similarly, in discussing children with disabilities as a general category, another woman said that "mentally retarded children are some of the most loving kids I've ever met." She went even further, claiming as her best friend an adult woman who is mentally retarded and whom she described as "an equal." One woman whose foster brother had a disability was eloquent in discussing the needless discrimination he suffered due to his speech and motor impairments. Yet, in keeping with the generally positive, and almost casual, voice many of the women used, she denied that her brother's conditions created any sort of problem for her parents and said that while he "had it rough for a while [he has] gotten over it fine." In these and in answers to other questions, images of what have been termed the "supercrip"[25] emerged—that is, special cases were created of people who "triumphed" or "overcame" disability, who were heroic, rather than simply people who had, among many other traits, a "disabling" one. Interestingly, children with disabilities were especially extolled. They were seen as especially loving and as examples for others. Adults were praised most, on the other hand, for acting "just as if they were normal." In fact, if the person's disability did not appear to alter their life in any way, the person with the disability was lauded and given a sort of provisional normalcy.

Yet, when each of these women was asked about the implications of a possible disability in a child of their own, the response was quite different. This difference seemed to go beyond the naturally greater concern one would expect to be expressed for one's own child. It was rather as though the women we interviewed suddenly switched from the political to the personal. Thus, not only their opinions, but their entire tone changed from casual and upbeat to emotionally charged, frightened, and negative. Thus, for example, the woman who had said that handicapped children were the most beautiful beings in the world said that if she were told her child had been born with a handicap, she would cry. The woman who said that handicapped people become better than the average person, said that if prenatal tests had shown a problem with her fetus she would have done whatever the doctor directed, including abortion. In addition, although the interviewer's question only mentioned a prenatally detected "problem," the image of disability spontaneously conjured up by this informant was a baby "who is going to be a vegetable and have to live off life support." The woman who claimed as a "best friend" a women who is mentally retarded stated later in the interview that, if she found out early enough in her pregnancy, she would terminate a pregnancy if the baby would be born mentally retarded because, "it would be selfish on my part to have this child that could never amount to anything. . . ." But perhaps most surprising was the response of the woman whose foster brother was disabled but who had "got over it fine." She said she might terminate a pregnancy because of a fetal abnormality. She feared that the child might ask "Why did you even have me?" and added, "I wouldn't want to bring a child into the world to suffer."

One of the most striking examples of the tension that may be created by a burgeoning disability rights discourse in the context of prenatal testing was seen in our informants' beliefs about Down syndrome. Everyone seemed to know about Down syndrome, even though the HMO specifically avoided discussing Down syndrome in connection with MSAFP. In fact, our informants' discussion of Down syndrome appeared to have been strongly influenced by recent popular media images, including television programs with Down syndrome actors, made-for TV movies about parents helping Down syndrome children achieve in school, and Down syndrome children pictured on the same cereal boxes as major athletes. The result was statements that show a dynamic and somewhat confused mix of old images of mental retardation and incapacity juxtaposed, with new images of different, but "special," children.

Thus, in responding to the question, "Can you tell me what Down syndrome is?," one woman said she wasn't sure exactly, ". . . just that it's not retardedness, not exactly. . . . It looks like they have mental retardation because of their movements, but their minds are fine." Another said that Down syndrome children can often be pretty much normal and it is primarily when their parents don't have high expectations and "treat them as if they're handicapped" that they wind up appearing mentally deficient. And when asked to define Down syndrome, a third said the only thing she knew was that "their eyes bulge out a little; they're actually smart but their mentality just isn't like ours."

Several women directly referenced a television series, popular at that time, which used a child with Down syndrome as one of the actors. One said, "I always thought [Down syndrome] was mental retardation [but] my husband corrected me the other night when we were watching 'Life Goes On.' " Another said that ". . . people with Down syndrome can grow up to have a normal life." When asked by the interviewer what was the basis of this belief she answered, "TV. That program on television [about the kid with Down syndrome]. Talk shows, things like that."

The struggle of these women to define the relationship between Down syndrome and mental retardation is particularly crucial since, elsewhere in the interviews, these same women reacted to a mention of the term "mental retardation" with great fear and indicated that it was one of the disabilities for which they would be most likely to consider abortion. The positive images they held of Down syndrome and "special children" had apparently not so much transformed their fears of mental retardation as led to the creation of a new subcategory for Down syndrome, one which lacked some of the negative attributes they attached to mental retardation in general.

The view among many of our informants that Down syndrome is not really mental retardation, and therefore not terribly handicapping, is significant since it contrasts with how most in the medical establishment view Down syndrome. The question that arises, then, is which image of Down syndrome would prevail if a pregnant woman were counseled following prenatal testing? Our data suggest that if a medical provider depicted Down syndrome as truly mental retardation, the more positive, new media image loosely held by many pregnant women would rapidly dissolve. This supposition is based in part on statistics that show that the vast majority of women whose fetuses are diagnosed with Down syndrome do in fact terminate.

In presenting these data, it is not my intention to be critical of women's attitudes toward disability. It is rather to show that criticism of the expressivist argument based on the legal and political gains of disability activists is considerably weakened by attending more closely to what pregnant women actually think about having a child with a disability. Ironically, greater social awareness and sensitivity about disability may be another factor making it more difficult to have an open public discussion about prenatal testing and selective abortion for disability.

The Role of Nondirective Genetic Counseling—
The Handmaid's Tale?

When Brock and Sutcliffe discovered that it was possible to screen for neural tube defects through maternal serum alpha fetoprotein levels, their intention was to develop a test that could lower the incidence of these anomalies because they saw NTDs as a public health problem in the United Kingdom. Nevertheless, neither they, nor any other proponent of prenatal testing, have suggested actively encouraging women/couples to terminate pregnancies following a confirmed positive result. The various factors that undergird the commitment to complete patient autonomy in these decisions must be seen to include a vigorous rejection of the eugenicist past. This past included, at its most benign, the promotion of breeding of "fit families" and, at its darkest, the involuntary sterilization of those deemed "unfit."[26] Some historians have traced direct links from the British and American eugenics movement of the early twentieth century to the Nazi plans to eliminate "unfit" populations beginning with those with disability.[27] As others have discussed, a desire to separate current prenatal testing from this past has contributed to making nondirectiveness and individual choice the central dogma of current genetics practice.[28]

A corollary of this central dogma is that the role of the genetic counselor is to be completely oriented toward working with, and thinking about, individuals or families one at a time. Their training leads them away from viewing their role as part of a structure that leads to so many amnioceteses or so many pregnancy terminations. Yet, genetic counselors do exist within a structure. Examination of that structure suggests that there are profound tensions surrounding the practice and profession of genetic counseling.

The first of these tensions concerns how genetic counselors are paid. Unable to bill directly for services, genetic counseling is generally billed under the rubric of a medical department, a genetics service, or, at its most explicit, a pathology department. Almost the only way these salary costs can be recouped is via the billable procedures to which genetic counseling services lead (e.g., amniocentesis). While genetic counselors are likely to be, to the best of their abilities, truly neutral about the outcome of their counseling sessions, if women stopped wanting amniocenteses, genetic counselors could probably not long be paid. The fact that this is not likely to happen would seem to speak to the demand for amniocentesis, not the role of genetic counseling for either good or bad in women's decisions.

This leads to the more profound tension—the fact that the profession of nondirective genetic counseling has grown in tandem with the expansion of prenatal testing, which has as its underlying purpose diminution in the incidence of birth defects. Two perspectives on this tension seem possible. The first is that genetic counseling is, in fact, a central safeguard put in place to counter any possibility of eugenic intent or explicit eugenic outcome to offers of prenatal testing. However, this possibility is severely compromised by the tension surrounding payment for genetic counseling and the fact that genetic counselors appear—in aggregate although certainly not in each individual case—to be ratifying existing demand for amniocentesis. The other possibility is that genetic counselors are, unwittingly and unconsciously, handmaidens of the system—a sort of bioethical window dressing that actually allows what Troy Duster has called a "backdoor" to eugenics.[29]

The latter suggestion may at first strike many—including this author—as too reductionist a reading in which the individual intentions and integrity of the genetic counselor are disregarded. However, one must consider what would happen if the number of pregnancy terminations following confirmed positive prenatal tests were to drop below the point where offering that test was cost effective. While it does not seem probable that—in our current historical and social space—women would be coerced to end their pregnancies, it does seem likely that enthusiasm for that prenatal test would diminish greatly. That is, if no public consensus (demonstrated through the action of abortion) exists that a particular anomaly should be avoided, it seems extremely unlikely that resources are going to be expended in developing and maintaining programs and procedures for offering that test. It thus seems an inescapable conclusion that while genetic counselors strive to provide unbiased information and nondirective counsel, the place at which they are located in the medical system reveals their actual role to be to the furtherance of the true, but unacknowledgeable, goals of prenatal testing.

Conclusions

The arguments presented in this chapter are not intended as direct support for the expressivist argument. It is hoped, however, that this exploration of the silences, discomforts, multiple discourses, and structural tensions underlying the arena of prenatal testing will demonstrate the need to think in a broader way about what constitute the "messages" of prenatal testing, and who are the senders and receivers. This is important not primarily because of the putative negative effects of an offer of prenatal testing on those with disability. More crucial are the effects of our silences and evasions about our attitudes, desires, and intentions as regards the main driving forces of prenatal testing— selective abortion and attitudes toward disability. As we continue with increasing speed down an ever-widening path of prenatal testing, we need to ask: What message are we sending to ourselves by being willing to do something which we cannot truly discuss?

NOTES

1. Marsha Saxton, "Disability Rights and Selective Abortion," in *Abortion Wars: A Half Century of Struggle, 1950–2000*, ed. Rickie Solinger (Berkeley and Los Angeles: University of California Press, 1997), pp. 374–95; Anne Finger, *Past Due: Disability, Pregnancy and Birth* (Seattle: Seal Press, 1987); Adrienne Asch and Michelle Fine, "Shared Dreams: A Left Perspective on Disability Rights and Reproductive Rights," in *Women with Disabilities: Essays in Psychology, Culture and Politics*, ed. Michelle Fine and Adrienne Asch (Philadelphia, Penn.: Temple University Press, 1988), pp. 297–305; and Deborah Kaplan, "Prenatal Screening and Its Impact on Persons with Disabilities," *Fetal Diagnosis and Therapy* 8 supplement 1 (1993): 64–69.

2. Adrienne Asch and Gail Geller, "Feminism, Bioethics, and Genetics," in *Feminism and Bioethics: Beyond Reproduction*, ed. Susan M. Wolf (New York: Oxford University Press, 1996), pp. 318–50, at 339.

3. Allen E. Buchanan, "Choosing Who Will Be Disabled: Genetic Intervention and the Morality of Inclusion," *Social Philosophy and Policy* 13 (1996): 18–46.

4. Buchanan, "Choosing Who Will Be Disabled."

5. See also Eva Feder Kittay, "On the Expressivity and Ethics of Selective Abortion for Disability: Conversations with My Son," in this volume.

6. James Lindemann Nelson, "The Meaning of the Act: Reflections on the Expressive Force of Reproductive Decision Making and Policies," in this volume.

7. Erik Parens and Adrienne Asch, "The Disability Rights Critique of Prenatal Testing: Reflections and Recommendations," Special Supplement, *Hastings Center Report* 29, no. 5 (1999): S1–S22 (same as introduction to this volume).

8. Nelson, "Meaning of the Act."

9. Simon Mawer, *Mendel's Dwarf* (New York: Harmony Books, 1998), pp. 178–79.

10. William F. Hanks, *Communication Practices* (Boulder, Colo.: Westview Press, 1996), pp. 234–37; and Nancy Ainsworth-Vaughn, "Is That a Theoretical Question? Ambiguity: Power in Medical Discourse," *Linguistic Anthropology* 4, no. 2 (1994): 194–214.

11. Some of the data reported in this section have appeared previously in the following articles: Nancy Press and Carole H. Browner, "Collective Fictions: Similarities in the Reasons for Accepting MSAFP Screening Among Women of Diverse Ethnic and Social Class Backgrounds," *Fetal Diagnosis and Therapy* 8, supplement 1 (1993): 97–106; Browner and Press, "The Production of Authoritative Knowledge in Prenatal Care," *Medical Anthropology Quarterly* 10, no. 2 (1996): 141–56; Press and Browner, "Why Women Say Yes to Prenatal Testing," *Social Science and Medicine* 45, no. 7 (1997): 979–89; and Press and Browner, "Characteristics of Women Who Refuse an Offer of Prenatal Diagnosis: Data from the California MSAFP Experience," *American Journal of Medical Genetics* 78, no. 5 (1998): 433–45.

12. D. H. J. Brock, A. E. Bolton, and J. M. Monaghan, "Prenatal Diagnosis of Anencephaly through Maternal Serum Alpha-Fetoprotein Measurement," *Lancet* 2 (1973): 923–24; and D. H. J. Brock and R. G. Sutcliffe, "Alpha-Fetoprotein in the Antenatal Diagnosis of Anencephaly and Spina Bifida," *Lancet* 2 (1972): 197–99.

13. N. J. Wald, H. Cuckle, D. J. Brock, et al., "Maternal Serum-Alpha-Fetoprotein Measurement in Antenatal Screening for Anencephaly and Spina Bifida in Early Pregnancy: Report of U.K. Collaborative Study on Alpha-Fetoprotein in Relation to Neural-Tube Defects," *Lancet* 1 (1977): 1323–33.

14. Neil Anthony Holtzman, "Prenatal Screening for Neural Tube Defects," *Pediatrics* 71 (1983): 658–60; Press and Browner, "Why Women Say Yes to Prenatal Testing"; George Annas, "Is a Genetic Screening Test Ready When the Lawyers Say It Is?" *Hastings Center Report* 15 (1985): 16–18; Neil Anthony Holtzman, "What Drives Neonatal Screening Programs?" *New England Journal of Medicine* 325 (1991): 802–04; and Richard Steinbrook, "In California, Voluntary Mass Prenatal Screening," *Hastings Center Report* 16 (1986): 5–7.

15. F. J. Meaney, S. M. Riggle, and G. C. Cunningham, "Providers and Consumers of Prenatal Genetic Testing Services: What Do the National Data Tell Us?" *Fetal Diagnosis and Therapy* 8, supplement 1 (1993): 18–27.

16. Press and Browner, "Collective Fictions."

17. G. Deukmejian, C. L. Allenby, and K. W. Kizer, "A Report to the Legislature: Review of Current Genetic Programs" (Berkeley: State of California Health and Welfare Agency, Department of Health Services, Genetic Disease Branch, 1990).

18. P. M. Layde, S. D. von Allmen, and G. P. Oakley, "Maternal Serum Alpha-Fetoprotein Screening: A Cost-Benefit Analysis," *American Journal of*

Public Health 69 (1979): 566–73; S. B. Meister, D. S. Shepard, and R. Zeck-hauser, "Cost-Effectiveness of Prenatal Screening for Neural Tube Defects," in *Prenatal Screening, Policies, and Values: The Example of Neural Tube Defects*, ed. E. O. Nightingale and S. B. Meister (Cambridge, Mass.: Harvard University Press, 1987), pp. 66–93; A. D. Sadovnick and P. A. Baird, "A Cost-Benefit Analysis of a Population Screening Programme for Neural Tube Defects," *Prenatal Diagnosis* 3 (1983): 117–26; S. H. Taplin, R. S. Thompson, and D. A. Conrad, "Cost Justification Analysis of Prenatal Maternal Serum Alpha-Feto Protein Screening," *Medical Care* 12 (1988): 1185–200; and L. L. Tosi, A. S. Detsky, D. P. Roye, et al., "When Does Mass Screening for Open Neural Tube Defects in Low-Risk Pregnancies Result in Cost Savings?" *Canadian Medical Association Journal* 136 (1987): 255–65.

19. S. L. Clark and G. R. Devore, "Prenatal Diagnosis for Couples Who Would Not Consider Abortion," *Obstetrics and Gynecology* 73 (1989): 1035–37; and Steinbrook, "In California, Voluntary Mass Prenatal Screening."

20. G. C. Cunningham and K. W. Kizer, "Maternal Serum Alpha-Fetopro-tein Screening Activities of State Health Agencies: A Survey," *American Journal of Human Genetics* 47 (1990): 899–903.

21. See Barbara Katz Rothman, *The Tentative Pregnancy* (New York: Viking, 1986) for similar stories from women undergoing pregnancy terminations for fetal anomalies.

22. Philip Kitcher, *The Lives to Come: The Genetic Revolution and Human Possibilities* (New York: Simon & Schuster, 1996).

23. Claudia Strauss, "Who Gets Ahead? Cognitive Responses to Hetero-glossia in American Political Culture," *American Ethnologist* 17 (1990): 312–28.

24. Press and Browner, "Provisional Normalcy and 'Perfect Babies': Preg-nant Women's Attitudes Toward Disability in the Context of Prenatal Testing," in *Reproducing Reproduction: Kinship, Power and Technological Innovation*, ed. Sarah Franklin and Helena Ragone (Philadelphia: University of Pennsylvania Press, 1997), pp. 46–65.

25. Harold E. Yuker, *Attitudes Toward Persons with Disabilities* (New York: Springer, 1988); and G. L. Albrecht, V. G. Walker, and J. A. Levy, "Social Distance from the Stigmatized: A Test of Two Theories," *Social Science and Medicine* 16 (1982): 1319–27.

26. Steven Selden, *Inheriting Shame: The Story of Eugenics and Racism in America* (New York: Teachers College Press, 1999).

27. Henry Friedlander, *The Origins of Nazi Genocide: From Euthanasia to the Final Solution* (Chapel Hill: University of North Carolina Press, 1995).

28. Thomas H. Murray, *The Worth of a Child* (Berkeley: University of California Press, 1996).

29. Troy Duster, *Backdoor to Eugenics* (New York: Routledge, 1990).

Adrienne Asch

Why I Haven't Changed My Mind about Prenatal Diagnosis: Reflections and Refinements

The arguments raised by colleagues and friends during this Hastings Center project on the disability rights critique of prenatal genetic testing are important, serious, and sophisticated. They are made by scholars and health professionals with deep commitments to creating a more just, caring, and inclusive society for every child and family. The arguments raised against the disability rights critique and in support for the social practice of prenatal diagnosis are put forward by those who support the legal victories and societal changes that the disability rights movement has struggled to attain.[1] In what follows I will try to explain why, despite the challenges to this critique, I and others still believe that support for prenatal diagnosis and selective abortion contravenes the goals of people with disabilities for full acceptance and inclusion in our society, and why it also threatens cherished values in the parent-child relationship. I continue to view the practice of prenatal diagnosis followed by selective abortion as both misinformed about the true nature of disability and as problematic in what it connotes about societal and parental willingness to appreciate the many forms of human variation.[2]

I will not here review in detail the components of the disability rights critique, discussed in the opening chapter and in several other contributions to this volume. I am aware that many of my views are shared by others who espouse similar critiques; I do not present what follows as endorsed by all those with disability-based objections to prenatal testing.[3]

Throughout this project, we have discussed the contentions that prenatal diagnosis is "morally problematic" and "misinformed." I take up these arguments as they are discussed in the opening of this volume. Misinformation and misinterpretation about disability pervade the construction of some moral arguments. Consequently, I address moral problems and misinterpretation throughout this discussion.

The "Message" of Prenatal Diagnosis and Selective Abortion

You are a professor in a philosophy department at a large urban university. In your class of fifty students, you notice that five students have pierced tongues and lips and that a few others have dyed their hair in unnatural colors. You have difficulty even looking at these students because of their style, and you ignore their raised hands when they want to participate in class discussion. Midway through the semester, a man with dyed hair comes to your office to raise questions about the work in the course, and you realize that he actually has some interesting observations to make about the class and find yourself chagrined at your avoidance of his raised hand, of which you were only half aware until he appears at your door. The characteristics of Down syndrome, spina bifida, cystic fibrosis, or hemophilia, you say, are not as trivial as piercings and dyed hair, and perhaps you are right, but recognize that prenatal testing gives only one piece of information about the embryo or fetus, that it carries a particular characteristic thought worthy of note by the medical profession. Prenatal testing is a clear case of first impression, and as with any such impression, it is an incomplete impression; when followed by selective abortion or by discarding an otherwise implantable embryo, that first impression includes a decision never to learn about the rest of who that embryo or fetus could become after its birth. Mary Johnson, the longtime editor of a major disability movement publication, writes in a similar vein when she says:

> A decision to abort based on the fact that the child is going to have specific individual characteristics such as mental retardation, or in the case of cystic fibrosis, a build-up of mucus in the lungs, says that those characteristics take precedence over living itself, that they are so important and so negative, that they overpower any positive qualities there might be in being alive.[4]

Writing in 1987, another woman with a disability underscores how incomplete is the information provided by prenatal testing when she says:

> I know that amniocentesis can't tell any parents what kind of child they will have. It can only tell what disability might exist in that child. Amniocentesis could never have told my mother that I would have artistic

talent, a high intellectual capacity, a sharp wit and an outgoing personality. The last thing amniocentesis would tell her is that I could be physically attractive.[5]

No matter how much we may find the previous self-description immodest, it is the description of someone who feels that she must justify the right of people with her disability to exist because she recognizes that its presence alone makes others ignore everything else about her and could make future parents reject a child they wanted once they learned of this unexpected characteristic through a prenatal test.

Those who object to the "expressivist argument"[6] contend that prospective parents who terminate a pregnancy after a diagnosis of a disability may do so for many reasons that are not overtly prejudiced or hostile to people with disabilities. The prospective mother and her partner may feel that they haven't the financial or emotional resources to "cope" with the "extra" demands that a child with a disability would entail. Or they may already have a child with the same or another disability and feel stretched to their limit and want a child whose needs and demands will not be "special." Or, it is argued, the prospective parent may herself have a disability identical to the one diagnosed and may feel that to transmit that disability is to pass along a harsh and painful part of life to her child. All these claims do not refute the view that this one characteristic of the embryo or fetus is the basis for the decision not to continue the pregnancy or to implant the embryo. That decision still concludes that one piece of information about a potential child suffices to predict whether the experience of raising that child will meet parental expectations. In most cases of preimplantation genetic diagnosis or prenatal diagnosis, the woman or couple desires to be pregnant at this time; the termination of the process only occurs because of something learned about *this child*.

The Any/Particular Distinction

James Lindemann Nelson argues that this "any/particular" distinction as applied to the case of disability could be used to call any abortion into question. He claims that the fetus who would be the fourth-born child is also a "particular" fetus, and that *any* decision to abort is always a decision to abort a *particular* fetus at a *particular* time.[7] However, Nelson errs in equating the fetus diagnosed with a disabling trait and the fetus that would become the fourth-born child in a family. As Nancy Press points out, the property of "fourth-bornness" does not inhere in the fetus/child in the same way that disability does; the fourth-born child could just as easily have been the first or only child if adopted into another family.[8] Moreover, being a fourth child, or even a family with four children, does not subject the child or the family to the invidious treatment that has marked the lives of people with disabilities. Fourth-born children have not been kept out of schools because of that trait; nor have they been subject to institutionalization, denied access to worship services with their families, or rejected by potential playmates for the characteristic of fourth-bornness.

What of other possible any/particular distinctions in prenatal testing? At least three other types of "selective abortion" present themselves for discussion: selecting for or against a fetus based on its sex; reducing the number of fetuses; or aborting a fetus if it is determined that Ted, rather than Jack, is the genetic father. Like most members of our project group, I am uncomfortable with using technologies to determine and select for or against a future child based on its sex, since it, too, uses one characteristic as determinative. Selective reductions, from triplets to twins or from twins to one for example, that are not undertaken to preserve the health or life of the mother or fetus/fetuses, pose some of the same moral dilemmas surrounding what prospective parents should be open to in undertaking a family that I will discuss shortly with regard to raising a child with a disability.

Abortion arising from uncertain or undesired paternity poses a challenge to those of us who distinguish between abortions based on fetal characteristics and those responsive to a woman's life circumstances. Ending a pregnancy because Ted, rather than Jack, is the genetic father of the baby a woman is carrying surely is a decision about a "particular" fetus and not "any" fetus; but the decision results from the woman's evaluation of the nature of the relationship with each of the men and what it means to her to imagine raising a child created out of a relationship with Ted or Jack. It may have little or nothing to do with any sense she has of wanting to carry on one man's genetic legacy but not the genetic characteristics of another. If she bears the child, her circumstances and those in which the child lives may be very much influenced by whether Ted, rather than Jack, is its father, but those intimate familial circumstances do not equate with membership in the category of "women" or "people with disabilities." Outside the circle of people who are aware of the child's origins, the child will not constantly have the badge "child of Jack" or "child of Ted"; for every day of the child's life, innumerable small and large occurrences will not be due to the world's regard for "children of Jack" or "children of Ted" as they will be due to the world's evaluation of "how girls should behave" or "if I talk to the man in the wheelchair I might say the wrong thing and offend him." The child of Ted or of Jack is not a member of a historically discriminated-against class, such as people with disabilities have been. The mother may have different feelings about having become pregnant with Ted's child rather than Jack's, and her feelings may influence her relationship with and treatment of the child either positively or negatively; but the feelings are about her relationships with Jack and Ted and the meanings of having the child of one or the other in her body and for her life. A woman might say to herself, "I could never fully love a child of Ted," but that statement is not the same as saying, "I could never love a child who has brown hair, or is female, or has Turner's syndrome." Rather, it is a statement about the child as a reminder of Ted; if those same characteristics—brown hair, being female, or having Turner's syndrome—occurred in the child resulting from her relationship with Jack, they would not necessarily pose a problem for her. A woman planning to raise a child on her own may be less concerned with knowing who the genetic father is than would someone planning to raise a child in an ongoing relationship with Jack or Ted; thus, the paternity question might resolve into "Do I want to be a mother at all at this time?" changing the question from "Do I want a particular child with a particular father?" to "Do I want a child?" I argue that the any/particular distinction is important only when someone knows that she wants a child at a particular time, and that a conception or pregnancy is desired, but only if testing determines a particular characteristic (being female) or rules out a fetus or embryo based on one characteristic or property inherent, intrinsic, inevitable in the embryo/fetus/child-to-be.

Although Nelson contends that the any/particular distinction collapses because all abortions are abortions about particular fetuses at particular times in women's (or couples') lives, the reports of researchers who have studied women's experiences of these abortions following prenatal detection of disability indicate that the women view them as very different from previous abortions or from abortions for other reasons.[9] Women who undergo prenatal testing typically are ending either a planned-for or very much desired pregnancy, based on their conviction that the disability in a future child will be gravely destructive for themselves and their families. Women are reported to think of the fetus as a baby they look forward to raising, and when they decide to end the pregnancy, they do so because they believe that the birth of a baby with this characteristic will be heartbreaking, difficult, disappointing, and not the joyful experience they had anticipated in accepting this pregnancy.

The Selection / Prevention Distinction

In her contribution to this volume, Bonnie Steinbock argues that preventing the birth of a child who would have spina bifida is no different from taking folic acid to try to ensure the health of the developing fetus.[10] For Steinbock, discarding the affected embryo or aborting the fetus determined to have spina bifida, like taking folic acid to protect the fetus against developing it, prevents someone from being born who will have this disability. To Steinbock or to Nelson, anyone who is pro-choice on abortion should not be troubled by the method of abortion if one accepts the act of prevention by taking medication. According to Nelson and Steinbock, I and others who differentiate among these actions must either have more concerns about the morality of abortion than we are acknowledging, or we must believe that disabilities are central, and desirable, aspects of identity. I reject both claims. Susan Wendell expresses views resembling mine when she writes:

> I would be terribly sorry to learn that a friend's fetus was very likely to be born with ME [myalgic encephalomeyelitis, the disability], but I would not urge her to abort it. In other words, many people with disabilities, while we understand quite well the personal burdens of disability, are not willing to make the judgment that lives like ours are not worth living. Every life has burdens, some of them far worse than disability.[11]

Ending an otherwise desired pregnancy after learning of a diagnosis of spina bifida or cystic fibrosis says that this one fact trumps everything else one could discover about the child-to-be, and says that the woman (or couple) cannot accept into her intimate life a child with this character-istic when she planned to accept a child. A health report card becomes precursor to membership in the family, making the family rather like "the club" Leo Kittay describes in the discussion with his mother captured in her chapter in this volume.[12]

I will return to this matter of "family as club" and to the effects of prenatal testing upon concepts of parenthood later. For now, let me restate my conviction that women or couples should be free to reject becoming parents for whatever reasons they wish, and thus they should be able to use techniques like abortion to fulfill their familial goals. The conviction that a life with a disabling trait is so distressing that it should not be undertaken if it can be avoided is quite different from saying that, if possible, one will try to aid the child one is now creating to be disability-free. Ending the process of becoming a parent because of a future child's likely disability, when one wished to become a parent at the time that the disability was discovered, in the network of relationships and amidst the life plans in which the disability was discovered, is saying that the disability is inimical to the life one wants for oneself, one's family, and one's child. The idea of a child's disability is so disturbing that it is best to delay parenthood or change the methods of parenthood (adoption, assisted reproduction with provided gametes) to avoid the child with the disability. Better to end any fantasy relationship begun with the child being created and to begin anew hoping for a different child at a different moment than to continue to nurture the life begun. (There is more on "parenthood," "nurturance," and "life" later.)

Undoubtedly, the prospective parents (whether with prior knowledge of disability or virtual ignorance of life with disability) sincerely believe that disability is best avoided by discarding affected embryos or delaying pregnancy after terminating the one with an affected fetus. Nelson, Steinbock, and others contend that this motive need express no devaluing of existing people with disabilities and no insult to anyone who might in the future be born with ones similar to those that can now be prenatally detected. Perhaps people who perceive insult do so because by expending substantial resources to determine the genes for some characteristics but not others, health professionals reinforce society's negative views about what disability means for a life. They endorse the idea that these traits are not acceptable if they can be avoided and that people should not be born with these traits if women and couples have the means to prevent their births. People with just the disabilities that can now be diagnosed have struggled against an inhospitable, often unwelcoming, discriminatory, and cruel society to fashion lives of richness, of social relationships, of economic productivity. For people with disabilities to work each day against the societally imposed hardships can be exhausting; learning that the world one lives in considers it better to "solve" problems of disability by prenatal detection and abortion, rather than by expending those resources in improving society so that everyone—including those people who have disabilities—could participate more easily, is demoralizing. It invalidates the effort to lead a life in an inhospitable world.

Urging abortion if an otherwise wanted child is found to have the trait of hemophilia suggests that having hemophilia could destroy a good life for a child and his family, rather than recognizing that hemophilia could occur to some people and that the society should consequently design its institutions to ensure that all members can participate. Prenatal testing and abortion suggest that perhaps it would be better if people with hemophilia didn't participate. "Don't participate at all if you will have a disability" differs markedly from "Let's do the best we can to make sure that all our future children avoid disability, but we will expect that people are born with and acquire disabilities, and we will include everyone no matter the disability." The first statement rejects potential people if they have the undesirable trait; the second acknowledges that the trait may be undesirable but rejects no existing or potential person who bears it.

Traits, Persons, and Disability Identity

Do people in the disability rights movement go beyond asserting the humanity of people who have disabilities, to actually valuing the trait of disability? Where does disability fit into a sense of personal identity? In a recent paper, Nelson suggests that the critique of prenatal testing springs from the place of disability in a sense of personal identity.

> As scholars and activists in disability studies have helped make plain, many conditions regarded as disabling are also identity constructing in this social world. This is so, I think, in the sense that disability is a deep fact about a person's identity that does much to fuel the sentiments behind the [expressivist argument], the sense that some disability scholars and activists have that prenatal diagnosis and selective abortion threatens "our children."[13]

Reportedly some Deaf community members and some people who have achondroplasia would like to use the technology to select for fetuses who would be deaf or who would have achondroplasia.[14]

I, perhaps Wendell as quoted earlier, and others in the disability community would disagree with some or all of the ideas in the foregoing paragraph. Disability is not, and need not, be either a "deep" or a valued part of identity for everyone who shares the disability critique. And, as I will discuss, it is just as problematic to select for a disabling trait, thinking it guarantees something important about family life, as it is to select against it for the same reasons. Disability is not, and need not, be "central" for everyone who shares this viewpoint about prenatal testing.

Some people with disabilities clearly see themselves as part of a disability community and subscribe to the notion of a disability culture.

Increasingly surveys of people with disabilities learn that respondents identify themselves as belonging to a disadvantaged social minority.[15] Recognizing membership in a numerical and disadvantaged minority group need not lead to assuming that the fact of disability is either central or positive, although it should be pointed out that a person could construct a sense of personal identity with disability central and positive, central and negative, or other combinations. During everyday life, people with disabilities do not think constantly about having a disability, but rather take necessary medications, use whatever methods they need to move, read, communicate, and get on with their lives of playing, studying, and working. A Chicago attorney lives with a woman who is one of the partners in their small law firm; together they travel to scenic parts of the world and enjoy exotic restaurants and foreign films. When the attorney is at home, she is involved in her local Episcopal parish and an urban neighborhood garden project. Muscular dystrophy affects her mobility, so that she must choose restaurants, theaters, and projects at her parish and with the garden group that she can negotiate on crutches or using a wheelchair. When the logistics work, she is more involved in thinking about the project or the next trip and what she wants to experience and learn; she factors in the crutches and the wheelchair as people who use glasses must factor them in.

Is muscular dystrophy central, positive, negative, or neutral to her sense of identity, and how does that influence her thinking about selective abortion to prevent others from having her disability? Like Wendell, she need not ignore the burdens imposed by trying to function in a world that is still not wheelchair-friendly.[16] She might sometimes work with others interested in disability issues to promote greater access to city parks. Knowing that she enjoys wheelchair sports, she suspects that she might have become an avid hiker if she could walk longer and more easily. She can say, if asked, that having muscular dystrophy has sometimes impeded her because it has reduced her energy; neither has she enjoyed the intermittent hospitalizations. She may hope that any child she has will be free of the condition of muscular dystrophy so that her child might forego the hospitalizations and have the chance to enjoy hiking; however, she is confident that just as she has enjoyed her life, any child who had muscular dystrophy would similarly recognize the condition as a frustration or complication that could be managed along with other life complications. The attorney can acknowledge "might-have-beens" for herself and hope for them for any future child, just as I, a serious amateur musician, might wish that perfect pitch would preclude me from singing sharp. She, or I, or anyone else can recognize that we lack capacities that others have (call them disabilities or traits) and appreciate the lives we have even without those enjoyable traits. Singing sharp keeps me out of certain music groups, and years of study and voice lessons haven't cured my musical problems. I must content myself with singing where and with whom I can, even though better pitch might give me more access to a much-loved activity.

Unlike the nonmusical Mary in Marsha Saxton's chapter in this volume, I needn't worry that "people like me" (without good intonation) will be told that the world would be better off if there weren't more people like us, when I am doing the best I can with the equipment I have in the world as it is.[17] I can try to change myself to be a better musician; I can find places that will accept me with my mix of talents and problems as a musician; and I can enjoy the rest of life that includes many activities and people having nothing to do with music. I do not need to have an emotional investment in the fate of nonmusical people because it is not yet a characteristic that carries social stigma and occasions discrimination; prenatal testing does not yet announce to prospective parents that they might wish to learn of the musicality of their next child and prevent the birth of anyone with impaired intonation. Disability becomes central, or salient, when circumstances in the world around us compel us to make it salient or central. Put another way: those people within the disability rights movement who challenge prenatal testing do so in much the same spirit as they challenge other practices that have historically kept people with disabilities from being accepted as customers, students, coworkers, friends, and loved ones. They do so because they needn't celebrate nor even like certain facets of their impairments, yet they recognize that their lives—impairments and all—are respectable, acceptable ways to live.[18]

I have argued that disability moves from being one component of identity to being emotionally charged, and perhaps central, because it has been so consistently the occasion for institutional and personal rejection or segregation. All of these practices are part of what the movement adherents term "the social construction of disability," contrasted with the medical model that locates all problems of people with impairments in the impairments themselves and not in the social arrangements that impose needless hardships upon them. Fortunately, everyone in our project affirms that much of disability is socially constructed; what has remained a contentious and painful divide has concerned just how much is "social," how much is irremediable, and how negative for child, family, or society those irremediable facets of disability turn out to be.

Challenges to the Social Construction of Disability

Australian philosopher Christopher Newell opposes prenatal diagnosis for much the same reasons as Saxton, Wendell, Kaplan, and I do: that it reifies disability as medical rather than social in its problems.[19] He has a rich understanding of the social constructivist account of disability when he argues for the

> social nature of disability, proposing that prenatal diagnosis and termination is a technology of oppression and control which serves to devalue the lives of people identified as having disabilities. . . . I suggest a social constructivist account, but this does not deny a physiological component. I have spent years of my life in hospitals and the symptoms were not just social! Rather, it is the social meanings given to "difference," "the disabled body" and the "disabled mind" which are important in terms of "social construction." Genetic conditions occur in a social context, and their meaning and impact are inherently social.[20]

Opposing prenatal testing does not commit us to trying to avoid physical pain or to deny the biological realities of less energy, shortened life span, difficulty in breathing, need for mechanical devices and human assistance that might accompany impairments like cystic fibrosis, muscular dystrophy, or sickle cell anemia. Newell articulates that how people understand and interpret biological realities is crucial.[21] Those realities can be viewed as only negative, destructive, and defeating of life's possibilities, or instead can be understood as an unenjoyable, but singular, part of a life that also contains many riches.

Although medicine, bioethics, and science imagine that physical pain, reduced life span, and other disability sequelae are the enemy and the problem, many people who live with the conditions themselves or as intimates of people affected by these conditions are able to incorporate them into the whole of a life, neither celebrating them nor having those difficulties overwhelm the rest of what life brings. To the surprise of social scientists, people with and families affected by cystic fibrosis and sickle cell anemia often reframed the experience of living with the condition. Describing one twenty-nine-year-old aspiring academic, the authors write:

Her biggest concern about health care is paying for her treatment. She told us she wanted to have free health care. "I want that even more than I want not to have CF."[22]

Some project group members have less trouble understanding a social-constructivist account of disability when that account is limited to conditions without cognitive/emotional components. Most troubling to anyone who prizes the intellectual life is an impairment such as Down syndrome that precludes people from engaging in discussion of abstract ideas, or perhaps from discussion at all depending upon its severity. Parents of young people and adults with significant cognitive/communicative/physical impairments participated in our deliberations and tried to indicate that although some conditions limited life experiences in many ways, skillful teaching and care in creating supportive social arrangements provided people with multiple impairments—no verbal communication skills, hard-to-measure intelligence, limited physical mobility—with life opportunities that they and those around them found rewarding.[23]

Illustrative is Dianne Ferguson's description of the life of her twenty-eight-year-old son, Ian:

The latest interpretation of self-determination for my husband and me came wrapped in a Christmas Eve invitation. Our son Ian invited us to his house for Christmas Eve. Although Ian has lived in his own home for almost 2 years, we have still spent holidays together in our home. At 28, perhaps Ian and we have reached the age when our children initiate that shift in relationship that sends parents to their children's homes for family celebratory rituals. What is hard to say is how this particular event occurred. Did Ian somehow arrive at the determination that it was time to shift our holiday celebrations to his own home? Did his housemates, Robin and Lyn, who had been helping him can fruits and vegetables, make jam and breads, and decorate and arrange baskets for weeks "support his choice" to invite us over or shape his choice on his behalf? Did they somehow teach him how and why he might want to request our presence at this holiday celebration?

. . . The challenge of Ian, and others with even more significant cognitive (and physical, and sensory, and medical) disabilities, is how close they seem to come to the absence of agency in key parts of their life. . . . It is not just that people's real and apparent passivity is enforced by limbs that do not move, or environmental and service barriers that trap them either physically, socially, emotionally, or politically. . . . [W]e cannot really conceive the social world of someone whose experience of concepts and communication is so uncertain and seems all too woefully inadequate to warrant . . . characteristics of autonomy, self-regulation, empowerment, and self-realization.

. . . I do not know what Ian realizes about himself, although I would dearly love to know. . . . Yes, we are all interdependent, but the truth of the matter is that the balance of interdependence in Ian's relationships is disproportionate in most matters compared to my own. He is more dependent. He requires more care. He determines fewer things in the course of a day, week, or year than I do. Yet he does contribute in some very important ways to what occurs in his life. Does he choose? Sometimes. But, more often, he sort of indirectly influences events to end up being more okay than not okay from his point of view. . . . We want Ian to have a life that is more okay than not okay from his point of view most of the time.

. . . His contributions on this occasion were his ebullient renditions of carols, his energetic opening of gifts, his enthusiastic greeting when we arrived, and his just-controlled crabbiness about the finger-food supper.[24]

I have quoted extensively because here we have a description of a life event imagined impossible by most in medicine and bioethics for someone with his array of cognitive, physical, and communicative impairments. His mother does not deny that his life differs in some important ways from that of adults his age without impairments; she describes him as a "co-author" of parts of his life, being more affected by his relationships with others than adults who can express and move more than he without others' help. Yet Ferguson emphasizes what makes Ian more like, than unlike, other people inviting their parents to their home for a holiday.

People with the impairments of Ian (and Sesha described in Eva Kittay's chapter in this volume) represent the largest challenges to the "social construction of disability."[25] Nelson, Steinbock, Ruddick, Botkin, Baily, and several others argue that these forms of human variation cannot be "constructed" so as to be neutral.[26] The heart of a "social construction of disability" is, perhaps, to appreciate what's more similar than different in the lives of people with the most significant departures from species typicality and to affirm the ways they benefit from and contribute to the world and the people around them. Increasingly, there are scholarly and personal accounts of people with these disabilities who live lives they and their loved ones consider more good than bad most of the time, and lives that enrich those they know. These writings also reveal stress and difficulty in trying to achieve the mix of independence and support that leads to interdependence, and the complex imaginative leaps required for people with these disabilities to succeed in home, school, work, and community.[27]

Philip M. Ferguson captures the social constructionist understanding of disability when he reminds us that under the right circumstances people with sensory impairments can enjoy beauty; those with mobility impairments can experience physical exhilaration; and people with cognitive disabilities can think and communicate about something they consider important.[28] That some people with "moderate" or "significant" impairments flourish does not mean that everyone does or will, any more than it indicates that every nondisabled child will grow into a productive, contributing adult. It does, however, demonstrate that people who depart in radical ways from species typicality can participate in what those of us who are typical define as "the human community." We can agree that our disabilities impose limitations we might sometimes wish were not there, and in that sense the trait of disability may not be neutral.

People with disabilities can also agree that to have their impairments is not to be "species-typical"; what they cannot agree to is that their impairments make them in Erving Goffman's words "less than human" or, to think again in terms of prenatal testing, less worthy than others of entering the world of humankind.[29]

Parenting and Disability: **Nakhes, Tsuris, and Abortion**[30]

Our Hastings Center project analyzed the disability critique of prenatal diagnosis principally in terms of the implications for family life. Sometimes people interpret the disability rights critics as "siding" with the disabled fetus against unthinking, unfair parents. The critique is focused principally on the professionals who advise parents, rather than on the parents themselves. Like Bruce Jennings, I am concerned about how genetic science suggests that people reimagine pregnancy, parenthood, and their future children; like Nancy Press, the critique is not so much with the choices made, but with the choices made available.[31]

I share much with those who have written eloquently about parental responsibilities and parental hopes. Along with Steinbock, I believe that parents should not bring children into the world if they do not feel they can help their children have rewarding lives.[32] Like Ruddick, I believe that parents legitimately can have hopes and dreams for themselves, as well as for their children, in creating families, and they can try to influence their children to adopt interests, goals, and values they hold dear.[33]

We differ primarily in whether we believe that a child's disability will deprive child or parent of a rewarding life. If I believed that disability in itself, now or in the future, thwarted parental dreams for themselves and their children, I would not be a critic. Since almost all people who have disabilities can give and receive love, contribute to others, appreciate the world around them, and make a social contribution, I am convinced that children and adults can have lives they and others will value without depriving parents of what they seek in family life.

Most project members believe that people with significant disabilities can have lives they experience as rewarding but worry that life with a disabled child would be more difficult than life with a child without disabilities. On this view, parents could or should not be expected to envision the family life that included a child with a disability as equivalent to family life where no children had disabilities. Skeptics about the research findings and interpretations summarized in this book by Ferguson, Gartner, and Lipsky suspect that the research reviewed does not tell the whole story and that a child with a disability poses substantial heartache, difficulty, and burden to families that far exceed in kind and degree the stresses modern parents typically face.[34]

Some members of the project recoil at unfettered parental selection because they share the tenet of the disability critique that urges parents to recognize the uniqueness of each individual child and to value the child for what that child is, rather than lamenting what a child is not. The parents' love and imagination should encompass people who will be tall or short, tone deaf, color blind, girls or boys, gay or straight, risk-takers or risk-averse. Disability strikes them as qualitatively different from all these other forms of human variation. They argue that even if the child can manage to have an acceptable life in this society with its inadequate set of supports for parents raising ordinary children, raising a child with a disability who requires anything "extra" is more than harried, frantic parents will or should want to do. Disability critics assert only that if society, and prospective parents, recognized how lives of people with disabilities and their families resembled other lives, they might decide that they could love, enjoy, welcome, and raise such a child.

The question for disability critics is what to make of the "extra burden" or "negative family impact claim." Families are indeed stressed as it is raising ordinary children. The society is not set up for disabled children; there is no support—financial or otherwise—for extra expenses disability entails for families. Kittay echoes this message when she points out how fortunate she is that her family has the financial, personal, and social resources to help their daughter.[35] She asks whether the disability rights critics of selective abortion shouldn't concentrate instead on changing health care, the educational system, and other social institutions so that existing disabled children and adults will live more easily and demand less parental sacrifice.

Disability rights critics, or at least this one, entirely support her social goals. The United States in the new millennium is hardly a perfect world for anyone regardless of disability, and the fight for social change must go on. It must be a fight that says, however, that the social arrangements for "ordinary" children should change to include the "special needs" of disabled children; since all children have special needs, but some of them don't have labels, some needs get met and others don't. All too often the children who have needs labeled by disability are still told that their needs are not ordinary and that ordinary school programs, after-school groups, baby-sitters, and daycare centers can't handle them. Only a fraction of children with disabilities have such complex and ongoing medical needs that those who care for them require specialized training. In manifold ways, the "extra burden" of raising a child who has a disability falls on family because the society still won't accept that children with disabilities are part of the human race and must be expected and planned for when we collectively create transportation, schools, housing, workplaces, or families.

I am heartened by data demonstrating that more families flourish than founder if they are raising disabled children, just as more families flourish than founder raising nondisabled children; yet I know that some families of both groups experience tremendous difficulty, upheaval, and stress. There are moving accounts of familial joy in disabled members, and wrenching stories of sorrow, anguish, rejection, and family dissolution.[36] But the data showing family problems when there is a child with a disability should not be used against families trying to do their best any more than data about divorce rates should be used to convince people to eschew marriage. The information is at least as valuable for lessons we can learn about how to do things better, just as we use data about divorce to try to avoid pitfalls in our marriages. That many marriages fail does not make us abandon the institution but rather try to find ways to help people survive and thrive. What does it say about our society that we are interested in abortion for disability, but we don't support divorce?

The wealth of empirical data about "the impact of the disabled child on the family" should not be used in the service of blaming the child with the disability for all problems or for saying that social arrangements are adequate because most families do well. Data about thriving or struggling families will not solve the moral question of what kind of society and family climate we want to create. If we learn enough about disability to locate problems in the interaction of biology with environment and not to view them as the inevitable consequence of impairment, we should put our professional institutions behind strengthening families; we should not use social resources to announce to prospective parents that a child's disability will ruin a family, because the data do not support these conclusions. Medical professionals and genetic counselors should learn about what works and why, as well as what is hard, and they should provide parents with the information. Program designers and policymakers should learn from the success stories and redesign services and laws to ameliorate problems when we can. We should work for funding and enforcement of a little-known federal law passed in 1994 that would increase the supports for families raising children with disabilities and better integrate that service network with the rest of the human service system.[37] Bioethics, medicine, and genetics must learn the lessons about the social nature of disability if they are ever to give wise guidance to people struggling to make hard decisions. Rather than giving up on societal acceptance and family appreciation of people with disabilities because some social institutions reject and some families abandon disabled members, I urge us to learn everything we can about what promotes inclusion and to stand behind laws, services, and innovations that promote that inclusion and enjoyment.

Mary Ann Baily argues that she and other decent parents expect to love any child they have, disability or no, but that they want to avoid whatever they can with selective abortion if they learn of a disability before a child is born.[38] She holds the view that if it is acceptable for women to end a pregnancy for any reason or no reason, the detected impairment of a future child is an excellent reason. Paraphrasing her metaphor: Why climb the Mount Everest of parenthood with problems I can predict and avoid if I have the chance to climb Mount Rainier? Mount Rainier will have its own twists and surprises!

I find the metaphor and attitude tempting but dangerous. It is dangerous because it again assumes that only the twists of detectable impairment are problems, that anything else is acceptable, but that disability is different, worse, unacceptable. It assumes that the attitude toward avoiding a detectable disability in a once-wanted child will not carry over into the attitude of rejecting or not appreciating the child who acquires a disability at two or twelve, the partner at twenty, the friend at forty, and parents when they are in their eighties. Why should playmates' parents, the neighbors, or the schools change to incorporate existing children with disabilities if families and professionals, government, insurance companies, and science work as hard as they do to avoid the births of people who will have these conditions? Where do we first learn justice, sharing, and cooperation, but in the family? If families are urged by their professional advisors and by experts not to welcome wanted children because those once-wanted children will now turn out to have disabilities, where will families learn for themselves and teach their existing disabled and nondisabled children to cooperate, to share, to respect difference, to see similarity within difference? I believe that disability is seen as a burden and only a burden because people forget that along with that negative characteristic of disability come hosts of other characteristics that are positive and negative, that enable people with very profound impairments to enrich the lives of those who discover the personality along with the impairment.

Let us grant that disability causes stress for parents and expense for them and for society. So does raising children with exceptional gifts. In June 1999, a family moved from Florida to Virginia so that their ten-year-old son could live at home while beginning his freshman year of college![39] This family has spent extra money in finding him tutoring, a college that would accept someone usually in fifth grade, and in moving for the sake of his education; that may be more money and more disruption than disability occasions for many families. Studies of gifted children show that their families revolve around the children with those gifts and can experience marital stress and sibling difficulties resembling the ones blamed on the disabled child's presence in the family.[40] However, parents, siblings, and society tolerate the stress because they value the trait and the person with the trait, seeing the gift as offsetting the stress. The gifted child brings *nakhes* (joy) and makes up for the trouble (the *tsuris*). In raising a typical child, parents count on joy and struggle and expect them to balance out in the years of family life. With the child who has a disability, professionals emphasize negatives and burdens and often suggest that there will be no joy (no *nakhes*) and only trouble (*tsuris*).

If the majority continues to see disability as a form of human difference that is worse than other types of difference, it is no wonder that the majority will resist social changes that would incorporate people who have these negatively valued characteristics. The goal of the disability rights movement is to persuade the majority to recognize that people with those disabilities are not lesser than others because of those variations; they are not lesser in what they have to offer and what they can contribute to family and social life. If we truly believed that it was acceptable to have a disability, we would subsidize more disability-related expenses than we do as a society; even if parents paid some of their own money to help with making life easier for their son or daughter, professionals and the public would see it as neither better nor worse, nor different from the expenditures to help other children flourish.

Our society, as exemplified by medicine, science, education, and government, should do more than it does to help parents. It takes a village to raise every child, and perhaps that village needs to expand and change to include one described as having a disability.

If we want to create a society willing to include people with disabilities as well as accepting of parental decisions to avoid the births of disabled children, we must radically change how we offer prenatal diagnosis and selective abortion. In addition to the recommendations for a revamped counseling process endorsed by our project, we should change some other "messages." Professional literature should speak about the "possibility" or "likelihood" of having children with Down syndrome or spina bifida, rather than insisting upon using the word "risk" in discussions with prospective parents. Let parents themselves decide whether the possibility of having a child with one or another disabling condition is a risk to their hopes for family life. Similarly, spina bifida and other nonlethal disabilities should not still be described as "devastating defects" in professional literature or in materials given to parents contemplating offers of prenatal testing.[41] We should eschew the temptation to accept some limits on testing for non-health-related characteristics, or for only what professionals decide are severe and burdensome conditions. Offered balanced, careful information about detected characteristics, parents should decide what they believe is in accord with parental and family goals. Saying that color blindness and tone deafness are too trivial, but that blindness and deafness are serious enough to warrant testing and abortion, will not increase recognition of the humanity of people who are blind or deaf.

Although I commit myself to a trend toward much more selectivity than I would wish by respecting parental autonomy, I avoid the tendency to perceive disability as radically different from and worse than all other human difference. Because I oppose using selective abortion to avoid any traits, I oppose efforts of deaf parents or parents with achondroplasia to abort fetuses that would not share those particular traits. People with disabilities who seek such likeness in a child make the same mistake as those who reject children based on one characteristic—believing that the presence or absence of a trait predicts a satisfying life for a child, a fulfilling parent-child relationship, and a happy family life. Rather than wishing to make disability central to identity, I would like a world in which it assumed the moral, social, and professional significance that being fourth-born or nonmusical assume in this world.

I am convinced that professional limit setting based on a committee's list of "acceptable" and "unacceptable" disabilities or variations will erode what cooperation exists among people across disabilities. It will weaken those alliances being built between disability organizations and other political groups pressing for changes in how society handles new technologies, thinks about families, or deals with human difference.

I and others who take a critical view of selective abortion have been viewed as hard on parents and as holding out expectations that are too high. My concerns are much more with the professionals who set the tones that prospective parents hear than with prospective parents themselves. Ruddick is correct in saying that I would prefer all parents to imagine themselves able to welcome and nurture whatever children they have, and to see that the extras perhaps occasioned by some aspects of a child's characteristics may yield extras in human relationship.[42] The hours spent in daily physiotherapy with a boy who has cystic fibrosis could be viewed as only a tragedy and chore, or they could come to be a special time for family or friend to help someone they care about, knowing that in other ways the boy gives to them in fun, love, and companionship. Ruddick is also correct that I think the process of parenting begins when a woman (or she and her partner) accepts the idea of a pregnancy as the beginning of a relationship with a child-to-be. I do agree with people who worry that making acceptance of parenthood contingent on a child's characteristics will fundamentally change what is precious and unique in the love of parent for child and in family life. I recognize that prospective parents have their own limits and differences (call them disabilities?). If parents can make their choices about selective abortion after information that helps them to imagine a worthwhile life for child and family, I support parents in the decisions they make. There has been much searching and struggling in our project group. I have been moved and heartened by the words of Leo Kittay:

> The argument you're making draws a major line between normal and retarded [sic] children, based on the difficulty of bringing them up. But beware the slippery slope, Mom. Are not all children a burden?
>
> If, someday, we could determine that a fetus will develop into a hyperactive child, or into one with recurring ear infections, will these children's births also have to be expressly willed? Children are a burden. But it is incredibly important to keep making them and tolerating them. . . . No human child is fit for survival without the help of elders. To start drawing the line about how much help they should need is extremely problematic. Some groups of children will start vanishing. And we do not even want a single species of animal to disappear. They are all intrinsically valuable. How do we show others how wonderful it can be to raise a retarded child, and how important and valuable her existence is?
>
> . . . What kind of message does aborting the retarded send to would-be siblings?
>
> . . . My parents wouldn't just love any child they might have, they love me because I possess the desirable properties or characteristics that make me who I am.
>
> What I am trying to say is that the family starts to seem more like a club, and less like a family. In a club the members are selected based on one characteristic or another. This leads one to believe that if, for some reason, that characteristic is no longer attributable to the individual, or if anyone in the club comes to believe that this characteristic never applied, the membership in the group and the "love" that results can vanish.[43]

Thank you, Leo! You confirm my belief that there can be appreciation of people with disabilities, and of the disability critique of selective abortion.

Acknowledgments

I would like to thank Alan Gartner, Ruth Hubbard, John Kelly, Deborah Kent, Abby Lippman, and Cara Dunne Yates for suggestions to improve this iteration of our shared views. I also express deep appreciation to Taran Jefferies for clarifying the expression of these ideas, keeping me on track, and showing remarkable resourcefulness and grace under pressure.

NOTES

1. I am profoundly indebted to Erik Parens for initiating the project, for permitting me to collaborate closely in its every stage, and for the countless discussions that have assisted me to rethink and perhaps clarify my beliefs. I would like to think that our collaboration has heightened my respect and compassion for people trying to do their best in difficult situations.

2. This project and this volume concentrate on prenatal diagnosis because it is the most frequent form of antenatal testing. For my purposes in evaluating the arguments for and against the merits of prenatal testing and abortion, I need not distinguish among types of procedures done on fetuses or embryos and whether the traits looked for are "genetic" in origin. I am concerned with the activity of seeking to use any method designed to select against the births of people with prenatally detectable disabling traits. My concern applies to preimplantation genetic diagnosis, or to any other procedure that could be devised, and it applies to people who seek testing to avoid the births of nondisabled, as well as disabled, children, such as are hypothesized about members of the Deaf community or of Little People of America.

3. For several other statements of the disability rights critique, see the articles by Marsha Saxton, "Why Members of the Disability Community Oppose Prenatal Diagnosis and Selective Abortion," in this volume; and Adrienne Asch, "Prenatal Diagnosis and Selective Abortion: A Challenge to Practice and Policy," *American Journal of Public Health* 89, no. 11 (1999): 1649–57, and the references they cite.

4. Mary Johnson, "Aborting Defective Fetuses—What Will it Do?" *Link Disability Journal* 14 August–September (1990), cited in Christopher Newell, "The Social Nature of Disability, Disease, and Genetics: A Response to Gillam, Persson, Holtug, Draper and Chadwick," *Journal of Medical Ethics* 25 (1999): 172–75, at 174.

5. Eileen Cronin-Noe, " 'Thalidomide Baby' Grows Up," *Houston Chronicle*, July 26, 1987.

6. Parens and Asch, "The Disability Rights Critique of Prenatal Genetic Testing: Reflections and Recommendations," in this volume; and James Lindemann Nelson, "The Meaning of the Act: Reflections on the Expressive Force of Reproductive Decision Making and Policies," in this volume.

7. Nelson, "The Meaning of the Act."

8. Nancy Press, "Assessing the Expressive Character of Prenatal Testing: The Choices Made or the Choices Made Available?" in this volume.

9. Jeanne Menary, "The Amniocentesis Abortion Experience: A Study of Psychological Effects and Healing Process" (Ph.D. diss., Harvard University, 1987); and Rayna Rapp, *Testing Women, Testing the Fetus: The Social Impact of Amniocentesis in America* (New York: Routledge, 1999).

10. Bonnie Steinbock, "Disability, Prenatal Testing, and Selective Abortion," in this volume.

11. Susan Wendell, *The Rejected Body: Feminist Philosophical Reflections on Disability* (New York: Routledge, 1996), p. 154.

12. Eva Feder Kittay with Leo Kittay, "On the Expressivity and Ethics of Selective Abortion for Disability: Conversations with My Son," in this volume.

13. James Lindemann Nelson, "Identity and Disability" (paper presented at the second annual meeting of the American Society for Bioethics and Humanities, Philadelphia, Penn., October 30, 1999).

14. Parens and Asch, "The Disability Rights Critique."

15. National Organization on Disability's 1998 Harris Survey of Americans with Disabilities, available at http://www.nod.org/press.html#poll, accessed August 29, 1999.

16. Wendell, *The Rejected Body.*

17. Saxton, "Why Members of the Disability Community Oppose Prenatal Diagnosis and Selective Abortion."

18. See Deborah Kent's essay discussing the difference between her own and her family's responses to the possibility that her child might inherit her genetic disability. Deborah Kent, "Somewhere a Mockingbird," in this volume.

19. Newell, "The Social Nature of Disability"; Saxton, "Why Members of the Disability Community Oppose Prenatal Diagnosis and Selective Abortion"; Wendell, *The Rejected Body*; and Deborah Kaplan, "Prenatal Screening and Diagnosis: The Impact on Persons with Disabilities," in *Women and Prenatal Testing: Facing the Challenges of Genetic Technology*, ed. Karen H. Rothenberg and Elizabeth J. Thomson (Columbus: Ohio State University Press, 1994), pp. 49–61.

20. Newell, "The Social Nature of Disability," pp. 172, 173.

21. Newell, "The Social Nature of Disability."

22. Troy Duster and Diane Beeson, *Pathways and Barriers to Genetic Testing and Screening: Molecular Genetics Meets the "High Risk" Family* (Washington, D.C.: U.S. Department of Energy, October 1997), p. 47.

23. See also Fredda Brown, Carole R. Gothelf, Doug Guess, and Donna H. Lehr, "Self-Determination for Individuals With the Most Severe Disabilities: Moving Beyond," *Journal of the Association of Persons with Severe Handicaps* 23, no. 1 (1998): 17–26; Dianne L. Ferguson, "Relating to Self-Determination: One Parent's Thoughts," *Journal of the Association of Persons with Severe Handicaps*

23, no. 1 (1998): 44–46; and Michael Wehmeyer, "Self-Determination for Individuals With Significant Disabilities: Examining Meanings and Misinterpretations," *Journal of the Association of Persons with Severe Handicaps* 23, no. 1 (1998): 5–16.

24. Ferguson, "Relating to Self-Determination," pp. 45, 46.

25. Kittay, "On the Expressivity and Ethics of Selective Abortion."

26. Nelson, "The Meaning of the Act"; Steinbock, "Disability, Prenatal Testing"; William Ruddick, "Ways to Limit Prenatal Testing," in this volume; Jeffrey R. Botkin, "Line Drawing: Developing Professional Standards for Prenatal Diagnostic Services," in this volume; and Mary Ann Baily, "Why I Had Amniocentesis," in this volume.

27. Brown, Gothelf, Guess, and Lehr, "Self-Determination for Individuals"; Ferguson, "Relating to Self-Determination"; Wehmeyer, "Self-Determination for Individuals"; and David Goode, ed., *Quality of Life for Persons with Disabilities* (Cambridge, Mass.: Brookline Books, 1994).

28. Philip M. Ferguson, personal communication, cited in Parens and Asch, "The Disability Rights Critique," note 51, in this volume.

29. Erving Goffman, *Stigma: Notes on the Management of Spoiled Identity* (Englewood Cliffs, N.J.: Prentice-Hall, 1963), pp. 5–6.

30. This title comes from an interchange during one of the meetings of our project group: "People are worried that the child with a disability won't give parents the 'nakhes' they want from a child." Rejoinder: "It's not the 'nakhes' I'm worried about; it's the 'tsuris.'"

31. Bruce Jennings, "Technology and the Genetic Imaginary: Prenatal Testing and the Construction of Disability," in this volume; and Press, "Assessing the Expressive Character of Prenatal Testing."

32. Bonnie Steinbock and Ron McClamrock, "When Is Birth Unfair to the Child?" *Hastings Center Report* 24, no. 6 (1994): 15–21.

33. William Ruddick, "Parenthood: Three Concepts and a Principle," in *Morals, Marriage, and Parenthood: An Introduction to Family Ethics*, ed. Laurence D. Houlgate (Belmont, Calif.: Wadsworth, 1999), pp. 242–51.

34. Philip M. Ferguson, Alan Gartner, and Dorothy K. Lipsky, "The Experience of Disability in Families: A Synthesis of Research and Parent Narratives," in this volume.

35. Kittay, "On the Expressivity and Ethics of Selective Abortion."

36. Zolinda Stoneman and Phyllis Waldman Berman, eds., *The Effects of Mental Retardation, Disability, and Illness on Sibling Relationships: Research Issues and Challenges* (Baltimore, Md.: Paul H. Brookes, 1993); Myra Bluebond-Langner, *In the Shadow of Illness: Parents and Siblings of the Chronically Ill Child* (Princeton, N.J.: Princeton University Press, 1996); and Meira Weiss, *Conditional Love: Parents' Attitudes Toward Handicapped Children* (South Hadley, Mass.: Bergin & Garvey, 1994).

37. Families of Children with Disabilities Support Act of 1994, P.L. 103-382 (October 20, 1994); Title 20, U.S.C. 1491 et seq.: U.S. Statutes at Large, 108, 3937.

38. Baily, "Why I Had Amniocentesis."

39. National Public Radio, "Nine-Year-Old Florida Boy Graduating from High School," *Morning Edition*, June 3, 1999.

40. Ellen Winner, *Gifted Children: Myths and Realities* (New York: Basic Books, 1996).

41. Martha M. Werler, Carol Louik, and Allen A. Mitchell, "Achieving a Public Health Recommendation for Preventing Neural Tube Defects with Folic Acid," *American Journal of Public Health* 89, no. 11 (1999): 1637–40.

42. Ruddick, "Ways to Limit Prenatal Testing."

43. Kittay, "On the Expressivity and Ethics of Selective Abortion."

Part Four

Making Policies, Delivering Services

Dorothy C. Wertz

Drawing Lines: Notes for Policymakers

The Hastings Center project began with the premise that some lines might be drawn with regard to which disorders did and did not warrant an offer of prenatal diagnosis. Some project participants believed that underlying criteria could be used to differentiate between "serious" and "minor" genetic conditions. For example, Botkin[1] posits four criteria: effectiveness of treatment, impact on the child and family, age of onset, and likelihood that someone with the gene will actually develop the disorder in question. According to Botkin, fetal PKU (treatable), Huntington disease (late-onset), and Tourette syndrome (limited impact on life) would not warrant offering prenatal diagnosis as a standard of care, while cystic fibrosis, fragile X syndrome, and Down syndrome would require such an offer. Left unstated is who makes, or should make, the decision as to how and why a particular disorder fits under each criterion, or if indeed it fits under a criterion at all. (For example, what about the family that cannot afford the extra $8,000 for special, low-protein PKU foods, whose child will inevitably cheat on the diet? Is PKU really treatable in this case?)

Many policy documents, both national[2] and international,[3] implicitly assume that lines can and will be drawn but make no attempts to do this. The word "serious"—undefined and perhaps undefinable[4]—appears in the health policies of many countries. One country, Norway, actually attempted to ration prenatal diagnosis by legally limiting procedures to a certain number per year.[5] In effect, this meant refusing prenatal diagnosis that women requested solely to relieve their own anxiety, with no other "indications." (Anxiety is considered a medical indication in some countries and accounts for up to one-quarter of prenatal diagnoses in parts of Europe.[6]) On the other hand, in some countries, such as China, the word "serious" applies to almost everything, including cleft lip and palate, because almost all forms of ill health are considered a burden to society.[7]

In view of the enormous cultural differences in defining seriousness, the 1998 World Health Organization's *Proposed International Guidelines*[8] drew lines against use of prenatal diagnosis only for "nondisease" situations, such as sex selection in the absence of an X-linked disorder or prenatal paternity testing in the absence of rape or incest. The *Guidelines* also recommended that prenatal diagnosis solely for maternal anxiety be given lower priority in health budgets than prenatal diagnosis for women at higher-than-average risk of having an affected fetus due to age, family history, or biochemical test results.

I myself have advocated drawing a line against using prenatal diagnosis for sex selection,[9] although such line drawing seems to be a losing battle almost everywhere.[10] Since I once proposed at least one type of line drawing, I was asked to try to answer the following three questions:

1. Can we draw meaningful lines between conditions that are disabling primarily because of their biological reality and those that are disabling primarily because of how they are socially constructed?
2. If we can, does it matter for practice?
3. Can we offer any guidance whatsoever to policymakers?

Unlike most of my colleagues on the project, I will not delve into profound existential questions. The following chapter is an experiment in various kinds of line drawing, at a *practical* level, with particular reference to managed care and to the multiplex tests that may soon be available.

In dealing with these questions, I will refer to data from a recent set of surveys that I conducted. Anonymous questionnaire surveys of ethical views were distributed to 4,594 genetics professionals (including medical geneticists and genetic counselors) in thirty-seven nations, including 1,538 in the United States. Similar, but simpler, questionnaires went to 710 persons visiting a genetics clinic for the first time at fourteen different sites (mostly in the "rust belt" of older eastern and midwestern cities) in the United States and Canada, and to 852 U.S. primary care physicians (pediatricians, obstetricians, family practitioners), selected at random from the American Medical Association's *Physician Masterfile*, which includes all U.S. physicians, whether or not they are members of the AMA. In addition, some questions were delivered door-to-door, in a printed format, to 1,000 adult members of the U.S. public, by Roper Starch Worldwide, a survey organization. In the international survey, 2,903 (64 percent) responded; in the United States, 1,084 geneticists (or 70 percent of those surveyed, equally divided between MD/PhD geneticists and master's-level counselors),

476 (67 percent) patients, 499 (59 percent) primary care physicians, and 988 members of the public responded. The "patients" were not "prenatal patients." Most were mothers of children (median age five years) coming in for evaluation of the child. A minority (16 percent) were having prenatal diagnosis for advanced maternal age, and an additional 8 percent said they wanted to find out about "tests on an unborn baby." Most were working class (sales, clerical, factory, or service occupations), with a family income of $25,000 to $45,000 and a mean of thirteen years of education (29 percent had finished college). The discussion refers mainly to data from the United States, for several reasons: (a) except in English-speaking nations, much counseling follows a pessimistically directive course;[11] (b) the disability critique has not reached the level of public discussion in most nations outside North America and Western Europe; and (c) economic realities in some other nations force the discussion into a different context.

Biology versus Social Construction

Question 1. Can we draw meaningful lines between conditions that are disabling primarily because of their biological reality and those that are disabling primarily because of how they are socially constructed?

Yes, but in very few places. The general typology in Table 1 is largely based on whether a condition is a "normal human variation," which in itself is a fuzzy term.

1. "Normal" Fetus / Nondiseases

There are only two clear cases of "non-disease" in Table 1: sex selection and the deaf couple who would abort a hearing fetus (column 1). *Sex is not a disease.* Half of the 2,903 geneticists in our international survey said exactly that, in those words. Although some philosophers may not find this a sophisticated argument, it reflects a deep-seated human intuition. Sex is biological, distributed fifty-fifty among the human population, and carries no biological deficits. Its social correlate, gender, causes social disabilities for women in some societies, but prenatal diagnosis identifies sex, not gender. Race, though not identifiable by prenatal diagnosis, is a correlate to sex.

Identification of a "normal" or "hearing" fetus for a deaf couple who will abort a hearing child is similar to sex selection in that it uses technology to identify and eliminate a normal fetus. There was a widespread feeling among providers and parents in the survey that these

Table 1. Categories of Disease/Nondisease

1. "Normal" Fetus/Nondiseases	1a. "Normal" Fetus with Special Social/Familial Characteristics	1b. "Normal Human Variations"	2. "Risk Genes" (Elevated Risk of Some Disease Before Person Dies of Old Age, But Not Certainty)	3. Everything Else
Sex selection	Prenatal paternity tests, in absence of rape or incest	Bisexuality	BRCA (breast cancer)	Only chromosomal abnormalities are identified in the course of testing; routinely offered for advanced maternal age
Deaf couple wants deaf child	Twins (reduction to a singleton)	Exclusive homosexuality (2–7% of population)	APOE4 (Alzheimer)	
		Left-handedness	Probably most behavioral disorders where several genes and/or genes and environment interact (bipolar disorder, schizophrenia, alcoholism)	In the future, thousands of conditions could be added to a multiplex
		Blue eyes		
		> 20% overweight (close to half of U.S. population), but less than some extreme limit, say 300 lb.	Provides "fuzzy information" to parents even if test itself is accurate	Structural abnormalities are identified by routine ultrasound
		Autosomal recessive or X-linked carrier status, in absence of symptoms		
		Low normal IQ		

two cases were a misuse and corruption of medical services. There was also a felt demarcation between these two cases and another situation involving a "normal" fetus: prenatal paternity testing. Although one cannot "do ethics" on the basis of opinion polls, responses of the various stakeholders must be dealt with in the long run. In this country, where autonomy reigns, there must be a strong potential for harm in order to outweigh autonomy. Sex selection is probably the only case where there is clear potential for harm to the wider society, by unbalancing the sex ratio or perpetuating gender stereotyping. Overriding individual autonomy would be justifiable in this case, though resorting to law or regulation would set a highly dangerous precedent for other restrictions.

Although there is probably little or no social harm from a deaf couple aborting a hearing child (the situation would be extremely rare), aborting a fetus simply because it is "normal" appears to pervert the goals of medicine (helping people to live to the fullest extent possible) in order to satisfy special interests. If lines are to be drawn, this case belongs in the same category with sex selection. Probably the only clear line that can be drawn is between column 1 and the rest of the table.

1a. "Normal" Fetus with Special Social/Familial Characteristics

The two cases in column 1a, prenatal paternity testing in the absence of rape or incest and reducing twins to a singleton are similar to the cases in column 1, in that they involve abortion of a "normal" fetus. However, the line is much less clear. Both these cases share a common situation with elective abortion generally, and courts have agreed that women have the right to choose. If one can abort a singleton, why not half of a set of twins? If a woman can abort a fetus because it has the "wrong" father when only one man is involved, why not when two men are involved? It could be argued that these cases are extensions of abortion rights generally. If prenatal diagnosis were not involved, this would be logical. A woman could abort because she thinks the fetus has the "wrong" father. Twins, identified as such in the course of usual prenatal care, could be reduced to a singleton at parental request, under *Roe v. Wade*. (There is usually no compelling medical reason to do so, as twins and their mothers are only at a slightly elevated risk. Reducing triplets or higher orders of multiple fetuses to twins may increase the likelihood of survival and health for the remaining fetuses.)

However, if prenatal diagnosis is used for the specific purpose of identifying the father or the condition of "twinship" (or to identify the twins' sexes), these cases become similar to the cases in column 1 in that they identify a "normal" fetus. (I have placed "normal" in quotes throughout, as we can never be certain that a fetus falls within average parameters until it is born and completes its life span.) If equal cases are to be considered equally, as John Rawls suggests, one could also draw a line against these cases. The German Genetics Society, in its code of ethics, forbids prenatal paternity testing in the absence of rape or incest. Use of prenatal diagnosis for the express purpose of identifying twins and reducing them to a singleton in the absence of medical necessity could also be forbidden under a code of ethics.

1b. *"Normal Human Variations"*

The conditions listed in column 1b—sexual orientation, left-handedness, and blue eyes and other cosmetic conditions, more than 20 percent overweight, recessive or X-linked carrier status in the absence of symptoms, and "low normal IQ"—are all shared by substantial portions of the population, though none is a characteristic of the majority. All of these have social dimensions, and some (obesity, handedness, and sexual orientation) are related to reduced life span, either through biological or social intermediacy (heart disease for obesity, accidents for left-handedness, and hepatitis or HIV for bisexual or homosexual orientation). For obesity, there is a fuzzy line between the average "too much" and a "really, really too much" that sets the person many standard deviations outside the general population. Nevertheless, so many people have one or more of these characteristics that the characteristics must be considered part of normal human variation. Statistically, these characteristics cannot be compared with the "population risk" of about 3 percent for having a child with a genetic condition or "birth defect." There are so many different genetic conditions that no one condition (with the possible exception of hemochromatosis, a treatable condition) even comes close to affecting 1 percent of the population. (Down syndrome, one of the most common, affects one in a thousand newborns, or one-tenth of 1 percent). As yet, and for the foreseeable future, there are no tests for anything listed in this column—except fetal carrier status for an autosomal recessive or X-linked disease. Parents learn about their own carrier status often only inadvertently when a child tests positive for the disease. If tests with real predictive values do become available, it would be possible—ethically speaking—to draw a line against providing tests for anything in this column, because, like the cases in columns 1 and 1a, these are "normal" fetuses. (Please be patient. I am going to speak practically in answering Question 2.)

2. "Risk Genes"

Many tests provide an elevated risk, but no certainty, of getting a common disease if one lives long enough. Examples are BRCA1 and 2 (significantly elevated risk of breast cancer) and APOE4 (elevated risk of Alzheimer disease). Most behavioral disorders (bipolar disorder, schizophrenia, alcoholism) probably fall into this category, with a complex interaction between several different genes and the environment. Individual genes may be associated with higher or lower risk but cannot predict severity of disease or age of onset, or even whether the disease will actually occur. Tests for the presence of what I will call "risk genes" would provide "fuzzy information" to parents, even if the tests themselves were highly accurate in identifying particular mutations. Most of us have trouble interpreting risk—we underestimate numerically high risks and overestimate numerically low risks.[12]

A note on testing children for adult-onset diseases. As a further complication, most of the "risk genes" point to adult-onset diseases that appear after the parents' period of caregiving is over. Unless the fetus is aborted, testing for these risk genes prenatally is tantamount to testing children for adult-onset disorders. The major professional societies (American Medical Association,[13] American Society of Human Genetics [ASHG],[14] National Society of Genetic Counselors[15]) have recommended against testing children for disorders that may occur later in life, unless there are proven methods of prevention or early diagnosis that are useful in childhood. No such methods exist for the diseases that may be predicted by "risk genes" (such as breast or ovarian cancer, Alzheimer disease, or adult-onset diabetes). Nevertheless, many parents may think that they can prevent the disease by drastically controlling a child's behavior, for example by enforcing a strict diet. (One woman in the survey said that if her daughter had a BRCA mutation, she would make the girl become pregnant at age sixteen and every year thereafter, because she thought early and continued pregnancy would prevent breast cancer.)

I would like to suggest that few people would abort for the conditions listed in column 2, at least on the basis of responses to the patient and public surveys. I would also like to suggest that abortion may not be the worst outcome of testing for these "risk genes." If the parents decide to carry to term after the test indicates the child carries mutations associated with such risk, the child could face a "genetically determined" future, clouded by risk, with the possibility of stigmatization by parents, schools, insurance companies, employers, and society in general. Every symptom or misbehavior could be regarded as a special cue, and (at least for behavioral conditions) parental expectations could become self-fulfilling prophecies. I would therefore suggest that unless the parents would consider abortion if they get a result identifying a given mutation, prenatal tests for "risk genes" for adult-onset disorders should not be offered. Counseling should follow the model proposed in the ASHG statement[16] on testing children.

3. Everything Else

The category "Everything else" (column 3) consists of "real disorders," all of which have a well-described "biological reality," as well as varying degrees of "social construction." It is impossible to draw lines within this category, because individuals have their own definitions of the word "serious." These definitions may be related to culture, socioeconomic status, religion, or personal experience. People also have different understandings of what is socially constructed and what is biological.

Many genetic conditions have a wide range of expression, from so-called "mild" to so-called "severe," and professionals would be hard put to place any firm label on them. Furthermore, placing labels may offend people from cultures that take a different view of a particular condition. Drawing lines within this broad category, which includes most prenatal tests, is not only practically difficult but also offensive, both to individuals' autonomy and to some people with disabilities, who might consider their conditions labeled inappropriately. It therefore seems most appropriate to let the people who will raise the child—the parents—make the decisions within this broad category.

Extenuating Circumstances and "Hard-Luck Cases"

In theory, we could draw a line against testing for situations in columns 1, 1a, 1b, and possibly even 2. However, there are always extenuating circumstances in which a medical professional might believe that the medical benefits gained from testing exceed the harms. Some examples include the parents with heart disease who feel that raising twins will kill them; the couple that will break up without prenatal paternity testing; the woman with "genetic" breast cancer who is morbidly anxious about her fetal daughter's future health; the parents who can't stand homosexuals and would make a gay son's life miserable, and so on. Many of these cases fall under the heading of individual or family mental health. Medical professionals usually feel some obligation to promote mental health, to reduce anxiety, to keep families together, and to prevent the stresses of family breakup on both parents and children. There will undoubtedly be cases where doing the test is the course of least harm. Probably the only place where a hard line might be drawn is column 1, sex selection and the deaf couple. And even here, there may be some allowances for "mental health." This brings us to the second question.

Question 2. If we can draw conceptually coherent lines, does it matter for practice?

Probably not, at least in terms of what is allowed. We have already lost the battle against sex selection, judging from the survey results in Table 2. There appears to be a growing trend in the United States and many other nations to honor such requests or at least to offer referrals.[17] Referrals are the Achilles heel of many professionals' attempts to draw lines. Most professionals feel they have an obligation to offer referrals

Table 2. Prenatal Diagnosis in Controversial Situations: Geneticists, Primary Care Physicians, and Patients

Situation	Geneticists (n = 1,084)	Primary Care Physicians (n = 499)	Patients (n = 476)
Sex selection[a]	34/38[b]	34/34[b]	59[c]
Deaf couple wants a deaf child	35/33	21/29	57
Paternity testing (no rape or incest)	56/35	62/29	87
Maternal anxiety alone	88/8	28/40	78

[a]A couple with four daughters desires a son.
[b]Percent who would perform/percent who would refer.
[c]Percent who thought doctor should honor patient's request.
Note: The majority of geneticists and primary care physicians thought insurers should not pay for testing in any of these situations.

for services to which they are morally opposed, including sex selection (Table 3). This is a function of an overriding belief in individual autonomy. Although the referral process might exhaust prospective parents in countries with universal health care systems (where the referral would likely also refuse sex selection, following system guidelines for payment), in the United States people with the initiative and the money will be able to get the services they want. Even some professionals who said, "Sex is not a disease," would offer referrals for sex selection or would perform prenatal diagnosis on grounds of autonomy.

The deaf couple who say they would abort a hearing child and the woman who asks for prenatal paternity testing are also likely to find someone who would provide the requested services (Table 2).

If a family has trouble getting what they want, they can always ask for prenatal diagnosis under the guise of another reason. Those who want sex selection can conjure up a false family history of chromosomal abnormality (with no centralized records in the United States, it will be difficult to check this out). The deaf couple, after one rebuff, may learn that the "correct" approach is to say they want prenatal diagnosis in order to abort a deaf child; they can do what they want once they have the information. The woman who wants paternity testing can take refuge under the umbrella of "maternal anxiety," which most providers regard as a legitimate medical indication for prenatal diagnosis (Table 2). So can parents who are afraid of homosexual offspring, breast cancer, or behavioral disorders. Thus, in effect, it would become virtually impossible to enforce lines even if they were drawn. People with the money will find a way to get most of the services in columns 1, 1a, 1b, and 2 (Table 1).

Probably the only place where lines can be drawn is in the area of payment by public funds or private insurance. This is the place where Americans usually like to draw lines. (So who cares if poor people are unable to get some of these tests, as long as I get mine?) It is not necessarily the most ethical place to draw lines. However, in the absence of a just system of universal health care, we must consider Question 3.

Question 3. Can we offer any useful guidance to policymakers?

Yes. Let's try the following exercise.

Imagine that you are a business manager of a health maintenance organization (HMO). You may have "M.D." after your name, but your priorities are:

Table 3. Views on Autonomy and Rights to Services: Genetics Professionals, Primary Care Physicians, and Patients[a]

Rights to Services	Genetics Professionals (n = 1084)	Primary Care Physicians (n = 499)	Patients (n = 476)
Withholding any requested service is paternalistic and a denial of the patient's rights	56	57	69
Prenatal diagnosis should be available to any woman who requests it	41	42	80
Patients are entitled to any service they request and can pay for out-of-pocket	36	26	60
When patients ask for a procedure that a provider is unwilling to perform for moral reasons, the provider owes patient a referral, if procedure is legal	90	82	86
If law forbids a procedure in state/country, should refer outside state/country	65	55	50
A provider who refuses sex selection should offer a referral	55	41	50
Genetic counselors should support all patients' decisions	90	not asked	80
A woman's decision about abortion should be her own, without any intervention from anyone	85	65	60
Parents should have the right to choose the sex of their children	10	11	13
Parents should be told fetal sex if they ask	91	87	92
After taking a test, patients should have the right not to know the results	82	62	40

[a]Percent in agreement.

1. To stay in business.
2. To provide sufficiently adequate care to beat (or at least equal) the competition from other HMOs and independent physicians.
3. To keep the bottom line in the black.
4. To avoid costly lawsuits.
5. To maintain a good public image (necessary in order to fulfill priorities 1 through 4).

This list sounds cynical, but HMOs, like most of American medicine, are businesses. Medicine has always been a business in this country; the difference is that now it's big business. This does not mean that doctors are necessarily callous or uncaring.

If yours is a for-profit HMO, your primary responsibility is to your stockholders, not to the income-producing biological units ("Biological Structures Yielding Cash [BSYCs]"[18]) that most people call patients. Actually, there is probably not too much difference between the criteria used by for-profit and non-profit HMOs in deciding what services to provide.

In reality, everybody can't have everything. This would also be true under universal health care. Costs of prenatal tests add up, so everybody will not be tested for everything, though some will be able to purchase everything privately if they pay out of pocket. What criteria can HMOs use to decide who gets offered what?

The HMO could draw a line against the services in column 1, Table 1 (sex selection and the deaf couple) without too much trouble. These are nonmedical services that do not diagnose disease and are not customary. (Clients cannot sue for nonprovision of services that are not customary.) The HMO could also draw a line against offering prenatal diagnosis for the cases in columns 1a (paternity testing, twins) and 1b (normal human variations), with exceptions for situations where there is a threat to physical health (twins) or mental health for parents or child. (Preserving mental health is possibly a big "out," unless monitored carefully, but mental health services are expensive.) To those who say it is impossible to differentiate clearly between "normal human variation" and "mild" genetic disorder, I would reply that while there is inevitable overlap, health systems have to make judgments of this sort all the time in deciding what medical (not necessarily genetic) tests to offer in attempts to diagnose puzzling symptoms and decide how far to proceed with treatment of disease. If a large portion of the population has a given condition and it's not the result of infection, malnutrition, toxic exposure, war, or accident, it seems simplest to deem it as a normal variation, and thus not an appropriate target for testing. Most genetic conditions have been medically labeled as needing treatment (if such is available), unlike brown eyes or homosexuality. Most are also sufficiently rare as not to provoke confusion with "normal human variations."

HMOs could also draw the line against offering tests for the "risk genes" in column 2, Table 1, on grounds that these tests do not provide certainty of disease and that most of the diseases in question do not appear until adulthood. Exceptions could be made for parents with a family history of the disease, if they express concerns about the possibility of their children having the disease. As explained above under "A Note on Testing Children for Adult-Onset Diseases," counselors should explain the potential harms of labeling and stigmatization if the child is tested for an adult-onset condition as a fetus and is subsequently born. Pretest requirements (for abortion) would be undesirable and restrictive of parental autonomy.

So how should an HMO determine what tests to offer among the literally thousands that are or will become possible in column 3 (Table 1)? The karyotyping offered routinely to women of advanced maternal age (thirty-five or over) identifies only chromosomal abnormalities (extra or missing chromosomes). (Criteria other than age—toxic exposure or multiple miscarriages, for example—may also lead to offers of karyotyping.) The routine ultrasound identifies some structural abnormalities. Everything else (e.g., cystic fibrosis, sickle cell anemia, PKU, familial hypercholesterolemia, fragile X, etc.) requires a special test. Today, these tests are done only if there is reason to suspect that there is a higher-than-average chance that the fetus will have the condition. Usually, this means a family history or birth of a previous child with the condition, or parents who have been identified as carriers of the gene in question. People with a family history should be offered tests for the condition in question, whatever its characteristics, on the basis that they have a *right to the information* if they wish it, not on the assumption that they will wish to abort.

Multiplex Tests

In the future, through DNA chip technology, it may be possible to offer tests for thousands of conditions for mere pennies per test. What criteria should be used in placing tests on a "multiplex" that could be offered to the general pregnant population, in the absence of family history? (Even at pennies a test, costs still add up.)

The great existential questions—"Is this life worth living?" or "Is existence in an 'impaired state' preferable to nonexistence?"—are *not appropriate in a policy-making context.* Considering such questions can lead to coercive eugenics, whether at the governmental, insurance, or HMO level. The Nazis had an elaborate bureaucratic apparatus for considering these questions and using the answers to send children to the gas chambers.[19] In a democratic society, only the parents have the right, and burden, of using such questions in their decision making.[20] The criteria appropriate for policymakers are more mundane and involve treatability and frequency of the condition. The criteria used by state public health officials in deciding what tests to include in routine newborn screening provide a good example. The basic criteria are (1) that early treatment for the condition is available and will benefit the new-born, and (2) the condition is sufficiently frequent in the general population (or ethnic/social subsets) to warrant expenditure of public funds. (Frequency may be one in ten thousand or even one in thirty thousand.)

These criteria can be translated into criteria for placing prenatal tests on a multiplex, as follows:

1. The condition can be treated before birth. This is direct medical care; probably no one would object to applying such a test routinely. At present, very few prebirth treatments exist.
2. The "medical management" of the birth itself can be prearranged to meet the needs of a child with the condition. This may mean early delivery, Cesarean section, moving the birth to a hospital with a neonatal ICU, avoiding some medications, and so forth.
3. Immediate treatment at birth offers a health advantage over waiting for the results of newborn screening. This may be an argument for moving some newborn screening to the prenatal period, particularly since some mothers leave the hospital before the optimum time for newborn screening.
4. Conceptions of fetuses with the condition in question are relatively frequent (excluding those that miscarry too early to be identified). Incidence (frequency of new occurrences) is a usual rationale in allocating medical services.

5. Parents are members of an ethnic/social group at elevated risk for the condition.
6. Accuracy and costs of the test.

None of the above criteria involve "seriousness." This is an individual parental judgment.

To these criteria will inevitably be added one more, after the HMO/insurance company has had some experience with multiplex testing. This last criterion will be the use that prospective parents make of the information provided by testing. If the information about a particular condition makes no difference in medical preparations for the birth or to parents' reproductive plans (for example, nobody has an abortion), the HMO may decide not to offer the test, unless, of course, someone asks for it. The information may have other uses than determining whether to abort, however, and these should be taken into account before discontinuing a test. For example, there may be a positive mental health benefit to knowing about the condition before the birth and being able to prepare. These benefits are not yet proven and would have to outweigh the costs and risks of testing for the fetus.

The criteria above will inevitably lead to some "frivolous" choices and some abuses. These may be few, however. It appears that the American public is not eager to abort for most fetal conditions (Tables 4 and 5). The alternative to allowing some abuses would be to establish a government "Bureau of Good Parenthood" that would rule on exactly who could have what tests. The French seem to think that this is possible. Most Americans would find it repressive and meddlesome.

Case Example: Prenatal Diagnosis for Webbed Toes

Suppose a woman wants prenatal diagnosis to determine if the fetus will have webbed toes. Will she get it from her HMO under the guidelines proposed above?

If she has a family history of webbed toes and wants prenatal diagnosis, the answer is yes. It is for her to decide just how great a "disaster" having webbed toes may be for a child. This is probably how most Americans want it. Even if they themselves would never abort for such a condition, they believe that others should have the right to make "wrong" decisions. If the HMO has trained its providers well, she (like other women who are offered prenatal diagnosis) will be told about the risks of the procedure to the fetus. If webbed toes are her

Table 4. U.S. Public's Views on Abortion (n = 988)[a]

Situation	Abortion Would Be Acceptable for Me or My Partner	I or My Partner Would Not Have Abortion, But It Should Be Legal for Others	Abortion Should Be Illegal	Don't Know
Mother's life in danger	69	12	10	9
Pregnancy caused by rape	63	13	13	11
Child would be severely retarded and would die within first few months of life	48	20	18	14
Child would be severely retarded, unable to speak or understand, with a nearly normal life span	47	20	18	15
Child would not be retarded but would be paralyzed from the neck down, with normal life span	41	22	19	18
Child would be moderately retarded (could communicate, but not live independently)	22	31	30	18
Child would get a severe, incurable mental disease at age forty	21	29	28	22
Child would be mildly retarded, but could work and live independently	17	35	30	17
Child would be grossly overweight, with no chance at successful treatment	18	29	35	20
Child is not the sex desired by parents	7	22	58	13

[a]Percent in agreement.

Note: Characteristics associated with acceptance of abortion in most situations above: male, aged thirty to forty-four, income over $50,000, college graduate, professional or white collar occupation, union member, residing in Northeast or West, single, Democrat, liberal politics.

Table 5. Personal Attitudes toward Abortion: Genetics Professionals, Primary Care Physicians, and Patients[a]

Condition	Genetics Professionals (n = 1,084)	Primary Care Physicians (n = 499)	Patients (n = 476)
Anencephaly	94	n/a	88
Trisomy 13	93	93	81
Hurler syndrome	91	n/a	77
Severe spina bifida	90	78	63
Down syndrome	80	62	36
Cystic fibrosis	62	47	52
Achondroplasia	57	29	24
Sickle cell anemia	52	39	72
Neurofibromatosis	51	37	40
XXY	49	48	22
PKU in fetus	44	45	n/a
45,X	42	37	9
Severe obesity	29	13	8
Cleft lip/palate	12	10	5
Child is not desired sex	3	3	1
Huntington disease	64	50	32
Familial hypercholesterolemia (homozygous)	48	10	9
Predisposition to schizophrenia or bipolar disorder	27	24	59
Predisposition to Alzheimer disease	20	16	5
Predisposition to alcoholism	10	8	4
Toxoplasmosis	80	72	20
Rubella	84	79	68
Mild retardation (could live independently)	n/a	n/a	20
Pregnancy result of rape	87	81	75
Mother's life in danger	96	95	71
HIV in fetus	85	74	64

[a]Percent who would abort.

only reason for having prenatal diagnosis, she may reconsider after hearing about these risks.

Suppose the woman does not have a family history of webbed toes or a history of toxic exposure. She asks for prenatal diagnosis because a neighbor's child has webbed toes, or perhaps because she has had dreams that her child will look like a frog. Will she get prenatal diagnosis from her HMO? No, except under the most unusual conditions. She would have to convince a mental health professional that without prenatal diagnosis she will suffer grave psychiatric consequences.

Will a test for webbed toes be on the multiplex offered to women of advanced maternal age? No. Knowing that a fetus has webbed toes makes no difference in terms of prenatal treatment or birth management. It makes no difference to most people's reproductive plans. Therefore, there is no reason to offer it or even to tell women about its existence, unless there is a family history.

The "webbed toes" case, although hypothetical, is the kind of circumstance that concerns bioethicists and people in the disability community who fear that fashion or a desire for perfection will submerge human diversity. The approach suggested above would prevent such tests from being offered routinely, while allowing sufficient flexibility for individuals with personal reasons (e.g., family history) to obtain the tests. We need a balance between personal autonomy and the requirements of a health care system that cannot offer everything to everyone.

Why Counseling Needs to Change

The preceding discussion assumes that people are receiving clear, comprehensive, unbiased, empathetic counseling. Although most professionally trained genetics specialists try to achieve this perhaps unreachable ideal in professional interactions, they also have personal viewpoints.

Most genetics services providers (particularly master's-level genetic counselors) said they would be nondirective in counseling about most conditions (Tables 6 and 7); however, they were personally much more willing to abort for these conditions than were primary care physicians (Tables 5 and 8) or patients (Table 5). This divergence between personal attitudes and reported professional behavior raises the question of whether the personal sometimes leaks into the professional realm and also whether counseling is as nondirective as claimed.[21]

The majority of primary care physicians, on the other hand, reported that they would be directive (Table 3). The apparent "pro-life" stance

Table 6. Counseling after Prenatal Diagnosis: Professional Approaches of U.S. Genetics Professionals (n = 1,084) including Master's-Level Genetic Counselors (n = 555)[a]

Condition	Emphasize Positive Aspects So They Will Favor Carrying to Term Without Suggesting It Directly	Try to Be as Unbiased as Possible	Emphasize Negative Aspects So They Will Favor Termination Without Suggesting It Directly	Would Present Carrying to Term and Placing the Child for Adoption as an Option
1. Neurofibromatosis	7	89/95	4	52/62
2. Sickle cell anemia	6	88/95	6	52/63
3. Cystic fibrosis	3	88/95	8	54/66
4. Achondroplasia	7	88/93	6	64/76
5. Trisomy 21	2	86/95	13/4	70/84
6. Huntington disease	4	86/94	10	42/49
7. Predisposition to schizophrenia or bipolar disorder	10	86	3	42/49
8. Predisposition to Alzheimer disease	12	85	3	40
9. Pregnancy result of rape	1	85/93	14/7	86
10. XXY	12/9	84/90	5	63/72
11. Predisposition to alcoholism	16	83	1	42
12. Familial hypercholesterolemia (homozygous)	7	83/90	11/3	43/52
13. 45,X	16	81/86	3	62/72

Table 6. *Continued*

Condition	Emphasize Positive Aspects So They Will Favor Carrying to Term Without Suggesting It Directly	Try to Be as Unbiased as Possible	Emphasize Negative Aspects So They Will Favor Termination Without Suggesting It Directly	Would Present Carrying to Term and Placing the Child for Adoption as an Option
14. Severe obesity, in absence of a known genetic syndrome	17	81	1	47
15. PKU in fetus	16	77[b]/82[c]	7	55[b]/66[c]
16. Toxoplasmosis in fetus	2	75/86	24	47/66
17. Hurler syndrome	2	73/86	27	N/A
18. Rubella in fetus	1	72/86	27	48/61
19. Severe, open spina bifida	1	70/79	29	52/68
20. HIV infection in fetus	1	69/78	29/10	52/64
21. Cleft lip and palate in boy	31/5	69	0	52
22. Cleft lip and palate in girl	32/4	67	1	49
23. Trisomy 13	0	63/75	7/10	N/A
24. Anencephaly	0	51/61	49/20	N/A
25. Child is not sex desired by parents	50/23	46	0	74
26. Mother's life in danger	0	44/50	56/35	17

[a]Percent of all genetics professionals including master's-level genetic counselors/percent of master's-level genetic counselors.
[b]All genetics counselors, including master's-level counselors.
[c]Genetics counselors only.

Table 7. Personal Attitudes toward Abortion: Genetics Services Providers
(n = 1,084)

Condition	% who would abort (1st trimester)	% who would not abort but thought it should be legal for others	% who thought abortion should be illegal
Childhood conditions			
Severe spina bifida	90	9	1
Down syndrome	80	19	1
Cystic fibrosis	62	36	2
Achondroplasia	57	40	3
Sickle cell anemia	52	46	2
Neurofibromatosis	51	46	2
XXY	49	49	2
PKU	44	52	4
45,X	42	55	3
Severe obesity	29	60	10
Cleft lip/palate	12	79	9
Child is not the desired sex	3	65	32
Adult-onset conditions			
Huntington disease	64	34	2
Familial hypercholesterolemia (homozygous)	48	48	4
Predisposition to schizophrenia or bipolar disorder	27	66	6
Predisposition to Alzheimer disease	20	72	8
Predisposition to alcoholism	10	80	10

Note: On average, 5% fewer would abort in second trimester.

of many was not "pro-disability," however. They shared the same pessimistic view of disability as did geneticists. Primary care physicians already do much of the posttest counseling for more common conditions such as Down syndrome and spina bifida and will do more in the future. Their knowledge of the functional aspects (life expectancy, presence or absence of mental retardation, ability to finish high school, hold a job,

Table 8. Primary Care Physicians' Counseling after Prenatal Diagnosis (n = 499)

Condition	Urge Parents to Carry to Term	Emphasize Positive Aspects So They Will Favor Carrying to Term Without Suggesting It Directly	Try to Be as Unbiased as Possible	Emphasize Negative Aspects So They Will Favor Termination Without Suggesting It Directly	Urge Termination
Neurofibromatosis	12%	18%	61%	7%	2%
Sickle cell anemia	12	12	58	13	5
Cystic fibrosis	5	14	61	13	8
Achondroplasia	18	23	54	3	3
Trisomy 21	4	10	63	13	10
Huntington disease	6	8	61	14	10
Predisposition to schizophrenia or bipolar disorder	12	15	65	6	3
Predisposition to Alzheimer disease	16	17	60	4	2
Pregnancy result of rape	2	4	66	11	17
XXY	8	11	66	9	6
Predisposition to alcoholism	23	16	57	4	0
Familial hypercholesterolemia (homozygous)	20	25	50	2	1

Table 8. *Continued*

Condition	Urge Parents to Carry to Term	Emphasize Positive Aspects So They Will Favor Carrying to Term Without Suggesting It Directly	Try to Be as Unbiased as Possible	Emphasize Negative Aspects So They Will Favor Termination Without Suggesting It Directly	Urge Termination
45,X	12	16	58	9	5
Severe obesity in absence of known genetic syndrome	32	20	47	2	0
PKU in fetus	14	16	52	12	7
Toxoplasmosis in fetus	4	7	44	23	21
Rubella in fetus	4	6	41	24	25
Severe, open spina bifida	3	5	51	22	20
HIV infection in fetus	6	7	43	18	25
Cleft lip/palate in a boy	30	29	40	1	1
Cleft lip/palate in a girl	24	33	39	3	1
Trisomy 13	1	1	28	23	2
Child is not sex desired by parents	58	19	23	0	0
Mother's life in danger	0	1	33	16	50

or become a biological parent) of even relatively common conditions such as Down syndrome or cystic fibrosis leaves much to be desired.[22]

At present, counseling focuses on the genetic and medical implications of a condition ("the biological reality") and usually gives short shrift to psychosocial aspects, such as effects on marriage or family life, financial costs, or what the child will be like as an adult. Time constraints on the training of master's-level genetic counselors and physicians, and on the time allowed for interactions with families, may push these issues aside. Both patient and counselor reports in my survey indicated that such issues were discussed in depth in about 1 to 2 percent of sessions. Support groups (for people with the condition at issue) were discussed in 4 percent.[23] Patients were not dissatisfied; according to their own reports, what they expected to learn from counseling was why a genetic condition occurs and the likelihood of its occurrence in their families. Most, however, considered the psychosocial aspects important, even if they did not expect a genetics professional to discuss these.

Who, if anyone, provides this important information remains unclear. Since medical and counselor training is already heavily burdened by learning genetic information, perhaps a new type of professional is needed who can discuss social and economic supports, effects on the marriage and daily living, and what the child will be like at age twenty-five or forty. The training of such professionals would have a dual focus: the functional aspects (not etiology) of genetic conditions and family life with genetic disabilities. Nurses, social workers, and perhaps some HMO consumer representatives could be trained to fulfill this role. Good policy requires good counseling.

Universal Health Care: Justice or an "Immoral Minimum"?

Bioethicists agree that universal, nationally funded health care is the most just and ethical approach. Ideally, all services that exist in a society ought to be equally available free of charge to everyone who may benefit from them. A service that cannot be made available to all would not exist for anyone. This radical egalitarianism exists today in no society in the world, with the possible exceptions of Cuba and the state of Kerala in southern India. In most societies, those who can afford to pay for services will not tolerate what they consider an abridgement of their rights, as evidenced by our figures on autonomy in Table 2. Therefore, a dual public/private system will develop, unless private services are forbidden by law. Prohibition would be seen as highly undesirable in most nations.

Universal health care of any kind is not currently on the agenda for the United States. About four-fifths of the population has some insurance, and most appear not to care about, or, more accurately, are unwilling to pay for, the care of those who do not have insurance. The fact that at least sixteen million people are uninsured, even by Medicaid,[24] has caused no public outcry or agitation for national health insurance.

In the United States, a universal health system is unlikely to provide just and fair answers in reproductive medicine. The politics of abortion could transform what should be a "moral minimum of care" into an "immoral minimum" that restricts abortion to a few life-threatening situations. Current Medicaid regulations, set by the states, may provide a clue to what could happen under national health care. Most states pay for prenatal diagnosis,[25] but only a handful will pay for an abortion following the prenatal diagnosis. Most women on Medicaid are in a position similar to that of women in Latin America, where women can get prenatal diagnosis, but nowhere (except in Cuba) can they get a legal, safe abortion.

At least one state—Iowa—has drawn its own lines. A woman on Medicaid can get an abortion for anencephaly or severe, open spina bifida, but not for Down syndrome, which officials have decided is not sufficiently serious. Typically, there is little or no involvement of potential users of services when such decisions are made. This is true even in relatively noncontroversial areas of state-provided genetics services, such as newborn screening.[26] Usually no mechanisms exist whereby communities or individuals can express their opinions.

Even if line drawing were to result from the involvement of all stakeholders, as described below, it could be far more restrictive of personal freedoms than many people want. Many people, including supporters of universal health care, would not accept constraints on their personal freedom, even in the name of justice. This is why universal health care—an admirable goal in less politicized areas of medicine—is unlikely to provide solutions.

Bioethicists—including those at The Hastings Center—are not the people to draw the lines or make the recommendations. This is a political process that should involve the primary stakeholders, namely the prospective parents, and, to a lesser extent, representatives of a broad spectrum of society. Consumers should be involved in social decisions about prenatal tests to a greater extent than they are currently.

NOTES

1. Jeffrey R. Botkin, "Fetal Privacy and Confidentiality," *Hastings Center Report* 25, no. 5 (1995): 32–39.

2. Lori B. Andrews, Jane E. Fullarton, Neil A. Holtzman, and Arno Motulsky, eds., *Assessing Genetic Risks: Implications for Health and Social Policy* (Washington, D.C.: National Academy Press, 1994).

3. World Health Organization, *Hereditary Diseases Programme: Proposed International Guidelines on Ethical Issues in Medical Genetics and Genetic Services* (Geneva, Switzerland: WHO, 1998).

4. Bartha M. Knoppers, Dorothy C. Wertz, Ruth Chadwick, Victor B. Penchaszadeh, and Sonia LeBris, "Defining 'Serious' Disorders in Relation to Genetics Services: Who Should Decide?" *American Journal of Human Genetics* 57, no. 4 (1995): A296.

5. Kåre Berg, "Ethics and Medical Genetics in Norway," in *Ethics and Human Genetics: A Cross-Cultural Perspective*, ed. Dorothy C. Wertz and John C. Fletcher (Berlin: Springer-Verlag, 1989), pp. 317–38, at 321.

6. Eric Engel and C. Dawn DeLozier-Blanchet, "Ethics and Genetics in Switzerland," in *Ethics and Human Genetics: A Cross-Cultural Perspective*, ed. Dorothy C. Wertz and John C. Fletcher (Berlin: Springer-Verlag, 1989), pp. 353–79, at 358; and Traute Schroeder-Kurth and Juergen Huebner, "Ethics and Medical Genetics in the Federal Republic of Germany," in *Ethics and Human Genetics: A Cross-Cultural Perspective*, ed. Wertz and Fletcher, pp. 156–75, at 161.

7. Xin Mao, "Chinese Geneticists' Views on Ethical Issues in Genetic Testing and Screening: Evidence for Eugenics in China," *American Journal of Human Genetics* 63, no. 3 (1998): 688–95.

8. World Health Organization, *Proposed International Guidelines.*

9. Dorothy C. Wertz and John C. Fletcher, "Fatal Knowledge? Prenatal Diagnosis and Sex Selection," *Hastings Center Report* 19, no. 3 (1989): 21–27.

10. Wertz and Fletcher, "Ethical and Social Issues in Sex Selection: A Survey of Geneticists in 37 Nations," *Social Science and Medicine* 46, no. 2 (1998): 255–73.

11. Wertz, "Eugenics is Alive and Well," *Science in Context* 11, nos. 3 and 4 (1998): 493–510 (special issue titled "Eugenic Thought and Practice," ed. Raphael Falk and Diane B. Paul).

12. Wertz, James R. Sorenson, and Timothy C. Heeren, "Clients' Interpretation of Risks Provided in Genetic Counseling," *American Journal of Human Genetics* 39 (1986): 79–88.

13. American Medical Association Council on Ethical and Judicial Affairs, *Testing Children for Genetic Status*, Code of Medical Ethics, Report 66 (Chicago: American Medical Association, 1995).

14. American Society of Human Genetics Board of Directors and American College of Medical Genetics Board of Directors, "Points to Consider: Ethical, Legal, and Psychosocial Implications of Genetic Testing in Children and Adolescents," *American Journal of Human Genetics* 57 (1995): 1233–41.

15. National Society of Genetic Counselors, "Prenatal and Childhood Testing for Adult-Onset Disorders," *Perspectives in Genetic Counseling* 17, no. 3 (1995): 5.

16. American Society of Human Genetics Board, "Points to Consider."

17. Wertz and Fletcher, "Ethical and Social Issues in Sex Selection."

18. Uwe Reinhardt, "Do you sincerely want to be rich? Get a life! Don't go to medical school. Just buy and sell docs, at a profit of course." Course handout for EC333, Financial Accounting, Princeton University, 1997.

19. Michael Burleigh, *Death and Deliverance: "Euthanasia" in Germany c. 1900–1945* (Cambridge, U.K.: Cambridge University Press, 1994).

20. Even for parents these questions may not be useful. As Bonnie Steinbock has pointed out, the only one who can answer them is the person involved, which in this case is a fetus. Surrogate exploration suggests that in almost all cases, life is worth living, so comparing life with non-life does not offer useful guidance.

21. Wertz, "Eugenics Is Alive and Well."

22. Wertz, "Primary Care Physicians' Knowledge of Genetics," *American Journal of Human Genetics* 61, no. 4 (1997): A193.

23. Wertz, "What's Missing from Genetic Counseling: A Survey of 476 Counseling Sessions," *Journal of Genetic Counseling* 7, no. 6 (1998): 499–500.

24. U.S. Census Bureau, *Health Insurance Coverage, 1996* (Washington D.C.: U.S. Census Bureau, 1997), Table B.

25. U.S. Congress, Office of Technology Assessment, *Cystic Fibrosis and DNA Tests: Implications of Carrier Screening* (Washington, D.C.: U.S. Congress, Office of Technology Assessment, August 1992), p. 183.

26. Elaine H. Hiller, Gretchen Landenburger, and Marvin Natowicz, "Public Participation in Medical Policy-Making and the Status of Consumer Autonomy: The Example of Newborn-Screening Programs in the United States, *American Journal of Public Health* 87, no. 8 (1997): 1280–88.

Jeffrey R. Botkin

Line Drawing: Developing Professional Standards for Prenatal Diagnostic Services

Genetic research and advances in imaging technology will produce an expanding array of tests that may be utilized in prenatal diagnosis. Conditions with genetic components that may be amenable to testing range in severity from the promptly lethal in the neonatal period to the relatively minor, such as susceptibility to allergies or migraines. In addition, genes conferring risk to diseases of adults, such as cancer or Alzheimer's disease, are detectable in embryos or fetuses. In the future, normal traits that have genetic influences may be targeted by genetic testing, including body build, intelligence, and personality characteristics. Of course, genes are not strictly determinative of any of these traits but genetic tests may be sufficiently determinative to foster promotion of commercial testing for these conditions in the future. Prenatal testing for gender has been available for a number of years and the controversy over the use of technology for this purpose heralds the broad social debate that will emerge over the genetic selection of embryos and fetuses for a wide range of characteristics.

A central question raised by The Hastings Center project on prenatal testing for genetic disability is whether society should articulate moral or legal limits on the application of this technology in prenatal diagnosis. Should society "draw a line" between those conditions that are deemed appropriate for offers of prenatal diagnosis to prospective parents and those that are considered not appropriate for offers of prenatal detection and selective abortion? This chapter will argue that some form of line drawing is inevitable and appropriate. I will advocate the development of a professional standard for health care providers that states that ethical practitioners need not offer or provide the full range of diagnostic tests. It is by no means clear where such a line should be drawn, and I will not develop an argument for a specific line in this chapter. Rather, I argue that prudent decisions should emerge from broad social dialogue about the appropriate use of this technology, as is being done across the spectrum of medical and nonmedical technologies in our complex society.

Participants in The Hastings Center project were unable to reach consensus on the line-drawing question. Critics of line drawing developed three kinds of arguments that will be addressed in more detail below. One argument is that there is no consensus on where to draw the lines, and that given the subjective nature of determinations of disease "severity," no consensus can be anticipated. A second argument is a rights-based argument, which suggests that parents have basic liberty rights involved in reproduction that should not be infringed by limits on access to prenatal information or diagnostic procedures. Limits on reproductive choice is viewed as paternalistic. While this line of argument is articulated in the literature by authors such as John Robertson,[1] this position was not fully developed by participants in The Hastings Center project. The third line of argument arises from within the disability rights community and was a significant focus of discussion in the project. The concern is that lines will explicitly segregate individuals with disabilities into two groups—those with disabilities judged sufficiently severe to warrant consideration of prenatal diagnosis and, potentially, selective termination, and those conditions that do not warrant such consideration. Line drawing is viewed as hurtful to those who "fall on the wrong side of the line," divisive to the community, and reinforcing of stigma and discriminatory attitudes.

These are each important and powerful arguments. Unfortunately, The Hastings Center project did not have sufficient time to develop the implications of these positions in terms of how prenatal diagnostic services should be provided if no lines are drawn. What are the alternatives to lines? What should be the obligation of an obstetrician to a pregnant woman with respect to prenatal diagnostic information? There are at least three alternatives that can be considered that do not involve lines. One is to simply not provide any information about prenatal diagnosis. While clear philosophic arguments can be developed for this position, it does not lead to a tenable policy given the current standards of care and well established legal liabilities in prenatal medicine—nor is it consistent with the critiques of line drawing sketched above. The second alternative would be to require the provision of information on all health risks and offers of all diagnostic services to all couples. This position appears to be consistent with the positions of the three critiques above. Third, an argument could be developed that permits lines to be drawn by individual practitioners. This approach would permit lines but would avoid a formal public policy and an "official" declaration of where lines should fall. This kind of argument might be supported by the first and third critiques above, but would not be supported by those advocating a parental liberty position. The question for those in the disability rights community is whether the hurtful aspects of lines would be avoided if ad hoc lines are drawn in the privacy of clinics, rather than through public dialogue resulting in the establishment of professional standards. Is it the fact that lines are drawn, or the public declaration of lines that is important?

In the absence of a well-articulated alternative to line drawing in this context, arguments here will be developed on the assumption that the primary alternative in mind by critics of lines is the second: a comprehensive set of information and services should be offered to all pregnant women/couples.

Many Potential Lines

The provision of prenatal diagnostic services to prospective parents entails a sequence of educational processes, decisions, and physical interventions. At the initiation of the provider-parent relationship, there is typically a significant discrepancy in knowledge between the provider and the prospective parents. Providers are aware of a broad range of congenital illnesses and malformations that might affect the child, the population-based risk of these conditions, and the available technologies to detect these traits in embryos or fetuses. Most prospective parents will have, at best, a limited knowledge of congenital malformations or illnesses and the kinds of tools used to detect these problems. The provision of diagnostic services typically requires the following sequence of events:

1. evaluation by the provider of the background risk for the specific couple through a history and physical;
2. education of the prospective parents about their risk of bearing a child with a disabling condition;
3. discussion of the tests and procedures available for prenatal diagnosis for conditions relevant to their history;

4. tests and procedures deemed appropriate by the provider are offered;
5. a decision by the prospective parents about the kinds of tests and procedures they want;
6. purchase and provision of the desired tests and procedures; and
7. disclosure of test results.

Given the complexity of this process, there are many opportunities for "line drawing" by both the provider and the prospective parents. Consider each of the stages outlined. (1) Providers will make a decision about how extensive a history and physical to perform in order to assess the couple's risk. (2) Given the thousands of genetic and congenital disorders that have been characterized, providers will make a decision about what specific risks will be discussed with the couple. For example, even the most thorough providers will not discuss the risk of cystic fibrosis with Asian couples or sickle cell disease with white couples due to the low (but not zero) background risk of these conditions in couples with these backgrounds. (3) Tests and procedures range from the routine, such as ultrasound, to highly experimental, so the provider will make a decision about which tests and procedures are appropriate at any given time. (4) Individual providers may think only selected tests are "indicated," there may be limited availability of certain tests, or she may be unwilling to provide prenatal diagnosis for certain conditions, such as gender. (5) Prospective parents will make a determination about what tests are desirable, if any. (6) Economic considerations of the couple, such as the extent of their insurance coverage, may limit the tests or procedures that can be purchased by the couple. In addition, couples may draw their own lines by requesting tests that were not offered initially by the provider. (7) Finally, the provider could choose to withhold some information obtained in the diagnostic testing; again, withholding information about the gender of the fetus (perhaps with prior notification of this policy) would be an example.

In our discussion of "line drawing" in prenatal diagnosis, we must be careful to stipulate which of these potential lines we are considering. Each of these lines has ethical and legal implications and will engender different levels of controversy. In addition, there may be different lines to be drawn within each of these categories, depending on whether the purpose is to define ethically appropriate behavior or simply behavior sufficient to avoid legal liability. In this discussion, I will be addressing the question of what tests need to be discussed with prospective parents as a standard of care. This question should not be confused with a determination of what conditions warrant selective abortion. That determination should be made only by the prospective parents, although, admittedly, there is a complex relationship between disclosure of information about prenatal risks and decisions about pregnancy termination. The standard of care may be determined, in part, by what prospective couples generally consider to be grounds for abortion, while, conversely, the very offer of prenatal diagnosis for a condition may suggest implicitly to couples that pregnancy termination is warranted. More succinctly, do professional standards follow popular attitudes or are popular attitudes shaped by professional standards? The answer is probably both. For the purposes of this discussion, I will focus on the threshold at which tests are offered and maintain that it is up to the couple alone to decide whether to accept testing and, if so, how to use the information obtained. To be clear, I am discussing what tests should be offered in certain circumstances, not suggesting which ones should be accepted by couples. It would be fine from my perspective if informed couples never wanted prenatal diagnosis.

As prenatal diagnosis is currently provided, lines are drawn routinely in many of the categories mentioned above. A thirty-two-year-old Caucasian woman without a family history of a genetic condition is likely to be offered only a triple screen (for Down syndrome and neural tube defects) and an ultrasound. If she is an Ashkenazi Jew, she will be offered carrier screening for Tay-Sachs. A thirty-eight-year-old woman with the same history may be offered an amniocentesis or chorionic villus sampling for the same limited set of conditions. Although now there are hundreds of tests available for prenatal diagnosis, the vast majority of these tests, and the conditions they target, are not being discussed with prospective parents, unless there is a specific indication. A "specific indication" generally means a substantially increased risk of a "severe" or relatively severe condition based on the age, medical history, or family history of the particular couple. Clearly, current practice involves "line drawing" at multiple points in the provision of services. Of course, describing current practice does not justify it. Yet, a position against line drawing in this context must be seen as having extensive implications. As noted above, critics of line drawing have yet to articulate how a rapidly expanding body of information and array of tests can be offered to all prospective parents without respect to level of risk or severity of condition.

Decision Theory

Decision theory suggests that the attractiveness of an option is based on the probability of an outcome and the value placed on that outcome. Contemporary doctrines of informed consent in medicine do not require that all information be provided, nor that all conceivable services always be offered. Typically patients are offered what a reasonable person would want to know in the situation or what other prudent practitioners would offer. While there are no hard and fast rules to this determination when discussing risks with patients, we can suppose that reasonable people are concerned about common adverse outcomes and serious adverse outcomes. Obviously, patients would be most concerned about possible adverse outcomes that are both common and serious. Patients and providers rarely have the time and interest to discuss remote risks, particularly remote minor risks. While there may be discrepancies in judgment between patient and physicians on what constitutes a sufficient level of risk and what constitutes a sufficiently serious adverse outcome to justify disclosure, very few patients, if any, expect all conceivable risks to be disclosed in all circumstances.

Informed Consent

Given the differences in knowledge levels between physicians and patients, it is typically the physician who makes the determination about what options are reasonably appropriate in a given medical situation. The physician's determination often is based, in turn, on what she believes a reasonable patient would want to know, or on her perception of what the standard of care calls for in the circumstance. In addition, physicians (and other providers) have their own ethical standards that dictate what kinds of services will be offered. Of course, patients may disagree, but physicians are not morally or legally bound to provide services that they do not feel are necessary or appropriate. Obviously, this is the whole purpose in investing in the medical professions; the exclusive authority to prescribe drugs and order medical interventions. Further, patients seek physicians in whom they can place their trust. Part of this trust is the expectation that the physician will use his or her judgment in recommending or offering services that are important and relevant to the primary needs of the patient. Patients simply do not want exhaustive lists of risks, benefits, and options; they want basic information, recommendations, and involvement in important choices. Though physicians can abuse this authority, this model of decision making is entirely consistent with respect for broad patient autonomy. The bottom line is that physicians draw lines with virtually every encounter. This is considered ethical and integral to the standard of care—indeed, lines and the categories they create constitute the standard of care.

Is prenatal diagnosis sufficiently different from other kinds of medical services that this familiar model should not apply? We can look at decisions in prenatal diagnosis in terms of levels of risk and the values placed on those risks. From the perspective of risk levels alone, I will argue there should be little ethical controversy over line drawing between relatively common conditions and extremely rare conditions. In contrast, line drawing based on values (that is, the "severity" of the condition) is more problematic in the context of prenatal diagnosis. These aspects of decisions will be discussed in turn.

Risk-based lines.   When we think in terms of genetic conditions or congenital malformations, we often mention relatively common conditions such as cystic fibrosis, Down syndrome, or hemophilia. Yet there are a large number of rare conditions that are virtually unknown to the majority of physicians, much less to prospective parents. For example, there are a host of "inborn errors of metabolism" that are quite rare, occurring in only one child in 200,000 individuals or less. Genetic tests are emerging for such conditions, but research is demonstrating that there are often many different mutations within individual genes that are associated with specific conditions. This molecular complexity makes genetic testing difficult and expensive; testing for a single condition may involve testing for hundreds of mutations. Nonetheless, with new technologies, such diagnostic tests may be feasible in the near future. When a family has an affected child with such a rare condition, prenatal diagnosis may be available for subsequent pregnancies. When there is no family history, the risk to any particular couple is remote. Should all couples be made aware of these remote risks and should testing be made available without respect to the risk for the condition and to the complexity of the testing procedures? Given that there are thousands of such conditions, how much information is sufficient to fulfill the obstetrician's obligation to the couple if no lines have been drawn?

If a discussion of all rare conditions with all couples does not seem ethically mandatory, then obviously a line is appropriate to delineate which conditions are too rare to justify routine offers of testing. Similarly, if the obstetrician declines to provide testing for all such conditions to an average-risk couple who "want everything," a somewhat different line has been drawn to the same effect. Is this obstetrician justified?

My argument is that she is, as long as there has been some social consensus on what level of risk is sufficiently low that offers of testing are not required as a standard of care. The prospects of having a meaningful conversation about thousands of rare conditions is simply too overwhelming to be even remotely feasible, much less obligatory.

Advances in prenatal diagnostic technologies, such as chip technology, may make testing for rare conditions easier and cheaper. These chips are postage-stamp-size wafers on which are embedded tens of thousands of DNA probes. By passing a sample of the patient's DNA over the chip, tens of thousands of genetic tests can be performed simultaneously with a prompt readout. This technology may reduce the cost barriers to extensive testing, thus potentially fostering testing for a wide array of rare conditions. Such testing could not involve an informed consent process for each test. A general disclosure about the spectrum of conditions targeted on the chip is likely to be the approach. This may leave some couples struggling with how to respond to a positive diagnosis for a condition they, and perhaps their physician, had never heard of, but this would be a price of efficiency in mass testing. Experience would tell whether this would be an acceptable price.

Yet cost is not the only barrier to wide-scale testing. Test validity is crucially important as well in deciding whether to offer testing. Genes play a major role in many illnesses, but only a relatively minor role in others. Gene-gene interactions, gene-environment interactions, environmental agents, and random events in the complex sequence of human development all have powerful influences on subsequent health and disease. Discordance between identical twins for illnesses such as diabetes, schizophrenia, bipolar disease, and alcoholism illustrates that such diseases have important causes other than gene action. So even if we develop inexpensive chip technology for a wide range of conditions, we still will have only a limited ability to accurately predict many conditions. Chip developers may decide to include genetic probes for common conditions like diabetes, despite poor predictive value, if this information is considered important by many couples. However, it still will be appropriate to exclude rare conditions on chips when genetic tests are of poor predictive value. Therefore, the cost of the test, the prevalence of the condition, and the predictive value of the test are, separately and in combination, the bases of lines that will continue to be drawn in this context. The point here is that the ability to do many genetic tests cheaply will not eliminate complex ethical issues in deciding what tests to include in the panel.

Contemporary policy and case law offer some guidance on current lines with respect to the risk levels that prompt offers of screening. Traditionally, amniocentesis is offered to a woman in the general population when she will be thirty-five years of age or older at the time of delivery. Before age thirty-five, the risk of bearing a child with a chromosome abnormality is 3.6 per 1,000 (1 in 278 births).[2] At age thirty-five, the incidence rises to 4.9 per 1,000 (1 in 204 births). Part of the justification for this particular cut-off was the perception that the risk of bearing a child with a chromosome abnormality at age thirty-five exceeds the risk of losing the pregnancy through complications of the procedure (approximately 1 in 200). Of note, this policy was not based on any empirical data that couples considered the risk at thirty-five to be sufficiently greater to justify screening. Nevertheless, current professional standards have established a risk of approximately 1 in 200 for chromosome abnormalities as sufficiently high to justify routinely offering a relatively expensive and invasive diagnostic procedure.

The wrongful birth suits offer additional insight on how the judicial system has judged the provider's obligation to offer prenatal diagnosis. Wrongful birth suits are brought by parents of a child with a disabling condition who claim inadequate counseling or provision of prenatal diagnostic services leading to the birth of the child.[3] Parents typically claim that, had they been offered information and services, they would have detected the abnormality in the fetus and terminated the pregnancy. Currently, twenty-six state jurisdictions in the United States have accepted the wrongful birth claim, which suggests broad social and legal support. The success of these suits clearly establishes the health care provider's obligation to offer some information and services relevant to prenatal diagnosis. However, the extent of the obligation based on these suits is unclear.

A substantial number of suits have been brought by couples with a child with trisomy 21 (Down syndrome) who were not offered amniocentesis despite a maternal age of thirty-five or older. Only one case provides insight into a court's perception of obligation under substantially lower levels of risk. In *Munro v. Regents of the University of California*,[4] a physician obtained a family history from a couple that indicated that neither of the individuals had Jewish heritage. Prenatal diagnosis was offered to the couple but testing for Tay-Sachs disease was not included. Subsequently, a child was born with Tay-Sachs disease. Further exploration of the family history revealed that the parents had ancestors who were French Canadian—a population that has a "slightly increased" risk for Tay-Sachs disease. The parents claimed that if the Tay-Sachs test was excluded because they were not Jewish, this fact should have been made known to them. They claimed that regardless of the rarity of Tay-Sachs disease in non-Jewish individuals, they would have wanted the $500 test. Dr. Michael Kaback, an expert witness for the defendants, stated that the parents did not meet the profile characteristics necessary to warrant Tay-Sachs testing and it was not the standard of care to perform such testing in this circumstance. The court found that the physician did not have an obligation to offer Tay-Sachs screening in the absence of recognizable factors indicating increased risk. Clearly, the courts have not been willing to demand that all tests be offered to all couples. (Indeed, in the absence of clearly articulated professional standards, it may be wrongful birth suits of this type that ultimately develop the "lines" by which providers understand their obligations in this context.)

These brief accounts of contemporary professional standards, as articulated by the profession and the courts, illustrate that threshold levels of risk already exist below which providers are not obligated to discuss specific conditions or offer diagnostic services. Again, describing current practice does not justify it. Nevertheless, new tests are emerging in an established context that supports "lines" in the provision of prenatal diagnosis specifically, and certainly in the practice of medicine more broadly. Reversing this established approach and requiring information and offers of testing for rare conditions to all couples—presumably with threats of wrongful birth suits if tests are not offered—would have unacceptable implications for the physician-patient relationship. At least until tests for rare conditions become safe, cheap, and highly accurate, it is reasonable and appropriate for society to define a rough line, say a prevalence of less than one in one thousand or one in ten thousand births, for example, below which physicians need not offer prenatal testing for the condition as a standard of care.

Value-based lines. Drawing lines based on the "severity" of conditions is more problematic than lines based largely on the prevalence of the condition or the accuracy of the test. The values inherent in such a determination are more explicit than determinations about levels of risk alone. In The Hastings Center project, the discussion about line drawing focused primarily on this kind of determination. Should society make decisions about what kinds of conditions justify offers of prenatal diagnosis? As noted, conditions with genetic influences range from the lethal to those with limited impact on daily living. Genes also influence adult-onset conditions and a broad range of normal traits. Are there distinctions that can be made between these kinds of conditions that enable justifiable lines to be drawn?

Numerous scholars and authoritative committees have raised concerns over the use of prenatal diagnosis for "mild" conditions or "trivial" indications. The President's Commission for the Study of Ethical Problems in Medicine and Biomedical and Behavioral Research focused primarily on prenatal diagnosis for sex selection, stating:

> The idea that it is morally permissible to terminate pregnancy simply on the grounds that a fetus of that sex is unwanted may also rest on the very dubious notion that virtually any characteristic of an expected child is an appropriate object of appraisal and selection. Taken to an extreme, this attitude treats a child as an artifact and the reproductive process as a chance to design and produce human beings according to parental standards of excellence, which over time are transformed into collective standards. . . . [T]he Commission concludes that although individual physicians are free to follow the dictates of conscience, public policy should discourage the use of amniocentesis for sex selection.[5]

The Committee on Assessing Genetic Risks of the Institute of Medicine took a stronger stand and recommended that

> prenatal diagnosis not be used for minor conditions or characteristics. In particular, the committee felt strongly that the use of fetal diagnosis for determination of fetal sex or use of abortion for the purpose of preferential selection of the sex of the fetus is a misuse of genetic services that is inappropriate and should be discouraged by health professionals. . . . The committee believes this issue warrants careful scrutiny over the next three to five years as the availability of genetic testing becomes more widespread, and especially as simpler, safer technologies for prenatal diagnosis are developed.[6]

The American Medical Association's Council on Ethical and Judicial Affairs supports limitation of prenatal diagnostic services to more serious conditions. The council suggests: "Selection to avoid genetic disorders would not always be appropriate. . . . [S]election becomes more problematic as the effects of the disease become milder and as they become manifest later in life."[7] The Council states that a variety of factors influence whether prenatal selection for specific conditions would be ethically acceptable. The Council encouraged additional work on the appropriate uses of prenatal diagnosis, stating: "[I]t is important to begin discussion of the issue now to ensure that appropriate ethical guidelines are in place when new applications become available."

Several scholars have taken similar positions. Thomas Murray, a Hastings Center project participant, concluded: "In short, we should not offer to provide prenatally information about traits or afflictions that are not substantial burdens on parent and child. We certainly should not assist couples in a misguided quest for the child that embodies their ideal collection of traits, including gender."[8] Like the President's Commission, other authors have framed the issue of limits of technology use around prenatal sex selection. Wertz and Fletcher provided clear recommendations: "[W]e believe that it is important that the medical profession take a stand now against sex selection. A posture of ethical neutrality on this issue could lead to unfortunate precedents in moral thinking about future uses of genetic knowledge. . . ."[9]

The courts have, on occasion, addressed the issue of "line drawing" based on the severity of the condition in the context of wrongful birth cases. The Supreme Court of Kansas wrote in a 1990 case:

> In recognizing a cause of action for wrongful birth in this state, we assume that the child is severely and permanently handicapped. By handicapped, we mean, in this context, that the child has such gross deformities, not medically correctable, that the child will never be able to function as a normal human being.[10]

Several authors have attempted to draw more explicit lines to preclude specific uses of prenatal diagnosis. Stephen Post, Peter White-house, and myself argued against the use of prenatal diagnosis for familial Alzheimer disease.[11] Carson Strong argues for no restrictions on prenatal diagnosis for disease-related conditions.[12] However, Strong's analysis would support a clinician who refused services for diagnosing non-disease-related characteristics, such as gender or personality traits. Dena Davis has written about the circumstance in which deaf parents consider using prenatal diagnosis to ensure that their child also will be deaf. Davis concludes:

> A decision, made before a child is even born, that confines her forever to a narrow group of people and a limited choice of careers, so violates the child's right to an open future that no genetic counseling team should acquiesce in it. The very value of autonomy that grounds the ethics of genetic counseling should preclude assisting parents in a project that so dramatically narrows the autonomy of the child to be.[13]

My own work published in the *Hastings Center Report* is perhaps the most concerted attempt to date to draw relatively explicit lines for the use of prenatal diagnosis.[14] The argument developed in that article is that practitioners should provide information on conditions that may significantly impair the legitimate interests of the parents. The claim is that the justification for prenatal diagnosis is the impact of the medical condition on the family (not the impact on the child or on society). Further, distinctions are made between conditions that often have a profound impact on families, such as Tay-Sachs disease, and those that do not, such as most cases of asthma. This analysis suggests that practitioners need not provide diagnostic information about "mild" conditions, late-onset conditions, or non-disease-related conditions.

A basic challenge in this discussion is to define what we mean by "severity." The first question is severity to whom—the parents, the child, or to society? While a full discussion of this issue is beyond this chapter, I will sketch a few points that are more fully developed elsewhere.[15] If we assume that prenatal diagnosis exists for the welfare of parents, then severity refers to the impact of the child's condition on the parents and family. There may be wide overlap between severity as measured from the child's perspective and that from the parent's perspective, but there are some cases in which the impact on the family might be profound, yet there is little impact from the child's perspective. Anencephaly is an extreme example where the impact on the child is absent, at least in one sense, since the child never had a conscious existence, yet the impact on the parents is profound due to the devastating malformation and early death of the child. I also will be careful to use the term "impact" instead of "burden" on parents since the former is more value neutral. Parents who spend large portions of their time caring for a disabled child, for example, might not consider this effort to be a burden, but it would constitute a large impact on their lives nonetheless. People may reasonably decide to avoid large impacts on their lives, like having a baby, whether or not the impact has a positive or negative valence (or both positive and negative influences). In this context, a large proportion of parents of children with profound impairments might not consider the child to be a burden but might describe a large impact that the child's condition has had on their lives.

Severity of impact on the family encompasses a range of factors that we understand at a common sense level. The early death of a child has a terrible impact on families. Other medical conditions for the child will entail time commitments for parents, mental and physical effort, substantial costs, lost opportunities, and psychological impacts including guilt, isolation, anxiety, and sorrow. Of course, positive impacts are present as well, as with any child, and may include a heightened sense of love and bonding with a unique child, a clearer sense of purpose in life, pride in hard-won achievements, and a restructured set of values about what is important in life. Using these kinds of rough measures, we can claim reasonably that Hurler's disease, for example, is more severe than, say, eczema or color blindness. The argument is that Hurler's disease has a profound impact on families, including chronic illness and premature death of the child, and therefore warrants a discussion of testing capabilities for at-risk families. Color blindness has a marginal impact on families, if any, and therefore would not warrant a discussion of prenatal diagnosis in at-risk families.

Of course, a few parents might claim severe impact of the birth of an infant with color blindness or of the "wrong" gender. While a plausible case might be made in individual circumstances based on idiosyncratic values, such exceptions need not form the basis of professional standards. Physicians should not be obligated to offer prenatal gender testing to all parents, even if we can find justification in isolated cases. In general terms, the impact of a child of the unwanted gender on the parents is not sufficiently severe to warrant offers of gender selection as the standard of care.

This discussion suggests that some distinctions can be made between medical conditions based on yardsticks such as impact on the family, although such measures do not lend themselves to precision. An effort to make such distinctions is justified on the practical and legal implications alone, as discussed above, but there are several more purely ethical justifications for making such distinctions as well. Arguments can be made that hinge on the welfare of the embryo/fetus, the welfare of prospective parents, and the welfare of children. First, while embryos and fetuses are not considered "persons" by many of those articulating these concerns, society still confers substantial value on these entities. The argument is that the destruction of fetal life for gender selection or for "mild" health conditions is not ethically justified in these circumstances because the benefits to parents are not balanced by the harm to prenatal life. This general conclusion does not mean that there can be no exceptions in individual circumstances but, as a standard of care, prenatal diagnosis need not be offered routinely for these purposes.

Second, there is legitimate concern about child welfare and the parent-child relationship if embryos and fetuses can be exhaustively analyzed and selected for traits that don't have a substantial impact on the family or on the child's health. While selection technology will not exactly create "designer babies," the implications are the same. To provide parents with a fine-grained control over the biologic nature of their children risks affecting one of the most intimate and profound relationships of people's lives—the relationship between parent and child. I believe a personal sense of independence and individuality for future generations are at stake in this debate, for these concepts would be threatened by the knowledge that our parents fashioned us to their liking and that we, in turn, fashioned our children to fulfill our own ideals.

If the justification of prenatal diagnosis is the promotion of the welfare of prospective parents, distinctions can be made between conditions based on whether testing will promote this goal without seriously compromising other values, such as respect for prenatal life and concerns over the detailed selection of babies. The legitimate interest of prospective parents in avoiding the birth of a seriously disabled child can be promoted without fostering testing for the full range of conditions amenable to prenatal diagnosis.

Addressing Counterarguments

Whether these justifications for lines based on prevalence and severity are determinative will depend on the strength of the arguments in favor of unlimited use of diagnostic technology. As outlined above, the first of these arguments appeals to autonomy or liberty. Insofar as reproductive decisions are personal and highly value laden, it is claimed that our respect for the autonomy and liberty of prospective parents precludes restrictions on these intimate choices. Indeed, some critics of lines in The Hastings Center project seemed to claim that the development of any lines in this context is paternalistic.

That is a powerful argument in Western culture. However, while autonomy is an important value in medicine, it has never been absolute. In recent decades, negative autonomy rights have become quite strong, meaning that autonomous patients have the right to refuse interventions (i.e., to be left alone), even when such refusals will lead to death. In contrast, positive autonomy rights are much more limited. By this I mean the patient's right to obtain information or services is limited to what reasonable people would want to know, what services are reasonably expected to be beneficial, and what services the provider believes are ethical to provide.

This distinction between positive and negative rights is essential in this context. Reproductive rights are primarily negative rights; an individual has the liberty to reproduce, or to refrain from reproducing, as he/she sees fit without interference from society. Positive rights in reproduction have been limited to the kinds of disclosures discussed above. Women thirty-five and older at delivery have a legally defensible right in many jurisdictions to be informed about their risk of bearing a child with a chromosome abnormality. Similarly, couples at substantially increased risk for specific conditions based on family history or ethnic background have established rights to be informed of those risks. There is certainly no context in medicine in which a patient's autonomy/liberty right requires a complete disclosure of all information or the offer of all services beyond what reasonable patients and professionals deem appropriate.

Is reproduction and prenatal diagnosis so value laden that exceptions to this general standard in medicine should be made? Certainly one's personal health is as important an interest as reproductive interests, yet there have been no calls for unlimited access to clinical diagnostic technology. Should physicians be obligated to offer and perform MRI scans on all worried patients with headaches upon the patient's request? Should I be able to order a bronchoscopy on myself whenever I want one, even if my physician does not believe it is indicated? Should physicians become educators alone and permit informed patients full access to all available technologies? This would represent a profound transformation of how medicine is structured in our culture. I see no reason why autonomy/liberty rights in prenatal diagnosis should be stronger than such rights in clinical medicine more generally. We don't require professionals to provide services that are not expected to be beneficial or that have, in the opinion of the professional, disproportionately negative consequences to other individuals or society.

To a certain extent, prenatal diagnosis has achieved a special place in medical services. The tradition of nondirectiveness for genetic counselors is strong and clearly states that counselors should not attempt to influence clients in their decision making about whether to obtain prenatal diagnosis or how to respond to the information. However, this tradition relates largely to how couples respond to offers of testing, not to what offers are made to begin with. As noted above, there are numerous lines drawn in contemporary prenatal medicine about what tests are offered to prospective parents. Once a test has been deemed appropriate to offer, then the nondirective counseling becomes relevant. Contemporary rights to information are entirely consistent with drawing a clear line that stipulates what information and services should be offered to patients by prudent practitioners in anticipated circumstances. A broad social dialogue in the development of such lines undercuts criticisms of paternalism (or at least criticisms of unjustified paternalism) for physicians who practice according to a resultant standard of care.

A second argument against line drawing based on the severity of the condition is that there is no consensus on where such a line might be drawn. As Dorothy C. Wertz has demonstrated through her survey research with geneticists, there is no consistent concept of disease severity.[16] This is not too surprising, since severity is a relative term, many medical conditions are highly variable, and the debate over this issue is young. We cannot conclude quite yet that the discussion of the issue is futile. Since severity is a relative term, it may be more productive to discuss severity in comparative terms rather than attempt to classify conditions as "severe" or not in isolation. If we simply ask professionals whether Down syndrome is a "severe condition," we will get differences of opinion since the respondent will want to ask, "Severe compared to what?" We would get a similar range of opinions if we asked whether Pittsburgh has a cold climate or whether a Toyota Camry is an expensive car. In contrast, there might be broad agreement that Pittsburgh is colder than Tucson, a Camry is more expensive than a Kia, and that sickle cell disease is more severe than hypothyroidism. At the extremes, we can dispense with comparisons—Fairbanks is cold, Bentleys are expensive, and Tay-Sachs is a severe medical condition by any standard. Again, we can imagine couples who might disagree with these conclusions based on idiosyncratic views, but such exceptions do not undermine reasonable policy judgments based on widely shared values.

There may well be serious difficulties in eventually placing any bright line in this context, but we can proceed by working from the edges. Society could conclude relatively easily that technology for prenatal diagnosis of gender and for normal physical and psychological characteristics need not be offered or provided without deciding where else lines would be drawn. Line drawing is a prime function of ethics, law, and policy development and these would cease to be meaningful social pursuits if we demanded consensus before tackling the problems.

The third argument against line drawing arises from the concerns over the impact of lines on those with disabilities. As articulated by Adrienne Asch, socially defined lines that indicate which conditions potentially justify termination of a pregnancy could be hurtful to those living with those same conditions. In that this concern predicts how large groups of diverse individuals will react to future professional standards, this is a difficult claim to counter. It can be noted, however, that through the discussions and writings emerging from The Hastings Center project, it is by no means clear whether prenatal diagnosis sends any unambiguous messages to those with disabilities. Parents who choose to terminate a pregnancy for a disabling condition may be saying very little about the value of lives of individuals living with the condition, just as a woman who terminates an unwanted pregnancy may be saying very little about the value of children in general. Prospective parents may be saying much more about how they choose to live their own lives. Of course, the message that is received by those with disabilities may be different than the message sent by those offering and seeking services. In any case, it would be valuable to carefully assess the attitudes in the community of individuals living with disabilities on these issues so that their voices can be heard clearly in policy development.

Perhaps more to the point, it hardly seems beneficial to the welfare of the disabled community to advocate that all conditions be subject to prenatal diagnosis and selective termination. This would appear to be the fast lane to "perfectibilism" and intolerance for progressively less severe disabilities. If society condones and promotes prenatal diagnosis for the full spectrum of medical (and nonmedical) conditions, what message does that send? If we want to promote inclusiveness, understanding, and support for those with disabilities, requiring the extensive provision of prenatal diagnostic information and services would appear to be a poor strategy. My concern is that the attempt to eliminate the hurtful effects of line drawing in prenatal diagnosis will fuel a broader set of discriminatory attitudes in society that will be much more hurtful to those with disabilities in the long run.

Conclusions

A failure to develop reasonable limits for the application of prenatal diagnosis would have profound implications. Suggestions that all tests be discussed and offered to all individuals seriously underestimates the complexity of this task for the professionals involved, even if conditions are described in broad classes. Problems at this pragmatic level are reinforced by the expectation that prospective parents would have little interest in discussing numerous rare conditions and trivial afflictions. More important, there may be profound harms to children and the parent-child relationship by the unbridled selection of children. I find none of the critiques of line drawing to be compelling enough to override these pragmatic and ethical concerns.

My conception of a line corresponds to a professional standard of care, not legal prohibitions on the provision of services. Under a professional standard, ethical practitioners need to offer information and services for some conditions (based on an assessment of individual risks), but need not offer information or services for others. Practitioners could choose not to conform to the standard, by offering either more or less testing than the standard (although they could be held legally liable through wrongful birth suits for failure to provide sufficient information). In this view, prudent standards of care would best promote substantial, although not unlimited, patient autonomy while fostering a measure of tolerance and unconditional love for children and the rest of us with imperfections.

Acknowledgments

I would like to thank all of the participants in The Hastings Center project on prenatal testing for genetic disability for the fascinating and valuable discussions that helped frame the issues in this chapter. In particular, I am indebted to Erik Parens, Adrienne Asch, and Ben Wilfond for their thoughtful critiques of this work.

NOTES

1. John A. Robertson, *Children of Choice: Freedom and the New Reproductive Technologies* (Princeton, N.J.: Princeton University Press, 1994).
2. L. Y. F. Hsu, "Prenatal Diagnosis of Chromosomal Abnormalities Through Amniocentesis," in *Genetic Disorders and the Fetus: Diagnosis, Prevention, and Treatment*, 4th ed., ed. Aubrey A. Milunsky (Baltimore, Md.: Johns Hopkins University Press, 1998), pp. 179–248.
3. Jeffrey R. Botkin and Maxwell J. Mehlman, "Wrongful Birth: Medical, Legal and Philosophic Issues," *American Journal of Law, Medicine, & Ethics* 22 (1994): 21–28.

4. *Munro v. Regents of the University of California*, 263 California Reporter 878 (California Appellate 2d. District, 1989).

5. The President's Commission for the Study of Ethical Problems in Medicine and Biomedical and Behavioral Research, *Screening and Counseling for Genetic Conditions* (Washington, D.C.: U.S. Government Printing Office, 1983), pp. 57–58.

6. Committee on Assessing Genetic Risks, Division of Health Sciences Policy, Institute of Medicine; Lori B. Andrew, Jane E. Fullarton, Neal A. Holtzman, Aubrey A. Motulsky, eds., *Assessing Genetic Risks: Implications for Health and Social Policy* (Washington, D.C.: National Academy Press, 1994), p. 105.

7. American Medical Association Council on Ethical and Judicial Affairs, "Ethical Issues Related to Prenatal Genetic Testing," *Archives of Family Medicine* 3 (1994): 633–42.

8. Thomas H. Murray, *The Worth of a Child* (Berkeley: University of California Press, 1996), p. 139.

9. Dorothy C. Wertz and John C. Fletcher, "Fatal Knowledge? Prenatal Diagnosis and Sex Selection," *Hastings Center Report* 19, no. 3 (1989): 21–27.

10. *Arche v. U.S. Dept. of Army*, 798 P. 2d 477 (Kansas 1990).

11. Stephen Post, Jeffrey R. Botkin, and Peter Whitehouse, "Selective Abortion for Familial Alzheimer Disease," *Obstetrics and Gynecology* 79, no. 5 (1992): 794–98.

12. Carson Strong, *Ethics in Reproductive and Perinatal Medicine: A New Framework* (New Haven, Conn.: Yale University Press, 1997), pp. 137–48.

13. Dena S. Davis, "Genetic Dilemmas and the Child's Right to An Open Future," *Hastings Center Report* 27, no. 2 (1997): 7–15.

14. Jeffrey R. Botkin, "Fetal Privacy and Confidentiality," *Hastings Center Report* 25, no. 5 (1995): 32–40.

15. Botkin, "Fetal Privacy."

16. See Dorothy C. Wertz, "Drawing Lines: Notes for Policymakers," in this volume.

PILAR N. OSSORIO

Prenatal Genetic Testing
and the Courts

Our Hastings Center working group on prenatal testing for genetic disability attempted, but failed, to reach consensus on a principled method for distinguishing prenatal tests that health care providers are permitted or obliged to offer from tests that providers should not offer.[1] We were left with several unanswered questions: What characteristics of tests, medical conditions, family medical histories and/or parental expectations should trigger the offer of a test? In what way, if at all, should the social construction of disability be taken into account in determining whether it is permissible or obligatory to offer a test? In legal language, we could ask—under what circumstances does the scope of a physician's duty to disclose information relevant to pregnancy risks include disclosure of the availability of prenatal tests?

While our working group could remain indecisive with respect to these questions, courts cannot. Parents may bring suit against a physician who fails to offer a prenatal test if a child is later born with a disability that could have been detected. A judge or jury must determine whether the physician is liable, and central to this determination is the question of whether the physician had a legal duty to offer the test.

Judicial decisions and legislative bans can constitute and reconstitute our society by altering goals and preferences.[2] What courts decide about duties to offer prenatal tests, or what physicians perceive them to have decided, will have a substantial impact on physicians' conduct. Ethical pronouncements to the contrary will not stop physicians from offering every prenatal genetic test possible if they believe that such behavior will diminish their likelihood of being sued for malpractice, or help them prevail should a suit arise.

The most likely causes of action for failure to offer a prenatal test are wrongful birth, wrongful life, and informed consent. Plaintiffs may also seek recovery under negligent infliction of emotional distress doctrine. All of these are torts—civil law causes of action in which the patient-plaintiff sues the physician-defendant for money damages.

Wrongful birth, wrongful life, and informed consent are all negligence torts (although in a small minority of jurisdictions informed consent is analyzed as battery rather than negligence). This means that a plaintiff must prove each element of negligence to prove her case. The elements of negligence are (1) the defendant had a *duty* to conform to a specific standard of conduct for the protection of the plaintiff against an unreasonable risk of injury; (2) the defendant *breached* that duty; (3); the plaintiff was *injured* (damaged); and (4) the breach actually and proximately caused the plaintiff's injury. Tort law is primarily state common law, which means that the requirements for proving each element of the tort may differ from state to state.

The issues our working group debated go primarily to the first element of negligence—did the physician have a duty to offer a prenatal test? If there was no duty, then the physician could not be found liable, even if a child was later born with a disability that could have been detected.

Tort Duties and Standards of Care

There is no magic formula for determining whether a tort duty exists. Duty is assessed by the court as the "sum total of those conditions of policy which lead the law to say that the particular plaintiff is entitled to protection."[3] Duty is the conclusion that a defendant ought to have acted in a certain manner in a certain situation, and that if she acted differently then she must bear the cost of injuries resulting from her behavior. Some factors courts consider in determining the existence of a duty include the foreseeability of harm to the plaintiff, the probability that the plaintiff would be harmed, the nexus between the defendant's actions and the harm suffered, the moral blame attached to the defendant's conduct, policy (or lack thereof) regarding prevention of the kind of harm suffered, the extent of the burden to the defendant in averting the harm, the consequences to the community of imposing liability, and the availability of insurance for the risk involved.[4] Thus, in determining whether a health care provider had a legal duty to offer a prenatal test, the courts will struggle with many of the policy questions considered by our working group.

To decide whether the defendant had a duty, the court first determines the standard of care. The standard of care is a uniform standard of behavior against which the defendant's conduct is to be measured. This uniform standard protects others from unreasonable risk of injury resulting from the tortfeasor's conduct. In most negligence cases the standard of care is that of a reasonable person of ordinary prudence acting under the same or similar circumstances as the defendant (the reasonable person standard). This standard of care is then used to specify the defendant's duties—the defendant had a duty to undertake or refrain from just those actions that would have been undertaken or refrained from by a reasonable, prudent person under the circumstances. The preceding is sometimes referred to as a duty of ordinary care.

While the reasonable person standard applies in most negligence cases, cases arising from the practice of a learned profession are generally tried under a *professional standard of care*. Professionals are expected to have skill and knowledge beyond that of the general public, and they are required to act in a manner consistent with their specialized skills. Professionals must still use "ordinary care," but what constitutes ordinary care in the practice of their profession is determined by comparison to others in their profession.

The Professional Standard of Care

The professional standard of care applies to physicians and other health care providers in most malpractice suits. The standard can be stated as follows: in diagnosis and treatment physicians must exercise that reasonable degree of skill, care, and knowledge ordinarily possessed and exercised by physicians in the same field under the same or similar circumstances.[5] The particular duties specified by this standard depend on the procedure or medical encounter at issue. For instance, it is well established that the professional standard imposes duties on obstetricians to offer amniocentesis to a pregnant women who is thirty-five years or older. The standard of care generally remains the same across medical specialties and circumstances, but the *duties specified by the standard differ* depending on the circumstances, the state of medical knowledge, and the availability of medical technology. The patient-plaintiff always has the burden of proving what particular duties were specified by the standard of care and proving that the physician-defendant breached her duties.

Note that the phrase standard of care is frequently used as a shorthand to describe specific duties imposed by the legal standard. Thus, physicians or the court will state that it is the standard of care to offer amniocentesis to a pregnant woman aged thirty-five years or older. When physicians use the phrase "standard of care," they are generally referring to specific practices that constitute proper or accepted medical management of a given disease or condition. Sometimes, physicians use the phrase in reference to practice guidelines or recommendations. However, under the law, whether or not a physician's practice falls within guidelines is not dispositive as to whether the legal standard of care has been met (discussed above). Remember, under the law, there are no particular standards of care for particular medical procedures or encounters. Rather, one standard of care imposes different duties in different circumstances.

Under the professional standard, physicians who undertake to per-form a certain procedure, test, or type of practice must possess the same degree of professional learning, skill, and ability that others simi-larly situated ordinarily possess.[6] If the physician is a general practitioner, the reasonableness of her actions will be judged by comparison to other general practitioners; if she is an obstetrician, her actions will be judged against those of other obstetricians. However, if a general practitioner performs a surgery, then she must employ the same learning and skill as a one who typically undertakes that type of surgery. Likewise, a physician who offers a prenatal genetic test should be competent to offer genetic counseling, interpret the test results, and communicate genetic information and test results to patients in a comprehensible manner. If she lacks these skills, she must refer the patient to a profes-sional who possesses them, such as a clinical geneticist or a genetic coun-selor.[7]

Context is extremely important in determining whether a physician has fulfilled her duties. Under the professional standard, "advances in the profession, availability of facilities, specialization or general practice, proximity of specialists, together with all other relevant considerations will be taken into account."[8] Furthermore, the physician's duties will depend on details of the patient's case. In a prenatal testing situation these include (but are not limited to) her family history, her age, her general health, and whether she has had past miscarriages or previous children with inheritable conditions.[9]

Expert testimony is used to determine the usual and customary degree of knowledge, care, and skill in a medical encounter. The physi-cian's legal duties generally coincide with a medical consensus because the duties are defined by medical experts testifying as to what the majority of physicians usually do. Thus, the medical consensus that amniocentesis should be offered to pregnant women thirty-five years or older has become a legal duty in addition to being a professional mandate.

The professional standard of care does not refer to best practices or high-quality practices but to usual and customary ones. In trying to prove duties under this standard, parties "normally present expert testimony describing the actual pattern of medical practice, without any reference to the effectiveness of that practice."[10] Commentators have noted that rigid legal adherence to medical custom could enshrine out-of-date, sloppy, or lazy practices as a physician's duties.[11] Some have recommended that the professional standard should reflect approved practices as opposed to those which have merely occurred with sufficient regularity;[12] however, no court has explicitly adopted this approach.

Defining legal duties according to medical custom also means that there is a dialectical relationship between law and medicine through which the practice of defensive medicine may create a self-defeating "race to the bottom." The more tests physicians order to prevent liability, the more likely it is that they will create a legal duty to offer these tests, regardless of whether testing is otherwise well advised.[13]

This "race to the bottom" may represent a particular problem for the use or overuse of prenatal genetic tests because there is an asymmetry in the costs physicians face for conducting or not conducting tests. In the absence of physical harm to the mother or fetus, parents are unlikely to sue because too many prenatal tests were done, even when they are dismayed by test results or feel that they have been coerced into testing. There are few legal avenues of recovery open for such parents, and the amount they would recover might not be worth the trouble of bringing suit. On the other hand, parents whose baby is born with a disability do bring suit on occasion and may prevail if a test was not done.

If only a fraction of parents sue when their child is born with a disability but few or none sue when too many tests are done, the legal system will provide incentives for physicians to offer every feasible prenatal genetic test. The system will participate in constituting a medical norm of offering tests, and once this norm becomes common practice, physicians will face legal duties to offer the tests. Without strong consensus statements giving guidance about the permissibility of not offering prenatal tests, physicians who refrain from offering will have little evidence to rely on in court. To be credible and weighty, such statements would have to come from medical associations, bioethicists, or other professional groups.

One question raised by our working group's failure to reach consensus is the following: "What duties does the law impose when professionals cannot agree on a best course of action under the circumstances?" There are several possibilities. The court could hold that the plaintiff failed to prove which duties were required by the standard of care. The court could identify a set of minimum duties and determine whether the physician-defendant breached those. Minimum duties in a genetic testing case might include the taking of adequate family and medical histories on a patient. Or the court could seek to determine whether the physician-defendant's behavior fell within a range of acceptable alternatives. When the physician chooses one approach from among viable alternative courses of treatment or management, she will not have breached her duties, even if the course she chose ultimately resulted in a bad outcome for the patient.[14]

The report produced by our working group could be considered as evidence that there is no consensus regarding when tests should be offered or which tests should be offered. A physician-defendant might use the report to argue that not offering a test was a valid alternative. However, legal duties are extremely situation specific, whereas our deliberations were quite general. A patient-plaintiff would argue that the standard of care mandated the offer of a test *in her particular situation*, regardless of whether experts could agree on overarching principles governing when tests should or should not be offered.

There are important exceptions to the general rule that a physician's legal duties will be equivalent to usual and customary medical practice. In rare cases, courts have found that regardless of an unambiguous, common approach to a particular problem, the entire community of physicians was not exercising reasonable care. The most notorious instance in which custom was held insufficient is the Washington state case *Helling v. Carey*, in which an ophthalmologist was found liable for failing to perform a pressure test to detect glaucoma, despite undisputed expert opinion that such tests were not usually given to patients in the plaintiff's circumstances.[15] In *Helling*, the court opined that "what is usually done may be evidence of what ought to be done, but what ought to be done is fixed by a standard of reasonable prudence, whether it usually is complied with or not."[16] The Wisconsin Supreme Court recently noted that when custom fails to keep pace with developments in medicine, then adherence to custom may constitute failure to exercise reasonable care.[17]

When considering prenatal testing, I believe that courts are more likely to find common medical practice falling below the standard of reasonableness if a test was not offered than if it was offered in a situation where most physicians would not do so. As genetic tests become cheaper and safer, courts may reason—as the Washington court did in *Helling*—that if offering and conducting tests can give parents the option of avoiding the birth of a child with very low probability, prenatally detectable disabilities, then the tests should be done. Perhaps a legally effective counterargument is that testing for very-low-probability events could lead to more false positives than actual positives and could therefore lead to parental trauma and to abortions of nondisabled, desired fetuses.

Other Standards of Care

To this point, I have referred only to the standard of care that is generally used to specify physician duties in medical malpractice cases— the professional standard. However, other standards may be relevant for cases involving the offer of prenatal tests. One such standard is the *reasonable patient standard*, which is used in informed consent actions in approximately half of U.S. jurisdictions (nearly all of the other jurisdictions use the professional standard). Because the offer of a prenatal test has to do with the exchange of information between physicians and patients, cases arising from failure to offer a test may include causes of action for informed consent. Physicians' duties under the reasonable patient standard are determined by answering the question, "What information would a reasonable patient in the same or similar circumstances have wanted to hear?"

Under standards of care other than the professional standard, the pronouncements and deliberations of professional bodies, including our working group, become less relevant to the legal determination of physician duties. Under the professional standard, experts testify as to what a physician should have done in the case *sub judice*. Under the reasonable patient standard, experts can only address background issues; no expert can testify as to whether the physician should have offered the test. Juries are thought capable of determining for themselves what information a reasonable patient would have wanted. However, under the reasonable patient standard, experts (including some members of our working group) could testify as to the results of empirical ethics research showing what proportion of people want the opportunity to take a particular prenatal test. Also relevant might be expert testimony showing that people's preferences for taking genetic and/or prenatal tests can be manipulated based on the manner in which the test is offered.

Legal Duties to Offer Prenatal Tests

There are many cases describing physicians' duties to offer two particular prenatal tests—amniocentesis and alfafetoprotein (AFP) tests.[18] There are as yet few cases addressing the duties of physicians to offer prenatal genetic tests that directly examine DNA sequences; however, several relevant principles can be extrapolated from other prenatal testing cases. In addition, at least one court has addressed the broader issue of physicians' duties to offer information pertaining to women's choices to continue their pregnancies.[19]

In attempting to identify general principles from which legal duties may be deduced, we should keep in mind that duties mandated by the standard of care (whichever standard is used) are situation specific. The court will take into account the peculiarities of each woman's/couple's circumstances, as well as parameters of the test, such as its clinical predictive value, the ease with which it can be interpreted, the pene-trance of the disease or condition, and the prevalence of the disease or condition. In other words, courts will consider many of the same issues that scholars have considered in attempting to draw lines concerning which tests should be offered and to whom.

Several trends can be observed in the accumulated jurisprudence on offers of prenatal tests and offers of diagnostic tests more broadly. First, courts generally have not found duties for physicians to offer or discuss tests in the absence of "medical indications" that the test would be appropriate. Second, if information in a patient's family or medical history even hints at an inherited disease, physicians may have duties to offer any relevant prenatal tests. Third, when a prenatal test becomes fairly routine, courts across the nation will find that physicians have a duty to offer that test.

Courts have recognized that it would be impossible for physicians to offer all conceivable prenatal tests, and therefore have been careful not to impose duties to offer a nonroutine test in the absence of medical indications. In a 1989 case, the California court held that defendant-physicians had no duty to offer Tay-Sachs prenatal testing to a patient who did not tell her genetic counselor that both she and her husband had French Canadian ancestors.[20] At the time, geneticists knew that people with Acadian ancestry have a greater-than-average likelihood of carrying Tay-Sachs alleles. The court relied on several previous cases in holding that physicians and genetic counselors have no duties to discuss Tay-Sachs testing with somebody who is not at risk because the predicate for disclosure of material facts is a proposed therapy, diagnostic test, or other intervention.[21] Doctors have no duty to disclose information about "noninterventions" because such a duty would be limitless.

In a case holding that the reasonable patient standard must be applied in determining physicians' duties of information disclosure relevant to pregnancy continuation, the New Jersey Supreme Court still limited physicians' duties of disclosure to the offer of tests that are "medically indicated."[22] Physicians have a duty to disclose "*medically accepted* risks that a reasonably prudent patient in the plaintiff's position would deem material to her decision [to continue or terminate a pregnancy]" (emphasis added).[23] The court cited numerous law review articles warning that under a reasonable patient standard, physicians might be held liable for any detectable disability, no matter how slight the likelihood of it materializing. It responded that physicians are not required to identify and disclose "remote" risks, and that the "medical probability of the risk manifesting in the patient is highly relevant to whether a reasonably prudent person would consider the risk material."[24]

One interesting question is how courts that use a reasonable patient standard might rule in a situation where empirical evidence showed that physicians have very inaccurate views about what most patients want to know, or what information is useful in their decision making. Such data should be admissible at trial and could persuade a court to deviate from reliance on medical indications in determining what a reasonable patient might want to know.

Whether the seriousness of a condition affects physicians' duties of disclosure has not been addressed by the courts. One could argue that it is not common medical practice to disclose information about genetic polymorphisms deemed inconsequential by the medical community, and thus, under the professional standard, physician's duties would not include disclosure of tests for "medically" inconsequential problems. Jurisdictions using a reasonable patient standard could follow the reasoning of the New Jersey Supreme Court, and find that medical assessments of seriousness determine the information's materiality to patients. Our working group's discussions and data presented by Dorothy C. Wertz suggest that medical seriousness may be a bad metric for ethical or legal line drawing, because experts cannot agree on which conditions are serious.[25] However, like our working group, courts have yet to arrive at a better method to avoid creating a limitless duty to offer tests.

Although courts have not imposed a duty to offer where a test was not medically indicated, they have imposed duties when there were only vague indications that the future child could inherit a disease. In *Ellis v. Sherman* a woman consulted with her obstetrician both before and during pregnancy, and when relaying her family history disclosed that her husband had a skin disease.[26] The obstetrician did not follow up on this information, and allegedly stated that it would have no bearing on the future child's health. The skin ailment was a mild form of neurofibromatosis,[27] and his physicians failed to tell the husband that the disease could be inherited. The Ellis baby was born with neurofibromatosis that resulted in seizures at the age of five months and "severe mental and physical disabilities."[28] The court upheld the Ellises' cause of action for negligence against the obstetrician and the husband's physicians because none of them warned the Ellises of the nature and possible consequences of Mr. Ellis's condition. Other courts could easily have decided this case differently; nonetheless, it signifies that at least some courts will impose on physicians stringent responsibilities of knowledge and history taking with respect to identifying inheritable diseases and offering prenatal tests.

Finally, we should note that when prenatal tests become part of routine practice, courts will find that physicians have a duty to offer them. The offer of amniocentesis for women over thirty-five years of age has become a uniformly recognized legal duty. The offer of alpha-fetoprotein (AFP) testing for all pregnant women probably has as well. For instance, in 1994 the parties in *Basten v. U.S.*, a federal court case in Alabama, stipulated that under the professional standard of care physicians had a legal duty to offer AFP to all pregnant women, and that this duty had been recognized nationally as early as 1986.[29] The court also held that physicians must document the acceptance or rejection of the test. In recognizing duties to routinely offer prenatal tests, courts are strongly influenced by consensus in the medical community and by forceful professional society guidelines, particularly those from the American College of Obstetrics and Gynecology (ACOG).

Physicians' duty to offer a prenatal test may include several specific, affirmative actions. *Basten* held that physicians' duties to offer an AFP test are not fulfilled if the patient receives only cursory information about the test during a group orientation.[30] The court held that physicians have the onus of initiating a conversation about AFP testing and of ensuring that the patient has sufficient information about the test. Furthermore, the court noted with favor testimony of an expert who stated that physicians have a responsibility to "convey with conviction the importance of taking an AFP test" and that a refusal rate of 30 percent indicated that the hospital was not providing sufficient information.[31] Implicit in the court's approbation is the notion that taking prenatal tests will lead to the birth of fewer children with disabilities, and that this is a good. What kind of good, and for whom, is not clear.

Wrongful Life and Wrongful Birth

To this point I have discussed how issues addressed by our working group are particularly relevant for the determination of tort duties. However, courts must also determine whether the plaintiff is a person to whom the defendant owed a duty. Furthermore, duty is only one element of the negligence tort. Lawyers' and judges' reasoning with respect to the other elements, particularly causation and harm (damages), also constructs attitudes towards disability.

The legal system both expresses and reflects social norms. Trials are discursive fields in which alternate narratives about harm, responsibility, and worth (among other things) compete for preeminence. Wrongful life and wrongful birth cases involve, in part, a competition of "stories" about the life of a person with disabilities and her family. These are narratives about the range of life plans available to the disabled person, about whether or to what degree she experiences pain from her disability, and about how her family is affected by the disability. For these reasons, I would now like to expand the focus of this chapter to discuss wrongful life and wrongful birth.

Wrongful life and wrongful birth can be alleged on the same set of facts. Wrongful birth is an action brought by the disabled child's *parents* against health care professionals, and wrongful life is an action brought by the disabled *child*. Both causes of action may be brought as a result of prenatal occurrences, including a physician's failure to offer or perform a prenatal test, an incorrectly performed test, or the failure to report prenatal test results to parents in a timely manner. These suits are also brought in response to preconception occurrences; however, my discussion here will focus on prenatal testing cases because prenatal testing was the topic of deliberation for our working group.

Although the two types of suit may arise from the same set of facts, courts have encountered several logical and logistical difficulties in construing wrongful life that they have not encountered with wrongful birth. Only three states (California, New Jersey, and Washington) currently recognize a wrongful life cause of action.[32] On the other hand, at least twenty-four states and the District of Columbia recognize a wrongful birth cause of action.[33]

Wrongful life. In a wrongful life case the child argues that she should not have been born, and that but for the physician's negligence she would not have been born. Had her parents been offered a prenatal test, they would have discovered her "undesirable genetic constitution" and terminated the pregnancy.[34] Because both wrongful life and wrongful birth are negligence claims, plaintiffs must prove each of the negligence elements—duty, breach, harm (damage), and causation.

One rule in tort law is that the defendant's duty must have been owed to the plaintiff. When a disabled child sues for wrongful life, she alleges that the physician owed *her* a duty to offer prenatal testing to her parents. It may seem strange that a physician could owe a duty to one party, the child or fetus, to offer testing to a third party, the mother/parents. However, the law recognizes duties that run to third parties in other contexts, for instance, with trusts and some contracts.

It may also seem strange that a physician's duty to the child could require the physician to act before the child is born. In other contexts courts have found that certain of a defendant's duties must be acted on before the obligee is born. For instance, a person who drives negligently and injures a pregnant woman and her fetus can have liability to the child once she is born. Had the defendant fulfilled her duty of driving with due care, the child would have been born uninjured. Commentators have noted that there is no logical inconsistency in having a duty to somebody who does not yet exist.[35] If an act performed now eventuates in a bad effect on a person who lives in the future then that person may have been wronged.

Compare the negligent driving case to wrongful life, in which the physician's fulfillment of a duty to the disabled child to offer prenatal testing could not have resulted in a nondisabled child being born. Instead, the child would never have been born at all (and this is her argument in court). It seems implausible to argue, as one must in wrongful life, that an obligor could have duties to an obligee to prevent her existence.

Assuming that physicians do have a duty in wrongful life situations, breach would occur if a prenatal test is not offered to the parents.

The next tort element—harm (damages)—presents insurmountable problems for many courts hearing wrongful life cases. To show that she has been harmed by being born, the child must argue that her life is worse than nonexistence. Courts are extremely reluctant to accept this claim, even if the child is born with numerous disabilities and requires substantial, lifelong medical care. As the New Hampshire court put it: "Compelling policy reasons militate against recognition of wrongful life claims. The first such reason is our conviction that the courts of this state should not become involved in deciding whether a given person's life is or is not worthwhile."[36] Furthermore, courts contend that they are ill-equipped to make sense of the counterfactual comparison between life with a disability and nonexistence: "Whether it is better never to have been born at all than to have been born with even gross deficiencies is a mystery more properly to be left to philosophers and the theologians."[37]

A plaintiff also could argue that she has been harmed because the physician's alleged negligence deprived her of her right to be born with a genome that meets a minimum quality standard. However, courts have consistently rejected this argument. In an often-quoted passage the New York court stated that the law recognizes "no fundamental right of a child to be born as a whole, functional human being."[38]

The courts have developed their own "expressivist" critique, one that acknowledges the law's role in shaping attitudes and which decries the message that would be sent if the state places differential value on its citizens based on the abilities with which they are born. "[T]he implications of [recognizing wrongful life claims] are staggering. Would claims be honored . . . for less than a perfect birth? And by what standard or by whom would perfection be defined?"[39] Although the word "eugenics" is rarely mentioned, we can detect the belief that having a branch of government pass quality-of-life judgments on citizens is a form of eugenics or could lead to more overt government interventions in reproduction.

We should note, however, that courts assign differential monetary value to people's lives in other torts. For instance, in wrongful death cases courts assign monetary value for lost income, loss of companionship, and emotional distress caused by the loss of a family member. In doing so, they place different values on people according to class and age, among other characteristics that seem morally irrelevant to a person's dignitary worth. They could even take into account a disability that would have affected the dead person's future earnings. Thus, the court's expressivist critique needs to be supplemented with arguments about why it is worse to put monetary values to ability/disability at birth than to other aspects of a person's life.

Even if courts were willing to describe life with a disability as a harm, there is still the problem of causation. To prove wrongful life, a disabled plaintiff must show that the physician's breach of a duty to her caused her to be born. Note that in wrongful life (and wrongful birth) claims plaintiffs do not allege that the physician caused the disability by physically injuring the child. The child's medical problems resulted from the stochastic processes that created her genome with a mutation or set of mutations leading to certain biologically problematic and socially disfavored characteristics. The plaintiff could not have come into existence with a different genome and different physical characteristics. So the plaintiff argues that the physician-defendant caused her to be born; if the physician had fulfilled her duties, the parents would have terminated the pregnancy and the plaintiff would not have been born to live life with a disability.

For the plaintiff to prove that she would not have been born, her parents testify that they would have had an abortion had they been offered a prenatal test and received undesired results. The claim that the parents would have had an abortion does not logically entail the conclusion that they do not love their child once born; but there is a high probability that such a conclusion will be drawn either by spectators or by the disabled child, particularly in light of current misinformation about and prejudices against people with disabilities. Although the causation element does not present logical or procedural problems for the court, the prospect that wrongful life suits will encourage the public display of less-than-unconditional acceptance of offspring underlies judicial concern that allowing wrongful life claims would be bad public policy. Many courts are reluctant to allow the "unseemly spectacle of parents disparaging the 'value' of their children or the degree of their affection for them in open court."[40]

Courts that recognize a cause of action for wrongful life do so for reasons of pragmatism and fairness. They argue that the child should not be deprived of reimbursement for medical care or education in the event that her/his parents cannot recover for wrongful birth. This may occur if the statute of limitations has passed for the parents to bring suit or once the child attains majority.[41]

No court has allowed damages to a disabled person for the very fact of her/his existence or the "pain and suffering" of living with a disability—no jurisdiction allows recovery of general damages in a wrongful life suit. The three jurisdictions that recognize wrongful life claims only allow a child to recover special damages for extraordinary expenses associated with her/his disability.[42] Thus, these courts compare the medical and educational costs of life with a disability and life without, even though the logic of wrongful life claims does not support this comparison, because the person bringing suit could not have come into existence without a disability. These courts are not comparing life with a disability to nonexistence, which would require compensation for the child's entire existence. While attempting to ensure that children with disabilities are adequately cared for, these courts have not actually accepted the underlying premises of the wrongful life cause of action.

Wrongful birth.   Recall that wrongful birth is the cause of action brought by the parents. In these cases, the physician's duty is to provide the woman (or couple) with information relevant to the continuation or termination of a pregnancy. This is because wrongful birth is "predicated on a woman's right to determine for herself whether or not to terminate her pregnancy. Persons 'have a right to determine whether to accept or reject a parental relationship, and the deprivation of that right by the negligent misconduct of another creates a cause of action for the parents.' "[43] A breach of the disclosure duty may occur if the physician fails to offer a prenatal test, if the test is done incorrectly, or if the results are misinterpreted.

Although duty in wrongful birth cases is straightforward, the harm (or damage) element is not. Early wrongful birth cases construed the birth of a child with disabilities as a harm to its parents. However, many courts have been reluctant to accept this position. The Michigan Appellate Court recently refused to follow earlier Michigan cases recognizing a cause of action for wrongful birth, largely because it was unwilling to endorse the view that the life of a disabled child could constitute harm to parents, or that the life of a disabled child should be construed as a burden on parents in a qualitatively different manner than that of a nondisabled child.[44] The Michigan opinion devotes several paragraphs to describing a slippery slope from recognizing wrongful birth cases to a state eugenics policy:

> If one accepts the premise that the birth of one "defective" child should have been prevented, then it is but a short step to accepting the premise that the births of classes of "defective" children should be similarly pre-

vented, not just for the benefit of the parents but also for the benefit of the society as a whole. . .[45]

There is also growing (although uneven) recognition in the legal system of patients as important decision makers and agents in the medical context. This and the courts' refusal to characterize the life of a disabled child as a harm has led to an evolution in wrongful birth analyses, whereby some courts now allow recovery under the theory that the harm is one to the parents' autonomy and decision-making capacity. The parents' protectable interest is characterized as their "personal right of self-determination."[46] These courts take pains to indicate that wrongfulness lies in the physician's unresponsiveness to the parents' autonomy interests, and not in the birth or life of the child.[47] If we accept this position, then the label, "wrongful birth", is inapposite because it associates the compensable wrong with the child's existence rather than with the alleged inappropriate interaction between the physicians and the parents.

These decisions highlight the fact that wrongful birth and wrongful life are two different causes of action, and the harm alleged by the parents is (or can be) different from the harm alleged by the child. Furthermore, this new formulation better reflects most ethical rationales for physicians' duties to provide patients with information. The standard rationale is that physicians' provision of information indicates respect for patients and enhances their ability to actively participate in their own health care. Courts following this new harm analysis have validated the idea that diminishing somebody's decision-making capacity can be a harm. The analysis and justification are similar to that used for informed consent.

The reconceptualization of harm in wrongful birth has created opportunities for courts also to reconceptualize the causation requirement. Traditionally, causation in wrongful birth was similar to that in wrongful life—parents had to testify that they would have taken the prenatal test and had an abortion when it showed a genetic anomaly. However, in at least one jurisdiction parents are no longer required to testify that they would have had an abortion. In 1998, the Federal District Court for the District of New Jersey, in *Provenzano v. Integrated Genetics*, stated that because harm in a wrongful birth case consists of the lost opportunity to make an informed decision, causation can be shown whenever the missing or incorrect information was material to the decision to continue a pregnancy.[48] In *Provenzano* the parents testified that they were uncertain as to whether or not they would have aborted if they had been informed of their fetus's trisomy 14. The court held that so long as abortion was a viable option for the parents, then causation had been shown because the plaintiffs had been deprived of "their right to accept or reject a parental relationship" based on complete information.[49]

The New Jersey Supreme Court has recently followed this analysis in *Canesi v. Wilson*, where the court stated that causation was shown when the risk was material to the parents' decision to continue pregnancy, the risk materialized, and it was reasonably foreseeable.[50] The court noted that proving causation under its new formulation will now be easier for plaintiffs, and that some might perceive this new approach as putting physicians in the role of "guarantors against birth defects."[51] However, it stated that the foreseeability requirement would prevent this.

Evolution of the harm and causation requirements in the parents' cause of action may change the focus of courtroom narratives away from portrayals of disabled children as burdensome, unwanted, or unbearable to their parents. The focus on family building and parents' choices in accepting or rejecting certain parental relationships is also consistent with a transformation in the ethical debate whereby the focus is shifted away from the hypothetical, imagined life of the future child with disabilities and towards the parents' goals and values. The courts' focus on parental autonomy in wrongful birth cases may substantially decrease the damages that parents could recover. There is a logical disconnect between claiming parental dignitary harm and asking for damages for the child's extraordinary medical and educational expenses. Thus, if parents' primary motive in bringing wrongful birth suits is to provide for the child, the newly developing theory of wrongful birth may preclude the kinds of damages that would achieve this goal.

Informed Consent

In many wrongful life or wrongful birth cases the alleged wrong involves inadequate conveyance of information. For this reason, there are many instances in which one set of facts can give rise to a cause of action for lack of informed consent, in addition to or instead of wrongful birth or wrongful life.

The legal doctrine of informed consent (as opposed to the ethical principle) developed from the law of battery and reflected the idea that people have a right to determine who violates their bodily integrity and under what conditions. In all but one jurisdiction, informed consent has now developed into a negligence cause of action, and, therefore, each element of negligence must be proved. When an informed consent case revolves around failure to offer a prenatal test, the elements are as follows: (1) the physician had a duty to offer the test; (2) the physician breached by failing to tell the pregnant woman about the test; (3) the woman was harmed (damaged) because she was deprived of the opportunity to make a fully informed choice about continuing her pregnancy and so she gave birth to a disabled child; (4) the physician's breach caused this harm because had the woman been offered the test she would have taken it, received information of a genetic anomaly, and terminated the pregnancy.

Whether the offer of a test will be analyzed as an informed consent issue depends in part on whether the jurisdiction in question conceptualizes consent as requiring an affirmative act on the part of the physician. The term "consent" implies that the physician proposes to do something to the patient, to which the patient must either give or withhold agreement.[52] If a physician took blood and conducted a prenatal test without obtaining the patient's agreement, then that would generate a straightforward informed consent case. However, when the issue is failure to offer a prenatal test, it is difficult to understand where the failure of consent occurred. Certainly women decide to continue pregnancies or to abort, but is this the same as consenting to continue their pregnancies? To whom would a women give such consent—to her physician? Does it make sense to say that a woman continued her pregnancy without giving consent to her physician?

On the other hand, if we think of informed consent more broadly, as an information-autonomy tort, then it makes sense to consider lack of a test offer under this rubric.

From the description given above, it may be difficult to distinguish informed consent from wrongful birth. In many jurisdictions the two causes of action are becoming quite similar, and the differences between the two vary by jurisdiction. One respect in which they are similar in nearly all jurisdictions (except New Jersey) is the causation analysis. The causation analysis in informed consent requires the plaintiff to prove that if she had received additional information she would have behaved differently than she actually did. Where the case revolves around prenatal genetic testing, the different thing the parents would have done is to terminate rather than continue the pregnancy. Thus, bringing an informed consent case leads to the same spectacle of parents appearing to reject their disabled child in public.

One could ask, why does it matter whether a case is analyzed as wrongful birth or informed consent? One reason is that different standards of care may apply. One could be in a jurisdiction where a professional standard would be used for a wrongful birth cause of action, but a reasonable patient standard would be used for informed consent. There is some possibility that a duty to offer a test would be found under the patient-centered standard, but not under a professional standard. The Maryland Court of Appeals, in *Reed v. Campagnolo*, explicitly declined to analyze failure to offer a prenatal test as an informed consent cause of action because it did not find the reasonable patient standard appropriate:

> ". . . [T]he rule cannot focus exclusively on the plaintiff. A fair rule would have to look at all of the possible tests that might be given and evaluate the reasons for excluding some and perhaps recommending one or more others. That approach requires expert testimony.[53]

Another reason it may matter is that informed consent may provide the means by which plaintiffs can recover in jurisdictions that do not recognize wrongful birth or wrongful life as causes of action. A third reason is that informed consent might allow the plaintiff to recover damages that she cannot recover under wrongful birth. For example, a jurisdiction that does not allow emotional distress damages for wrongful birth may allow them for informed consent. A fourth reason is that litigating a case as informed consent may, in some jurisdictions, allow plaintiffs to escape statutes of limitations or recovery caps imposed on medical malpractice actions by various states' tort reform laws.

Infliction of Emotional Distress

Emotional distress doctrine as applied to pre- and peri-natal events is new and still evolving.[54] I include a brief discussion here because parents have successfully recovered damages from physicians under this doctrine after the birth of a child with prenatally detectable disabilities. In addition, I believe that emotional distress doctrine could be expanded to permit recovery for anguish associated with overly aggressive prenatal test offers or overutilization of prenatal tests. Such an expansion could partially redress the imbalance between legal incentives to offer prenatal tests and legal incentives not to offer them; it could provide some legal checks on the inclination to offer all possible tests and to promote prenatal testing aggressively.

Courts have traditionally limited the applicability of emotional distress doctrine to a narrow range of cases because they assumed that a generous cause of action for emotional distress would result in inappropriately high liability and speculative claims. They feared that emotional distress without physical injury could be easily feigned.[55] However, exceptions are developing, and the modern trend is to allow recovery in a broader range of cases.[56]

Traditionally, negligent infliction of emotional distress (NIED) damages were only allowed if the psychic injury flowed from physical injuries the plaintiff suffered in an impact (the "impact rule"). Many jurisdictions have now relaxed the impact rule to allow plaintiffs a cause of action if they were within the "zone of physical danger" of a negligently caused impact. Thus, the plaintiff could recover if she was nearly hit and reasonably feared that she would be. Parents are unlikely to have a cause of action for either the overly aggressive offer of a prenatal test or for failure to offer a test in a jurisdiction that strictly adheres to either the impact or zone of danger rules. As one court noted, "it is readily apparent that in the vast majority of instances a plaintiff will find it impossible to establish that [she] was within a zone of danger created by a medical misdiagnosis of a family member. Diagnoses, by their nature, tend not to create immediate danger to others."[57]

When courts allow recovery for NIED in the absence of a physical impact, they frequently still require that the emotional disturbance have some physical manifestation such as vomiting, hypertension, or sleeplessness. They also require that the emotional distress be a foreseeable result of the negligence, and that it is more than a temporary disappointment, regret, or fright.[58]

Some courts have allowed parents of disabled or stillborn children to recover for NIED, even in the absence of substantial physical manifestations of the emotional disturbance. Recovery is predicated on the fact that the physician had a preexisting relationship with the parents and because emotional injury was a foreseeable consequence of the physician's actions. The California Supreme Court found that the parents could recover for NIED when a physician negligently caused their child to be stillborn.[59] The North Carolina Supreme Court held that parents could recover for NIED when their physician negligently failed to tell them that they were both sickle cell carriers and they later gave birth to a child with the disease.[60]

Doctrine in jurisdictions such as California or North Carolina could be expanded to include instances in which the overly aggressive offer of a prenatal test caused parents to become distraught and affected their choices or the course of the pregnancy. For instance, physicians might instigate or exacerbate extreme parental fear about a future child's condition as a byproduct of strenuously encouraging parents to take prenatal tests. If this fear caused the parents to choose an amniocentesis or other procedure that put their nondisabled fetus at risk, parents might have a cause of action for NIED. If the stress had physical manifestations in the mother that altered the course or outcome of the pregnancy, then the parents would have the elements of a preexisting relationship with the physician, a foreseeable emotional trauma, and a physical manifestation of the emotional distress. With these elements present, a court could reasonably allow a cause of action for NIED to proceed.

Even in jurisdictions that still adhere to the impact rule, courts have created some specific exceptions. For instance, a plaintiff may have an NIED cause of action if she is negligently and erroneously told that a family member is suffering from a deadly disease or if she is negligently and erroneously notified of a family member's death.[61] Courts have also created exceptions for parents who were negligently told that their future child would not have a disability. In *Naccash v. Burger* the Virginia Supreme Court upheld an NIED cause of action for parents whose physician negligently informed them that the husband was not a Tay-Sachs carrier and the couple's child was later born with Tay-Sachs.[62] The *Naccash* court noted that the public policy reasons for limiting recovery to situations in which the plaintiffs suffered direct physical injury were inapposite here—nobody suggested that the parents' emotional suffering when they watched their baby die was feigned or that their claim was fraudulent.[63]

Courts might also create impact-rule exceptions for parents who were subjected to extreme pressure because they chose not to take a prenatal test, or when the overly aggressive offer of a test could reasonably be interpreted as suggesting an unusually high likelihood that their child would be born with a disability.

Allowing parents to recover for NIED when a child is born with a disability may appear to promote an inappropriate focus on disabled children as sources of parental anguish, while ignoring the pleasures and benefits they bring. It may emphasize or legitimize ideologically motivated and poorly controlled research claiming that families with disabled children are overwhelmingly worse off than other families.[64] However, it may also reflect the fact that families have a wide variety of reactions to the birth of a child with disabilities, and that disabilities vary substantially in their manifestations. Parents who must watch their child die an early and perhaps painful death, or parents who must watch their child endure numerous painful operations and therapy, may indeed be deeply traumatized. The question is whether we characterize their pain as a sad but unavoidable part of life or an avoidable experience for which they can be compensated.

If we do endorse recovery under some circumstances, there are advantages to allowing recovery under NIED rather than informed consent or other causes of action—under NIED parents need not argue that they would have aborted their child, or that they would have been better off without their child in their lives. Furthermore, NIED is a cause of action that is not limited to issues of disabled children; a third party's mistreatment of a nondisabled child might also lead to NIED liability. One drawback of NIED as a sole means of recovery for the birth of a disabled child is that parents probably would not be entitled to extraordinary medical or educational expenses for their children, so NIED is not as satisfactory a means of obtaining care and support for children and families.

Conclusions

Issues addressed by our working group are significant and problematic for the courts. One of the working group's central questions— under what circumstances does a physician have a duty to offer a prenatal test—is addressed directly in the tort law element of duty. Courts have tended to find a legal duty to offer prenatal tests when the medical profession has routinized the offer of the particular test, or if there are medical indications of an inheritable disease in the family. Even jurisdictions that are moving toward a patient-centered standard for assessing duty rely heavily on medical indications to signify the materiality of test information for a patient. Courts have not found a better rationale for distinguishing those tests that are permitted or required to be offered from those that are not. They fear that other methods of line drawing would create unclear or unending duties for physicians to offer tests. Vague or ambiguous legal duties can lead to the waste of resources, for instance, through inefficient use of tests and excessive litigation.

Jurisdictions are divided on how and whether they allow recovery for the birth of a child with a prenatally detectable disability when a test was not offered, and to a large degree their divisions mirror those in our group. Many courts are deeply disturbed by the sociocultural apparatus surrounding prenatal testing for genetic disabilities, including the justifications for it, the manner in which it is offered, the way in which those who do not accept it are treated, and the messages litigation sends about disability. Some courts have begun to recharacterize the alleged harms to parents as involving diminishment of parents' decision-making capacity rather than as the birth of their disabled child. This approach is more sensitive to the legal system's role in perpetuating the indignities and stereotypes visited on disabled people. It is more consistent with pluralistic views on the role of children in families and the nature of parenthood.

Incentives produced by the current legal framework weigh in favor of genetic testing. In part, this is because there are rarely (if ever) legal ramifications for physicians who overutilize tests, while there may be legal ramifications when tests are not utilized. I note that NIED doctrine could be expanded to allow a cause of action for the overutilization of tests, and thus, partially redress this imbalance.

Acknowledgment

I would like to thank Clement Hsiao and Erica Linden for their research assistance.

NOTES

1. Erik Parens and Adrienne Asch, "The Disability Rights Critique of Prenatal Genetic Testing: Reflections and Recommendations," in this volume.

2. Laurence Tribe, "On Not Banning Cloning for the Wrong Reasons," in *Clones and Clones: Facts and Fantasies About Human Cloning,* ed. Martha Nussbaum and Cass Sunstein (New York: W. W. Norton and Company, Inc., 1998), pp. 221–32.

3. William L. Prosser, *Handbook of the Law of Torts,* 4th ed. (St. Paul, Minn.: West Group, 1971), pp. 325–26.

4. *Klein v. Children's Hospital Medical Center of Northern California,* 46 Cal. App. 4th 889 (1996).

5. *Bardessono v. Michels,* 3 Cal. 3d 780 (1970).

6. *McAllister v. Khie Sem HA,* 347 N. C. 638 (1998).

7. Carolyn Brown, "Genetic Malpractice: Avoiding Liability," *University of Cincinnati Law Review* 54 (1986): 857–81.

8. *Reed v. Campagnolo,* 332 Md. 226 (1993), p. 233.

9. Brown, "Genetic Malpractice," pp. 857–81; *Berman v. Allan,* 80 N.J. 421 (1979); and *Phillips v. United States,* 566 F. Supp. 1 (1981).

10. Barry R. Furrow et al., *Health Law: Cases, Materials and Problems* (St. Paul, Minn.: West Publishing Co., 1991).

11. Joseph H. King, "In Search of a Standard of Care for the Medical Profession: The 'Accepted Practice' Formula," *Vanderbilt Law Review* 28 (1975): 1213–76; and *Nowatske v. Osterloh*, 198 Wis. 2d 419 (1996).

12. King, "The 'Accepted Practice' Formula."

13. Such an argument was made in *Reed v. Campanolo*: "In argument before this Court, counsel for the defendants also presented an 'overutilization' argument. The submission is that, faced with the possibility of liability, . . . physicians will order tests for which there is no medical justification, and that this form of defensive medicine will become so widespread that it would create the appearance of the standard of care" (*Reed v. Campagnolo*, 332 Md. 226 (1993), p. 240).

14. Mark A. Hall, "The Defensive Effect of Medical Practice Policies in Malpractice Litigation," *Law and Contemporary Problems* 54, no. 2 (1991): 119–46; *Lama v. Borras*,16 F. 3d 174 (1994); and *Hood v. Slappey*, 601 So. 2d 981 (1992).

15. *Helling v. Carey*, 83 Wash. 2d 514 (1974).

16. *Helling v. Carey*, 83 Wash. 2d 514.

17. *Nowatske v. Osterloh*, 198 Wis. 2d 419, p.435.

18. Amniocentesis detects genetic anomalies at the chromosomal level, and AFP detects abnormal levels of protein circulating in the mother's blood that could indicate genetic anomalies such as trisomy 21.

19. *Canesi v. Wilson*, 158 N.J. 490 (1999).

20. *Munro v. UC Regents*, 215 Cal. App. 3d 977 (1989) (rev. denied).

21. *Munro v. UC Regents*, 215 Cal. App. 3d 977, p. 987.

22. *Canesi v. Wilson*, 158 N.J., p. 490.

23. *Canesi v. Wilson*, 158 N.J., p. 506.

24. *Canesi v. Wilson*, 158 N.J., p. 510.

25. Parens and Asch, "The Disability Rights Critique."

26. *Ellis v. Sherman*, 478 A. 2d 1339 (Pa. Super 1984) (aff'd 512 Pa. 14).

27. Neurofibromatosis is an autosomal dominant but incompletely penetrant disease that affects the nervous system, muscles, bones, and skin. Its manifestations range from extremely minor (café au lait spots) to extremely disfiguring skin tumors and tumors on cranial, acoustic, and optic nerves.

28. *Ellis v. Sherman*, 478 A. 2d, p. 1340.

29. *Basten v. U.S.*, 848 F. Supp. 962 (1994), p. 967.

30. *Basten v. U.S.*, 848 F. Supp., p. 969.

31. *Basten v. U.S.*, 848 F. Supp. 962, p. 968.

32. *Procanik v. Cillo*, 97 N.J. 339 (1984); *Turpin v. Sortini*, 32 Cal. 3d 220 (1982); and *Harbeson v. Parke-Davis*, 98 Wash. 2d 460 (1983).

33. Six states bar claims for wrongful birth by statute, and one state, Missouri, bars most compensatory damages arising from wrongful birth cases but does allow plaintiffs' claims for emotional distress because of failure to be advised of a genetic or congenital anomaly (675 N.E. 2d 1119). Two states, Georgia and North Carolina, bar wrongful birth claims by judicial decision. The Court of Appeals of Michigan has refused to recognize a wrongful birth cause of action in the absence of either legislation or Michigan Supreme Court decisions in favor (236 Mich. App. 315., 675 N.E. 2d 1119). See also *Bader v. Johnson*, 675 N.E. 2d 1119 (1997), pp. 1122–23.

34. If preconceptive negligence is alleged, the child argues that had her parents had proper information (genetic counseling, carrier testing, diagnosis of an earlier born child, etc.), then they would not have conceived the plaintiff.

35. Melinda A. Roberts, *Child versus Childmaker: Future Persons and Present Duties in Ethics and the Law* (Lanham, Md.: Rowman and Littlefield Publishers, Inc., 1998); and Derek Parfit, *Reasons and Persons* (New York: Oxford University Press, 1984).

36. *Smith v. Cote*, 128 N.H. 231 (1986), p. 248.

37. *Becker v. Schwartz*, 46 N.Y. 2d 401 (1978), p. 411.

38. *Becker v. Schwartz*, 46 N.Y. 2d, p. 411.

39. *Becker v. Schwartz*, 46 N.Y. 2d, p. 411.

40. *Taylor v. Surender Kurpati*, 236 Mich. App. 315 (1999), p. 3335.

41. In most jurisdictions, awards to the parents for a child's medical expenses are calculated to end when the child reaches the age of majority. However, some jurisdictions have recognized a "duty imposed on parents to support their children who continue to be disabled beyond their majority" (848 F. Supp. 962).

42. *Procanik v. Cillo*, 97 N.J. 339; *Turpin v. Sortini*, 32 Cal. 3d 220; and *Harbeson v. Parke-Davis,* 98 Wash. 2d 460.

43. *Canesi v. Wilson*, 158 N.J., p. 501.

44. *Taylor v. Surender Kurpati*, 236 Mich. App., p. 334.

45. *Taylor v. Surender Kurpati*, 236 Mich. App., p. 349.

46. *Canesi v. Wilson*, 158 N.J. 490; *Provenzano v. Integrated Genetics*, 22 F. Supp. 2d 406 (1998); Keel v. Banach, 624 So. 2d 1022 (Ala. 1993).

47. *Viccaro v. Milunsky*, 551 N.E. 2d 8 (1990), p. 10.

48. *Provenzano v. Integrated Genetics*, 22 F. Supp. 2d, p. 406.

49. *Provenzano v. Integrated Genetics*, 22 F. Supp. 2d, p. 416.

50. *Canesi v. Wilson*, 158 N.J., p. 490.

51. *Canesi v. Wilson*, 158 N.J., p. 516.

52. *Reed v. Campagnolo*, 332 Md. 226 (1993), p. 241.

53. *Reed v. Campagnolo*, 332 Md., p. 244.

54. *Klein v. Children's Hospital Medical Center of Northern California*, 46 Cal. App. 4th 889.

55. *Chizmar v. Mackie*, 896 P. 2d 196 (S. Ct. AL 1995).

56. *Chizmar v. Mackie*, 896 P. 2d 196.

57. *Cauman v. George Washington University*, 630 A. 2d 1104 (D.C. Dist. Ct. App. 1993).

58. *Johnson v. Ruark*, 327 N.C. 283 (1990).

59. *Burgess v. Superior Court*, 2 Cal. 4th 1064 (1992).

60. *Johnson v. Ruark*, 327 N.C. 638.

61. *Klein v. Children's Hospital Medical Center of Northern California*, 896 P. 2d 196.

62. *Naccash MD v. Burger*, 223 Va. 406 (1982).

63. *Naccash MD v. Burger*, 223 Va., p. 415.

64. Philip M. Ferguson, Alan Gartner, and Dorothy K. Lipsky, "The Experience of Disability in Families: A Synthesis of Research and Parent Narratives," in this volume.

STEVEN J. RALSTON

Reflections from the Trenches: One Doctor's Encounter with Disability Rights Arguments

As a perinatologist, an obstetrician who specializes in high-risk pregnancy, I care for pregnant women with medical problems or obstetrical
complications. I also take care of women who are seeking information
about the health and status of their unborn children. I perform ultra-
sounds looking for structural abnormalities or subtle signs of genetic
disorders, and I offer amniocentesis for the prenatal diagnosis of many
abnormalities ranging from Down syndrome to cystic fibrosis to Tay-
Sachs disease. Along the way, I provide counseling about genetic testing,
abnormal results, and even termination of pregnancy. Much of what I
do in the arena of prenatal diagnosis is to reassure parents about the
health of their fetuses. However, the abnormal results I give create
much distress and anxiety about the pregnancy. And although this
information may allow a woman and her family time to prepare for a
child with special needs, the abnormal results often lead to decisions
to terminate pregnancies.

In the spring of 1997, I was invited to attend the annual meeting
of the Society for Disability Studies (SDS) and subsequently the meetings
being held at The Hastings Center to discuss the ethics and social impact
of prenatal diagnosis for genetic disability. Since a large part of my job
is devoted to the prevention of birth defects and the prenatal detection
(and often termination) of abnormal pregnancies, I approached the SDS
meeting with a bit of trepidation. It was not clear to me how I would
be received: Was I the enemy?

Well, I think my fears were actually baseless, as the vast majority
of people I met at the meeting, including those with disabilities, were
thrilled to have someone like me in attendance, if only because a
prevailing sentiment at the meeting was that the medical community
wanted little to do with and had limited knowledge about the "disability

community." Many of the people I met at the conference expressed to me a belief that medical professionals have very little direct contact with people with disabilities and that our experience with disability is largely confined to what we have learned in the classroom or in the acute setting of a hospital or clinic. Although it is difficult for me to generalize about all medical professionals, my sense is that this belief is probably true.

Of course, some physicians deal almost exclusively with patients with disabilities in their daily practices—geneticists and rehabilitation medicine specialists come to mind. Obstetricians, however, primarily see young healthy women; even perinatologists like me who see many women with a variety of medical problems rarely see women with the typical disabling traits or conditions being screened for during pregnancy, such as spina bifida, Down syndrome, cystic fibrosis, and the like.

I cannot comment on all doctors' medical training because it varies from medical school to medical school. In general, what I was taught in medical school and in my training is that disability—no matter what its form—is a bad thing and to be avoided at all costs. Lectures or seminars on Down syndrome or other genetic syndromes were geared toward the description of the abnormalities and the efforts that can be made to prevent the problem in the first place; that children with congenital diseases may find their lives to be rich and valuable was hardly recognized, much less stressed.

I must, however, mention an episode that occurred early in medical school, which, because it was so exceptional, remains quite vivid in my memory even ten years later. We had a special guest lecturer, a neurologist, who gave the case histories of two men with spinal abnormalities: one with spina bifida, the other with cerebral palsy. He brought each of these patients out before us in wheelchairs and demonstrated their individual musculoskeletal deficiencies—this one had spasticity here, that one weakness there, and so on. He then wheeled the patients out of the room, came back, and asked us to describe the findings on their physical exams and the limitations these men might have in the real world. He asked us to imagine what kind of difficulties they would have with their ADLs—activities of daily living—and then to come up with the kinds of jobs for which they might be suited or capable.

The neurologist then asked the two patients to come back into the room, which they both did, fully dressed in business attire, ambulating: one with crutches, the other with leg braces. Then they spoke to us, telling us they were professionals—an accountant and a lawyer—and dispelled a number of myths, misconceptions, and prejudices we had about persons with disabilities. They spoke of their friends, their families, their sex lives. For me—and I suspect most of my classmates—it was an emotional, eye-opening experience. The lesson was clear: contrary to our preconceptions, people with disabilities have depth and breadth to their personhood that extends well beyond their disabling traits.

Unfortunately, this was a unique experience in my medical school career. I recollect no similar lectures, nor was anything so affirming ever said about the lives of people with congenital impairments, especially those that are associated with mental retardation. Much time and effort were devoted to learning how to diagnose and categorize these traits, but certainly at no time in my training did anyone ever suggest that the experience of raising a child with a disability might be as rewarding and frustrating as that of raising any child.

Nevertheless, I don't think my experience with disability and disease in my own life has been limited by any means. I grew up in a family with its fair share: my brother was born with a single kidney that failed in his teens, leading him to undergo transplantation in his early twenties; my sister was born deaf; my uncle had multiple sclerosis and was institutionalized in his forties; and a cousin was born blind. Now, how this compares with other physicians' families and personal experiences with disability is not clear, though I suspect it is somewhat broader than most. Moreover, the ways in which these various disabling conditions and traits were handled in my family I think helped shape my attitudes toward disability today.

What I learned growing up is that not all disabilities are debilitating, and that the outcome for a person with a disability is dependent on much more than the mere nature of the disability itself. My sister, who is deaf, was mainstreamed from an early age and received extensive speech therapy; she is completely oral and functions extremely well in the hearing world. She works, supports herself, and leads a full life. The message from my parents growing up was clear: this is a hardship for her, but one that in no way should preclude her from leading a successful and fulfilling life. My cousin who was born blind, however, did not have nearly as successful an outcome. Her blindness was never treated as anything short of a tragedy and, unable to care for herself, she was placed in a nursing facility in her early forties. I grew up feeling that these different outcomes had little to do with the differences in the disabling traits—deafness versus blindness—than how the disabled person was treated, motivated, and perceived.

At the SDS meeting I was heartened, impressed, and (naïvely) amazed at the tremendously successful lives and careers being led by the men and women with disabilities I met there. And over the next year while attending the meetings at The Hastings Center, I found myself continually questioning my underlying assumptions about prenatal diagnosis, genetic testing, parenthood, families, and disability. I wouldn't say I was thrown into an existential crisis, but I certainly spent a lot of energy trying to resolve what for me was clearly a conflict: my belief that society would be better if it were more tolerant and accepting of those with different abilities and needs, and my belief that insofar as the world is not yet ideal, the decision to terminate a pregnancy with an abnormal fetus is reasonable.

This conflict was complicated further by the fact that a large part of my work involves diagnosing abnormal pregnancies. Over the period of time I was attending The Hastings Center meetings, I was becoming more aware and concerned about the ways in which prenatal testing is offered and results are given. As testing becomes more complicated and time constraints preclude extensive counseling for patients, our ability to obtain truly informed consent for tests and to offer unbiased "nondirective" counseling about test results seems limited.

Even a single prenatal test can require extensive consideration and counseling. I recently learned I was a carrier for cystic fibrosis (CF): I was screening myself to see if I was a carrier for CF as well as several degenerative neurological diseases more common in Ashkenazi Jews. Although I didn't feel my CF carrier status would influence my reproductive decisions—I personally wouldn't consider termination of pregnancy for an affected fetus—the mistake I made was that I assumed that the test had relevance only for me. But the laws of Mendelian genetics make my test an implicit test of my parents' genetic make-up: since I am a carrier of the CF gene, then so is (at least) one of my parents. And though my parents may be long past their reproductive endeavors, I do have three reproductive-age siblings, each of whose risk of being a CF carrier was now 50 percent. What should I tell them? What about my cousins who have a 25 percent chance of being carriers?

I think this story illustrates one more aspect of the complicated nature of even one simple prenatal screening test. Although maternal serum or amniocentesis screening for Down syndrome and spina bifida is relevant only for the involved couple and fetus, there are much broader ramifications for entire families when screening for parental genetic carrier status. And with emerging biochemical technologies making more and more genetic tests available and cheap, these tests are going to be offered and taken with increasing frequency. This story also demonstrates (much to my chagrin) that it is very difficult to be fully and adequately informed about these tests before taking them. The time and expense required to provide pertinent information and adequate counseling about these tests may be an unwelcome addition to our already overburdened health care system.

So where does this leave me now? How have all these experiences affected me? What impact have the meetings of the SDS and The Hastings Center had on my views and on the details of my daily professional routine?

First, my views on abortion have not changed. I am pro-choice and I believe all women and couples should have the right to and access to abortion services regardless of their motivations. Period. I think perhaps, though, I have become less able to see myself rejecting an abnormal pregnancy, or perhaps I see myself as more able to accept the idea of raising an "imperfect" or challenging child. Some of this has stemmed from meeting people with disabilities, and some of it from meeting parents of disabled children. Certainly some of this reflects where I am in my life at this particular moment in time. The reality is, of course, that I won't know how I will meet such a challenge or treat such a decision about an abnormal pregnancy until I am faced with it.

Second, I am much more cognizant and wary—if not worried—about the impact and power of the language I use while counseling patients. No longer do words like "risk," "abnormality," or "problem" seem innocent or devoid of judgment and bias. And although I try my best to present the information I have as accurately, succinctly, simply, and clearly as possible, the task of being a nondirective, unbiased counselor and an effective communicator is daunting, if not impossible. I had a patient last year berate me months after the fact for telling her that her fetus had a 1 in 400 risk of an abnormality but neglecting to tell her that this was indeed less than 1 percent. This experience made it obvious to me that it is not only important to present the information clearly and in language and terms that patients can understand, it is just as vital to listen to patients to know what their assessment of the risks might be. The language we use in talking to patients is so crucial, and yet so unpredictable in its impact.

Third, I am also more keenly aware now of the kinds of information we give patients and the manner in which we give it before a test is offered and after a diagnosis has been made of a fetal "abnormality," as well as the types of resources we provide them in helping them (a) understand the diagnosis and (b) make a decision about pregnancy continuation or termination. Again, I think that this part of the process is fraught with difficulties and biases. For a couple with a fetus newly diagnosed with Down syndrome, how do we tell them about the outcomes for these children and their families? What information should we give them? The medical literature may stress the medical complications and rates of mental retardation; the sociological literature may stress the impact, both good and bad, on families; and support groups will undoubtedly have their own biases. Alas, Michael Bérubé[1] is not available to personally counsel and advise each and every one of these couples.

Ideally, patients would know all they need to know about Down syndrome or spina bifida or cystic fibrosis or any other congenital disease prior to embarking on a searching expedition with maternal serum screening, ultrasound, or amniocentesis. Ideally, they would already know children who have these particular diseases; they would see families around them raising these children; and the media and popular culture would provide positive images of them. But the reality is that parents are often presented with a diagnosis of an unfamiliar disease entity, given limited information about the disease, and told they have three to four weeks to make a decision about whether they want to carry this fetus to term. As hard as we try to do this job empathetically and responsibly, at times it seems dishearteningly difficult to do it well. I think the best we can do as medical professionals is to help patients discover the answers to these questions on their own, with as complete information as possible, and without projecting onto them our own personal and professional biases. This is not a simple task but it is one of the many challenges that make my job satisfying, interesting, and compelling, and it is a task that I think I understand better as a result of my encounter with the arguments and concerns posed by people with disabilities.

NOTE

1. Michael Bérubé's *Life As We Know It: A Father, a Family, and an Exceptional Child* (New York: Pantheon, 1996) is a recounting of the early years of raising his son who has Down syndrome. It is a wonderful book, which begins as a paean to the joys and pains of parenthood and then becomes a cogent critique of our society's failure to accommodate those among us with disabilities.

BARBARA BOWLES BIESECKER AND LORI HAMBY

What Difference the Disability Community Arguments Should Make for the Delivery of Prenatal Genetic Information

Genetic counselors and other professionals working with people faced with the option of prenatal testing, and disability scholars, researchers, and advocates, have an ongoing need to inform one another about the use and implications of prenatal testing. Both groups have much to offer one another in broadening societal views about disability and in enhancing the ways that prenatal services are provided.

While some view prenatal testing as an opportunity to maximize a couple's reproductive options, others emphasize the ability of such testing to provide reassurance concerning the fetus's development or, alternatively, the chance to be prepared for the birth of a child with special needs.[1] Professionals such as genetic counselors, who work with women (and their partners) prior to prenatal testing, are well positioned to consider the ramifications of this testing both for individual families and for society as a whole. In addition to our understanding of the science and technology involved in prenatal testing, our experience with women undergoing prenatal testing offers some insight into the needs of women and their partners. However, in order to be truly helpful to women exploring prenatal testing, genetic counselors and other professionals benefit from the perspectives of those who know personally about the lives and experiences of individuals affected with disabilities.

One of the agreed upon goals of counseling prior to prenatal testing is to aid women/couples in making personal decisions about the use of such testing.[2] Opinions regarding the effectiveness of genetic counselors in aiding in decision making vary. Although many clients state that their decisions are influenced by the counseling process, research data have shown that client decisions before and after counseling are similar.[3] It could be that the process of counseling often helps to solidify decisions that clients have already made. While not changing these clients' decisions, genetic counseling may have been influential in the decision-making process. The process strives to help couples live contentedly with their decision, one way or another. It could also be the case that genetic counselors are not generally taking an active role in the decisions of their clients.

Genetic Counseling

Genetic counseling has long ascribed to an ethic of nondirectiveness. The concept was adopted in genetics largely in response to previous eugenic practices. It intends to prevent the persuasion or coercion of reproductive decisions for an individual or couple whose fetus is found to be affected with a certain condition. Unfortunately, the label of nondirectiveness has led to misunderstandings about the practice and objectives of genetic counseling. Given the expertise of the counselor and the expectations of the client, as the term "counseling" itself suggests, the counseling interaction will always in some sense be "directive." Yet, a client-centered counselor works to explore and support the values and beliefs of the client. A short-term therapeutic relationship can be established in order to help clarify the needs and desires of the client and family.

Genetic counselors often provide scientific information to disabled individuals and their family members when disability is caused by a genetic condition. In the pediatric or adult genetics setting, counselors help families to understand how a condition occurs. But families attend genetics clinics seeking to understand more than simply how a condition occurs. They struggle to make sense of the event in their lives, much in the same way a family adjusts to an accident or other inexplicable occurrence that leads to disability. Genetic counselors support families in their adjustment and help them to recognize and employ their personal strengths and resources.

Commonly, families who have a child or other relative affected with a genetic condition, or who have lost such a child, often say that they have found strengths (in character and coping skills) that they never knew they had.[4] The meaning of life or family may be forever changed for them because of the presence of the condition in the family, and often it is described as for the better. Families adapt, grow, and open their hearts to new meanings for successful or rewarding lives. They learn tolerance, acceptance, and joy in the context of different achievements. Counselors who share aspects of this journey with families often remark that witnessing these experiences is a rewarding aspect of their work.[5] Counselors live this celebration of human variation in a manner that can expand the meaning of their own lives as well.

How then can counselors who value and endorse the lives of those affected with a myriad of genetic conditions promote or offer prenatal testing for the option of aborting affected fetuses? The answer is complex but is often reduced to a commitment to the freedom of reproductive choice. Counselors adhere to a code of ethics that promotes autonomous, reproductive decision making.[6] Some couples may not have the resources or emotional fortitude to raise a child who may have to learn or live differently in order to grow and flourish in our society. Some couples may not even be interested in discussing parenting a child with special needs, rejecting outright the notion of continuing a pregnancy. Yet counselors recognize that many people do not know what they can handle, what they can cope with, what they can embrace, or what they can celebrate until they've experienced it firsthand.

How can counselors help clients consider a broad interpretation of "normal" and valuable? How do they help clients consider a developing fetus as an evolving person with a condition and not as the condition itself or as simply "abnormal?" This chapter will address these difficult questions as we attempt to explore the role of genetic counselors in the offering of prenatal testing and in advocating for the value of the lives of those affected by genetic or nongenetic disabling conditions.

Voluntary Nature of Prenatal Testing

Prenatal testing should always be voluntary. The client or couple should freely choose whether or not to undergo testing. Prenatal testing is not medically indicated and is not useful for everyone eligible to pursue it. In order to uphold the voluntary nature of prenatal testing, genetic counseling should precede it. Even if counseling is not offered, at minimum, obstetric providers should take care to reinforce the voluntary nature of the test and to help patients consider some of the risks and benefits. Ideally, extensive prenatal counseling ought to precede prenatal testing.

One of the countervailing forces to the voluntary nature of testing is that providers are legally liable if eligible patients are not made aware of the availability of prenatal testing.[7] Professional medical societies have endorsed this responsibility.[8] Unfortunately, this responsibility to offer testing often gets misconstrued as an obligation to perform prenatal testing. Obstetric providers may view a woman's choice not to undergo testing as a professional liability. Thus, they may promote rather than offer prenatal testing.[9]

Genetic counseling rarely accompanies prenatal screening such as the use of ultrasound or triple screening (see Press, this volume). Counseling does often precede the decision whether or not to pursue amniocentesis or chorionic villus sampling (CVS) (see Powell, this volume). Yet, prenatal screening can result in an alarming result that raises the option of prenatal testing and the need for counseling quite unexpectedly.[10] Regrettably, the provision of prenatal counseling is not uniform.[11] This makes it difficult to accurately describe prenatal genetic counseling. Four models will be discussed to capture this variation. We will argue that the most extensive model in terms of engaging with the client is the most desirable in helping couples make personal choices about whether or not to pursue prenatal testing and about acting on the results.

Models of Prenatal Counseling

The most basic approach to prenatal counseling is the *minimalist model*. It consists of a conversation between provider and client that occurs before routine prenatal testing (amniocentesis or CVS) for women over the age of thirty-five and those otherwise at increased risk of carrying a fetus with a condition that can be detected. The "counseling" emphasizes the risks of the test procedure itself rather than the information that the test may reveal about the fetus. This model assumes inherent benefit in the information about the procedure and does little to educate the patient or prepare her for any difficult decision making that could lie ahead. Patients should object to the minimalist model for these reasons, yet they tend to be satisfied with it because the majority of them go on to have "normal" outcomes of the testing that are reassuring.[12] Patients also do not know what to expect from prenatal counseling and so satisfaction seems to be relatively easy to achieve.[13] It would be useful to know whether the couples faced with difficult information about their developing fetus, who received minimal information prior to testing, felt sufficiently prepared to make a decision about whether or not to continue the pregnancy.

A somewhat expanded model of prenatal counseling can be described as the *informational model*. The informational model involves a discussion of chromosomes and nondisjunction as a cause of chromosomal trisomy, the most likely "abnormal" finding from testing. It emphasizes information that providers have deemed important to patients facing testing. While patients may find the genetics information interesting, since many of them have little prior understanding of genetics, studies have not consistently shown whether such an introduction to genetics is useful to patients. It assumes the benefit of the genetic information and neglects to consider the personal meaning patients make of it, which may not resemble the providers' priorities.[14] The informational model fails to emphasize topics such as abortion, the only intervention for most identifiable conditions, and what a commitment to life parenting an individual who is disabled may mean for parents. Research suggests this is a common model and that the failure to discuss these additional topics is not rare, yet despite this, patients are reportedly satisfied.[15]

An *informed consent model* assumes that a couple needs information about the conditions that may be identified and what options and resources are available in order to make a personal decision about the use of prenatal testing. This model involves a more extensive discussion of the risks and benefits and strives to uncover personal meaning of the information. Couples may be asked to explore what they would do if they received a result that indicated the fetus was affected with various conditions. The consent model is deliberative and may be described as a dialogue between the client and the counselor.[16] Genetic counselors are trained to provide this type of decision-making counseling, but restraints on time, agendas that conflict with physicians who may prefer a minimalist model, and limited reimbursement for such time-consuming services restrict its availability.[17]

The most extensive model, the *psycho-educational model*, includes offering information on the conditions under study but also explores thoughts and feelings that the information elicits in the client. It is collaborative; the counselor asks what information is most useful to the client in making a decision about prenatal testing. The client's experience with people who are affected with a variety of different types of disability may be explored in conjunction with her expectations for her own family. Working within this model, the counselor attempts to achieve an empathetic understanding of the client's values as they relate to having a baby, terminating a pregnancy, and establishing a family. This model of counseling requires a great deal of skill and flexibility on behalf of the counselor. No two sessions are the same as they are shaped by the needs of the individual client. One of this model's assumptions is that a client may not make the same decision about prenatal testing from one pregnancy to the next, depending on her circumstances.

The psycho-educational model allows counselors to confront clients with the notion that an abnormality in the fetus may be found. It helps couples to absorb information that could threaten their family plans and their personal identities as parents. The possibility that something could go "wrong" with the fetus is entertained by most couples during pregnancy and may be understood cognitively, but women and couples defend themselves against the possibility emotionally.[18] Since it is unlikely to happen and stress-invoking to entertain, most couples endure (and enjoy!) their pregnancies by assuming the best possible outcome—a "healthy" baby. When this hope is challenged, the couple's defenses are down; they feel vulnerable and scared by the unknown and the lack of control they have over the developing baby's health. Maintaining feelings of personal emotional control is important in coping with stressful life events.[19]

A skilled counselor can establish a sufficiently therapeutic relationship with a couple that allows them to relax their defenses enough to explore how they may feel if something is found to be "wrong" with their fetus. With an empathic connection, the counselor can work with the couple to imagine their role as parents of a child who may have special needs of a medical or cognitive nature, or both. If a couple has addressed this possibility (emotionally) prior to counseling, the session is likely to be more productive. If it is the first time a couple has explored or shared their feelings, most likely it begins an exchange that the couple will need to continue. Either situation will help to prepare those few couples who unexpectedly will be faced with frightening information about their developing baby. The majority of couples who will receive normal results may benefit from this counseling in several ways. It may help prepare them for unrelated and unpredictable struggles that may arise later for their child. It may also bring couples closer in understanding one another's values. Lastly, it may assist in expanding their sensitivity to other families with disabled members, having personalized the likelihood that this indeed could happen to them.

For those few who do face a prenatal finding, prior counseling may expand the amount of time/opportunity they have to make a difficult decision. Regardless of the value and joy that children with special needs may bring to their parents and family, assuming the role of parenting them involves an adjustment of large proportions. Adding the element of personal choice may actually enhance the burden. Parents need to "grieve" for the child they expected and readjust their expectations for the new child. This does not mean they are grieving over becoming parents of a child who is different; it is the plans and expectations that are lost—not that the child is of less value to them. The child's inherent value and their acceptance also become less abstract to parents once the child is born.

The psycho-educational model takes time and is difficult to implement but represents a more ideal model. It requires that factual information be shared with couples effectively and that it be processed in a meaningful way. Couples will likely resist entertaining their fears and worries knowing they are not likely to be realized. They may feel they are being stripped of an opportunity to enjoy their pregnancy by being asked to consider an outcome that is less desirable or unexpected.[20] The expectations and agendas that couples come to genetic counseling with greatly affect the outcome. Many obstetric providers refer their patients for prenatal testing rather than to explore the option of prenatal diagnosis.[21] It is surprising to couples when they learn that genetic counseling offers the exploration of emotions, differentiating it from other types of medical care.[22] If clients were better prepared for prenatal counseling and anticipated an opportunity for a bit of self-exploration, the overall benefit of the service would be enhanced.

Moral Responsibilities of Prenatal Counselors

There are practical considerations to the dynamic in prenatal counseling and its success at both preparing couples to make decisions about using prenatal testing and about whether to continue a pregnancy when a condition is identified. As discussed, these include the referral source and expectations, conflicting agendas of providers, constraints on time and reimbursement, and common coping strategies of pregnant women/couples. But genetic counselors and other providers have moral responsibilities to their patients when offering prenatal diagnosis as well. What are the inherent goals in offering prenatal testing? There is no denying the inherent endorsement of abortion as an option for dealing with a variety of genetic (chromosomal) conditions. How do the goals relate to the perceptions of members of the disability community that prenatal testing is an attempt to eliminate them or people similarly affected? Herein lies a serious issue for genetic counselors who must ask themselves very difficult questions about their role in supporting reproductive freedom. Does a pro-choice stance mean that termination of pregnancy for any indication should be supported by a genetic counselor? If counselors support some decisions to terminate but not others, that suggests counselors are placing judgment on the worth of life with certain disabilities versus others. Counselors have long avoided any differentiation, claiming that even sex selection, if an informed choice, should be upheld.[23] Yet, being born with a cleft lip or a clubfoot has completely different implications than being born affected with trisomy 13, where a baby will have severe mental and physical problems. Should a counselor not stress these differences directly with the couple facing a decision about the pregnancy? Is it not the responsibility of the counselor to indicate how successfully a cleft lip or clubfoot can be repaired and how likely the child is to otherwise have a successful life? Beyond the ability to fix or repair certain birth anomalies, when and how should counselors support the birth of children affected with conditions that cannot be repaired? If a child were to be born blind (a condition that usually cannot be prenatally detected or "repaired"), shouldn't the counselor emphasize the availability of support resources as well as the potential for successful adaptation, normal cognition, and life success? Is this not an opportunity to expand parents' acceptance of a diversity of characteristics in their children as well as to remind them of the many aspects of our children's lives that we don't control but can accept and value? In contrast, should counselors support parents' efforts to have "normal" children and encourage them to terminate the pregnancy in preference of having a future child who would not be blind?

   In the psycho-educational model, the counselor explores with a couple the implications of specific prenatal findings for the couple's family. The counselor, knowing the feelings and values of the couple, is prepared to discuss in a more direct manner what the implications for the life of the child might be. The counselor may point out the personal resources and strengths that the couple previously identified in their hypothetical consideration of potential outcomes of pregnancy.[24] This may allow the couple to more clearly envision life parenting a child with certain needs. It is a dialogue that appreciates the child as a whole and not as a "finding." It is exploratory and requires a great deal of work on behalf of both the counselor and, most important, the client/couple. Within this model the client is not simply told that the counselor will support any decision she makes, thereby abandoning the client in an important time of need. Rather, the counselor strives to understand what would be a good decision for the client/couple and directs them toward it. The counselor must be exquisitely self-aware and insightful about her own beliefs. If the counselor does harbor ideas that life with certain conditions is not worthwhile, s/he needs to self-disclose these feelings to the client if they are likely to play a role in the decision-making exchange. The counselor can use it as an opportunity to help the client, or couple, clarify whether s/he shares similar or different views. The most successful counseling is likely to be conducted by prenatal counselors with a wide tolerance for a variety of decisions and few strongly held opinions about life lived with specific conditions that may lead to disability.

Training and Continuing Education of Prenatal Counselors

In order to adhere as closely as possible to the psycho-educational model described, prenatal genetic counselors need to be skilled in many areas. Currently, the majority of prenatal counselors are trained at the master's level in programs specifically designed for educating professionals in genetic counseling. The curricula vary across programs, but generally include coursework in human genetics, technological applications of genetics, decision-making aides, and supportive counseling techniques.[25] Programs may differ considerably in their emphasis on each of these topics, but in order to be accredited by the American Board of Genetic Counseling, they need to include a minimum of coursework in each area.[26] Programs also differ in their coverage of psychotherapeutic counseling techniques and exposure to the community of people with disabilities. The extensive counseling required by the psycho-educational model necessitates graduate education in these areas as well. In addition, prenatal genetic counselors endeavoring to practice this model of counseling need to have skills that will enable them to become increasingly self-aware, allowing for a continuous personal dialogue regarding the effects of their own values and beliefs on their interactions with clients.

For those counselors who are just embarking on their education, expansion of existing graduate curricula in areas of self-awareness, exposure to actual life experiences of those with disabilities, decision making as a partnership between counselor and client, and training in the development of a therapeutic relationship is needed. However, if the profession is to embrace a psycho-educational approach to prenatal clients, newly trained genetic counselors will also need to have professional role models who are striving to practice in such a fashion. While the literature suggests that some genetic counselors endeavor to achieve such a model, our clinical experiences suggest they may be a minority.[27] Additional education for practicing genetic counselors may be offered as workshops within professional conferences, short courses, voluntary community experiences, and discussions with or supervision by professionals in related fields. With regard to the latter, it would be beneficial, for instance, to discuss prenatal cases or practices with members of the disability community who could provide further insight into the impact of such interventions.

As mentioned earlier, prenatal genetic counselors are faced with many difficult questions that cannot be ignored. Self-awareness training is crucial in helping us as professionals to consider our goals for our clients as well as our responsibilities to the women that we serve, their families, and the larger community of which they are a part. Without a method for exploring the meaning that such concepts as disability and reproductive freedom have for ourselves, we have little hope of aiding others in similar deliberations.

Experience of and with people with disabilities should be added to the training of professionals who offer prenatal counseling.[28] Although master's-trained genetic counselors are prepared for practicing in the pediatric and adult settings described earlier as well as the prenatal setting (and thus have exposure to families who may be affected by various conditions), many prenatal genetic counselors focus only on prenatal counseling after their graduate education is complete. Because of the nature of their work, many of these counselors have limited exposure to individuals with disabilities and their family members. Much of their information comes from articles appearing in textbooks and journals, presentations at professional meetings, or from discussions with other medical professionals who care for adults and children in the clinical setting. Even those counselors who maintain some contact with families by splitting their practices between pediatric and/or adult settings and prenatal settings are limited by the clinical nature of their exposure. Without realizing it, many counselors may carry an overly "medicalized" view of genetic and nongenetic disabilities, with little sense of the actual experiences of the families living with such conditions. In order to be able to help give women exploring the option of prenatal testing a true vision of the experience of having a child with a disability, a prenatal counselor should have experience with people across the life span who are living with such circumstances. Through exposure to such families in educational workshops, community volunteer opportunities, or even support groups, counselors can gain a firsthand understanding of how families are able to adjust and flourish. They can learn more about the people affected rather than about the conditions in isolation. Counselors are already pursuing such training.[29] Such genetic counselors are not only better prepared to help families identify resources as they are needed but also better equipped to aid couples in considering their abilities to cope and how these might relate to their feelings about prenatal testing.

Enhancing the Effectiveness of Prenatal Counseling

When sitting in a room with a couple prior to undergoing prenatal testing, one of the primary objectives a counselor may be considering is how best to prepare these individuals in the event that an "abnormality" is discovered. In considering prenatal testing, couples may head down a path that could lead them to further decisions about the pregnancy. Couples struggle with the unknowns involved in the potential of parenting any child, let alone a child with special needs. How can genetic counselors best help families to prepare for these possibilities? Widespread adoption of the psycho-educational model of prenatal counseling could bring us closer to helping prospective parents with such preparation.

Some might argue that such preparation is not only excessive but also perhaps even unfair to the majority of families who will receive normal results. To date, no studies have examined the effect of discussing potentially threatening events on a couple's pregnancy experience. We have tried to make a case for the importance of helping women/couples to consider the personal impact of prenatal testing prior to undergoing such procedures, in the event that they are among the small percentage who are faced with unexpected news. For those who receive "normal" results, having a discussion with a prenatal counselor could foster a deeper understanding of their personal values as parents and aid them in accepting the inevitable uncontrollability involved in parenthood. One might argue that all potential parents might benefit to some degree from this sort of examination of values and beliefs.

Upon examining the goals outlined thus far in the chapter, it might seem that prenatal genetic counselors practicing under the psycho-educational model should be well equipped to enable women to wholly consider their values, beliefs, and strengths in order to make decisions that match their own personal meanings of life. In the time-limited sessions of genetic counseling (often only one session), however, this is a nearly impossible task. Unless a family has given much prior consideration to these topics, the genetic counselor probably can hope only to start a process—perhaps one that will lead to further exploration and discussion in the absence of the counselor. There may be a need to encourage more preconception counseling as well as additional follow-up sessions in the event that an abnormality is found. In order to have the maximum ability to consider the meaning of disability and the implications of prenatal testing, families would be best served by being encouraged to examine these issues throughout their lifetimes. Genetic professionals can aid in such encouragement. However, people will not truly be prepared for considering the relevant issues during genetic counseling until society as a whole begins to embrace these very same topics.

In keeping with what we said earlier about the benefit of discussions for even those families who will receive "normal" prenatal testing results, we propose that *all* members of our society would benefit from a broad, public examination of how we do—and should—understand "normal" and "valuable." To help our society better handle difference, it might be logical to begin by developing programs for elementary and secondary school classrooms. Encouraging community members to accept people with a wide range of abilities from an early age might be the most effective means of promoting long-lasting acceptance. Many schools are already on the cusp of developing such programs. Increasingly, students have exposure to other students with disabilities through mainstreaming and inclusion in the classroom. However, exposure in the absence of a well-developed educational curriculum designed to promote understanding and acceptance fails to encourage students to develop their own conceptions of normalcy.

Although classroom programs would be the most effective way to reach the majority of the public at a moment in which they are primed for learning, elementary school programs are unlikely to help prospective prenatal counseling clients for several years to come. Further, if such values are not reinforced by parents and other adults in the community, they are unlikely to have a lasting effect on the attitudes and beliefs of the children as they age. Thus, communities need to strive for similar awareness at the adult level. Over the years, there have been numerous successful health education campaigns aimed at promoting healthy life-styles. Perhaps we could borrow from the techniques used in such campaigns to encourage the public to consider feelings regarding a range of disabilities in relationship to reproductive decisions. Community educational programs would be different, depending on the concerns of the members of each community. In some areas, continuing education programs designed to promote discussion could be offered through local schools, churches, or town councils. The experiences of "temporarily abled" community members would be enriched by opportunities to be involved with community members with disabilities. Opportunities for such involvement could take many forms, from shared volunteer work to shared participation in seminars led by people with disabilities.

To reach a large percentage of some communities (especially those that are currently being referred for prenatal testing and counseling), it might also help to encourage discussions between physicians and their patients within routine medical appointments. The vast majority of women referred for prenatal counseling are referred through a physician. If, at a minimum, women were encouraged by their referring physicians to consider their feelings about disability and parenting prior to coming to genetic counseling, genetic counselors might be better able to help women consider the potential impact of information from prenatal testing on their lives. Perhaps the more time people have to consider their values, the clearer those values become. Along these lines, if couples are encouraged by their physicians prior even to embarking on pregnancy to think about some of these issues, they may have an even greater advantage when faced with a decision about testing.

Overall, it may be that the types of community discussion and awareness that disability advocates would like to promote for the good of those with disabilities are the very same interventions that would promote more effective prenatal genetic counseling. Finding ways to move thought and discussion about disabilities (both genetic and non-genetic) into the everyday lives of members of society, rather than isolating them to limited sessions with professionals, may not only encourage increased acceptance of difference, but may also allow genetic counselors to explore the values of their clients more deeply in order to help them make choices about prenatal testing. Thus, attaining such a goal may involve a cooperative effort among genetic counselors, other health care providers, the disability community, and society as a whole.

Remaining Research Questions

Although we have proposed ways to help women/couples who are contemplating prenatal testing, it is clear that many unanswered questions remain. We have outlined ways in which communities might increase their awareness of feelings and values related to difference in order to enhance their decisions regarding prenatal testing. Although we have anecdotal evidence that more aware clients are able to explore relevant issues more deeply within genetic counseling sessions, studies are needed to help us understand the true impact increased community awareness might have on counseling interactions, reproductive decisions, and acceptance/embracing of children and adults with disabilities.

In addition, genetics professionals need further information about the impact of prenatal genetic counseling interventions on women/couples who receive results that show an abnormality. We need to develop a deeper understanding of counselors' ability to affect the readiness of clients to make decisions. We also need a deeper understanding of the abilities clients draw on to cope with abnormal findings. On the other hand, questions also remain about the actual impact of intensive psycho-educational prenatal counseling on clients who do *not* receive abnormal results. Are we actually increasing pregnancy-related anxiety unnecessarily by discussing uncomfortable topics, against which many individuals may seek to defend themselves psychologically? If so, what are the effects of such an increase on the pregnancy and on the parenting of the future child?

With so many unknowns, genetics professionals must be prepared to consider the implications of future research on both the process and goals of genetic counseling. Counselors need to be prepared to interpret the results of such studies in terms of our own values and beliefs with regard to our clients in order to reshape our goals for our individual clients and for society as a whole.

What the Disability Movement Has Suggested for Prenatal Counseling

In the realm of prenatal testing, it is obvious that there is still much to learn. As genetics professionals, we (and our clients) can and have benefited a great deal from the knowledge and experiences of members of the disability community. Even in the psycho-educational model, which emphasizes an exploration of each client's individual feelings and experiences over the provision of specific facts, the ability of clients to make choices with as much information as possible continues to be of paramount importance. We are reminded that complete information is information that strives to convey the wholeness of life with a particular condition, rather than information that is merely medically correct or comprehensive. People with conditions should be discussed as people in and of themselves, not merely as medical conditions. Couples who are not given the opportunity to carefully explore their potential for raising a child with special needs, and their feelings about the potential joys as well as pains, are not truly informed about the impact prenatal testing may have on their lives.

As Thomas Murray has reminded us, prenatal testing gives us the opportunity to help families reexplore their goals and values with regard to parenthood in general.[30] Rather than promoting the idea of the possibility of the "perfect child," we can offer couples a chance to discuss their hopes and fears regarding parenthood in terms of the love that they potentially have to offer as the parents of any child. In addition, we can help them clarify and accept their personal limitations as parents.

Those involved in the disability movement might also remind us, as genetics professionals, to stay in touch with the meaning of our professional requirement for the provision of "nondirective" counseling. Rather than allowing us to avoid the responsibilities related to the potential ramifications of increased prenatal testing, our duty to enable our clients to make autonomous decisions increases our need to help clients explore their feelings related to decisions concerning prenatal testing. To help women/couples take a journey through their values related to difference, parenting, and reproductive decisions, we must be aware of our own values on an ongoing basis, and must be aware of how these values affect our counseling practices.

Lastly, consideration of the disability community's concerns regarding prenatal testing should encourage us to increase our skills as genetic counselors so that we might better help couples understand the joys as well as the limitations of living with a variety of disabilities. Consideration of these concerns may also help us better understand how our dealings with clients may be related to our own feelings about parenting a child with special needs. As we suggested earlier, genetic counseling skills may be fine tuned through additional training in self-awareness, psycho-educational counseling techniques, and exposure to and understanding of individuals living with a variety of disabilities. In addition, our practices should be informed by further research into the most effective ways to help women/couples make decisions about genetic testing, as well as research into the needs of couples who receive "abnormal" results.

NOTES

1. Mark I. Evans et al., "The Choices Women Make about Prenatal Diagnosis," *Fetal Diagnosis and Therapy* 8, supplement 1 (1993): 70–80; and Ann P. Garber and Helen E. Hixon, "Prenatal Genetic Counseling," *Clinical Perinatology* 17, no. 4 (1990): 749–59.

2. F. Clarke Fraser, "Genetic Counselling," *American Journal of Human Genetics* 26 (1974): 636–59.

3. F. Abramovsky, "Analysis of a Follow-up Study of Genetic Counseling," *Clinical Genetics* 17 (1980): 1–12.

4. See, for instance, Philip M. Ferguson, Alan Gartner, and Dorothy K. Lipsky, "The Experience of Disability in Families: A Synthesis of Research and Parent Narratives," in this volume; and Eva Feder Kittay, "On the Expressivity of Selective Abortion for Disability: Conversations with My Son," in this volume.

5. Luba Djurdjinovic, "Psychosocial Counseling," in *A Guide to Genetic Counseling*, ed. Diane Baker, Jane Schuette, and Wendy Uhlmann (New York: Wiley-Liss, 1998), pp. 127–66.

6. National Society of Genetic Counselors, "National Society for Genetic Counselors Code of Ethics," in *Prescribing Our Future: Ethical Challenges in Genetic Counseling*, ed. Dianne M. Bartels, Bonnie S. LeRoy, and Arthur L. Caplan (New York: Aldine de Gruyter, 1993), pp. 169–71.

7. Ellen Wright Clayton, "Reproductive Genetic Testing: Regulatory and Liability Issues," *Fetal Diagnosis and Therapy* 8, supplement 1 (1993): 39–59.

8. American College of Obstetricians and Gynecologists, "Antenatal Diagnosis of Genetic Disorders," ACOG Technical Bulletin no. 108 (Washington, D.C.: American College of Obstetricians and Gynecologists, 1987).

9. Barbara Bowles Biesecker and Theresa M. Marteau, "The Future of Genetic Counseling: An International Perspective," *Nature Genetics* 22 (June 1999): 133–37.

10. Nancy A. Press and Carole H. Browner, "Why Women Say Yes to Prenatal Diagnosis," *Social Science in Medicine* 45, no. 7 (1997): 979–89.

11. B. Meredith Burke and Aliza Kolker, "Variation in Content in Prenatal Genetic Counseling Interviews," *Journal of Genetic Counseling* 3, no. 1 (1994): 23–38; and Ellen Matloff, "Practice Variability in Prenatal Genetic Counseling," *Journal of Genetic Counseling* 3, no. 3 (1994): 215–31.

12. Shoshana S. Shiloh, O. Audor, and R. Goodman, "Satisfaction with Genetic Counseling: Dimensions and Measurement," *American Journal of Medical Genetics* 37 (1990): 522–29.

13. Barbara A. Bernhardt, Barbara Biesecker, and Carrie Mastromarino, "Goals, Benefits and Outcomes of Genetic Counseling," *American Journal of Medical Genetics,* in press.

14. Melanie F. Myers et al., "Involving Consumers in the Development of an Educational Program for Cystic Fibrosis Carrier Screening," *American Journal of Human Genetics* 54, no. 4 (1994): 719–26.

15. B. Williams, J. Coyle, and D. Healy, "The Meaning of Patient Satisfaction: An Exploration of High Reported Levels," *Social Science in Medicine* 47 (1998): 1351–59; and Dorothy C. Wertz, James R. Sorenson, and T. Heeren, "Communication in Health Professional-Lay Encounters: How Often Does Each Party Know What the Other Wants to Discuss?" *Work and Occupations* 15 (1988): 36–54.

16. Mary T. White, "Respect for Autonomy in Genetic Counseling: An Analysis and a Proposal," *Journal of Genetic Counseling* 6 (1997): 297–313.

17. Barbara Bernhardt, J. Weiner, E. Foster et al., "The Economics of Clinical Genetics Services. II. A Time Analysis of a Medical Genetics Clinic," *American Journal of Human Genetics* 41, no. 4 (1987): 559–65.

18. Shelley E. Taylor, "Adjustment to Threatening Events: A Theory of Cognitive Adaptation," *American Psychologist* (November 1983): 1161–73.

19. M. Berkenstadt, Shoshana Shiloh, and G. Barkai, "Perceived Personal Control (PPC): A New Concept in Measuring Outcomes of Genetic Counseling," *American Journal of Medical Genetics* 82 (1999): 53–59.

20. A. Brewster, "After Office Hours: A Patient's Reaction to Amniocentesis," *Obstetrics and Gynecology* 64, no. 3 (1984): 443–44.

21. Barbara A. Bernhardt, Gail Geller, Theresa Doksum et al., "Prenatal Genetic Testing: Content of Discussions between Obstetric Providers and Pregnant Women," *Obstetrics and Gynecology* 91 (1998): 648–55; and T. M. Marteau, J. Kidd, and M. Plenicar, "Obstetricians Presenting Amniocentesis to Pregnant Women: Practice Observed," *Journal of Reproductive Infant Psychology* 11 (1993): 3–10.

22. Bernhardt et al., "Goals, Benefits, and Outcomes of Genetic Counseling."

23. Dorothy C. Wertz and John C. Fletcher, "Ethical and Social Issues in Prenatal Sex Selection: A Survey of Geneticists in 37 Nations," *Social Science in Medicine* 46, no. 2 (1998): 255–73.

24. V. Wake, "Prelude to Future Decisions: Using Questions of Hypothetical Future in Prenatal Genetic Counseling," *Journal of Genetic Counseling* 7, no. 6 (1998): 498.

25. Ann Walker, Joan Scott, Barbara Biesecker et al., "Report of the 1989 Asilomar Meeting on Education," *American Journal of Human Genetics* 46 (1990): 1223–30.

26. American Board of Genetic Counseling, Inc. (Bethesda, Md.), "Requirements for Graduate Programs in Genetic Counseling Seeking Accreditation by the American Board of Genetic Counseling," adopted January 25, 1996.

27. Seymour Kessler, "Psychological Aspects of Genetic Counseling. IX. Teaching and Counseling," *Journal of Genetic Counseling* 6, no. 2 (1997): 287–95; Kessler, "Psychological Aspects of Genetic Counseling. XII. More on Counseling Skills," *Journal of Genetic Counseling* 7, no. 3 (1998): 263–78; and Barbara Bowles Biesecker, "Future Directions in Genetic Counseling: Practical and Ethical Considerations," *Kennedy Institute of Ethics Journal* 8, no. 2 (1998): 145–60.

28. Adrienne Asch, "Reproductive Technology and Disability," *in Reproductive Laws for the 1990's*, ed. Sherrill Cohen and Nadine Taub (Clifton, N.J.: Humana Press, 1989), pp. 69–124; Marsha Saxton, "Disability Feminism Meets DNA: A Study of an Educational Model for Genetic Counseling Students on the Social and Ethical Issues of Selective Abortion" (Ph.D. diss., Brandeis University, 1996).

29. Saxton, "Disability Feminism Meets DNA."

30. Thomas H. Murray, *The Worth of a Child* (Berkeley and Los Angeles: University of California Press, 1996), pp. 115–41.

Contributors

ADRIENNE ASCH is the Henry R. Luce Professor in Biology, Ethics, and the Politics of Human Reproduction at Wellesley College, Wellesley, Massachusetts.

MARY ANN BAILY is a fellow at the Institute for Ethics of the American Medical Association, Chicago, Illinois.

BARBARA BOWLES BIESECKER is the National Human Genome Research Institute (NHGRI) Director of the Johns Hopkins University–NHGRI Genetic Counseling Graduate Program, Bethesda, Maryland.

JEFFREY R. BOTKIN is professor of pediatrics and medical ethics at the University of Utah School of Medicine, Salt Lake City.

PHILIP M. FERGUSON is an associate professor and senior research associate in the Department of Special Education and Community Resources at the University of Oregon, Eugene.

ALAN GARTNER is codirector of the National Center on Educational Restructuring and Inclusion, City University of New York.

LORI HAMBY is a third-year graduate student in the Johns Hopkins–NHGRI Genetic Counseling Program, Bethesda, Maryland.

BRUCE JENNINGS is senior research scholar at The Hastings Center, Garrison, New York.

DEBORAH KENT is a freelance writer living in Chicago, Illinois.

EVA FEDER KITTAY is a professor of philosophy at the State University of New York at Stony Brook.

LEO KITTAY is an actor in New York City.

DOROTHY K. LIPSKY is director of the National Center on Educational Restructuring and Inclusion at the Graduate School, City University of New York.

JAMES LINDEMANN NELSON is a professor of philosophy at Michigan State University, East Lansing.

PILAR N. OSSORIO is an assistant professor of law and medical ethics at the University of Wisconsin, Madison.

ERIK PARENS is the associate for philosophical studies at The Hastings Center, Garrison, New York.

CYNTHIA M. POWELL is an assistant professor of pediatrics in the Division of Genetics and Metabolism at the University of North Carolina, Chapel Hill.

NANCY PRESS is an associate professor in the Department of Public Health and Preventive Medicine at the Oregon Health Sciences University, Portland.

STEVEN J. RALSTON is an assistant professor of obstetrics and gynecology in the Division of Maternal and Fetal Medicine at Tufts University School of Medicine/New England Medical Center, Boston, Massachusetts.

WILLIAM RUDDICK is a professor of philosophy at New York University, New York.

MARSHA SAXTON is a lecturer in disability studies at the University of California, Berkeley, and a research associate at the World Institute on Disability in Oakland, California.

BONNIE STEINBOCK is a professor of philosophy, public policy, and public health at the State University of New York at Albany.

DOROTHY C. WERTZ is research professor of psychiatry at the University of Massachusetts Medical Center, Shriver Center Division, in Waltham, Massachusetts.

Index